WAX & GOLD

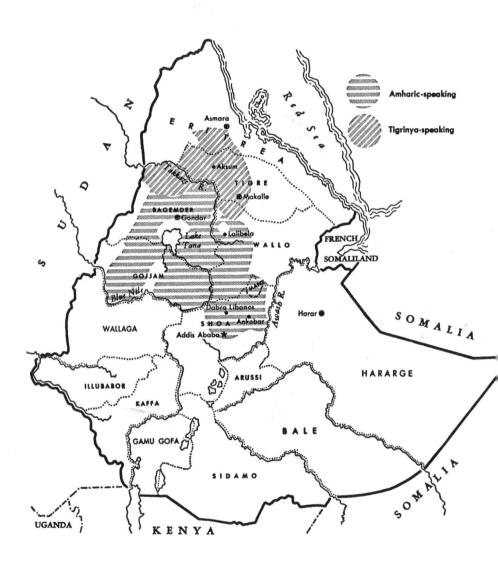

Amharic-speaking

Tigrinya-speaking

Red Sea

S U D A N

E R I T R E A

Asmara

• Aksum

TIGRE

• Makalle

BAGEMDER

• Gondar

Lake Tana

• Lalibela

WALLO

FRENCH SOMALILAND

GOJJAM

Blue Nile

Dabra Libanos •

SHOA • Ankober

Addis Ababa ✕

Awash R.

Harar •

SOMALIA

WALLAGA

HARARGE

ILLUBABOR

KAFFA

ARUSSI

BALE

GAMU GOFA

SIDAMO

SOMALIA

UGANDA

K E N Y A

WAX & GOLD

TRADITION AND INNOVATION IN ETHIOPIAN CULTURE

Donald N. Levine

The University of Chicago Press
Chicago and London

International Standard Book Number: 0-226-47563-8

Library of Congress Catalog Card Number: 65-18340

 THE UNIVERSITY OF CHICAGO PRESS, CHICAGO 60637

THE UNIVERSITY OF CHICAGO PRESS, LTD., LONDON

Designed by Adrian Wilson

ላለፉት ፡ ኩሩዎቸና ፡ በአሁኑም ፡ ዘመን ፡
ፈልሳፊ ፡ ሰሆኑት ፡ ኢትዮጵያዊያን ፡
ደራሲው ፡ ይህንን ፡ መጽሐፍ ፡ በአድናቆት ፡
ያበረክታል።

To the proud Ethiopians of the past and
the creative of the present

PREFACE

This book is the outgrowth of a relatively uninhibited encounter of a mind bearing some of the ideas and methods of contemporary social science with the dominant traditional culture of a developing nation. As a result it embodies a variety of interests which, in more conventional work, would be pursued through separate writings. Broadly speaking, *Wax and Gold* is animated by three different forms of curiosity, each of which moves to the fore at different times. Proceeding first of all as an empirical social scientist, I have been curious about the nature of traditional Amhara culture. Shifting at certain junctures to the viewpoint of the social analyst, I have been concerned with examining the situation of action faced by thoughtful Ethiopians today. And throughout I have been moved, as a sociological theorist, to raise questions and suggest hypotheses regarding the more general significance of the phenomena examined in the course of my Ethiopian studies. If the book is therefore somewhat disjointed at moments, I hope the reader will be compensated by sharing some of my satisfaction in refusing to suppress one or another of these interests.

The motive which lies behind any scholar's effort to characterize an exotic culture is ultimately aesthetic. I freely admit to having been seduced by the charm of traditional Amhara life. Played out by an extraordinarily handsome people in a setting of great natural beauty and a climate often called "idyllic," it offers a gate through time to a state of being that is richly medieval. Such sights and sounds! A minstrel singing his subtle lyrics as he bows a one-stringed fiddle; in the dark interiors of church, barefoot deacons holding beeswax candles and swinging vessels of smoking incense; the pomp of a nobleman moving cross country with his crowded entourage; a young girl washing the feet of her father's guest; warriors boasting with their martial chants; the stately rhythms of clergy chanting and dancing under the mid-day sun; the open marketplace, offering all manner of livestock, grain, and spices; the counsel of an elder, resolving a dispute; the simple dignity of the bow when two men meet.

The scholar's job is of course to transcend such a medley of impressions and to discern the patterns of order through which such details are bound together in a living whole. In carrying out this task I have not imposed any one methodological framework on my materials. Rather, as the reader of Robert Redfield's methodological handbook, *The Little Community,* will readily appreciate, I have sought to organize these materials in terms of half a dozen of the more common viewpoints used in the study of human communities. Roughly speaking, I have looked upon Amhara culture as a history (chapter ii), an outlook on life (chapter iii), a way of growing up (chapter iv), a social structure (chapter v), a kind of psychological orientation (chapter vi), and as "a combination of opposites" (chapter vii). The observational techniques employed in the course of this study have been accordingly diverse, ranging from the analysis of literary texts and oral traditions to the use of questionnaires, projective tests, interviews, and participant observation.

Yet however gratifying the contemplation of a traditional culture may be, the student of traditional societies today finds it difficult to remain aloof from the historical changes which now permeate the world. As he talks with the bright young men of the cities, he finds considerable ambivalence regarding the value of traditional ways. He finds Ethiopians acutely conscious that their traditional life, for all its charm, has been chronically afflicted with war, pestilence, famine, and disease, and that their traditional social order has encouraged the many to toil and the few to live in idle luxury. He sees them bitter that Ethiopia has remained backward—"*wada hwāla qaratch!*"—and isolated from the great advances of the human spirit achieved elsewhere. They are anxious to enter the modern world.

And thus the aesthetic impulse is joined by the moral. The sociologist feels drawn to contribute what he can to elucidate the sometimes desperate problems faced by societies trying to make a rapid transition to modernity. In this he is inspired in part by the history of his discipline. The contrast between traditional and modern society has constituted the central substantive problem in sociology since Auguste Comte named the discipline well over a century ago, and some of the foremost proponents of sociology—notably, Émile Durkheim, Max Weber, and Karl Mannheim—have understood their calling to involve the sympathetic analysis of problems created by the great transition to modernity.

In the case of Ethiopia the temptation is particularly compelling. The literature on Ethiopia is conspicuous for the absence of thoughtful social analysis. With few exceptions it is divided between the esoteric treatises of specialists and the insipid blandishments of partisans.* I have therefore offered certain analyses and suggestions regarding Ethiopia's dilemmas, not on the presumption that they are in every case the most sound, but with the aim of raising questions and formulating issues in public which heretofore have been politely overlooked or furtively concealed, or of promoting their discussion in a more exploratory manner than has previously been the practice.

In so doing I trust that my words will not be taken as the preachings of an omniscient Westerner to a backward congregation. On the contrary, I am fully aware that the problems faced by Ethiopia today are simply variants of the basic problems faced by all of us throughout the world, problems which stem from the accelerated rate of historic change in our time and the persisting difficulties of institutionalizing a rational civilization in any human society. If I have sought to throw light on the dilemmas facing Ethiopians, it has been in part with the end of providing a mirror against which the dilemmas of Western societies might also be viewed.

For this and other reasons, our discussion touches now and then on matters of more universal concern. I have done this by means of allusion either to the comparable experience of other societies or to more abstract ways of conceptualizing the phenomena under consideration. Such references to comparative sociology or social theory represent the intrusion, beyond aesthetic interest and practical concern, of a purely intellectual impulse. I have, in other words, permitted myself to linger awhile with certain questions which emerged in the course of my work on Ethiopia—such as the nature of ambiguity, the functions of oral literature, or the concept of individualism—for their intrinsic theoretic interest.

In a way, this type of digression, more than any specific proposals set forth herein, embodies the chief message I would wish to convey to those now shaping the fate of developing nations. The upheavals of our time do not only confront us with dilemmas of action and moral emergencies; they and the work of scholars who study them also afford great opportunity for the cultivation of those faculties of "sociological imagination" and "sociological sensibility" which can enrich our lives as we live them, here and now, from day to day. To readers who may be offended by parts of this book which may seem critical, I can only say that to be modern means—for all of us—to be joined to

---

* The chief exception is Margery Perham's book, *The Government of Ethiopia,* which remains far and away the best general introduction to contemporary Ethiopian society.

a world-wide dialogue about the limitations and potentialities of human experience. For by any reckoning, a key defining characteristic of modernity is the prominence of education; and education in its truest sense, as Robert Redfield has put it, is "conversation about the meaning of life, as each sees some part of it, on behalf of everyone."

It is in the spirit of Robert Redfield that this book was conceived. I should like to place this remembrance of him at the head of the list of acknowledgments which follows. The debt owed by those who had the fortune to study the art of questioning with him is not to be measured.

There are numerous other debts I wish to acknowledge as the author of this book, with the regret that they cannot all be identified individually. I am deeply grateful to:

the Foreign Area Training Fellowship program, for a grant which financed my field work in Ethiopia;

the Committee for the Comparative Study of New Nations, University of Chicago, for providing me the time to complete this inquiry as well as a stimulating seminar on kindred problems;

Lloyd Fallers and Morris Janowitz of the University of Chicago for invaluable practical assistance and moral support at times when work on the manuscript was jeopardized;

a number of friends and colleagues, in the United States and abroad, who read parts of the manuscript and contributed helpful suggestions;

librarians in many institutions, including the Library of Congress, Northwestern University, the University of Chicago, the Istituto Pontificio Biblico at Rome, and the libraries of Addis Ababa;

my wife Joanna, for the generous use of her amazing talents both as a perceptive observer and as a literary critic;

and Ethiopians in many walks of life, whose sensitive hospitality and rewarding confidence it was our privilege to enjoy.

D. N. L.

CONTENTS

ILLUSTRATIONS

TABLES

1

INTRODUCTION

AMHARA TRADITION AND
ETHIOPIA'S MODERNIZATION

THE FACT OF AMHARA DOMINANCE

Of the many traditions which are alive in the empire of Ethiopia—those of the nomadic Danakil and the sedentary Wollamo, the hippopotamus-eating Woyto and the ensete-eating Gurage, the age-graded Konso and the patri-lineal Somali, the Judaic Falasha and the Muslim Bani 'Amer, and many others—clearly the dominant tradition is that of the people known throughout history to the outside world as the Abyssinians. Living on the temperate highland massif in the northern and central regions of the country, these people have gained their subsistence through the plow cultivation of cereal grains, have organized their polity as a feudal kingdom, and have remained steadfast in their Monophysite Christian faith since its introduction to the land in the fourth century.

The Abyssinians comprise two linguistic and geographical groups—the Amhara and the Tigre.* The Tigre inhabit the northern part of Ethiopia, above the Takazzē River; their lands fall in what are now the province of Tigre and the former Italian colony of Eritrea. Their language, Tigrinya, is

---

* Abyssinians object to the term "Abyssinian," since it has been used pejoratively by foreigners, even though they do use its indigenous counterpart, "Hābashā," among themselves. The term apparently derives from the name of one of the South Arabian tribes which migrated to Ethiopia in antiquity—the Habashat. In deference to this objection, I shall use the compound "Amhara-Tigre" in place of "Abyssinian" wherever feasible. The name "Ethiopia" will be used consistently to refer to the national polity which, throughout its history, has included other peoples and traditions as well as the Amhara-Tigre.

related to Ge'ez, the ancient and liturgical language of Ethiopia, much as Italian is related to Latin.[1] It was in Tigre country that, during the first seven centuries A.D., the kingdom of Aksum reached heights of civilization never again attained in Ethiopia's history. Because of the antiquity of their region and the glory of their past, the Tigre are to some extent the cultural aristocrats of Ethiopia.

The Amhara inhabit vast areas of what are today the provinces of Bagemder, Gojjam, Wallo, and Shoa. Their language, Amharic, is the official language of Ethiopia.* Since the beginning of what is called the restored Solomonid Dynasty (1270), all but one of the emperors of Ethiopia have been Amhara.† The exception was a Tigre, Emperor Yohānnes IV (1872–89), though he sojourned for many years at Dabra Tābor in Amhara country, and Amharic was commonly spoken at his court.

The differences between Amhara and Tigre culture have not yet been studied systematically. Even so, one can say that their differences are not nearly so great as what the two groups have in common. Language forms the chief difference. Like Ge'ez and Tigrinya, Amharic is a Semitic language, ultimately descended from old South Arabic, but Amharic has been molded to a greater degree by indigenous Cushitic tongues. Other differences relate to minor variations in custom, greater communal orientation in some Tigre areas, and differences in temperament. But the two groups share the legacy of Aksum, the Ethiopic alphabet, Ge'ez literature, Monophysite Christianity, similar political and social institutions, and the same style of life. One would be justified in treating their traditional Abyssinian culture as a unity, as virtually all authors have done in the past.

In this book, however, I have chosen to focus on Amhara culture as the dominant tradition in Ethiopia. This has been done, first of all, because of my limited competence to deal with Tigre materials, since I am neither familiar with Tigrinya nor fortunate enough to have done field work in Tigre areas. But a less fortuitous reason is that any serious account of contemporary Ethiopia must begin with the fact of Amhara dominance. With respect to numbers, true, the Amhara are in a minority: Amhara probably comprise no more than one-quarter of Ethiopia's total population (now estimated at around twenty-two million). Their dominance is to be measured, rather, in political and cultural terms. On the political side it is manifest in the perpetuation of the Amhara monarchy and the preponderance of Amhara in top political offices. On the cultural side it appears in the spread of Amhara customs throughout the empire by officials, soldiers, settlers, and teachers, and in

---

* English is the second official language.

† A number of Amhara emperors since the mid-eighteenth century were partly of Galla stock, however.

the continuous Amharization of the peoples of the empire through the required use of Amharic in schools and government offices and through the substitution of Amharic names for indigenous place-names in many parts of the country. If the national institutions and culture of Ethiopia are essentially Abyssinian, more particularly they are Amhara.[2]

The domination of Ethiopian national life by the Amhara, and the related fact that the modern Ethiopian nation was the creation of the Amhara and not of European colonists, are characteristics which distinguish Ethiopia from all other African societies. For Ethiopia is the only country in Africa with a large number of ethnic groups where one of these groups has imposed its rule and its language over the rest and has preserved indigenous national institutions, elites, and culture patterns from displacement by Western forms and authorities.

This condition has imparted a basically conservative tone to the character of public life in Ethiopia, especially when compared to the new nations of sub-Saharan Africa. Because Ethiopians did not have to participate in the postwar struggle for independence, they did not experience the rise of agitational politics or the related phenomenon of political parties or movements. As a corollary of this, the Ethiopian populace was not exposed to oratory promising dynamic social and economic changes, and therefore developed no mass base of support for populist leaders who might seek to promote more rapid forms of change.

Yet if modernization has proceeded more slowly in Ethiopia than elsewhere in Africa—and speed in such matters has at times been associated with recklessness—the pattern of virtually unbroken Amhara rule for at least seven centuries stands in refreshing contrast to the somewhat anguished struggle for nationality within the new nations. Elsewhere in sub-Saharan Africa no indigenous cultural tradition exists at the national level. There are many degrees to this cultural fragmentation. At one extreme are countries such as the Ivory Coast which, with some sixty disparate tribal groups in a population of about three million, can as yet appeal only to French culture as a basis for unity at the national level. Somewhat less fragmented are the nations, like Nigeria, in which a small number of important tribal traditions dominate the national scene. Still more consolidated is Uganda, whose kingdom of Buganda has long supported a strong quasi-national tradition, but whose non-Baganda tribes have remained largely outside the pale.

In Ethiopia, by contrast, Amhara rule has long provided a minimal basis for national unity. While this rule has been secured by coercive means, it has accustomed the various tribes in Ethiopia to live under a common sovereignty and to some extent has enabled their leaders to communicate with one another by means of a common native tongue.

One need not be blind to the drawbacks of Amhara dominance to recognize in it these and other important advantages for Ethiopia. These drawbacks have been those of any imperialism. During the great Amhara expansion under Menelik (1889–1913), many peoples were maltreated. Independent tribesmen were reduced to slavery; unique cultures were decimated; proud kings were dragged in the dust. Those who held down the Amhara position in these occupied territories seized land from the indigenous peoples and exploited them much as would any invader. The unfavorable reputation of the Amhara in the non-Amhara provinces has been due largely to the example of these governors and soldiers whose worst impulses were at times allowed free play.

One can scarcely single out the Amhara for criticism because of their imperialistic behavior in the past. Nor is it fair to judge the Amhara people as a whole by the character of their provincial officials in conquered areas, any more than one may judge the British, French, Portuguese, or Russian people by the behavior of certain imperious and sadistic colonial administrators. This distinction was self-evident to more discriminating observers of the Ethiopian scene like Augustus Wylde, who wrote in 1901:

> There is no harder worker than the Abyssinian peasant, and no more harmless and hospitable person when left alone and properly treated; and no more truculent, worthless, conceited, lazy and useless individual than the Abyssinian soldier, who formerly did nothing but prey upon the defenceless cultivator.[3]

Indeed, if any imperialism of modern times should be granted special consideration, it might be that of the Amhara. The Amhara were to some extent merely reconquering lands that had been taken from them in earlier centuries. Furthermore, they needed additional strength to help withstand threats to their own independence. Finally, it can also be argued that if the Amhara had not conquered the other peoples now within the Ethiopian boundaries some European power might have colonized them instead.

However one may assess the fact of Amhara dominance in Ethiopia, it is a given of the present situation. It is a fact that leads naturally to two outstanding questions. One concerns the relations between the Amhara and the non-Amhara peoples of the empire: is it possible for the latter to be integrated more effectively and justly into the texture of a common national life? If not, the present state of tribal calm may prove to be but a long prelude to a wasteful storm. The question demands serious and sustained inquiry by a number of scholars, Ethiopians and foreigners alike.

The other question concerns the nature of Amhara culture, as the dominant tradition in Ethiopia, and its implications for the processes of Ethiopia's modernization now at work and yet to come. To this question we now direct our attention.

THE GENIUS OF AMHARA CULTURE

The Amhara as a whole are not much given to aesthetic concerns. They are practical-minded peasants, austere religionists, and spirited warriors. Their interests and achievements as a nation are chiefly in the spheres of military activity and government. And yet, if we seek some theme with which to gain an entree into the spirit of their society and culture, we will do well to attend to the sphere of poetry. For it is a poetic phenomenon—that represented by the title of this book—which constitutes both a key to the genius of Amhara culture and a highly distinctive Amhara contribution to Ethiopian culture.

Sam-ennā warq ("wax and gold") is the formula used by the Amhara to symbolize their favorite form of verse. It is a form built of two semantic layers. The apparent, figurative meaning of the words is called "wax"; their more or less hidden actual significance is the "gold."

In its generic sense, the expression *sam-ennā warq* refers to a number of poetic figures which embody this twofold meaning. The use of such figures distinguishes the Amhara equivalent of true poetry from ordinary verse, in which everyday language is merely embellished with rhyme and rhythm. In the genre known as *qenē,* the original and more elegant kind of *sam-ennā warq* poetry, the lines are composed in Ge'ez and depend primarily on religious symbolism. But *sam-ennā warq* constructions also appear in some types of secular verse in the vernacular Amharic and, indeed, at times inform Amharic conversation.

Masters of the art of *qenē* composition have analyzed these poetic figures into about a dozen different types.[4] *Sam-ennā warq* in its more specific sense refers to one of these types of figures—the prototype of them all. It consists of an explicit comparison in which the subjects being compared—the wax and gold—are presented in apposition, while their predicates are rendered jointly by a single verb which carries both a wax and a gold meaning. (This terminology is derived from the work of the goldsmith, who constructs a clay mold around a form created in wax and then, draining the wax, pours the molten gold into that form.) So, for example, if the poet's aim is to praise a hero like Emperor Menelik, he creates a wax model, like "the lion," in terms of whose actions the gold, Menelik, is depicted: "The lion Menelik crushed the wolf Italy."[5]

Keeping this dual imagery consistent throughout the stanza is a primary rule of wax-and-gold composition. A poet who mixes his metaphors is sometimes rebuked with the epithet "hermaphrodite." The following example presents an Amharic couplet which properly embodies the *sam-ennā warq* figure:

Etsa balas balto addām kanfareshe
Madhānē alam lebē tasaqala-leshe.

Since Adam your lip did eat of that Tree
The Savior my heart has been hung up for thee.

In this couplet the wax of Adam's sin and Christ's crucifixion in his behalf
has been used as a form in which to pour a love message. A literal translation
of the wax of the couplet is:

Because Adam ate of the apple from the Tree of Knowledge
The Savior of the World has been crucified for thee.

To savor the gold of the couplet fully, one must know that the verb meaning "was crucified," *tasaqala,* may also signify "is anxious to be near." So a
literal translation of the gold would be:

Because of your [tempting] lips
My heart is anxious to be near thee.

In other more commonly used figures, the duplexity of the message becomes less explicit. In figures known as *hiber and merïmer,* the wax and
gold are combined in the same word or phrase instead of being put side by
side. These figures thus correspond to the English pun. In verses which employ these figures the wax is often but a contrived and transparent excuse for
getting to the real point, which appears only in the pun line. Such verses are
highly prized, however, for the Amhara tends to regard the pun as a very
high form of humor. Here are two examples of Amharic couplets based on
simple puns:

(1) *Ya-mïn ṭïqem ṭallā ya-mïn ṭïqem ṭajji*
    Tallāt sishañu bunā adargaw enji.

    Of what use is *ṭallā,* of what use is *ṭajji?**
    When seeing an enemy off, serve him coffee.

(2) *Yābbāt eddā la-lïjj yebāl nabar dero:*
    Bāyāt eddā gabāhu ennē-mā zandero.

    In olden times a father's debt was passed down to his son;
    But here I have a debt today by grandfather begun.

The pun in the first example lies in the phrase *bunā adargaw* ("serve him
coffee"), which by elision becomes *bun adargaw* ("reduce him to ashes"). In
the second couplet the pun hinges on the word *bāyat,* which signifies "grandfather" but may also be understood to represent *bāyhuāt* ("because I saw
her"). The gold meaning of this couplet is thus: It used to be said that one
inherited the debt of one's father, but in my case it was the sight of her that
put me into debt.

---

* *Ṭallā* is a kind of beer made from barley. *Ṭajj* (pronounced *ṭajji* here for the sake of rhyme)
is mead.

Ethiopic verse becomes most obscure in the figure known as *weṣṭa wayrā* ("inside of olive tree"). Here only the wax is given, and the listener must work to unearth the gold. Often this can be done only when the circumstances under which the verse was made up are known. The author of a *weṣṭa wayrā* often refuses to reveal anything that may help the listener to grasp its hidden meaning.

The expression *weṣṭa wayrā* alludes to the fact that the inner core of the olive tree is a hard substance encased by bark of a different color. The implication is that the inner sense of a *weṣṭa wayrā* poem is concealed by a veneer which conveys a quite different sense and is difficult to penetrate. This figure is thus especially suitable for expressing insults in a safe way and for esoteric philosophical or religious message. Here is an instance of the latter usage:

> *Ya-bāhetāwi lïjj sifalleg le'ullennā*
> *Ya-ḵristosn mesht talānt washama-nnā*
> *Qeṭal betābalaw hono qarama-nnā.*

> The son of a hermit, high rank to display,
> Made love with Christ's wife yesterday;
> When she fed him leaves he wasted away.

The surface meaning of this tercet describes an ambitious man who had relations with "Christ's wife" in order to raise his status, for in Ethiopia having relations with a woman of high rank is one way to gain prestige. Instead of advancing his position, however, this man lost all his power when the woman fed him (medicinal) leaves. The esoteric meaning, on the other hand, refers to the experience of a hermit. His "son" is intended to symbolize his hunger, and "Christ's wife" symbolizes fasting. The "inside" meaning, the gold, is therefore that the hermit's hunger is heightened by its relations with fasting, but it diminishes when he is fed leaves, the hallowed diet of a hermit.

The mode of the various poetic figures collectively designated as *sam-ennā warq* is intellectual rather than sensuous. The chief delight of Ethiopic poetry is to attain a maximum of thought with a minimum of words. This effect is reached, as we have seen, through subtle allusions and plays on words. The point may be a serious moral comment, the understanding of which requires one to decipher hidden references to biblical passages or sacred legends; or it may be a jest about love based on a pornographic pun. In any case, the more ingeniously compact and obscure the construction of the verse, the more pleased will be the poet and his audience. Weighty (i.e., mysterious) verse is the ideal, for as the Amhara say, "weighty verse, like heavy clothing, warms the insides."

The creation of the wax and gold figures was an integral part of the development of *qenē,* the genre of verse composed to be sung at the conclusion of devotional services in the church. And *qenē* appears to be a specifically

Amhara invention. Though exact documentation is not available on the matter, *qenē* appears to be one of the flowers of the literary renascence which took place during the centuries following the ascendance of the Solomonid Dynasty. The earliest specimens of *qenē* extant date back to the reign of Emperor Eskender (1478–94).[6] Ethiopian traditions trace the invention of *qenē* to the work of a man named Tawānay, who is said to have lived in Gojjam in the fourteenth century.[7] The important schools of *qenē* have always been located in Amhara country, primarily at the monasteries of Wā-delā, Wāsharā, and Gonj in Gojjam Province. While the choristers of Tigre have long since mastered the canons of *qenē* composition in Ge'ez, the use of wax and gold in the vernacular occurs much more often in Amharic than in Tigrinya. Indeed, wax and gold is so important in Amharic that some Amhara maintain that one does not properly speak the language unless he is well versed in the art of exploiting its numerous ambiguities. One of the more common indictments of Tigre character by Amhara is that the Tigre are "dry" (*daraq*); they say just what they feel and do not know how to be ambiguous. Conversely, many Tigre as well as other non-Amhara people in the empire complain about the excess of symbolism and subtlety in Amhara discourse.

Educated Amhara traditionalists extol wax and gold as a unique creation of their culture. One of them has written that *qenē* is as distinctive of Ethiopia's spiritual culture as *tēff*, a species of grass grown as a cereal grain only in Ethiopia, is distinctive of her material culture.[8] They further maintain that Ge'ez *qenē* contains a unique kind of wisdom, dark and deep. Instruction in this occult art of verse composition has traditionally been regarded as propaedeutic to the study of religious texts.* Partly this is because Ge'ez grammar, which must be known in order to understand these texts, is normally taught only in the schools of *qenē*. The more philosophical reason given, however, is that by affording exercise in fathoming secrets it "opens the mind" and thereby enhances the student's ability to approach the divine mysteries.

Important as such functions may be in the high culture of Ethiopia, wax and gold represents more than a principle of poetic composition and a method of spiritual gymnastics for a small class of literati. The ambiguity symbolized by the formula *sam-ennā warq* colors the entire fabric of traditional Amhara life. It patterns the speech and outlook of every Amhara. When he talks, his

---

* The course of instruction in *qenē* takes from two to five years, according to the talent of the student and the degree of mastery he desires. Ge'ez grammar and *qenē* prosody are taught side by side. The former, usually studied in the evening, is learned by rote. The latter is taught by running the student step by step through the gamut of figures and stanza forms. Instruction by example begins in the dark, before sunrise. The teacher extemporizes on a given theme in each of the stanza forms. His productions are memorized and discussed. In the daytime each student goes off by himself to a secluded place and composes one stanza. When finished—it may take him all day to perfect a couplet—he recites it to the master, who makes appropriate critical comments.

9 / *Tradition and Modernization*

words often carry *double-entendre* as a matter of course; when he listens, he is ever on the lookout for latent meanings and hidden motives. As one of my Ethiopian colleagues has said: "Wax and gold is anything but a formula—it is a way of life."

In essence, wax and gold is simply a more refined and stylized manifestation of the Amhara's basic manner of communicating. This manner is indirect, often secretive. Amharic conversation is larded with vague remarks like *Min yeshāllāl?* ("What is better?") when the speaker has failed to indicate what is the issue at hand, or *Tādyās!*, an interjection which can mean almost anything. Often, when the speaker is then quizzed about the issue at hand, he will give an answer that does not reveal what is really on his mind at all, and even when he does, the person with whom he is talking is likely to interpret his response as a disguise.

Wax and gold embodies this fundamental indirection in speech by means of the studied use of ambiguity. Apart from its literary and religious manifestations, wax and gold appears in the common life of the traditional Amhara on a variety of occasions and serves a number of diverse functions.

It provides the medium for an inexhaustible supply of humor, among a wry people who prefer the clever, double-edged remark to comic actions or incongruous situations. This includes the wit of daily life—the invention of puns and sly retorts, the telling and retelling of good anecdotes and famous lines—as well as the more formalized humor on festive occasions, where minstrels sing the *sam-ennā warq* verses extemporized by the guests.

It provides a means for insulting one's fellows in a socially approved manner, in a culture which requires fastidious etiquette in social relations and punishes direct insults by heavy fines. *Sam-ennā warq* insulting, too, has its more stylized expressions, as at the drink-house, where one may find persons competing in a prolonged exchange of more or less disguised insults, or in time of political or military conflict, when opposing lords were wont formerly to satirize one another with ambiguous couplets.

It provides a technique for defending the sphere of privacy against excessive intrusion, in a social order that thrives on rumor and gossip and puts most of its people at the mercy of superiors. While vague and evasive responses often suffice to dampen the enthusiasm of the tax collector or the curious neighbor, *sam-ennā warq* constitutes another potent weapon of self-defense.

Finally, it provides the one outlet for criticism of authority figures in a society which strictly controls every kind of overt aggression toward authority, be it parental, religious, or political. Thus it has been a safety valve for certain social tensions, enabling, for example, witty individuals to satirize the monarch himself and still live to repeat the witticism—so long as its subject was himself duly appreciative of the cleverness of the lines.

TRADITION AND MODERNITY

Insofar as Ethiopia is committed to the pursuit of modernity, she cannot fail to be embarrassed to some extent by the wax-and-gold complex. For nothing could be more at odds with the ethos of modernization, if not with its actuality, than a cult of ambiguity.[9]

It is true, of course, that cultural formations analogous to wax and gold in their exploitation of ambiguity have been prominent throughout the history of the West, not to mention the whole non-Western world. The Christian tradition has always made much of parables and allegories. The classical teaching of rhetoric, following Cicero, placed great stress on the use of paradox; and a major philosophical tradition, stretching from Plato to Marx, has been founded on a logic which assumes that reality can be known only by combining opposite concepts and that any single term is subject to dual interpretation. The flowering of symbolist literature, to take a more recent example, created an audience as partial to subtle allusion and *double-entendre* as the most obscurantist proponent of *wesṭa wayrā*.

Yet there can be little doubt that the pace-setting spirit of modern Western culture rests on a commitment to unambiguous communication. It is predicated on the proposition that A must be A or not be A. It was no accident that one of the more characteristic philosophical movements of the present century, logical positivism, should have had as its primary motif the desire to maximize precision in the use of language. For the decisive institutions of the modern world—technologies based on logico-experimental science, rational legal systems, and bureaucratic organizations in government, commerce, and industry—depend intimately on the unambiguous definition of terms and the utmost clarity of expression. Whether the task be one of constructing a legal contract, outlining a job description, designing a nuclear reactor, classifying genera and species, or defining variables and their interrelations, these characteristic modern activities are informed by the need and intention to eliminate, as far as possible, all traces of linguistic ambiguity.

The incorporation of these aspects of modern culture into Ethiopian life must inevitably produce a certain amount of strain in a culture which makes such thoroughgoing use of analogy and equivocation. Indeed, tension generated by this issue has been manifest in a variety of ways. Among the modern-educated Ethiopians, one finds demands for greater clarity in the specification of responsibilities in administration. One finds increased impatience with the devious, equivocal talk involved in joint action of any sort. One finds a slowly growing disposition to structure and fulfil expectations in literal terms, and occasional outbursts of protest against the vagueness and the conspiratorial mentality of those schooled only in the traditional way. In order to escape what they feel are the burdensome subtleties of Amharic, some Ethiopians prefer to speak in English in their offices. An alternative solution is proffered by those Amharic writers and journalists who have attempted to adapt Amharic to the modern idiom, replacing the florid, intricate sentence of yore with short, simple, straightforward declarative sentences —an effort that parallels changes in other countries, such as Japan, where an intrinsically more ambiguous language than Amharic in the traditional culture has been revised to facilitate more precise modes of expression.[10]

The opposition between the wax-and-gold complex and the rationalistic aspects of modern culture which some Ethiopians now seek to assimilate is of interest here as an instance of the more general phenomenon toward which this book as a whole is oriented. It is the dilemma posed in all the nations of Asia and Africa by the confrontation of their traditional cultures with their rather recently activated modernist aspirations. To study what is transpiring in these nations in terms of the encounter between tradition and modernity, rather than in terms of the more bland and less biased category of social change, is to focus our attention on a very important aspect of their actual situation: many members of these societies have suddenly been forced to grapple with a number of intellectual and moral dilemmas of great magnitude. The concepts of tradition and modernity are symbols to which they are more or less passionately attached. All of them have concepts symbolizing the sanctity of tradition, like the Amharic *hāymānot abāw* ("faith of the fathers"); and all have concepts symbolizing the goal of modernity, like the Amharic *sel̪t̪ānē* ("civilization"). And in all these nations the conflict between the two sorts of orientation has produced acute forms of disorientation, on the one hand, and extraordinary challenges to creativity, on the other.

Adopting this perspective for the study of "transitional" societies probably opens the door more widely than usual for the intrusion of the biases of the observer. For the observer's own attitudes regarding tradition and modernity naturally affect the order of questions he will ask and the kinds of data he will examine in making his analysis of the "actual situation." They influence, for example, how much attention he pays to the weakening of norms governing traditional kinship systems and whether he views this primarily as a form of social disorganization or primarily as a precondition for more effective societal organization. Accordingly it is fitting that we introduce the analyses to be presented below with a brief statement of the philosophy which guides the author's approach to these questions. This may be done most effectively by surveying the range of positions that might be taken. In considering the encounter between traditional and modern culture patterns currently experienced in acute form in most nations of the world, one may discern, at a high level of abstraction, these five positions: (1) the Traditionalist, (2) the Modernist, (3) the Skeptic, (4) the Conciliatory, and (5) the Pragmatist.

The Traditionalist may be defined as one who is oriented to the maximization of traditional values. What these values are of course varies considerably from culture to culture, but in all cases they include the values of kinship and religion. The Traditionalist sees modernization in general as a radically demoralizing force, yet may favor those elements of modern culture which serve to strengthen traditional patterns: modern military techniques to defend the nation's integrity, modern media to propagate inherited beliefs and values, etc. The questions inspired by this approach would be: What are the traditional values? In what ways are they threatened by modernization, and how may they be saved?

The Modernist is, in one form or another, a child of the Enlightenment. He asserts the superiority of reason over mere custom and locates the most important human values in the effort to subject man's physical and social environment to rational control. The Modernist views traditional patterns instrumentally, as potential aids or obstacles to modernization. The main questions he asks are: What are the modernizing elements in the society? What potentially useful resources are latent in the traditional system? What are the traditional obstacles to modernization, and how can they be overcome?

The Skeptic feels that no really worthwhile values can be realized in transitional societies, since their traditional orders have been fatally undermined and yet they are incapable of sustaining a modern institutional order. The reality alluded to here has been depicted in Colin Turnbull's poignant book, *The Lonely African.* Turnbull sees the urban, modern-educated Africans as adrift, accepted neither by the Western masters of modern culture nor by their own people, and the rural traditional people as no less vulnerable because they have lost the power and isolation necessary to sustain the ancient ways. This condition is regarded by some observers as justification for a position of skeptical detachment. Their commitment is to orders of integral value impossible in a society so disrupted, and their intellectual interest in transitional societies is, to paraphrase Max Weber, to see how much they can bear.

The position I have labeled "Conciliatory" stresses the minimization of tension and violence rather than the maximization of values, traditional or modern. The Conciliatory sees the transitional situation as one inherently fraught with increased conflict, and he is concerned more with the maintenance of security and order than with the quality of life in the social order involved. Insofar as he sees modernization as desirable, his main concern is that it be gradual. Questions natural to this approach include: What are the main lines of cleavage in a transitional society? What are the tendencies toward radical polarization between traditionalist and modernist elements in the society, and what conditions promote the reduction of such polarization?

The Pragmatist position differs from the Skeptic and the Conciliatory chiefly in its more affirmative emphasis. The Pragmatist is committed to the optimum realization of *all* values possible in a given historic situation. He affirms the human values of modernization, yet conceives of modernity not as of a single, fixed nature but as relative to the cultural context in which modernization takes place. Given the commitment to modernization he would sustain traditional values wherever possible; would modify them where feasible; and would reject them where necessary. The chief questions raised from this point of view will be outlined presently, since it is the approach we ourselves shall be following.

All of the intellectual positions just identified have been taken by respectable thinkers. All are to be found among the members of the transitional societies, distributed according to the individual's position in the social structure and, secondarily, according to his psychological makeup. Within the social sciences, moreover, the subject matters of the various disciplines incline them to one or another of these positions. Roughly speaking, one may say that heretofore the anthropologist has tended to take the Traditionalist position; the economist and the Marxist sociologist have been Modernists; the political scientist has leaned toward the Conciliatory position; while sociologists have been oriented as Skeptics and Pragmatists.

THE QUESTIONS OF A PRAGMATIST

Our intention in this book is to analyze a number of aspects of the confrontation between Amhara tradition and Ethiopia's quest for modernity from the viewpoint of a Pragmatist. Three general questions express the main concerns of this viewpoint: (1) What is the nature of the traditional culture, and what are its more enduring beliefs and values? (2) What aspects of modern culture are of interest to the society, and what are the processes by which they are introduced and institutionalized? (3) Given this interest in modernization, in what ways has it been frustrated by certain features of the traditional culture?

These three questions divide the following chapters into three pairs. Chapters ii and iii attempt a sympathetic understanding of some aspects of Amhara culture and an assessment of their positive relevance for Ethiopia in transition. Chapters iv and v deal with aspects of Amhara culture which have been found inadequate for modernization and with the natural processes by which they have been replaced in part by modernizing structures. Chapters vi and vii then explore aspects of the traditional Amhara culture which appear to be obstacles to the realization of the modernist goals.

We shall begin by exploring one of the traditional bases of cultural identity among the Amhara, one of those primordial sentiments whose integrity is a condition of vitality for a traditional people.[11] Vis-à-vis outsiders, the Amhara identify strongly with their religion, language, and racial characteristics, though not so fanatically as to preclude their toleration of other groups as part of a common nationality. Among themselves, however, the Amhara place great stress on region of origin. Deeply sentimental about their home-lands, they regard those whose families have long dwelt in the same area almost as kinsmen vis-à-vis Amhara from other regions. In chapter ii, two of these areas which hold a special place in Ethiopian history are explored in some detail. The history, ethos, and cultural significance of Manz and Gondar are discussed, partly to provide an introduction to Amhara culture that has some historical depth, and partly as background to the general ques-tion of the place of primordial sentiments like regionalism in a modernizing society.

Chapter iii proceeds to examine the matrix of Amhara culture, the world of the peasant. Its rhetorical aim is chiefly to bring the little-known peasant into sharper focus, to reaffirm the peasant world as one worthy of attention and respect. This will be done, first, by describing the social setting of peas-ant life, and the main events which make up the daily round and annual cycle of the typical Amhara. Then we shall explore the world view of the Amhara peasant, the main ideas and attitudes through which he interprets his experience. In conclusion, we shall discuss the relation of some aspects of this world view to certain aspects of modern culture.

Chapter iv proceeds from the fact that the skills and values needed for effec-tive participation in a modernizing society cannot be imparted by the tradi-tional processes of socialization during adolescence. With the establishment of a government school system a new and separate pattern has come into being that exists largely, though not wholly, in isolation from the traditional agents and mechanisms of secondary socialization. The subject of this chap-ter is thus the contrasting conditions in which an Amhara youth is brought up in the traditional and modernizing sectors of Ethiopian society. This ac-count is followed by a portrayal of the outlook of Ethiopian students today, with emphasis on the question of the continuity and discontinuity of their beliefs, tastes, and values with those of traditional Amhara culture.

In chapter v our attention shifts to the elite structure of Amhara-Tigre society. In this sphere modernization has proceeded, not by the addition of a novel structure as in the case of secondary socialization during adolescence, but through a process of differentiation within the existing order and delib-erate co-ordination by the sovereign. We shall discuss, first, the traditional elites of monarchy, nobility, and clergy; and then the changes in the status of these elites and the emergence of the new elites of government officials and a modern-educated "intelligentsia."

A key question to emerge from this chapter concerns what appears to be the relative ineffectuality and passivity of the modernizing intelligentsia as a whole. This is a complex and difficult question, only partly to be explained by the political conditions which are referred to in the chapter. We shall sug-

. 1.—*School of* qenē (*Wāsharā Māryām monastery, Gojjam*)

FIG. 2.—*Nagāssi's church, Agāntchā, Manz*

FIG. 3.—*Fāsil's castle, Gondar*

FIG. 4.—*Two Manzē elders*

FIG. 5.—*Manz: the sale of* bānnā

gest that it also reflects certain psychological and social characteristics deeply rooted in the culture of the land of wax and gold. These characteristics will be the subject of analysis in the two concluding chapters, which deal, respectively, with the phenomena of orality and of individualism in Amhara culture.

It should be evident from the foregoing that I have refrained from attempting a comprehensive assessment of the relationship between Amhara tradition and Ethiopia's modernization. By limiting myself to problems for which I had both prior theoretical interests and data obtained at first hand, I have sought to gain in accuracy of detail and depth of understanding what I might lose in breadth of coverage. It is hoped, moreover, that these studies may stimulate other scholars to extend this mode of analysis into such crucial areas as law, economic behavior, family life, religion, and military institutions.

On the other hand, by treating the relation between tradition and modernity as it appears in a variety of social and cultural phenomena rather than by concentrating on a single problem, I have found it easier to articulate some of the complexities of that relation. For traditional patterns and modern aspirations are related in many ways. Oftentimes they are fully compatible, the traditional either positively supporting the modern or else presenting no conflict with it. When conflict does obtain, on the other hand, it may work toward resolution in a number of different ways. One alternative is straightforward displacement of the old by the new, through a varying combination of coercive and persuasive measures. Another alternative is through structural differentiation, as mentioned above, either through the incorporation of a novel form from outside or through processes of internal differentiation. Still another way is through a subtle transformation of traditional forms so that they continue to be meaningful but are redefined to fit the modern situation. In its most creative outcome, the conflict may involve so genuine a dialogue between traditional and modern patterns that novel values emerge and authentic variants of modern culture are developed.

Perhaps the most important insight in this connection is that while traditional patterns may stand in conflict with modernity in some respects, the same patterns may support modernity in other respects. It is to this sort of complex relationship that the Pragmatist is most likely to draw attention. Theoretically the relationship follows logically from the realization, hard won by sociologists during recent decades, that no modern society can exist without substantial reliance on patterns which must be regarded as traditional and not rational. For a concrete example of this dual relationship, let us turn once more to the phenomenon previously discussed, that of wax and gold.

We have argued that the ambiguity and equivocation symbolized by the Amharic formula wax and gold stands in opposition to the semantic dimension of modernization which, because of the ascendance of technology, contractual relations, and bureaucratic organization places great stress on the unambiguous use of language. Yet we may now argue that the intellectual habits associated with the wax-and-gold pattern are also valuable assets in Ethiopia's pursuit of modernity.

The experience of history has demonstrated the futility of attempting the revolutionary implementation of a clear and distinct ideal in human society. No matter how bold and sweeping the program, traditional patterns persist tenaciously. The only real alternatives are whether they are to be maintained in isolation from the modern culture, or whether traditional and modern patterns can be fused sufficiently to produce a relatively homogeneous sort of culture. As Gabriel Almond's analysis suggests, the latter alternative appears to be conducive to stability and effectiveness in modern political systems.[12] For that to take place, however, traditional symbols must be interpreted with sufficient ambiguity as to permit their fusion with modern ones. The problems of "cultural management" faced by the elites of the transitional nations can only be handled in the long run by a deliberate effort to exploit the ambiguity of traditional symbols.

Enrico Cerulli's interpretation of the Aksumite inscriptions provides an interesting precedent for such manipulation of language in the service of induced culture change in Ethiopia.[13] Cerulli has remarked on the cautious and ambiguous language with which Emperor Ēzānā recorded his conversion to Christianity in the fourth century. For example, Ēzānā refers to his new deity, not as "God of the Christians," but with the traditional pagan symbolism, "God of the Heaven" and "God of the Earth"; and he attaches to his new God the same epithet—"Who has not been conquered by enemies"—which traditionally belonged to the pagan god Mahrem. So interpreted, Ēzānā's inscription may be seen as an antique expression of that cultural disposition which centuries later the Amhara were to crystallize in the canons of *sam-ennā warq* poesy. At the same time it illustrates how the sacred symbols of a traditional culture may be used to facilitate radical innovation.

What is true at the level of national leadership is no less true for the leadership of less inclusive social systems. Wise politicians at all levels have always been aware that to gain support and preserve solidarity it is not advisable to adhere scrupulously to a single literal interpretation of any system of beliefs or code of norms. This perception has been affirmed by recent sociological investigations, which show that the most effective administrators of complex organizations are those who have a high tolerance of ambiguity and who are skilled in the use of ambiguous language for the purpose of reducing interpersonal tensions.

In addition to serving these instrumental functions, the ambiguous use of language belongs in the most modern of cultures because it is the foundation of a humane literary style. The rationalist emphasis on clear and distinct ideas and the puritanical emphasis on honest, straightforward, and plain talk are indispensable in running the machinery of modern society but by themselves are insufficient to represent the savor of human experience. The ascendance of unambiguous communication in American culture has resulted in the triumph of "a journalese," which is characterized, as one critic has put it, by "words of flat signification . . . and with none of the broadly ruminative phrases which have the power to inspire speculation." As he further observes:

> The essential sterility of such a style is one of the surest signs we have that modern man is being dessicated. For the "modern" style is at once brash and timid: brash enough to break old patterns without thinking, and timid before the tremendous evocative and constructive powers immanent in language.[14]

If the aim of modern culture is a fuller life for man, it neglects its ends if strictly cognitive and instrumental considerations become so dominant that its very matrix becomes flat and dry. For modernity to be complete, the tremendous evocative powers immanent in language must also be unleashed.

The distrust of ambiguity arises in a modernizing society because those processes most obviously associated with the culture of modernity—chiefly those having to do with rational mastery over the environment and the rational co-ordination of human activities—take place in contexts where unambiguous communication is imperative. The successful development and operation of institutions in these areas do require, as we have suggested, the setting-aside of devious and equivocal habits of mind. But in those areas involving the creation of solidarity, the management of tensions, and the expression of intuition and sentiment, criteria of effectiveness would seem to permit, indeed to require considerable reliance on the uses of ambiguity. From this it follows that the wax-and-gold mentality should be regarded not only as an obstacle to Ethiopia's modernization but also, by virtue of its contribution to the continuing effectiveness of her social organization and the continuing richness of her expressive culture, as a beneficial agent.

2

The Legacy of Manz and Gondar

The six centuries of Ethiopian history that end with the conquests of Menelik —a historical unity which circumscribes the matured Amhara culture—may be divided into three main episodes: synthesis (1270–1527), in which the might and Christian culture of Ethiopia were consolidated and expanded; shock (1527–1633), in which the Ethiopian body politic was dealt a series of severe blows; and recovery (1633–1900), in which Ethiopia labored to resurrect itself —first through Gondar, then Tigre and Shoa—until its ancient order began to be threatened by the demands of a modern world.

Synthesis

Following the ascendance of the Shoan Amhara in 1270, Amhara-Tigre society attained a kind of medieval prosperity. Monophysite Christianity, incorporating many features of indigenous animist cults, was increasingly diffused among the peoples of the land. Though Amharic advanced as a vernacular tongue, Ge'ez was understood by the learned of both the Amhara and Tigre regions, and served as a ready medium for expressing the piety and fantasy of the age. The clergy were fruitful and multiplied, and produced sufficient heresies to keep the fires of theological disputation well fueled.

A hereditary line of Christian monarchs, claiming descent from King Solomon, had been made secure. The armies of the emperors and their powerful governors were active and usually successful. Though intrigue and revolt at

18

times brought dissension to the state, the legitimate Crown was triumphant most of the time.

In the history of Ethiopian literature the period has been called a Golden Age.[1] The important works composed during this time include *The Glory of Kings,* which contains the story of the Queen of Sheba, Solomon, and their offspring, Menelik I, legendary first king of Ethiopia; *The Book of the Mysteries of Heaven and Earth,* a compilation of occult theology and numerology, with a Miltonic account of the struggle between Michael and Satan; *The Christian Romance of Alexander the Great,* a fantastic portrayal of Alexander as a Christian hero who traverses the Land of Darkness and the miraculous Land of the Living; the moralizing tracts of the greatest emperor of the period, Zar'a Yā'qob; as well as numerous lives of saints and translations of Christian writings from Arabic.

Connoisseurs of Ethiopian art attribute the most original and refined paintings to the latter part of this period. Using translucent colors and austere shapes and design, Ethiopian monks brought to expression an intense spirituality in the form of miniatures in illuminated manuscripts.[2]

At the same time this was the Heroic Age of Ethiopian warfare. Amda Tseyon vanquished sixteen Muslim chiefs to the south and west; the valor of Sayfa Ar'ed was celebrated in medieval Arab tales of chivalry; Dāwit I pushed his victories against the Muslims as far as Zeila on the Gulf of Aden. Improved military equipment and organization under Yeshāq brought the imperial forces to a new level of discipline and power, which Yeshāq used to establish his authority in many southern areas. Zar'a Yā'qob, famous for endowing churches and monasteries and for encouraging literature and art, was a successful warrior in his own right.

A close-up of Ethiopia at the height of its medieval synthesis is provided by Father Francisco Alvares, Portuguese emissary to Abyssinia during the years 1520–27.[3] We see a prosperous kingdom, its far-flung dominions headed by hereditary rulers and royal appointees, all of whom pay tribute in kind to the emperor. The tribute consists of horses and mules, blankets and cloths, silk stuffs and gold, all in impressive amounts. The provincial heads, and the armies they must make available, live off the land they govern. The numerous priests and monks are supported by lands granted them by the king. Justice is administered at three levels, with the possibility of appeal from the local judge, to the provincial governor, to the royal court itself. The king's mobile camp, large as a town, is his capital, so that he spends his years marching about from one corner of his domain to another.

The monarch at the time of Alvares' visit was Lebna Dengel (1508–40), a man of pride and temper. He refused to heed counsel that the kingdom was imperiled by threats from the outside. Indeed, legend has it that he was discontented with the prevailing civil harmony and begged God to send an adversary, so that his people might be roused from their peacetime habits and the nation could have a chance to prove its might. Ethiopia never fully recovered from the shock that came in the middle of his reign.

Shock

Amhara-Tigre society was convulsed by one disaster after another during the succeeding century. In 1527 began a series of conflicts with the Muslim kingdom of Adal led by a fearful warrior, Imam Ahmad ibn Ibrahim al-Ghazi, surnamed Grāñ. Equipped with firearms from the Ottoman Turks and hordes of Somali soldiers, Ahmad Grāñ proceeded to overrun Ethiopia, causing destruction and massacre wherever he tread. Only after most of the country had been laid waste, its inhabitants forced to embrace Islam, its churches looted and burned, was Ahmad Grāñ at last killed. His troops were routed by an Ethiopian force that had been revived by the expedition of Portuguese match-lockmen under Christopher da Gama.

The wars with Ahmad Grāñ left the country impoverished and disorganized. In this state it lay vulnerable to another shock: the massive tribal movements of the Galla from the south. The Galla advanced through periodic invasions of their warrior age groups. Coming first in furtive raids, then concerted warfare, finally by slow migration, these hardy nomads managed to penetrate deeply into Amhara lands. By 1563 the Galla had invaded over a third of the empire.

Ethiopia was further shaken in 1557 when the Ottoman Turks occupied the port of Massawa. This action introduced a problem that was to harass Ethiopia intermittently until the present: the danger of occupation by European powers. The Ethiopians were able to repulse the Turkish invader as he pushed farther inland, but Massawa remained in foreign hands until 1941.

In seeking to recover from the destruction wrought by Grāñ's holy war, a number of emperors turned to European Christian powers for religious support as well as for political and technical assistance. Some of them became converts to Catholicism and, encouraged by Portuguese Jesuit missionaries, attempted to promote the new faith among their subjects. The outcome was only further bloodshed. Emperor Za Dengel's conversion in 1603 aroused civil strife and led to his downfall at the hands of nobles who did not share his Catholic sympathies. More serious trouble appeared during the reign of Susneyos (1607-32). He, too, adopted the Roman faith, and allowed one of the more impetuous Jesuits, Alphonzo Mendez, to direct a number of reforms in the Ethiopian Church. Mendez insisted that all priests be reordained by himself, that the population be rebaptized, and that the liturgy be rewritten. He forbade circumcision, and defined the previously unknown crime of witchcraft. Such measures antagonized the populace and provoked "horrid uproars, bloody wars, and the slaughter of many great Personages," as Ludolphus put it.[4] At length, unable to witness the further decimation of his people because of religious controversies, Susneyos abdicated in favor of his son Fāsil. Fāsil lost little time in deporting the Jesuits and restoring the Orthodox status quo.

Recovery

In the wake of all these collisions, Ethiopia made two valiant attempts to regain equilibrium and glory: through the splendor of Gondar in the seventeenth and early eighteenth centuries, and through the force of three emperors of the nineteenth century—Tēwodros II, Yohānnes IV of Tigre, and Menelik II of Shoa.

Gondar was founded as a new and stationary capital by Fāsil. It served as imperial headquarters for many generations. Later, the kingdom of Tigre knew a resurgence of power that led to control of the empire under Yohānnes (1872–89). His castle at Makalle symbolized one last rally for the north—after an interregnum of a thousand years—before being eclipsed by the Shoan throne.

The shock which began with the invasions of Ahmad Grañ shattered Ethiopia's medieval synthesis once and for all. The political consequence of those disruptions was an increase in provincialism, reaching its climax in the famous "Age of the Princes" (1755–1855) when each province had its own sovereign and for all practical purposes was a polity unto itself. The Solomonic line, the matrix of Ethiopian political unity, was splintered in several directions, leaving contenders in each of the provinces. Though the official imperial line remained at Gondar, Tigre was able to reassert its ancient claims and Gojjam recurrently voiced its separatism, and what may be called the "House of Manz" came to compete with Gondar as a center of national consciousness.

This political division was accompanied by a peculiar cultural bifurcation. Elements of the national culture that had been rather evenly distributed before Ahmad Grañ now became relatively specialized in Gondar and Manz. The recovery of Ethiopia produced a geographical division of manners and morals as well as several lines of Solomonic royalty.

HISTORICAL PROFILES

The Role of Gondar

Gondar is the only city in Ethiopia with charm and character expressive of Amhara culture. Even today, despite modern accretions, the remnants of its castles, walls, bridges, and sanctuaries transmit a stately calm, redolent of past nobility and African grandeur.

The town is situated on a flat volcanic ridge at seven thousand feet above sea level. It is surrounded by three rings of high mountains, which afforded military protection in times past and today provide handsome scenery. Only toward the south is a direct land route alluring, as the ridge descends toward the fertile plains of Dambiyā and the waters of Ṭānā, largest lake in Ethiopia.

Because of its intermediate altitude, Gondar escapes the chill of higher regions and the intense sun of the lowlands: its climate is among the most pleasant in Ethiopia. Water is supplied by two streams—the Angarab and the Qīha—which enclose the town, then flow together down to Lake Ṭānā twenty-one miles away. Adequate rains throughout the year assure two, some-

TABLE 1

THE HOUSES OF GONDAR AND MANZ

Gondarine Emperors Who Ruled with Full Power		The Line of Independent Shoan Rulers		
Name	Dates of Reign	Name	Highest Rank Attained	Dates of Reign
Fāsil (Fāsiladas)......	1632–67	Nagāssi (Nagāssē Kristos)	Abēto	169?–1703
Yohānnes I (the Pious)	1667–82	Sebstē (Sebstyānos)......	Marīdāzmātch	1705–20
Iyāsu I (the Great)...	1682–1706	Abbīyē...............	Marīdāzmātch	1720–45
Takla Hāymānot I...	1706–8	Amhāyas (Amhā Iyasus)..	Marīdāzmātch	1745–75
Tēwoflos............	1708–11	Asfā Wassan..........	Marīdāzmātch	1775–1808
Yosṭos.............	1711–16	Wassan Sagad.........	Rās	1808–13
Dāwit III (the Singer).	1716–21	Sāhla Selassie..........	Negus	1813–47
Bakāffā (the Inexo-		Haile Malakot..........	Negus	1847–55
rable).............	1721–30	***		***
Iyāsu II (the Little)...	1730–55	Menelik II.............	....	....
		As ruler of Shoa.......	Negus	1865–89
		As emperor of Ethiopia.	Negusa Nagast	1889–1913

times three, crops in the hinterland. Ṭēff and other grains, oilseed, honey, and livestock are produced in abundance.

The population of Gondar approached seventy thousand during the city's time of power.[5] Thereafter it declined to but a few thousands. The townspeople of Gondar have been chiefly traders, priests, scribes, soldiers, artisans, and drink-house proprietresses. Like the inhabitants of Aksum, they are more conscious of Ethiopian history than people elsewhere in the country, as well they might be.

Gondar was founded by Emperor Fāsil about 1635. Legend says that he was inspired to plant his capital there because of a prophecy that Ethiopia would attain its greatest power if its capital were established in a place whose name began with the syllable Go. More practical considerations were surely the proximity to water, the protective rings of mountains, and the healthy distance from Galla tribes.

When Fāsil arrived at Gondar, then no more than an insignificant village, he pitched his tent near a large sycamore. This magnificent tree, one of the landmarks of Gondar, became the site of popular celebrations on holidays. Not far from this tree Fāsil decided to construct his castle, the largest and best preserved of the castles of Gondar. Thus began an ambitious program of building, which included the construction of seven churches, a number of bridges over the streams around Gondar, and a large bath, next to which Fāsil placed a three-story pavilion. In the course of the following century Fāsil's successors added many more buildings, including a total of twenty-one additional churches. Of the secular buildings, the castles of Bakāffā and Empress Mantuāb and the "Recreation Hall" of Dāwit III were the most outstanding.

In their political endeavors, Gondar's monarchs began by upholding the Abyssinian tradition of a warrior king. Though unable to secure definitive victories over his enemies, Fāsil was continually joining battle with them. He spent all but five of his thirty-five years of rule on the warpath. The reign of Yohānnes the Pious was marked more by religious than military preoccupations, but warfare on a small scale was carried out during half the years he ruled. Yohānnes' son, Iyāsu the Great, seized the spear with renewed vigor and brought Gondar to the pinnacle of its might. Iyāsu's campaigns carried him to far parts of the empire, some of which were not again to be visited by a triumphant Amhara king until two centuries later.

On Iyāsu's return from one of his famous field tours, Gondar suffered a misfortune that ushered in a long era of political disorganization. Learning that his favorite concubine had died and been buried while he was away, the grief-stricken Iyāsu withdrew to one of the monastic islands of Lake Ṭānā. His son, Takla Hāymānot, took advantage of the situation to have himself proclaimed emperor; and shortly after, probably encouraged by those of the clergy who mistrusted Iyāsu's sympathy for Catholicism, he had his father assassinated on the isle.

The next four emperors had short and brutish reigns. Takla Hāymānot, Tēwoflos, and Yosṭos were occupied mainly with the quashing of conspiracy and rebellion. Even so, they had time for the favored sports of hunting wild animals and raiding Galla and Negroid tribes. Dāwit III, it seems, did not even accomplish that. The chief slaughter in his reign was of the local clergy; he brought Muslim Galla to massacre hundreds of the monks and priests of Gondar, for they had opposed his theological views. All four emperors ended ignobly. Takla Hāymānot was stabbed to death; Tēwoflos was probably poisoned; Yosṭos, not of the Solomonic line, was forcibly deposed; and Dāwit III was poisoned. Bakāffā was more careful to protect himself from pretenders than were his predecessors. He spent his days breaking the power of the feudal lords and strengthening the hand of the monarchy, and died a natural death.

Iyāsu II was the last of the Gondar emperors to rule with full power. He, too, had to spend much of his military energy suppressing conspirators. One pretender maintained a long siege of Gondar, and although his troops never succeeded in storming the castle, they destroyed much of the capital. After checking the rebels, Iyāsu II withdrew from the political affairs and became absorbed in private pursuits. Later, stung by the popular ridicule of his inactivity, he launched a major campaign against the Fung kingdom of Senaar. The net result of that venture was eighteen thousand dead and the depletion of his treasury. The subsequent subdual of Lāstā, a rebel region for generations, and Iyāsu's raids against tribes in the Atbārā district were not sufficient to redeem that defeat or restore the force of Gondar.

The political history of Gondar after the assassination of Iyāsu the Great is that of a fairly steady decline. The power of the monarchy was weakened by frequent coups d'état: no fewer than twenty-five emperors were deposed in the century and a half between Iyāsu I and Tēwodros. The power of central government was weakened by the increased strength of the nobles, each pursuing his personal interests. The power of the Abyssinian nation was weakened by the influx of Galla, who entered Gondar as prisoners and mercenary troops and finally, with the marriage of Iyāsu II to the daughter of a Galla chieftain, reached the royal court itself. The succession of emperors after Iyāsu II is largely a list of figureheads, living their brief spells in the dreary pomp into which the court had fallen, while the real power was wielded by independent lords throughout the land.

The history of Gondar, however, is more than a chronicle of military expeditions and political intrigues. It is above all a history of the Amhara's most concentrated attempt to cultivate their religious and aesthetic culture, some aspect of which stimulated most of Gondar's sovereigns.

Fāsil, we have seen, was greatly interested in architecture. In addition to his many constructions in and around Gondar, he rebuilt the old cathedral at Aksum, which had been in ruins since the pillage of Ahmad Grāñ. Fāsil's interest in religion, moreover, extended beyond the building of churches. He sought to promote the integrity of the Ethiopian Church by expelling the Jesuits, and assisted its restoration by fixing rules for the ministration of church services.

Yohānnes the Pious was devoted to the furtherance of religious studies. He built a library to house religious manuscripts, as well as two new churches. Possessed of an unusual decorative bent, he had the walls of the library covered with a yellowish plaster and raised designs in stucco, and he himself painted miniatures on some of the manuscripts. His queen, Sebla Wangel, sponsored the translation of works from Arabic. Among these were *Laws of the Kings,* a collection of civil and canon laws which became the official basis for judication, and a penitential manual, *Spiritual Medicine,* the last major production in Ge'ez literature.

Yohānnes also continued Fāsil's work of "purifying" the church. He decreed that descendants of the Portuguese must leave Ethiopia unless they joined the Orthodox Church and that Muslims must reside apart, either in their own villages or in ghettos. Ordained as a priest before becoming emperor, Yohānnes followed keenly the theological disputes of his day. Toward the end of his reign he convoked a synod in Gondar to discuss the nature of the Holy Spirit in Christ, the chief theological question in Ethiopian history.

Iyāsu I, like many of Ethiopia's rulers, appears to have been moved by deep religious feeling. Describing Iyāsu's religiosity, one of the priests of Gondar wrote an eulogy a few years after his death:

> The king used to stand at the window of his palace . . . and listen from his tower on high to the singing of the priests and learned men, to their gentle hymns which moistened the bones by their exceeding tenderness. When their offerings pleased him greatly he was pierced with affection for them and drawn by the harmony of their heavenly peace. For this reason . . . he would prepare for them dinners filled with delights, and bid them eat with him in his royal chambers, ornamented all about with the beauty of pure gold and wrought silver. He would take off his gold necklace and present it to them. He adorned them with garments of purple and of staffs interwoven with gold from the treasury of his kingdom. . . . None of the kings before him had done such as he, and none of the clergy of yore had been treated as were his priests and learned men. After the dinners, the king and his priests together sang hymns of joy and jubilation all night long in the palace—in their time of pleasure, in the sweetness of divine ministry.[6]

Iyāsu the Great did much to establish Gondar as the most important center of religious culture in Ethiopia. To this end he brought outstanding priests and learned men from all over the country to his capital. From Gojjam, for example, he brought the great master of religious verse, Kǐfflē Yohānnes, whose lines are remembered even today. The number of teachers in Gondar in his time exceeded five hundred; there were one hundred and fifty at his church Dabra Berhān Selassie alone.* It was under Iyāsu I that the classic subject matter of the higher religious studies in Abyssinia—*zēmā* ("religious

---

* Dabra Berhān Selassie, one of the two churches built by Iyāsu I, is the only one of the original churches of Gondar which survived later conflagrations of the city. The original paintings which covered its walls have been preserved, as well as the remarkable ceiling from which rows of wide-eyed angels look down from between wooden beams. The church provides separate places for nobility and commoners, and a balcony for the emperor.

chant"), *qenē,* and *tergum* ("interpretation")—is said to have received its definitive organization.

Dāwit III appears to have had a pronounced interest in Amharic folk song, for the more perfect enjoyment of which he built a special hall in the imperial compound. Because of this he has been called "Dāwit the Singer"—no term of praise in a land where minstrelsy is looked down on and where serious deportment is expected of royalty. Actually, this epithet, with its connotation of "playboy," was not deserved. Dāwit was a religious man, and in his brief reign built two churches. Knowledgeable Gondarēs today insist that, at first, even the priests were happy to join him in the amusement hall to listen to the one-stringed fiddles and the witty songs. Only after Dāwit's partiality to the Unctionist doctrine (that the humanity of Christ was made divine through the unction of the Holy Spirit) led him to persecute the Unionist clergy (who hold that humanity and divinity are blended in the single nature of Christ) did they abuse his music hall and tarnish his name.[7]

Interest in architecture was revived by Bakāffā. He constructed a long U-shaped castle which, together with the new castle of his Empress Mantuāb, completed the major complex of buildings in Gondar. Mantuāb's castle is noted for bas-reliefs of the Ethiopian Cross, while her other castle at nearby Qusquam is decorated with bas-reliefs depicting saints and animals as well.

The tastes of Iyāsu II were especially refined. He cultivated extensive gardens and orchards, an unusual pursuit for an Amhara monarch. He built a large and handsome church. He began to construct a palace, in the lavish decoration of which he took a personal interest. Budge writes of this:

> A number of Christians who had fled from Smyrna took refuge in Gondar, and the king employed them to decorate his palace with filigree work. The upper parts of the walls of the throne room were covered with three rows of Venetian mirrors set in gilded copper frames, and their lower parts . . . with slabs of ivory. The roof was made of painted cane mosaic, the work of the Falasha. . . . Iyāsu II spent his days with the workmen, and himself learned to do some of the work under the direction of the Greek workmen.[8]

The decline of imperial power at Gondar after Iyāsu II did not produce a slackening of the cultural activities that had been concentrated there. During the reign of Takla Hāymānot II (1769–77), for example, when the actual power at Gondar was in the hands of a lord from Tigre, seven more churches were built. One of these, Ba'ātā Māryām, eventually became one of the most famous schools for the teaching of *aquāquām* ("religious dance"), and in its heyday boasted 276 masters. Another, Abi Egzi, became noted for instruction in *tergum,* and is still a leading school for such studies.

The composition of verse, in forms which had become canonized during the early Gondar period, continued to flourish. As political turmoil often kindles artistic expression, so the poet could wax eloquent over Gondar's decadence at the close of the eighteenth cntury:

Beautiful from its beginnings, Gondar, hope of the wretched!
And hope of the great, Gondar, without measure or bounds!
O dove of John, Gondar, generous-hearted, mother!
Gondar, never bowed by affliction!
Gondar, with its merry name!
Gondar, seat of prosperity and of savoury food!
Gondar, dwelling of King Iyāsu and of mighty Bakāffā!
Gondar, which emulated the city of David, the land of Salem!
She will be a myth unto eternity.
How is it she has been destroyed like Sodom, and without any guilt?[9]

So, while the reputation of the Gondar monarchy grew dim, that of the town as a center for religious studies continued unabated. Gondar was the most famous place in the country for instruction in art, music, dance, poetry, and the great books of the Ethiopian Church, and young men continued to travel great distances to drink at such sources. The descendants of royalty somehow made their adjustment. In the middle of the nineteenth century, Arnauld d'Abbadie finds them making paintings and illuminating manuscripts.

At this late date, one more personality of stature emerges from Gondar. This time it is not a king but a *dabtarā,* or man of religious learning—Alaqā Gabra Hānnā. Gabra Hānnā was born in the district of Foggarā on the east coast of Lake Ṭānā. His pursuit of religious studies as a youth took him to Gondar, where he did well and before long became a teacher in the church of Ba'ātā Māryām. Subsequently he was made head of the church, receiving the customary title of *alaqā.*

While at Ba'ātā, Alaqā Gabra Hānnā invented a new style of dance for the clergy. In the traditional style of *aquāquām,* the bodies and sticks of the dancers move up and down, punctuating the flow of chant with alternately gradual and abrupt vertical movements. Alaqā Gabra Hānnā, inspired by the lateral movement of the waves at Lake Ṭānā and of the bamboo reeds in the breeze at its shore, taught that bodies and sticks should sway from side to side. This innovation was rejected by the conservative clergy at Gondar, but it was carried by his son Taklē to Dabra Tābor and from there spread elsewhere.

Alaqā Gabra Hānnā became most famous, however, for his quick and biting wit. So prolific and beloved were his witticisms that in a collection of some three hundred old parables and anecdotes published in Addis Ababa in 1955, no fewer than 25 per cent are devoted to stories about him.[10] After reaching prominence through his teachings and sayings, Alaqā Gabra Hānnā left Gondar for Shoa, where he became a favorite at the court of Emperor Menelik.

Alaqā Gabra Hānnā was not the only one to leave Gondar in the latter part of the nineteenth century. Conditions there had become increasingly miserable. In 1866 Tēwodros, angered by the opposition of the Gondarē clergy to his plans for unifying the country through a standing national army, turned his wrath against them into a fearful pillage of the churches of Gondar.* The next emperor, Takla Giyorgis, worked feverishly to rebuild Gondar during his few years in power (1869–72). It was to no avail. In 1887 a large army of dervishes invaded Ethiopia from the Sudan and sacked Gondar, destroying it more completely than had Tēwodros.

The priests and monks who survived carried on. Gondar remained an important center for instruction in *aquāquām* and *tergum,* though Gojjam became more important for the study of *qenē* and other schools in Bagemder and Tigre for the study of *zēmā.* The civil order, however, was thoroughly demoralized. Gondarēs left in large numbers for the countryside or made their way to Lāstā and more distant provinces.

At the time of the dervish invasion, the churchmen of Gondar appealed to Emperor Yohānnes for succor. The text of their message—the last utterance from the old capital—began as follows:

> O master! The heathen have come into thine inheritance; thy holy temple have they defiled; they have laid Gondar in heaps. The dead bodies of thy servants have they given to be meat unto the fowls of the heaven, the flesh of thy saints unto the beasts of the earth. Their blood have they shed like water round about Dambiyā; and there was none to bury them.[11]

Yohānnes responded at once. It was to revenge defenseless Gondar that he led the expedition against the dervishes which cost him his life, thereby leaving the way open for the accession of the House of Manz.

The Role of Manz

Manz is a rugged rural area of about 850 square miles located in the northeast horn of Shoa Province.[12] It lies on a broad plateau at a height of ten thousand feet above sea level. This plateau is crosscut by a number of rivers which flow westerly to become part of the great Blue Nile Basin. The valleys of the rivers are flanked by fairly abrupt cliffs, which make travel from one part of Manz to another slow going. These rivers form boundaries between the geographical divisions within Manz, which is divided into three major parts: Māmā Meder in the south, Lālo Meder in the center, and Gērā Meder in the north. The entire area of Manz is itself bounded by steep mountains.[13]

---

* Fortunately he preserved hundreds of manuscripts from Gondar's churches which eventually found their way to the British Museum after the Napier Expedition against Tēwodros in 1868.

The history and customs of Manz are more obviously related to its geography than is the case with Gondar. The encircling wall of mountains has been a source of isolation and protection, two factors of great moment in the history of the area. Peculiar eating and clothing habits have developed in response to a climate which, owing to the altitude of Manz and its position at the edge of an escarpment that leads down to a desert of the Rift Valley, is one of the coldest in Ethiopia. The temperature often approaches the freezing point, and in the colder months (October and November) standing in the sunshine at high noon is no defense against a shrill wind that pierces the bones.

Barley is the only crop that thrives in the highest parts of Manz, though wheat, beans, peas, and chick-peas grow in the slightly lower altitudes. But *ṭēff*, the grain preferred by Abyssinians for the preparation of their staple food —a kind of pancake known as *ǐnjarā*—cannot be cultivated at those heights, so the Manzē typically eats *ǐnjarā* made of barley.

Sheep are a major item in the Manz economy. The average farm has a herd of 100 to 150 sheep, which provide a heavy wool as well as the Manzē's favorite meat. This wool is used to make the *bānnā*, a warm blanket which is wrapped around the body and constitutes the standard dress of the Manzē. The *bānnā* distinguishes him from other Abyssinians, who wear a white cotton toga called *shammā*. Wealthier men wear the *barnos*, a tailored cape made of dark wool. Manzē wool is also used for the weaving of rugs which ornament the homes of the well-to-do.

No dyes are used in working their wool, so a crowd of Manzēs in natural-colored *bānnā* seen at a distance resembles a flock of their sheep. This is one of the touches contributing to the impressive aesthetic unity of the Manz landscape. The effect is also produced by the fact that the Manzē's house is built of stone, the same stone that is seen everywhere on the terrain; and its conical roof is made of thatch, which makes the roof look like the piles of grain in the fields. The churches are also built of stone with thatched conical roofs. Everything one sees in Manz bespeaks a harmony with the natural environment.

The cold climate of Manz is invigorating. It prevents food from spoiling quickly and discourages diseases which flourish in lower altitudes. The Manzē boasts that his climate keeps people healthy and gives them long lives, and indeed it is not uncommon to find men sprightly in their eighties and nineties. But only the hardy survive, for life there is as rugged as the land, and the people—like their landscape—are stony, bleak, and full of dark recesses.

Manz does not occupy so conspicuous a place in Ethiopian history as Gondar. Indeed, most books on Ethiopia do not even mention the area. While

Gondar has been described at first hand by numerous travelers and scholars, from the time of Poncet (1699) to the present day, only two foreign authors had penetrated Manz prior to my field trip there, and then hastily—the British missionary Krapf, for two days in 1842, and Soleillet, a French explorer (and friend of Rimbaud), for two days in 1882.[14]

Nevertheless, two circumstances of the era of recovery give Manz a special historical significance. First, since Manz was practically the only part of Shoa not overrun by the Galla, it was able to provide a base from which an Amhara offensive to reconquer the south was launched. It is for this reason that Shoans sentimentalize Manz as *ya-amāra mĭnçh* ("the Amhara's source"). Second, Manz was the birthplace of a line of rulers which culminated in the present imperial family of Ethiopia.

Both of these circumstances have been endowed with supernatural significance by latter-day supporters of the Shoan throne, much as *The Glory of Kings* added religious sanction to the Shoan Dynasty of the thirteenth century. In *Darsāna Rāguēl,* a homily in honor of the archangel Raguel which came to light during the early part of Menelik's reign, they are made the subject of a prophecy of Emperor Lebna Dengel.[15] In this homily Lebna Dengel, overcome by the destruction wrought by the forces of Ahmad Gragn, prays to the Virgin Mary for seven days. When Mary at last appears, she rebukes the king for forsaking the piety of his fathers and urges him to repent. She is followed by the angel Raguel, who announces to the humbled king what is to be the fate of his country and his children. "For two hundred and fifty years there will be many pagans throughout the land of Shoa . . . but not in Manz, for it is the land guarded by Uriel, the angel who gathered the pure blood from the side of Christ."[16] As for the sons of Lebna Dengel, Yā'qob—who is said to have sojourned in Manz during and after the time of Grāñ, and from whom the House of Manz claims descent—"will dwell in your land, in peace and safety. . . . Among the children of the king Yā [the prophecy alludes to persons and places by their initial syllables] one will remain in Manz, by the will of our God, for this son of Yā will love the angel Uriel. . . . The King beloved by the angel Uriel and issue of the house of Yā will govern Shoa."[17]

To some extent, moreover, Manz is noted for its connection with important events and sovereigns of earlier centuries. According to Ethiopian tradition, Manz was the refuge of the sole survivor of Aksumite royalty, Anbasā Wedem, who is believed to have fled south to Manz when Aksum was sacked in the tenth century.[18] Manz was the object of some attention under Emperor Zar'a Yā'qob (1434–68), who established a monastery at Ferkutā in eastern Manz, and during whose reign was written a biography of the "apostle of Manz," Yohānnes the Oriental, who converted wild beasts and overcame the dragon.[19] His successor, Ba'eda Māryām (1468–78), made his camp for a while at Masala Māryām in Manz. His sojourn there, remembered to this day, is recorded in the amusing rhymed formula with which he exacted tribute from the various districts near his camp:

From Agāntchā/fifty *ḳoretchā* ("saddles"); from Hulu Dehā/fifty *dehā* ("servants"); from Aftanaṭ/fifty *naṭ* ("rugs"); from Godambo/fifty *gambo* ("jars of drink").

It was from Manz that Ba'eda Māryām brought priests to officiate at his coronation in Djagno.[20] According to Shoan beliefs, finally, Manz also served as a refuge during the invasions of Ahmad Grāñ for the fourth son of Lebna Dengel (1507–40), Yā'qob, who is said to have fled there with the royal raiments and received succor from the local inhabitants.

According to *Futuḥ el-Habacha,* Manz was ravaged by the forces of Grāñ in 1531.[21] Scarred timbers identified as pillars of churches burned during that invasion may be seen there today. Local legends concerning the history of Manz relate for the most part to the miraculous feats of strength which Grāñ is said to have performed there and to the resettlement of Manz after Grāñ. These legends speak of the "founding" of Manz by three men—Māmā, Lālo, and Gērā—who were sent by one of the emperors to settle and govern that territory. As the story goes, the emperor offered each of them as much land as he could cross in a single day. They set out from the Adabāy River, today a western boundary of Manz, and the result of their long day's journey was the present tripartite division of Manz into Māmā Meder, Lālo Meder, and Gērā Meder. This explains why Gērā Meder is the largest of the three districts—for Gērā's horse was the strongest!

Although their deeds are recorded only in the form of legends, Māmā, Lālo, and Gērā were historical personages. They appear to have lived in the latter part of the seventeenth century.[22] Gērā was the most powerful of the three, as the legend of his horse suggests. He controlled most of the land of Manz, including Afqārā, an impregnable mountain fortress which was used for generations as a garrison for political prisoners. He set aside a large stretch of grassland to be used by local people for grazing cattle and providing thatch for roofs, where still today it is forbidden to plow or build houses.

Not these three lords, however, but one of their rivals—Nagassē Kristos Warada Qāl, commonly known as Nagāssi—put Manz on the map. Nagāssi was born to a wealthy proprietor in the district of Agāntchā. As a young man he showed outstanding valor and skill at arms. His success in battle won him many followers, who helped him advance from enlarging his possessions at the expense of his neighbors to the conquest of Galla territories southeast of Manz.

Nagāssi's ambition was fed by his victories. He proclaimed himself ruling prince of Shoa, and vanquished those who disputed this claim, including the mighty Gērā, in a long series of skirmishes. At length, around 1700, he proceeded to Gondar to gain official recognition from the emperor, then Iyāsu the Great. After presenting tribute from his area Nagāssi told the emperor of his achievements in Shoa, where he had established settlements and churches in lands taken back from the Galla. Pleased by such good news, Iyāsu agreed to award Nagāssi a title and a seal.[23]

For this accomplishment Nagāssi is generally acknowledged to be the founder of the modern ruling family of Shoa.[24] Nagāssi did not live to enjoy his long-sought investiture on Shoan soil; before he was able to return home he died of smallpox. He was buried with great honors at one of the churches built by Fāsil, Fit Abbo, where his grave—as well as the field he camped on, Nagāssi Mēdā—remain objects of historical interest today.

In the will proclaimed before he died, Nagāssi bequeathed his "throne" to Akāwā; his spear, silver cutlass, and gilded shield to Sebstē; and his land and money to his five other sons. As Akāwā began to rule, however, Manz was afflicted by drought and famine. Blaming this misfortune on their new ruler, the nobility deposed Akāwā and installed Dāñā, another of Nagāssi's sons, in his place.

Meanwhile Sebstē, dreading the fraternal conflict he knew would arise over the succession, had fled to the lowlands of Merhābētē, where he attached himself to the local governor. He served well; on one occasion he reportedly saved his liege's life by a brave thrust of his spear at an onrushing wild buffalo. Yet the governor feared Sebstē as the son of his father, and such bravery only alarmed him all the more. He decided to do away with Sebstē before he became too powerful and laid plans to have him seized during the next feast. In the meantime Dāñā was beginning to suffer losses. Sebstē's relatives sought a way to lure him back to Manz, for they needed his leadership in combatting their enemies and, no doubt, they feared for his safety in Merhābētē. They sent a messenger to tell him that his mother was sick and he should return to Manz at once. The message arrived the day that Sebstē was to have been killed. The ruse worked. Unwilling to mar the festivities by announcing his departure, the unwitting Sebstē slipped away without bidding farewell.

After a few seasons the superiority of Sebstē over his brother Dāñā became clear. Sebstē's victories over the Galla brought him much wealth, which enabled him to acquire his own followers. A showdown with Dāñā was inevitable, and Sebstē won. He decided that the meaning of Nagāssi's bequest to him was "Rise and rule." To confirm his new position Sebstē called an assembly of all his kinfolk and countrymen from all parts of Manz and adjacent regions, ostensibly to hold a day of mourning in honor of his father. When the mourning ritual was over, Sebstē proclaimed to the assembly:

"People of Manz, follow me! Henceforth my title shall be *marĭdāzmātch.**
Whosoever does not call me Marĭdāzmātch Sebstē in the future I shall punish
severely."[25]

The succession question was thus settled. After Sebstē the Shoan chief-
taincy passed from father to son for seven generations without serious contests. The next question was how to increase its power.

Sebstē proved himself worthy of Nagāssi's mantle. He conquered most of
the province of Yefāt and there securely established his authority. His reign
was terminated by a curious accident. Sebstē's son Abbĭyē, eager to replace
some of the churches destroyed by Gragn, decided to build a church in honor
of St. Michael in the town of Doqāqit. To this end he brought by stealth the
holy ark of St. Michael from Aynē, where Sebstē was living. Sebstē could
only conceive of this action as an expression of disloyalty, and set out with
some troops to capture Abbĭyē and reprimand him. In the ensuing encounter,
to Abbĭyē's dismay, one of his servants killed Sebstē.

Abbĭyē thereupon became the new ruler of Shoa. Though his reign began
on a note of insecurity he was able to pursue successfully the goals of his
father: strengthening control of the Amhara districts of Shoa, conquering
and resettling lands occupied by the Galla, and asserting Shoan independence
vis-à-vis Gondar.

Despite Nagāssi's efforts to unite the Amhara enclave in northern Shoa, it
was still broken up into a number of petty independent districts. Manz was
no exception. Now that Nāgassi's line had established its headquarters in the
lowlands southeast of Manz, some of the lords of Manz refused to live in
subordination to it. Gērā had been defeated, but his grandson Golē still
claimed independence. One of Abbĭyē's achievements was to defeat Golē and
so bring Manz once again under a regional authority. Abbĭyē also moved
further into Galla territory. He pushed beyond Doqāqit to Hār Ambā where
he built a town. After a reign of twenty-five years he met his death on the
battlefield fighting the Karayu Galla.

The novel feature of Abbĭyē's reign was his relationship with Gondar.
Sebstē had not gone to Gondar bearing tribute, for he declined to acknowledge the supremacy of the emperor. When Sebstē died, the emperor, then
Iyāsu II, sent an expedition to Shoa to collect tribute. According to the Shoan
historians, Abbĭyē defeated the expedition; according to other sources, Abbĭyē
was spared by the intervention of the emperor.[26] In any case, his attitude
toward the men who came on the expedition was conciliatory. He bade the
Gondarē lords teach him the ways of Gondar's court and administration, and
even made one of them a district governor. He ordered the Falasha artisans

---

* *Marĭdāzmātch* is an honorific title that was formerly used in the province of Shoa.

who trailed the Gondar camp to make spades and plowshares, spears and swords, and so improved the quality of agriculture and warfare in Shoa.

The reign of Abbïyē's son Amhāyas was long and prosperous. New lands were conquered, new settlements founded, new churches built. Amhāyas seized the strategic mountain of Ankobar, to which the mountainous plateaus of the north and the vast plains to the south were equally accessible, and set up his official residence there. The last of Shoa's princes to pay his respects to the court at Gondar, he was received there as an emissary of his father with great honors and treated more like a sovereign ally than a vassal.[27] When Amhāyas died, he left for his son Asfā Wassan what had by then become the vast principality of Shoa.

Asfā Wassan's youth was spent in a monastery in Manz, where he became proficient at composing *qenē* under the tutelage of a master from Gondar. As a ruler he resembled many of Gondar's monarchs, preferring to spend his time in religious pursuits and the embellishment of his capital (Ankobar) than on the warpath. The actual business of warfare he entrusted to his generals, who in a string of victories subjected dozens of Amhara and Galla districts to his authority. Nevertheless, when forced to fight, he lost no time in showing who was *marïdāzmātch*. When two of his generals rebelled, he defeated them in what Cecchi called "the most terrible and bloody battle which the Shoans remember."[28]

Asfā Wassan deserved his name, which means "Expand the Border." He brought nearly all the petty states of Shoa under his rule, by alliance or by conquest. A famous exchange of couplets between Asfā Wassan and Ṭedu, governor of Morat, formed the prologue to one instance of this expansion. Ṭedu, fearing the absorption of his territory, made the following rhyme:

Asfā Wassan Yefāt ṭankeraw yerrasu
Morat ṭeduāl belaw ḳamamalālasu.

O Asfā Wassan, stoutly plow Yefāt
Rather than eye what's baking in Morat.

There is gold in the verb in the second line, *ṭeduāl,* which may signify not only "is baking" but also "Ṭedu is there." The couplet may thus be read:

O Asfā Wassan, stoutly plow Yefāt
Rather than think about Ṭedu in Morat.

Upon hearing this couplet Asfā Wassan composed the following reply:

La-mofar la-qanbar yamihonaññen
Sālquarṭaw alqerem zandro ṭedun.

To get me yokes and plowbeams in this year
I will not fail to cut the juniper.

The pun here is on the word *Ṭedu,* for the name of Asfā Wassan's adversary means "the juniper." Morat soon began to pay him tribute.[29]

Asfā Wassan also accomplished much in the field of administration. He organized his realm into four large provinces, which were in turn subdivided into thirty-nine districts—half Amhara lands, half lands taken from the Galla. He improved the laws and introduced a more orderly system of finance. He supported agriculture and encouraged trade.

Such prosperity could scarcely be viewed with indifference by Gondar. Takla Giyorgis I (1779–84), who was trying vainly to restore imperial authority at Gondar, marched to Shoa with a large force. Asfā Wassan, not ready for an open clash with the emperor's troops, handled the situation with characteristic Shoan adroitness. He heaped gifts upon the emperor and his lieutenants. Protesting his fealty, he noted that if he had extended his own dominions, it had been at the expense of their common enemy, the Galla. Finally, he said he was willing to pay tribute to the emperor, but at the same time was ready if necessary to meet him in battle. The lords who accompanied Takla Giyorgis sympathized with the Shoan, and the emperor was not strong enough to prevent their defection.

Worried by a monkish prophecy that his life would be short, Asfā Wassan emptied the state coffers in order to subsidize churches and monasteries. He lived to fill them time and again, during a reign that lasted thirty-three years. Throughout that time he never forgot his church schooling, and frequently invented *qenē* to be repeated in the churches on holidays. But Asfā Wassan was a true son of Manz, and left the memory, as Harris noted, of "a great Nimrod and an unparalleled warrior."[30]

The next ruler, Wassan Sagad, was the offspring of a fortuitous union between Asfā Wassan and Woizero Atmotch Hono, a relative of the imperial family at Gondar and owner of vast properties in Wallo. En route from Manz to Ankobar at the end of his student days, Asfā Wassan was given hospitality at the home of this genteel woman. Not aware that the lady had in fact been brought by his father with the hope of siring offspring from her, Asfā Wassan spent the night with her. When she bore a son, and Asfā Wassan learned who she really was, he fled in terror to the monastery of Ferkutā. After sending scouts to all the monasteries in the area, Amhāyas had his son brought back and granted him pardon.

Wassan Sagad was thus kin to the highest nobility through his mother as well as his father. His noble blood, haughty disposition, and clever mind moved him to great ambitions. He convoked a large assembly of Amhara and Galla, and proclaimed himself Rās of Shoa.* Then he sent word to Rās Gugsa, power behind the throne at Gondar, that he was coming to fight, "for

---

* *Rās* is the highest ranking secular title in Abyssinia after *negus* ("king"). Cf. chap. v, p. 158.

I am the descendant of Nagāssi, and who put you, a Galla, on the throne of my fathers?"[31] He began his campaign by sending an expedition against the Wallo Galla, who were dependents of Rās Gugsa. But before he was able to persuade the reluctant Shoan nobility to venture forth against Gondar, Wassan Sagad's ambitions were cut short, in the fifth year of his reign, by the dagger of a slave.

The assassination of Wassan Sagad brought Shoa a moment of anarchy. In the absence of central authority, vicious passions were unleashed—"at Debra Libanos alone there fell no fewer than eight hundred victims to private animosity, of whose murder no account was ever taken."[32] The Galla burned hamlets over a wide area; they captured the heir apparent and prevented him from reaching the Shoan capital, then at Qundi. At this point Sāhla Selassie, younger son of the late *rās*, left the seclusion of his studies and presented himself to the Shoan nobility. His daring and quick wit won their consent. They named him Rās of Shoa at eighteen years, and he soon began to style himself as king (*negus*) of Shoa as well.

In the ensuing decades Sāhla Selassie completed the process of conquering and consolidating Shoa that his father had initiated. His rule was strong and beneficent, though tribes which did not pay tribute were shown no mercy. He led forays into Galla country three times a year, during which delinquent or independent settlements suffered sudden and total devastation.

A major crisis during the reign of Sāhla Selassie was the rebellion of one of his commanders, a man named Matako. Matako had risen to high position from that of minor retainer by dint of his fighting ability, but he antagonized the king by requesting that the king's daughter be married to his son. This was a double breach of etiquette, for the king's daughter would normally be given only to someone from a high-ranking family, and in any case the request should be tendered by some mediating elders, not in person. In the wake of the tension that ensued, Sāhla Selassie had Matako imprisoned. Matako escaped, however, and raised an army of Galla tribesmen to fight his campaign for revenge. The royal forces were in serious trouble. Sāhla Selassie sent a desperate message to the people of Manz: "My brothers, my relations, come and help me!"[33]

Such help could not be taken for granted. The men of Manz were then, as ever, fiercely independent, unwilling to subordinate themselves to distant authorities. At the time of Sāhla Selassie, in fact, Krapf observed that

> [His Majesty's] power and influence in that part of his dominions is very limited and loose. The Mansians openly declare, "We know little about Sahela Selassieh." Nobody would venture to say so in Efat.[34]

Still, the Shoan line had been infused with new Manzē blood by the marriage of Sāhla Selassie's father to Zanaba Warq, the grand-daughter of Golē, grandson of Gērā. Thanks to the intercession of his mother, Sāhla Selassie was able to reach his truculent kinsmen. In response to his appeal for help against the Galla forces, the Manzēs came in great numbers and saved the day. A vivid reconstruction of the final battle is provided by Harris:

> [Matako] and his gallant sons were everywhere in the thickest of the fight. His shout, rising high over the storm, animated the faint-hearted, and his presence roused to new life and exertion the successful partisan. Many of the Amhara bands were already reeling from the repeated shock of the wild riders of the Hawash [the Galla horsemen], when suddenly, in the very heat of the action, a large body of warriors, clothed in black mantles, and armed with long heavy spears, rushed down the hill on foot, and, prostrating themselves as they passed the royal unbrellas, descended fresh into the arena. The fierce inhabitants of Mans had sped to the rescue from their hereditary estates, and their savage ferocity and reckless bravery was well known throughout the land. The relations and the household retainers of the rebel attempted to breast the storm, but they were scattered like autumnal leaves before the angry blast; and the chief arrived to the succour only to behold the spot strewed with the bodies of his stoutest partisans. . . . A panic seized the pagans; and, dismayed and brokenhearted, they fled tumultously in every direction.[35]

Of the arts of peace, Sāhla Selassie was particularly absorbed in the development of manual crafts. He brought masons and carpenters from Gondar and took a personal interest in the work of his metalsmiths. He was eager to learn of European technical skills and showed much hospitality to missions from the British and French governments, with whom he concluded treaties of friendship and commerce.

In Gondar, Sāhla Selassie's province was known as "the most populous and most wisely governed" in the country.[36] His assumption of the title of *negus* had been urged by some of the Gondar nobility and clergy, for they looked to him for help in combatting the spread of Islamic influence by the Muslim Galla chief, Rās 'Ali. Sāhla Selassie needed little urging; his sights were set on the highest title of all—*negusa nagast* ("king of kings," or "emperor"). Yet he, like his father, was premature. Two more generations were to be needed before that triumph.

Abyssinia could not wait. The dissolution of imperial power and the inroads of Islam had proceeded too far. Unification of the country under a powerful monarch was the obvious need of the day. The process was begun by a rebel from Qwārā, who vanquished in turn the Rāses of Gojjam, Bagemder, and Tigre, and proclaimed himself emperor in 1855 as Tēwodros II.

Shoa could not long remain untouched by Tēwodros. The successor to Sāhla Selassie, his son Haile Malakot, tried to save Shoa's autonomy by leading an expedition to fight Tēwodros in Wallo, but found his camp impregnable. As the rainy season was approaching, Haile Malakot retreated to Shoa, where he fell sick and died. For the first time since Nagāssi, Shoa was left without an effective leader. Tēwodros marched into Manz from Wallo, and Shoa capitulated with little struggle. Eleven-year-old Menelik, son of Haile Malakot, was taken hostage.

Ten years later Menelik escaped from the camp of Tēwodros and regained Shoa. Slowly and carefully he built up his power. Tēwodros' reign raced to its tragic end. Takla Giyorgis II reigned briefly at Gondar, the last emperor to sit there. Yohānnes IV of Tigre governed the country for seventeen years. When Yohānnes died, Negus Menelik was forty-five and ready. Nagāssi's seed, eight generations later, reached the throne of all Ethiopia on November 3, 1889.

CULTURAL PROFILES

The Manzē Ethos

The goals of Nagāssi and his descendants, apart from simple increase of power, were to recover the lands taken from their fathers and to stiffen the authority of Christianity in Shoa. Their success was virtually unbroken by reason of exceptional soldierly prowess and political perseverance. These are ideals and qualities embodied par excellence in the people of Manz.

Sanctity of *rĭst,* or land inherited from one's parents, is a cardinal value in the Manzē scheme of things. Such land must not be given or sold to anyone who is not a close relative. People generations removed from actual residents of Manz still retain claims to family land there, still cherish the idea that if they so desired they could go back and live on it. As an urbanized Manzē once told his nephew in Addis Ababa: "No matter how far you travel abroad, no matter how long you stay away, you will always be able to think of your family land in Manz as your true home." This sentiment is expressed in a proverb:

Ya-Manz rĭst be-shi amatu/la-bālabētu.
Manz *rĭst* to the thousandth year/belongs to the owner.

A squatter may fight to keep his land from falling to some stranger who claims it as having belonged to his grandfather, but in his heart he respects the values that support such a claim.

By Manzē standards the good man is thus one who defends the land of his fathers, seeing that it is not sold to outsiders or that foreigners do not come to take it. If someone plows another's land without permission, he must be punished. If the matter can be settled through litigation, well and good; if it requires recourse to violence, so be it. To let such an offense go unavenged would be the worst sort of shame. Grievances concerning their "hereditary estates" make up the most common subjects of litigation in Manz, and hardly a day passes in the courts there without a hearing on some case about *rĭst*. The Manzēs are as stubbornly loyal to their fathers' faith as they are to their land. They take much pride in the strictness with which the Orthodox fasts are observed in Manz, and in the fact that non-Christians are not to be found there. A number of legends told locally represent Manz as an especially hallowed Christian territory. One legend says that after the Crucifixion the angel Uriel gathered some of Jesus' blood on his wings and flew to Manz. Standing on the hill of Dabra Qopros in Māmā Meder, he shook his wings and thereby sprinkled the holy blood over the entire area. Another story dates the sanctification of Manz by the blood of Jesus to the time when a portion of the true Cross was brought to Ethiopia and tells of how on the way to its repository at Gishēn Māryām, in Wallo, some drops spilled from the relic onto Manz soil.[37] Still another legend relates that the Virgin Mary sojourned in Manz when Jesus was a young boy. Lake Alo Bāhr in western Gērā Meder is said to be the product of Mary's wrath—her punishment of the people who lived on what was dry land at the time for judging against her in a dispute with a local woman.

To defend his land, church, or honor, the typical Manzē is ready at short notice to fight to the death. In their own eyes, as in the eyes of others, the men of Manz are reputed for hardiness and combativeness. *Mot ged yallam* ("Never mind about death!") is the motto one governor from Manz volunteered as the key to the ethos of his people. The Manzē wants his son to be *guabaz* ("brave") and uses this term, like that of *waṭādar* ("soldier"), as a favorite compliment. The names which are characteristically given to children in Manz express this determination:

Ahidē	"Thrasher"	*Goshemē*	"Shover"
Asdangaṭ	"Frighten"	*Laṭybalu*	"Let Them Bow"
Atāmantā	"Don't Hesitate"	*Mān Yāzhāl*	"Who Orders You?"
Balātchaw	"Give It To Them"	*Nādaw*	"Wipe Him Out"
Balāy-metā	"Hit On The Top"	*Ṭālārgē*	"Powerful"
Chabudē	"Squeezer"	*Tāsaw*	"Smash Him"
Chafchefē	"Hacker"	*Weqātchaw*	"Thrash Them"

Female names in Manz sometimes reflect this virile emphasis; for example, *Hijibātchaw* ("Go Against Them") or *Asagadatch* ("She Makes Them Bow").

A common symbol of physical bravery is the *dulā*, a hardwood staff about three feet long. The Manzē is rarely seen without his *dulā*. It has many purposes—to brace his shoulders on long treks, to carry loads, to ward off dogs when he goes visiting, to support his body while listening to litigation or standing at the long church services. Above all it is a weapon of offense and defense, and every Amhara male is supposed to be skilled in its use. When the *dulā* is so employed in Manz, the *bānnā* blanket is usually wrapped around the left arm to form a quick shield, the *dulā* raised high with the right to bring down on the adversary's cranium. The blows are sometimes fatal. The Manzēs are proud of their facility with the lethal stick, and nearly every district in Manz boasts that it is real *"dulā* country."

The Manzēs also excel at *shīllalā,* the Abyssinian war chant. This is a form of boastful verse—partly intoned, partly shouted—which is declaimed by warriors to "heat their blood" before hitting the warpath. Children in Manz start practicing *shīllalā* almost as soon as they leave the breast. The following is a good specimen of Manz *shīllalā:*

> *Agarātchn Māmā agarātchn Lālo wanzātchn Dangazē;*
> *Mān abātu yāzzāl imbi senīl gizē.*
>
> Our land is Māmā, our land is Lālo, our stream the Dangazē;
> What father will order us when *imbi* we say!

Imbi is an interjection used by children to express "No!" There is a double pun in this couplet. *Mān abātu* ("Who is the father?") is a profane idiom meaning "bastard." "To say *imbi*" is another idiom, meaning "to refuse." The second line may thus be also rendered as:

> What bastard dare shove us around when we tell him to keep off our lands!

The Manzē code asks that a man be ready to defend his land and church by force. It does not approve wanton aggression. But the Manzē's disposition is notoriously aggressive, for his emotional life is relatively devoid of warmth and, on the other hand, fighting is so highly rewarded. Children are urged to be adept with the *dulā.* Their temper tantrums are welcomed as signs that they are brave. As a result the men of Manz are often overcome by the impulse toward physical aggression; assault and murder are recurrent events on their fields and trails and at their marketplaces. The discrepancy between the *norm* of physical bravery, which is operative *in certain specified circumstances,* and the *general character trait* of aggressiveness comprises a major theme in their emotional life: they feel obliged to look for justification for the aggressive actions which they have been conditioned to want to carry out. This disposition is illustrated in the words of the Manzē youth who said:

> I want very much to kill somebody. The only problem is I'm not strong enough. Perhaps one day I will be. Why is it all right to kill? People kill sheep, don't they? And sheep are innocent, they don't know anything, don't do any wrong. But man knows, he knows much, and still he does wrong: every man is bad. I wouldn't kill everybody, only the bad ones. If I had an enemy, I would kill him. Maybe I will become a soldier, and kill my country's enemies.

Perhaps this sort of disposition was not unrelated to the part Manz played in sparking the restoration of Amhara rule in Shoa, thereby preparing the way for the dramatic resurgence and expansion of the Ethiopian state at the end of the nineteenth century.

The Gondarē Ethos

The unique character of Gondar derives first of all from the fact that it was a city. During the whole period of Ethiopian history reviewed in this chapter, the Gondar period was the only time in which the emperors resided in a fixed capital, and Gondar was the only permanent population center that grew beyond the contours of a large village. As in ancient Egypt before the rise of Thebes, the concept of the city had played scarcely any role in the political thinking of the Amhara, and so anomalous was the rise of Gondar that Ludolphus, writing in the fifth decade after the founding of Gondar, could not believe stories that Gondar was a large city and predicted that "perhaps in a few years there will be nothing to be seen of it."[38]

Like many oriental cities, Gondar consisted more of a collection of small homogeneous societies than of a diffused heterogeneous urban population. The city was divided into several quarters, each of which lived its own life. The imperial compound was of course foremost of these. It contained the great complex of buildings erected during more than a hundred years, from Fāsil to Iyāsu II, and was the seat of affairs of state. The compound was separated from the rest of the city by a stone wall, whose twelve well-guarded gates each served a special function or class of people.[39]

The nobility resided in a quarter known as Gaing Bēt. Here the dwellings were spaced at comfortable distances, and nearly every house was surrounded by a garden. Abyssinians of lower rank lived in the more densely populated sections of Faras Bēt and Denkākē.

The Christian hierarchy had its own quarters. The *abuna,* an Egyptian monk appointed by the Coptic Patriarch at Alexandria as spiritual head of the Ethiopian Church, lived with his retinue in one sector.[40] Another area, Eçhagē Bēt, was reserved for the Amhara monk who served as administrative head of the Church. Each church compound, moreover, was the focus of another residential section, where its clergy kept their modest huts. The Eçhage Bēt and the church compounds were considered sanctuaries and thus, in theory at least, were secure from plunderers. The Gondarēs and wealthy people from the country used these areas as a safety vault for their valuables.

The ethnic groups which settled in Gondar had their respective ghettos. The Muslims lived in the lower part of the city adjacent to the river Qīha, which was convenient for their ritual ablutions. They were looked down on by the Christians, and meat slaughtered by one group would not be touched by the other. Poncet observed that when an Abyssinian met a Muslim in the streets, "he salutes him with his left hand, which is a mark of contempt."[41] The Falasha, potters and metalsmiths of Judaic faith, were similarly segregated, and plied their arts and crafts in another quarter.

Though many different peoples came together in Gondar, and though it was a meeting-point of trade routes from the Sudan, the Red Sea ports, and the African interior, Gondar's cultural role was not primarily that of a melting pot of diverse traditions. It served rather as an agent for the quickened development of the Amhara's own culture.[42] And thus it became a focus of national pride. The countryfolk looked on Gondar not as a hotbed of alien custom and immorality, as they often regard Addis Ababa today, but as the most perfect and advanced embodiment of their own traditional values.

The Gondarē himself, as denizen of this second Jerusalem, was prouder still. A snobbish pride became one of the conspicuous marks of Gondarē character. This pride is manifest in many ways. On the one hand, it appears as incorrigible vanity. Hence arise the many caricatures of the Gondarē—as one who goes hungry in order to purchase fine clothes in which to strut about, or as one who satisfied his hunger at home before going out in order not to appear needy at his host's table. (Perhaps the most famous of the stories about the Gondarē is the one about the man who spent the night naked and shivering because, for form's sake, he hung up his only garment as a curtain about himself.) On the other hand, Gondarē pride appears as the immense dignity with which the Gondarē carries himself, his sensitivity to the nuances of personal relations, his choice use of the Amharic language, his noble bearing. If there is a polarity in Gondarē life comparable to the Manzē polarity of bravery versus aggression, it is pride versus vanity.

Gondar's role as political and cultural capital of the nation for so long produced two other distinctive aspects of the Gondarē ethos. One is the love of shumat, or political appointments. Despite the unfortunate denouement of the Gondar monarchy, Gondar's importance as chief administrative center for such a long period had a deep influence on the ways of the people. "Give the Gondarē any office whatsoever," it is said, "and no matter what the salary, he will be happy."

The Gondarē's love of shumat is expressed in two phenomena which contrast strikingly with their Manzē counterparts. In the naming of children, the Gondarē prefers names which express an ambition for political honors, such as Makonnen, meaning "nobleman," and Negusē ("my king"). Furthermore, litigation in Gondar is characteristically concerned with disputes regarding mādariyā, land which has been given as an award for service to the government, as well as with disputes over rĭst.

The other prominent aspect of Gondar's ethos relates to its position as the center of Ethiopia's Christian literati. The fact that it was the ecclesiastical capital of the country is not the most important consideration here. Of course, priests and monks celebrated mass and prayed in every direction. But the ritualistic and ascetic aspects of Ethiopian Christianity did not monopolize the attention of Gondar, for they were balanced by the sensuous leisure that prevailed in the city. Gondar could be, as European travelers found it before the middle of the nineteenth century, "a town of pleasures" and of "boundless debauchery."[43]

A preoccupation with the symbols of the religious tradition, however, was quite consistent with a less than puritanical atmosphere. This—the work of teachers, students, painters, copyists—represented the genius of Gondar's cultural activity. Generation after generation traversed the mountainous highlands to reach this mecca of learning. Painters were drawn or formed there in such numbers that a special section of the city, the "picture market," was reserved for the sale of parchment and pigments. Under such circumstances the prestige of the literatus was bound to affect the common culture.

Gondarēs have traditionally been eager to send their children to the church schools. An unusually high percentage of people is said to have learned to read the *Dāwit* (Psalms of David, the final step in the traditional elementary curriculum) in and around Gondar than in any other part of Ethiopia. The Gondarēs have been notoriously proud of their literary and general cultural level. Indeed, they claim to speak the purest and most elegant Amharic in the land. The stability and number of Gondar's religious institutions permitted religious culture to flourish there. This gave the Gondarē occasion to become especially proficient in the religio-literary virtues as they were defined in Amhara culture.

Manz versus Gondar

As church and army were among the chief institutional developments of Abyssinia, so religious culture and military culture were among the chief products of the Amhara-Tigre spirit. Both aspects of its culture were important all over Abyssinia throughout its history, but in Gondar and Manz, respectively, they underwent a more specialized development.

Gondar grew as a center for religious culture because the materials necessary for such a growth were concentrated in one place over a long period of time. The abundance of churches, masters, and pupils created a dense climate in which religious dance, painting, poetry, and textual studies flourished. Such innovation as the traditions permitted was encouraged by the coming of clergy to Gondar from all parts of the country.

The city failed as a military and political center because only a mobile capital could control the distant regions of Ethiopia and because, as Trimingham observes, "a fixed capital enabled court intrigue to thrive more insidiously [so that] coups d'état and the killing or imprisoning of monarchs became the rule."[44] Gondar's political integrity was weakened, moreover, by the influx of many Muslims and Galla, a migration favored by its urban situation. Manz, surrounded by hostile Galla, was forced for survival to cultivate its fighting powers, and for ultimate security to reconquer the surrounding areas. It was aided in this by whatever special geographical and cultural factors helped to produce the peculiarly militant and defiant character of the Manzē. But because of the annihilation of most of Shoa's churches and monasteries in the sixteenth century, and the isolation of Manz from the renascence of Amhara culture at Gondar, it was left illiterate and culturally impoverished. Its religious life remained limited to a narrow adherence to the ritual requirements of Ethiopian Christianity.

The dispersion of the Solomonic line over the several provinces was thus accompanied by the formation of distinct mores for Manz and Gondar. There is evidence that the differences were quite pronounced by the early nineteenth century. Just a few years before the fierce inhabitants of Manz sped to the rescue of Sāhla Selassie against the rebel Matako, Gondar was similarly threatened by a rebel band under a man named Mersu. Compare Rüppell's account of the behavior of the Gondarēs:

> In this general alarm the pitifulness of the local inhabitants was all too conspicuous. Far from uniting to defend their property with arms against the dreaded plunder—which would have been easy, in as much as there were at least four hundred rifles in Gondar, while not a single one of Mersu's men possessed a firearm—instead they carried the rifles into the churches, in order to keep them from being plundered along with the other booty.[45]

The distinction between Manz and Gondar suggested here is drawn in terms of "ideal types"—generalized dispositions which will, of course, not be true in every case and which will be found elsewhere in Ethiopia to a greater or lesser degree. It is interesting to note that in their own stereotypes, Ethiopians tend to view the Manzēs as fighters, the Gondarēs as literati, but not vice versa. Thus, an officer of the Imperial Bodyguard who commanded Ethiopian troops in the Korean War has said:

> The Manzēs were excellent soldiers. They were independent, not so ready to obey commands as the Galla, but they had good ideas about fighting and were very brave in the battlefield. The soldiers from Gondar tended to be independent and insubordinate, too, but they were not very good soldiers, either.*

On the other hand, Ethiopians commonly consider Manz as much a land of the backward as they regard Gondar the home of the learned. Krapf observed

---

* This stereotype of the Gondarē is combatted by Garimā Tāfara's book, *The Gondarē with His Shield* (*Gondarē Ba-Gāshāw* [Addis Ababa: Tasfā Gabra Selassie Press, 1957]), which records in great detail the contributions of individual Gondarēs to the fight against the enemy during the Italian occupation.

over a century ago that the people of Manz had the reputation of being "brave, daring, and ignorant."[46] The caricatures of the typical Manzē usually have to do with his *qilnat* ("stupidity"), such as the old story about the Manzēs at the bottom of a hill who were warned about some rolling boulders and replied: "That's all right, we'll just put our heads under the blanket and then we won't see the stones." As one Manzē himself put it: "We look to Gondar as our older brother. We know we are ignorant and illiterate."

Although in each other's eyes the Gondarē may be arraigned as haughty and cowardly and the Manzē berated as ignorant and hostile, a comparative view enables one to see the differences between Manz and Gondar as complementary, representing a specialization of interest and function within a common culture. An Amhara priest expressed this idea to me by saying: "The people of Gondar and Manz are really the same. Only Gondar is the head, and Manz the foot." (In Amharic thought the leg symbolizes force.) The pursuit of different interests and the perfection of different functions led to the cultivation of different virtues and, by the same token, the indulgence of different faults. The result was what might be called a moral division of labor along a geographical axis.

The primary axis of this division of labor in Amhara culture was vocational. The separate virtues of soldier and cleric were cultivated through distinct roles, pursued part or full time by two different sets of individuals. This permitted both sets of values to be realized without arousing the cultural and psychic conflicts that would inhere in their joint cultivation by the same persons.

It was by historical accident that Manz and Gondar came to provide an additional axis for this division of labor. At Gondar, through the political circumstances described above, the military function withered away, while the religio-literary culture was enabled to flourish. In Manz, the latter was destroyed and never recovered, while the energies of her people were consumed in fighting.

The historical advantage of this was that the Amhara thereby found the occasion for a massive revitalization of their religious culture through the facilities at Gondar, yet were able to accumulate a military momentum, through the years of incubation in Manz, that favored a political comeback which put them in a position to assert their might over an area larger than ever before in Ethiopian history. The moral consequence was that the Gondarē and the Manzē developed in pronounced form the virtues of the literatus and the soldier, respectively. The total culture was perhaps thereby enriched. Alaqā Gabra Hānnā, cultivated literatus, was in a sense the epitome of the Gondarē ethos, just as Menelik II, determined fighter as well as shrewd politician and tactful diplomat, was morally as well as genealogically akin to the men of Manz. The imperial court at the end of the nineteenth century, flushed with the reports of Menelik's conquests[47] and embellished by the wax and gold of Alaqā Gabra Hānnā, was a kind of traditional climax, a final expression of the integrity of traditional Amhara culture.

THE CONTEMPORARY SCENE

Gondar Today

A renascence of Gondar began during the Italian occupation, when it was made the capital of Amhara, one of the five large provinces into which the Italians divided Ethiopia. They equipped Gondar with modern buildings and roads, restored parts of the old castles, and made it the transportation center of northwestern Ethiopia.

After the liberation, Gondar retained some administrative importance by becoming the capital of Bagemder, one of the twelve provinces of postwar Ethiopia. A further impetus toward development of the town came in 1953 with the selection of Gondar as site for Ethiopia's first public health college. The existence of this college, with its enthusiastic staff of WHO and AID personnel, has stimulated the improvement of transportation and public utilities as well as local medical services. The population has increased to twenty thousand.[48] The progress shown by the city inspired one Ethiopian journalist to write, in the *Addis Zaman* of April 19, 1960: "By virtue of its annually increasing growth, sanitation, and modern appearance, one is emboldened to say that the city of Gondar takes second place only to Addis Ababa."

With the turn of Ethiopia's interest from the old church curriculum to a modern educational program, the traditional importance of Gondar has necessarily declined. It remains the place to go for the study of *aquāquām* and for a "diploma" in textual studies, but the total number of students now pursuing these subjects is probably less than a hundred. Almost none of the young people of Gondar itself attend the higher church schools. Still in the vanguard of learning, Gondar's youth prefer the currently more advantageous government schools. The elementary schools of Gondar receive many more applicants than they can accommodate each year. Gondar's secondary school is, next to that of Harar, the oldest and largest in the provinces.

Nevertheless, the life of Gondar is still dominated by its clergy. Nine church schools in Gondar are supported by government funds. Unlike other cities in Ethiopia, Gondar is partly governed by a town council of clergymen. The city is divided into districts marked by the location of the churches, and the town council consists of the heads of these churches—some of whose positions are so important that they are assigned directly by the Emperor. This council is convened to handle disputes over land and other matters, and to communicate the mayor's proclamations to the people. An accusation signed for a plaintiff by a priest carries much weight in the local courts. The ecclesias-

Fig. 6.—*The Amhara countryside*

Fig. 7.—*An Amhara homestead, Manz*

Fig. 8.—*Building a house*

Fig. 9.—*The weekly market*

Fig. 10.—*The market: weighing cotton*

tical character of Gondar has been implanted deeply enough so that one young Gondarē, commenting on the absence of dance halls such as are found in other Ethiopian cities, remarked: "This place is one big monastery."

In accord with Haile Selassie's program of centralization, the chief provincial administrators in Gondar are not local men. This has created a subtle problem for the national government. The Gondarēs cannot forget that their city was the capital of Ethiopia for more than two hundred years. They view the Shoans as political upstarts and love to refer to the Shoan Amhara as "Galla." As a result, Shoans in high offices at Gondar have found themselves boycotted by the natives. Their wishes have frequently been ignored by local subordinates or the local populace. They have not been invited to take part in the social life of the Gondarēs. All this has made the lot of Shoan emissaries in Gondar frustrating and lonely.

In order to increase the Gondarē's identification with the national government, its representatives in Gondar have tried in various ways to assert the symbolic supremacy of Addis Ababa. The traditional site for celebrating the festival of Masqal—the great sycamore near Fāsil's castle—has been shifted to the modern Haile Selassie I Square. An imposing sculpture is to be placed over the tomb of Nagāssi, and a principal street in Gondar has been named after him. Plans are afoot to outshine the traditional marketplace with one enhanced by modern facilities, to be named Haile Selassie I Market.

Despite the evident satisfaction with which one Shoan administrator noted that "the Gondarēs are not so proud any more," even for Shoa's purposes the traditional prestige of Gondar cannot be completely eradicated. The government gains much profit by extolling Ethiopia's long history. The flight to Gondar has become a standard part of the itinerary for foreign dignitaries. Gondar remains, after the stelae of Aksum and the monoliths of Lalibela, the most impressive visible reminder of the Ethiopian past.

Manz Today

The accession of the House of Manz to the throne of Ethiopia has given Manz much prestige in the national capital. Because Menelik and his successors filled the government with people from their home area, numerous higher officials of the imperial Ethiopian government are also of Manzē origin. Partly for these reasons, partly because of their scanty knowledge of Ethiopian geography, many Ethiopians born and raised in Addis Ababa claim to be of Manzē ancestry, even though their families may in fact have come from Merhābētē or Bulgā or other parts of Shoa.

Due to the close tie between the present imperial family and the homeland of Manz, a special affection persists between Haile Selassie and the Manzēs. The latter are said to have a standing invitation at the palace, including the right to a direct audience at any time. The Emperor is known to glow with pleasure when a subject with whom he is speaking reveals that he comes from Manz. The Manzēs, for their part, proudly refer to their area as *ya-negus agar* ("king's country"). They are perhaps the most devoted of all Ethiopians to the present Crown. However, many stories are told to show that this loyalty has not dissolved their intractable spirit. For example, when asked to select a representative for Ethiopia's first elected parliament in 1957, some of them were indignant: "We already have *our* representative in the capital, and if he isn't able to do the job himself, let him step down and hand it to somebody else."

Despite their expressed loyalty to Haile Selassie, the Manzēs stubbornly oppose the program with which he is publicly most associated and whose portfolio he has retained, as Minister of Education, from 1943 to the present day. The adults of Manz object to having their children attend the government schools. In many cases where a child has elected to attend school on his own, his parents have cut off all support. The four schools in Manz thus have an enrolment far below capacity, totaling (as of 1960) less than four hundred in this area of perhaps fifty to sixty thousand families.[49] Those hardy youngsters who do attend school often do so in rags and with an empty stomach.

One reason for this determined opposition to the government schools is the obvious economic one: children must stay at home to tend the herds. This is a problem all over rural Ethiopia, but still the schools in many other areas are overcrowded. Another reason is that, as we have seen, Manz was not interested in education in the old days. Few Manzēs learned to read in the church schools. When a boy showed unusual talent and interest in traditional studies he had to travel to Gondar, which often meant running away from Manz.

The crux of Manzē defiance of the new educational system, however, is cultural fundamentalism. The Manzēs keep their children away from the government schools because they fear that the students there are learning something that threatens the old ways. In particular, they do not like their children to learn the language of the *faranj* ("European") or to be exposed to Ethiopians who have been taught by *faranj* and thereby infected by alien ideas. Tending the farm, keeping the fasts, defending land and self—that is the sum and substance of Manzē education, beyond which there is nothing a boy needs to learn.

Undoubtedly part of this dread of *faranj* learning is based on the Manzēs' one experience with the white man: the Fascist occupation. As one of the strongholds of patriotic resistance to the occupation, Manz and the Manzēs became the object of the invader's unyielding fury. Over miles and miles of Manz not a home or church was spared. The inhabitants were either killed, or fled to safer areas in Galla country, or joined the underground opposition—

in such numbers that "Manzē" virtually became a synonym for "underground patriot."

After the liberation, as after the routing of Ahmad Grāñ's forces, the Manzē once again returned to redeem a ravished land. Slowly, the houses were rebuilt, the land was plowed once more. Churches which had been rebuilt after Grāñ's destruction only to be razed by the Italians were again put into place. Tough in his spiritual as in his physical life, the Manzē doggedly re-established the culture of his own. Now as before the occupation, a man of Manz sits on the throne, promising to let no foreigner take his country's land,* while the young braves celebrate the royal line in their festive boasting:

> *Ya-Manz ababā, ya-Manz ababā! Yābbabāl genā!*
> The flower of Manz, the flower of Manz! It will bloom yet again!

The Legacy of Manz and Gondar

Thus far the significance of Manz and Gondar has been discussed from the point of view of an outsider. We have attempted to assess, on the basis of the best available evidence, the respective historical and cultural roles of these two noted Amhara regions. We turn now to a different though related question, namely, the significance of these two places in the minds and feelings of Ethiopians themselves.

Two kinds of reaction are conspicuous. To the Ethiopian Modernist, Manz and Gondar are seen primarily as outlying pockets of conservatism. Their commitments to the past move them to resist certain changes promoted by the national government, with Manz protesting modern education and Gondar defending itself against nationalist centralization. They are regarded as backward areas, representative of the many forces that are "holding Ethiopia back," and to a certain extent are disdained.

To their inhabitants, on the other hand, these places are objects of intense loyalty. For differences of identity among the Amhara are defined chiefly in terms of their *agar,* or "home country." The size of one's *agar* is relative; it depends on the context in which the symbol is used, and may be as small as a district or as large as a province. Whatever the referent, one's *agar* signifies more than a place of residence or provenience. It means "home," and all those whose families live there are regarded with special affection, while those out-

---

* On certain festive occasions the following antiphonal chant is declaimed in praise of "Ṭaqel" (the affectionate, "horse" name of Haile Selassie):

[Leader:] *Mĭn āla ṭaqel mĭn āla?*
[Chorus:] *Agarē la-saw agarē la-saw alsaṭem ala!*
[Leader:] What did Ṭaqel say, what did he say?
[Chorus:] "My country to outsiders, my country to outsiders, I will not give!" said he.

side are regarded with reserve and suspicion, if not hostility. For this reason the word of native local authorities has always carried more weight than that of imported or distant authorities. For this reason the names of bars and cafés around Addis Ababa today are to a large extent place names. For this reason the type of voluntary association which has aroused the most enthusiastic interest in Addis Ababa in recent years is the association based on a membership drawn from the same *agar*.[50] Regionalist sentiments are so intense in connection with these groups that some members of the Manz association, for example, have asserted that they would not admit to membership a person whose family originated in a district only a few kilometers outside the boundaries of Manz.

This type of orientation to Manz, Gondar, and the many other regions in Amhara country may be regarded as an instance of the more general phenomenon referred to above as "primordial sentiments." These are sentiments which are based on the awareness of certain given qualities shared by the members of a group, qualities such as race, language, religious affiliation, tribal affiliation, as well as region of origin. The primordial sentiments account for much of the cohesion and much of the vitality among the members of any traditional society. How these allegiances are affected in the course of modernization has considerable bearing on the future shape of the rapidly developing nations.

A number of factors inherent in modernization work to erode the primordial sentiments. Increased physical and social mobility tend to uproot the individual from the settings of family and home community in which these sentiments are produced and reinforced. Occupational position comes to replace membership in primordial groups as a primary determinant of status and identity. Secondary education, military training, and the development of national institutions and symbols promote the sentiment of nationalism to which these narrower allegiances are subordinated.

Other aspects of modernization, however, work in the opposite direction to intensify primordial sentiments. The education of members of minority groups gives them both a heightened sense of grievance and a voice with which to protest. The creation of new forms of wealth and power provides new bases for competition and conflict, processes which tend to be structured along lines already laid out by cleavages based on primordial differences. The insecurity aroused by the threat to tradition inherent in modernization also produces defensive reactions which often take the form of heightened allegiance to such groups.

This intensification of primordial loyalties during modernization presents a problem which, for all their differences, nearly all the nations of Africa and Asia have in common. Whether the critical differences revolve about language, as in India; religion, as in Lebanon; geography, as in Indonesia; or tribal affiliation, as in sub-Saharan Africa—the passions spent in the conflict of primordial groups have impeded the development of a civil society at the national level. The problem is of such moment that Clifford Geertz has defined the nature of the effort required to cope with it as of a revolutionary order.[51]

Because of the disintegrative implications of primordial loyalties, so conspicuous in transitional societies, the ideas usually set forth for dealing with them have a tendency to reflect what we have called the "Conciliatory" perspective. On the one hand are those who conceive of tribalism or its counterparts as a major obstacle to the development of a national community, and see the chief hope for transitional societies in the effort to promote symbols and situations which excite the sentiment of nationalism as a substitute for primordial loyalties. On the other hand are those who appreciate the psychological advantages of retaining primordial identifications, and look rather for political and social mechanisms which will keep under control the explosive aspects of primordial loyalties.

Without denying the practical importance of such ideas, we would like to suggest an alternate emphasis, an emphasis on the positive aspects of traditional patterns—on their potentialities for reformation rather than for elimination or control. There is advantage in defining the durable aspects of tradition. The vitality of a people springs from feeling at home in its culture and from a sense of kinship with its past. The negation of all those sentiments acquired in childhood leaves man adrift, a prey to random images and destructive impulses. The only plausible alternative for a society which has been so uprooted is an order based on a rigid ideology and secured by a high degree of coercion. The most productive and liberating sort of social change is that built on continuity with the past.

This assumption may be elucidated by considering the nature of personality development. The human ego grows by incorporating new elements, discarding some old ones, and constantly reorganizing what it retains. The strongest egos, however, are those which have retained some solid identifications from childhood. The man with a strong ego may have substituted new religious, political, and occupational values for those of his father, but he has kept some general sense of oneness with his father, or original father-figures, all his life.

It is with respect to such general, archaic identifications that traditional primordial sentiments can be of positive use in times of rapid change. The specific content of early identifications can be replaced without sacrificing the deeply rooted, vitalizing sense of oneness with the original objects. In the Amhara case, Manz, Gondar, and other regions constitute such objects of identification: widely diffused symbols whose content must be modified with the times but which can endure as sources of inspiration in a changing society.

In what ways may the content of a primordial symbol be revised to benefit the developing national society? One way is through enlarging the scope of the referent. This is particularly feasible in the case of regionalist sentiments among the Amhara, for their concept of *agar* is, as we have seen, highly flexible. A native of Agāntchā, for example, may think of his *agar* now as Agāntchā, now as the sub-district of Gērā Meder, now as the district of Manz, now as Shoa Province, or even as Ethiopia as a whole. In each case, a feeling of inclusiveness would attach to anyone within the boundaries of the region in question, and he would be defined accordingly as *yāgarē saw* ("my countryman"). Thus a focus on the more inclusive reference of *agar* in the mass media and in educational institutions may serve to diffuse the libido invested in regional symbols and so expand, rather than destroy, the psychologically integrative functions of regional identifications.

A different process of reorientation is that which, instead of broadening the object of the particularistic attachment, focuses on aspects of the culture of the primordial group which are valuable in terms of universalistic criteria. One remains attached to the symbols of one's primordial groups, not because it is uniquely "chosen" in some way, not only because of the accident of birth and upbringing, but also because it embodies certain qualities which are intrinsically valuable according to the beliefs of the larger culture and/or which relate to some special function performed in behalf of the larger community. It involves a process of redefinition that might be termed a "rationalization" of primordial sentiment.

This process was exemplified, with an understandably high degree of self-awareness, in the personal experience of Sigmund Freud. Cosmopolitan though he was, Freud had a very intense primordial attachment to the Jewish people. As is well known, he rejected the particularistic beliefs of the Jewish tradition, both the religious mythology of Judaism and the chauvinistic concept of a Jewish nation. Yet throughout his life he maintained, and drew strength from, a lively sense of his identity as a Jew. In his own words, he was attracted to the symbolism of Jewish identity by "many obscure emotional forces, the more powerful as they are ineffable" and by "the clear consciousness of an inner identity, the secret of sharing the same type of soul."[52] In addition, he thanked his Jewishness for two qualities which he found of essential importance in his career: freedom from prejudices which hamper the full use of the intellect, and the readiness to accept a position of solitary opposition.[53]

In Freud's assessment of what it meant for him to be a Jew, we find an articulation of the three elements which constitute this process of rationalization of primordial sentiment: (1) rejection of exclusivist, particularistic beliefs and values, (2) retention of the basic emotional tie and identification with the group in question, and (3) elaboration of the virtues of the group in terms of universalistic criteria.

This is a type of orientation to the primordial sentiments which has the effect of maximizing both traditional and modern values, for it retains the sources of security and identity provided by tradition yet defines them in ways that promote national solidarity and the creative resources of the national culture. It is an approach which may be illustrated, in concluding this chapter, by the cases of two modern-educated Amhara who identify themselves, in part, as a Manzē and a Gondarē.

"Balātchaw" is an American-educated official of the Ethiopian government. Born and raised in Addis Ababa, his family originated in Manz, and he still has relatives who reside there. He is an ardent modernizer, anxious to see progressive leadership and the expansion of educational facilities provided in the provinces; yet he is also very sentimental about Amhara traditions and, in particular, his *agar* Manz.

To Balātchaw, Manz symbolizes hard-core loyalty to blood and to land. It also symbolizes the will to fight stubbornly for one's rights and for what one thinks right. He sees the government's keen concern for its territorial boundaries as a direct reflection of the Manzē's determination to retain and acquire land. Balātchaw gets much pleasure out of telling stories about the Manzē's almost foolhardy bravery in combatting the Italian invader. He reveals a "clear consciousness of an inner identity" with the Manzē in this regard, and says of himself: "You know, even as a child, and ever since, I have not been afraid of anybody."

"Makonnen" is a government official who was trained in western Europe. His family lives in Gondar, though he spent little time there after leaving for secondary school in Addis Ababa. In the course of his studies abroad, he had become estranged from the traditional ties and symbols of his Gondar-Amhara background. And yet now he speaks with great respect of the virtues of Gondarēs, their cultivated manner in personal relations, and their pride and wit in the use of language. The meaning of Gondar came to him almost in the manner of a revelation:

> In the midst of my studies in Western Europe I had the chance one summer to visit a number of West African countries and then to return home and spend some time in Gondar. I had not thought very highly of my people before that trip, and what I experienced was a great surprise. What I found—what we have, that I did not find in the African countries I visited—is a special sort of dignity of manner. When I talked with the elders at Gondar I was moved to tears. That is something priceless; that is a great and irreplaceable national resource.

It is spare vision to regard the Ethiopian past only as a source of obstacles to modernization, or as a matrix of primordial loyalties whose only issue can be discord and disruption. It is likewise constricting for Ethiopians to regard their past as useful only as a façade for exacting admiration from outsiders. The Ethiopian past can be, as the cases of Balātchaw and Makonnen demonstrate, a source of identifications which are associated with specific virtues of national significance, and which Ethiopian cultural leaders can draw upon to help define for their country its unique composite character in the company of transitional societies.

3

The world of
The amhara peasant

The life of the peasantry has been a constant setting for the Amhara drama. It is the faithful pedal point against which the ups and downs of Ethiopian history have been played. We cannot savor that history fully without becoming closely acquainted with the peasant himself.

If understanding the peasantry is important for a truer picture of the Abyssinian past, it is indispensable for a sensible approach to Ethiopia's future. Ethiopia is and will remain for a long time a predominantly agricultural nation, one whose exports—chiefly coffee, skins, and oilseeds—depend almost exclusively on rural output. The one economist to have discussed the problem at any length in print maintains that agriculture is the one area in which Ethiopia can reasonably expect significant economic development in the foreseeable future.[1] Conscious efforts to stimulate peasant productivity, however, may issue in stagnation or even setbacks if they are not based on a realistic understanding of the peasants' own attitudes and conditions of life.

Ethiopians who are striving to modernize their country have for the most part lost touch with the peasantry. If they were born and raised in one of the cities, they may have had no direct contact with the peasantry at all. If their origins are rural, they have been oriented all their school days toward gaining a modern education and tend, wittingly or not, to ignore what they can of their past. Nor are they helped much in this regard by foreign technical experts, who tend to have a modernist bias and typically know still less about the indigenous peasantry. Understanding of the peasantry by scholars, on the other hand, has hitherto been impeded by two characteristics of humanistic and social studies. The historian's view has been limited by his reliance on written records that deal chiefly with the activities of men of power and the conceptions of literati. The ethnographer or traveler who tries to give the peasantry its due has usually concentrated on the more evident and accessible facts of custom—activities related to work, play, kinship, and ritual. The peasant's inner feelings and notions have perforce been neglected.[2]

In default of a widely disseminated sensibility to peasant realities, modernizing Ethiopians have thus come to view the peasantry in terms of misleading stereotypes: either romantically, as an embodiment of virtue, awaiting only proper leadership to realize their suppressed aspirations for freedom, justice, and progress; or else as inhabitants of a dark hinterland, barbarous in custom and blind with superstition. In this chapter we shall attempt a more empirical account of one part of the Ethiopian peasant's world—that of the Amhara—with particular emphasis on the beliefs and values of the peasant himself. Our account is based on seven months of residence among the Amhara peasantry, using the observational techniques of participant observation, discreet questioning, analysis of folk expressions, and Thematic Apperception Tests (TAT).[3]

THE INSTITUTIONAL SETTING
OF PEASANT LIFE

The homestead is the basic ecological and social unit of the Amhara peasantry. The average homestead consists of from one to six small round structures, built of wattle (or stone, as in Manz) and capped with conical thatched roofs. A well-equipped homestead will have one building for eating and sleeping, one for animals, one for grain storage, one as a kitchen, and one for entertaining guests; though for many peasants all these functions are served by a single large building. The homestead is normally located on land worked by the peasant. While most peasants plow land whose use is theirs by hereditary right (*rĭst*), some are tenants on estates owned by the king, lords, monasteries, or older relatives.

The smallest homesteads consist simply of husband, wife, and unmarried children. Sometimes a young married son will remain within the family home and, much less frequently, a young married daughter. Occasionally an older relative will be sustained there, or a younger relative will be brought up there. One or more servants—slaves, until a generation ago—complete the household. The wealthier the peasant, the more relatives and servants will be found in the homestead.

At times hamlets will be formed by the clustering of households of a number of married brothers or other kin. These tend to have a patriarchal cast; if the father is no longer living, the oldest male relative usually assumes jurisdiction for the affairs of the hamlet. But the nucleated village, contrary to erroneous impressions conveyed by much of the literature on Ethiopia, is not a normal ecological unit in Amhara society.

Each homestead gives the appearance of self-sufficiency and autonomy, but it is bound to a wider social context in a number of ways. While satisfying most of its consumption needs by its own efforts, every household depends on the market for certain items. The highland peasants must go to market for their chili, onions, peppers, hops, and cotton; while lowland peasants must barter for barley and sheep there. Salt and foreign fabrics must be imported from afar, and iron and clay products must be bought from specialists who bring their wares. Limited needs for currency—chiefly for rifles and, since 1942, taxes—are also met at the market.

The markets normally are held once a week. Every homestead is within walking distance of at least one market; though often the trip may take several hours, at times the greater part of a day. Markets in the same region are often scheduled on different days, so that, for example, the family which misses the one five hours to the north on Saturday can catch another four hours to the south on Tuesday. The virtual absence of roads throughout the countryside makes travel to market slow and tedious, but wealthier peasants nonetheless manage to transport quantities of grain and livestock to the provincial capitals for better prices and a wider selection of consumers' goods.

The household is linked to a wider world politically as well as economically. By providing tithes, revenues, military service, and corvée labor, the peasant has traditionally been obliged to support an extensive political hierarchy. In return for this he has received an organization for defending the country against enemies, and a structure of legitimate authority sufficient to maintain order and settle disputes.

The peasant's relations with this political hierarchy have been mediated by the office of *chīqā shum*, a district headman. This office is circulated, usually annually, among a small number of men whose eligibility is based on their ownership of certain pieces of land. As the land passes from father to son, so does the eligibility for being *chīqā shum*.

Traditionally the *chīqā shum* was a role of considerable importance. It carried the duties of tax collection, adjudication, promulgation of official decrees, supervision of occasional work projects, levying of men for military service, and officiating at civil marriages and divorces. Through his work the *chīqā shum* received a variety of fees and bribes. In cases of flagrant misbehavior the local people were able to dismiss him from office. The reorganization of provincial administration since 1942 has deprived the *chīqā shum* of many of his former powers, but the office still exists and plays a modest role in peasant life.

The district over which a *chīqā shum* has authority is the closest thing to a village unit among the Amhara. It is usually coterminous with the area surrounding a local church, and therefore "parish" may be the more appropriate term for it than village. The *chĭqā shum* and the local church authorities work closely on occasion, particularly in connection with the construction and maintenance of church buildings.

The church represents the third main link between the peasant hamlet and the broader Abyssinian life. As the peasant depends on the local market to mediate between his production unit and the external economy, and on the *chĭqā shum* to mediate between his domestic polity and the higher political authorities, so he depends on the local clergy to mediate between his home culture and the "high culture" of Abyssinia as embodied in the institutions of the Orthodox Church.

The peasant supports the church by following its main ritual requirements and by contributing, according to his means, a certain quantity of grain each year. If the peasant works land owned by the church, a considerable part of his produce is transmitted automatically to individual priests, or gifts are offered to the church according to the occasion. In return, the church symbolizes for him the integrity of his moral order and provides moral support during personal crisis.

Such, in broad outline, is the structural setting of peasant life among the Amhara.

THE WORLD OF ACTIVITY

The Daily Round

Work begins in the peasant's home well before daybreak. His wife or maidservant rises with the first cockcrow to grind grain. It is pitch dark as she feels her way across the earthen floor and begins to push and pull a large flat stone over little heaps of barley, wheat, or *ṭēff.*

An hour or two later cold light seeps in through cracks in the door and, if it is in bad repair, the thatched roof. The noises of chickens and livestock become more audible, and the rest of the household begins to stir. The man of the house starts his day by reciting a prayer or, if he has some education, by reading a passage from some sacred text. Then he or one of the boys takes the oxen and cows out for breakfast, to a pile of hay in the yard or a spot of pasture rich with grass. Donkeys, mules, and perhaps horses are also sent to graze.

One of the women pokes the embers that spent the night under a blanket of ash. She blows them into flame through a bamboo pipe, filling the room with smoke and her eyes with tears. Over the fire she sets a clay pot to warm up leftover pepper sauce. The peasant sits on a sheepskin spread over the clay bench that adjoins the wall. Water is poured from a gourd for him to wash his hands, and *ĭnjarā* and sauce are brought for his breakfast. He eats by himself, slowly, pondering the work for the day.

When he has eaten and washed his hands, the children take their breakfast quickly. One or two of them then lead the remaining animals out to pasture—the cows, which have already been brought back and milked; the sheep and goats; the young draft animals. They spend the day roaming the hills with their flocks in the company of shepherds from nearby farms, unless it is harvest time when each must stay close to his family's fields where the herds feed on stalks and chaff.

The peasant leaves with his older sons or manservants for the fields. (If it is a fasting day, they go directly to work without any breakfast.) The day's activity may consist of cutting the ripe crops with a fine-toothed sickle, or threshing the harvest under the hooves of cattle and mules, or winnowing grain by tossing it up in the breeze. More often than not it will consist of plowing, virtually a year-round occupation. For each crop a field must be plowed at least twice: first to loosen the crusted soil, and then to cover up the seed that has been sown. Planting occurs in several months, the schedule varying according to region. In some regions, for example, barley, wheat, and chick-peas are sown in September and October; corn, beans, and peas in May and June; and *téff* in July. In many areas a January planting is also common. The central position of plowing in the world of the Amhara peasant is shown by the fact that the word for his vocation, *irshā*, literally means "plowing."

On plowing days, the wooden plow with its single iron share and the yoke are carried to the field, and the oxen are driven along with sticks and shouts. If it is sowing time, bags of seed are loaded on donkeys which join the procession. On his way to work the peasant is likely to see a neighbor at a distance and cries of "How did you spend the night?" are exchanged. At the field the team of oxen is yoked and the work begins. It lasts for about five hours, and the peasant is indeed wretched who does not have a helper with whom to take turns steering the heavy plow and cracking the whip as the oxen trace furrow after furrow.

The peasant's wife is too busy in the morning to sit down for a regular breakfast, so she takes bites of food at will as she works about the house. There is much ado in the house as she and her daughters, and perhaps maidservants, carry out a variety of chores—baking *injarā*, preparing *tallā*, spinning cotton, collecting dung for fuel, sweeping rubbish off the floor, carrying water from the spring, weaving straw baskets or mats. The impression of business is heightened by the chickens, which hop in and out of the house as they please, though they must be shooed away from grain drying in the sun.

Toward noon a fresh batch of pepper sauce is prepared. If the peasant is working in a distant field, his wife carries lunch out to him—or else risks being beaten with a stick. If he is not too far away he comes home for lunch, which he eats together with his wife. They talk about what each has done in the morning and what remains to be done. The peasant may retire for a nap, and perhaps to lie with his wife, before taking up the afternoon's work. He returns for about three more hours of plowing after his noon rest. The afternoon sun burns down on him; the plow is harder to wield; he plods on. At home the women continue their work, no sooner finishing one task than they attend to another. The mother puts the child who rides on her back to the breast whenever it cries.

The shepherds do not come home for lunch. They have taken some *injarā* or *dābo* ("whole wheat bread") along with them. In harvest months they enjoy a special treat, roasting grains or pulse which they have snatched from somebody's field. Though their responsibility is great—a boy will be whipped if an animal in his charge gets hurt or lost or if it gets into fields of grain—their work is light. They spend the day running idly, practicing war chants, playing at various adult activities. Their mood is as free as the great spaces about them. As the day grows hotter they are likely to discard their sheepskin covering and move about naked. Toward dusk, the shepherds' spirits quicken. Their songs become more excited; lively melodies are heard from their wooden flutes. It is time to go home to family, supper, and fire.

When father and sons enter after the day's work, they start munching on roasted grains, *injarā,* or *dābo.* They may drink some *ṭalla* and relax. It begins to get chilly. The room is dark and smoky, the fleas bite them—but it is the easiest time of the day. The family is together, and everyone enjoys talking and hearing about the homely events of the day. A few hours after dark, supper is served. Parents and older children eat together out of a common basket. Younger children and servants stand respectfully, awaiting their turn, grateful if someone places a large bite of food in their mouths.

After dinner there is a great washing of feet—the father's by his wife or children, the others' by themselves. The peasant recites or reads his evening prayers and lies down on his bed made of strips of cowhide. The children settle for the night on the clay benches. Last of all, the mother covers the embers with ashes, sets out the grain she must grind before dawn, and places her weary body next to that of her husband's.

This grueling schedule is not repeated every day. On nearly half the days in each month heavy labor is not permitted—men may not plow or harvest, women may not grind or spin. These are holy days: Saturdays and Sundays (both of which are honored as the Sabbath in Abyssinia) and the monthly and annual commemorations of the saints.

The woman's schedule on such days is only lightened, not radically altered. Food and drink must still be prepared and served. Except for a possible trip to church with her husband Sunday morning before breakfast, a woman's hours are still confined to the home compound and its obligations. The shepherds must still take care of their herds, though some boys may get together for games with sticks and cloth, or wooden, balls. The adult males may do odd jobs around home, such as loading and moving bags of grain, or repairing farm equipment. But they are likely to gather at some convenient spot, perhaps at a boundary between fields, and discuss land disputes, arrange marriages, reconcile quarrels, or tell stories.

The daily activity of the Amhara peasant is somber and severe. It is guided by the constant awareness that one must provide for oneself everything he needs in this world. His is a life of deadening exertion, devoid of casual gaiety. Even in his diversions the mood is generally serious and tense.

One of the Amhara peasant's principal diversions is litigation. On days when heavy labor is forbidden the judge's yard is filled; nor is it ever empty on work days. Some peasants spend as much as twenty to twenty-five per cent of their waking days at court. (Because of its importance in Amhara culture, litigation will be discussed at greater length in later chapters.)

Going to market is another diversion. The trip is made by the peasant or his wife, or both, according to the needs of the household. The wife usually is responsible for transactions dealing with cooking equipment and spices, the husband for animals and farm equipment, while either is competent to negotiate about the great common denominator of Amhara life—grain. Exchanges are made either by barter or currency, which in olden times consisted of salt bars, pepper, and iron, as well as silver.

The market provides an occasion for seeing distant relatives and friends, catching up on the latest news of the area, and generally countering the normal isolation of the peasant's life. It is especially stimulating for children, who may be treated to a piece of sugar cane if they are lucky. But the marketgoers are less absorbed with being sociable than they are with the serious business of locating the items they lack, haggling over the terms of exchange, and getting on the trail in time to arrive home before dark.

Finally, the peasant's day may be devoted to one of the many celebrations that constitute the brightest moments in his life. Huge feasts are held on the occasion of weddings, christenings, and memorial anniversaries. Feasts and special festive activities mark the various religious holidays. Indeed, apart from the alternation of the rainy season (June-September) and the long dry season, and the related alternation of planting and harvesting the different crops, it is the cycle of holidays and weddings that defines the pattern of the Abyssinian year. Yet even these holidays have a fundamentally serious tone. Apart from the feasting, they are chiefly times for the veneration of sacred symbols and the real or symbolic letting out of aggression.

The Yearly Cycle

The new year falls on St. John's Day in September. For this occasion the floor of the peasant's home is strewn with freshly cut grass, tall and green after the long rains. Children go singing from house to house in small bands, or take bunches of wild flowers to relatives, in hopes of getting a bit of *dābo*. In most homes an animal is slaughtered—in some areas superstition decrees that it be a white-headed lamb or a red chicken—and there is much eating and drinking, the basic activity of every holiday.

A little more than two weeks later the much more important festival of Masqal is observed, celebrating the discovery of the true Cross by Empress Helena. By this time the heavy rains have subsided, and the air is filled with something of the spirit of spring. (Although Ethiopia lies north of the equator the summer rainy season is known as "winter" because of its coldness.) The landscape is colored by acres of yellow wildflowers, which are cut and fastened to the poles each family brings to a central clearing where a huge bonfire is built. In late afternoon, after the tepee of poles has been constructed, the priests begin the ceremony by intoning appropriate chants. Then each status group circles the poles three times, in honor of the Trinity—first the local lord, then the clergy, the lesser nobility, the peasant men, women, and finally the children. In the evening the festival takes a more secular turn. The bonfire is lit, and the young braves dance around it shouting their war chants. As the fire blazes on, these fellows seize burning brands and playfully hurl them at one another.

In November the monthly St. Michael's Day is honored with special celebrations. The peasants travel distances to attend the ceremonies at any church consecrated to "Mikā'ēl." Holy water and hot springs sanctified by Mikā'ēl's name are drunk and bathed in by those with many kinds of disease. The rituals involve carrying the Mikā'ēl *tābot* ("holy ark") out of the church and elaborate chanting and dancing by the clergy. After the *tābot* has been returned, in a procession in which the laymen follow shouldering their rifles (undoubtedly spears in older times), folk dancing and singing go on until late afternoon. This provides an occasion for the more enterprising adolescent male to spot a potential bride, about whom he may diffidently ask his father to make inquiries.

Christmas, celebrated in early January, is marked chiefly by the playing of secular games. The common word for Christmas, *gannā,* is actually the name of an outdoors game played with sticks and a wooden puck. Played by boys, young men, and occasionally elders on the afternoon of Christmas Day, *gannā* is marked by a spirit of aggressive license. Accustomed norms of deference are held in abeyance. The game is played in so rough and disorderly a manner that it often results in broken limbs and scarred faces. Staged by two teams made up on the spot, *gannā* is concluded at dusk by volleys of abusive limericks with which the victors revile their adversaries.[4]

This is the season for special festivities on saints' days. St. Gabriel is particularly honored in December, as are St. Mary, St. George, and again St. Michael in January. But the giant of holidays in this season is Epiphany, about a fortnight after Christmas. The holiday commemorates the baptism of Jesus; the name of the holiday, *Ṭïmqat,* means "baptism." In preparation for Ṭïmqat new clothes are given to children and the adults' *shammā,* grown very gray over the months, are washed in every household.

The program for Ṭïmqat is long and complicated. At sunset on the eve of the holiday, the people don their white clothes and repair to the local church, from whence they escort the *tābot* to a place where it will spend the night—near some stream or pool. They go home for supper, and return to that site for singing and dancing until late at night. About two o'clock in the morning Mass is performed, after which quantities of *dābo* and *ṭalla* are consumed. Toward dawn, or shortly after, the clergy bless the water and sprinkle it on those assembled. Many like to bathe in the sanctified water at this time. It is the occasion for baptizing the children of syphilitic mothers and those who want to be rebaptized.

By noon on Ṭïmqat Day a large crowd has assembled at the ritual site, those who went home for a little sleep having returned, and the holy ark is escorted back to its church in colorful procession. The clergy, bearing robes and umbrellas of many hues, perform rollicking dances and songs; the elders march solemnly with their weapons, attended by middle-aged men singing a long-drawn, low-pitched *haaa hooo;* and the children run about with sticks and games. Dressed up in their finest, the women chatter excitedly on their one real day of freedom in the year. The young braves leap up and down in spirited dances, tirelessly repeating rhythmic songs. When the holy ark has been safely restored to its dwelling-place, everyone goes home for feasting. In the meantime, the eyes of gamesome men and women have met and secret rendezvous have been arranged.

Ṭïmqat ushers in a season of weddings, which comes to an abrupt end with the onset of the great fast before Easter. For eight long weeks, body and spirit are depressed by the heavy fasting requirements. The mood reaches a climax in the final week of Lent. Then no heavy work is allowed, and the more devout peasants go to church many times and intensify their daily schedule of prayers. Total abstinence is practiced for the forty-eight hours preceding the final Mass, performed in the middle of the night before Easter.

Gluttony follows this long deprivation. It is a season of the highest spirits. For eight weeks the inexorable requirement to fast on Wednesdays and Fridays is waived. The bins are full with the harvest of wheat, barley, and chickpeas. New crops of pulse start to appear in the fields. It is the most favored time of all for weddings.

And then, as the Amhara themselves view it, June brings another time of sadness. With the onset of the heavy rains come attacks of malaria in the lowlands, typhus in the highlands. Swollen streams make travel difficult and hazardous. Moisture and chill lower the resistance of man and beast to respiratory infections. The weekly fasting schedule is resumed, and the more devout observe the thirty-day fast of the Disciples. In August, finally, the sixteen-day fast in honor of the Assumption of Mary is observed by everyone older than six or seven years.

On the thirteenth day of that fast occurs the strange holiday of Buhē. Before and during this day, which is marked by the baking of special *dābo* for the shepherds, the countryside crackles with the reports of shepherds' whips. In this season when the humid air lends an explosive sound, the shepherds crack their whips for fun; but older boys and men join in great whipping battles on Buhē,* in which two teams lash each other until the members of one can stand it no more. On the evenings of Buhē, small bonfires are lit all over the countryside, and more *dābo* is eaten and whips cracked.[5] A few days later the fast of the Assumption is over. Young and old look forward to the end of the rains and the festivities that commence with the new year.

These are the days and years of the Amhara peasant. Some other aspects of his life that come to the fore when more analytic perspectives are applied will be discussed in later chapters. But this calendar of activities forms the immediately observable setting for the "inner world" of the Amhara peasantry: those ideas, sentiments, and values which constitute its outlook on life.

THE WORLD OF MEANING

The Natural Universe

The Amhara peasant is not familiar with most of the cosmological notions found in the Great Tradition of Abyssinian culture, as transmitted through books like *Qalamsis* and *Aksimareos* and the oral traditions of learned churchmen. It is unusual for him to have a precise image of the layers of water, fire, and air beneath the earth, and it is still less likely for him to be familiar with the complicated hierarchy of invisible worlds, watery skies, and seven "real" heavens which are enumerated in the Abyssinian cosmology. He believes that stars influence human affairs, but leaves the possession of astrological knowledge to the *dabtarā*. The presence of cultural specialists who know about such matters has relieved him of the burden of dealing with ideas about the cosmos, ideas which are more widely diffused in more homogeneous societies.

The peasant's working conception of the cosmos is thus a very simplified version of that of his Great Tradition, together with certain pagan notions. Like his more learned countrymen, he divides the universe into two main parts: the world, *alam,* consisting of the earth, sun, moon, and stars; and

---

* This custom is now extinct in many Amhara areas.

heaven, *samāy,* the abode of supernatural beings and the souls of the dead. The earth is seen as flat, though some believe its shape to be square, others think it is round like a disc, and still others imagine it to extend without limit. That the terrain of Ethiopia is so obviously not flat is explained by reference to the great flood, after which the parts which dried quickly became high-lands (*dēgā*), the parts slow to dry becoming lowlands (*qolā*). The peasant explains the greater heat of the lowlands by saying that they receive less wind than the highlands.

Beneath the earth's surface is an obscure area called *maq,* a depth to which the bodies of evildoers drop after burial. There is also a large subterranean ocean, *weqniyānos,* into which all the rivers and lakes on earth descend. The earth itself is held up, according to some, by a Y-shaped piece of wood; accord-ing to others, by two serpents; still another view is that no support is needed other than the will of God, as the saying indicates:

Ay, My God! Lord who stretched forth the heavens without a pillar, and the earth without tent-pegs.

The rotation of the sun *above* the earth causes the alternation of night and day. The imagery of this rotation is that of someone going home at night and coming out in the morning. Attitudes toward the sun are quite ambivalent. The sun is appreciated for dispersing the morning chill and for causing seed to germinate, but it is feared as a source of sickness and death.*

The moon is highly regarded, which is probably a vestige of pre-Christian moon worship. At the Ethiopian latitude the moon is functional, for its bright illumination facilitates night travel, especially desirable in the hotter regions. Beyond this, the moon is considered a powerful agent. It is chief of the sky, commander of an army of stars and it is the force which causes crops to grow after the sun has brought forth seedlings.

In the heavenly realm there are two regions located on either side of God's dwelling-place. To the right is an area where good souls repair for an eternity of ease after being judged shortly after the death of their bodies. Known both as the "kingdom of heaven" and "paradise"—terms which refer to quite dif-ferent spheres in the Orthodox cosmology but are fused in the vulgar mind —it is regarded as a home where food and clothes are plentiful and freely dis-tributed. To the left is the place where wicked souls are taken by the devil to be scorched eternally in the fire of Gehenna, also called *Si'ol* (again a fusion of concepts which are distinct for the learned). This treatment of the damned is made worse by alternate dippings in icy water, though some believe that the wicked souls get a respite from their tortures on weekends.

---

* The TAT's revealed a great dread of the sun; nearly every respondent interpreted one or another of the cards in terms of the sun's dangerousness.

As for the beginning and end of the world, all Amhara believe that the world was created at one time by the will of God. When the eighth millennium arrives, moreover (A.D. 2508), God will bring about a major upheaval, either destroying the world completely or, as others believe, turning it upside down. According to the latter view, all those who live at that time will perish, while those who died first in the world's history will return to life, to a time of renewal, when a little grain will go a long way and the milk of one cow will nourish a multitude.

The Amhara peasant's view of nature is matter-of-fact. There are a few traces of animism, such as the association of certain kinds of trees with holy places and the belief that whatever is planted on the monthly commemoration of Christ's birth will dry up and die. There are a few touches of aesthetic appreciation, such as the peasant's wonderment over a remarkable view when it is thrust upon him and his desire, when feasible, to locate his home in an attractive locale. But there is certainly no idealization, religious or secular, of the great outdoors. The peasant much prefers to get out of the bright sunshine and rest in the dark, smoky interior of his hut. When he sits gazing over the hills and slopes of his gorgeous country, he is probably counting his livestock or noticing how the grain is growing.*

The Amhara peasant's life is so much a part of nature that he does not view it as a separate category of experience; there is no word for "nature" in his vocabulary. Nor is there a sense that the things of nature have minds or laws of their own. Nature is simply the passive agent of God's rewards and punishments; for example, the man who fails to keep the Orthodox fasts will find that his crops are ruined.

For his part, the peasant's adjustment to nature is a straightforward practical one. He has no drive to conquer or to be master over nature; he has no inclination to fuse or lose himself in nature; he has no need to keep nature in equilibrium through a system of rituals. His perception of natural objects is in terms of what will assist or hinder eking out a subsistence. The farm animals are his friends, and must be taken care of properly or else they will die and he will be without their help. The wild beasts are his enemies, and they must be guarded against or else they will eat his crops, his livestock, or himself. The fields must be plowed at the right time each year or the bins will become empty, and knowing the right time depends upon a sufficient knowledge of weather to judge the coming of the various kinds of rain.

Thus, the motif in the Amhara peasant's orientation toward nature is to get what one can out of what nature readily provides, neither neglecting one's responsibilities to keep things running as nature requires, nor inflicting any

---

* All the TAT respondents interpreted card No. 4, showing two men sitting on a ridge overlooking a natural panorama, in terms of taking care of the grazing animals and becoming wealthy.

drastic changes on the familiar natural order. Insofar as there is a special affect regarding nature, it takes the form of a sentimentalization of the useful—as in the great respect felt for young cattle, the thrill aroused by the sight of newly sprouted grain, and the deep nostalgia about one's land.

The Supernatural

The peasant's conception of God is closer to that of the learned clergy than is his cosmology, since the Abyssinian clergy have tended to avoid systematic theology, believing that to probe too deeply into the nature of God verges on blasphemy. Abyssinians view God above all as *mystery*.

Nevertheless, they do have a sense of the various attributes of their God. God is the creator of the world. He is, as the name *Egziābhēr* signifies, Lord of the earth; and He is Lord of the seas, Lord of the King of Kings, and Lord of the angels. He is eternal and possesses knowledge without limit.

The Amhara peasant has a keen awareness that wherever one goes, God is there. "If you say no one is looking," goes an Amharic saying, "still God will see you." This consciousness of God's presence is reflected in the habit of referring to God scores of times every day. A number of common expressions contain references to God:

For greeting and farewell	"May He give you health for me."
For showing gratitude	"May God give you for me."
For responding to queries about one's health	"God be praised!"
For thanksgiving after meals	"Be praised, my Lord!"
For swearing by a statement that has been challenged	"By God! By the Savior!"

Prayers to God are spoken on numerous occasions. God's blessing is sought when an animal is slaughtered, when a group of people sits to eat, when a new house is begun, and when it is completed. Each day begins with a prayer something like this: "May He cause me to spend the day in peace. May He keep trouble from me. May He pardon my sins." When the peasant begins planting, he also prays: "God bless the seed; feed me, keeping birds away from it; bless it for the mouth of man."

It is probably the attribute of God's omnipotence, however, that appears most vivid to the Amhara mind. Everything that happens reflects His active will. The thunder expresses His anger, a flood the visitation of His wrath upon the sinful. He is ever active, bringing births and deaths, prosperity and hunger, leading one traveler to safety and another to disaster. He controls the homeliest details of everyday life. One boy, troubled that he was not selling his goods in the market, confessed that God must be angry with him about something. Another, asked what he wanted to do the following year, replied:

"If God wants me to, I may go to school; but it is hard to know what God will want."

As a corollary of this outlook, the main way for man to achieve anything on earth is to pray to the Almighty. If one prays properly, God's power can be invoked to punish one's foes. In former times at least, the peasant went to church and prayed for vengeance, then expected his enemy to fall sick or die. If he could not pray effectively himself, he would give money to a priest and the latter would do the job for him. It is commonly believed by the Amhara peasantry today that their praying and fasting were a major factor in ridding the country of the Italian invaders.

This conception of deity is at heart that of the early Old Testament, a powerful Lord who punishes, rewards, and avenges. But it is suffused with the pagan feeling for a plurality of deities. The Amhara is constantly aware of a number of supernatural beings other than *Egziābhēr* who affect his life for better or for worse.

Some of these are the simple agents of God in everyday affairs. Each individual receives at birth a pair of guardian angels of his own sex, one for daytime and one for night. They serve to protect him from accidents, sickness, and enemies. When some misfortune befalls a person, it is because God has ordered his guardian angels to neglect their duties.

More important are the many supernatural beings with wills of their own. Among the benevolent spirits the main figures are:

Mikā'ēl	The archangel Michael
Gabre'ēl	The archangel Gabriel
Giyorgis	St. George
Madhānē Alam	Savior of the World
Selassie	Trinity
Māryām	St. Mary
Abbo	Gabra Manfas Qeddus, an Abyssinian saint
Takla Hāymānot	Another Abyssinian saint

Most Amhara are particularly devoted to some one of these sacred figures. Partiality to one or another may be due to the fact that it is the patron saint of one's father, or represented in one's Christian name, or commemorated by the church in one's area. In time of sickness, a man will drink holy water from the church of a certain saint, and make a vow, for example, "If Giyorgis cures me, I will give money to the church in his name, I will kill a lamb for him, and I will drink in a Giyorgis *māhebar* ("religious fraternal association") every month thereafter."

These sacred figures are represented by numerous holy arks, or *tābot*. A *tābot* is a hollow oblong box containing some sacred script. It is identified with the saint for whom it has been named, and personalized. The extent to which the ark is regarded as human is shown by the following remark of a peasant who looked at the picture of a church on a TAT card and explained: "When the ark has been given incense, it will be happy. . . . If this church is given a new roof, the ark will be very happy and give *ĭnjarā* to the people."

The saints and the *tābot* which represent them are the objects of much veneration and prayer. They figure so prominently in the Amhara's outlook that at times they appear to be on a par with *Egziābhēr* himself. Two differences may be noted, however. The saints do not take the initiative in interfering in human affairs, as does *Egziābhēr*, but intervene only when appealed to. Their function, moreover, is that of protecting and healing spirits; it is not their portion to administer the punishments which *Egziābhēr* inflicts on those who disobey the religious laws, though they may mete out punishment to someone who breaks a vow he has made to them.

Malevolent spirits, on the other hand, do intervene in human affairs without being invited. Of the evil spirits, the devil—known as *Diabolos, Sayṭān,* or *Agannent,* which are names of different spirits to the learned but counted the same in the peasant's mind—is the most powerful. He is imagined as a dark, Negroid type, the least favored sort of racial stock in Ethiopia. He dwells in deep waters, woods, and caves, and likes to roam about at noon and at midnight, especially near dirty places. Amhara avoid going near a lake or pool known to harbor the devil, for fear of being pulled in and drowned. They likewise stay away from dirty places at noon, for fear that he will make them sick. The devil brings epileptic fits. He tries to push people into fire. He also tries to harm human beings by tempting them to some misdeed—stealing, murder, getting drunk—and then have them suffer the consequences. Finally, when the human soul appears for judgment after death, he strives to gain possession of the soul and put it into the fire. Sometimes he is pictured as chewing the souls he manages to obtain.

Despite his inimical gestures toward the human race, the devil is respected as well as feared, for he has much power. Many peasants pray to him for this reason. In time of sickness some choose *Sayṭān,* rather than (or in addition to] *Giyorgis* or *Māryām,* as the one to whom they pray and make promises. On New Year's Day, Christmas, and Easter, prayers to *Sayṭān* are surreptitiously repeated in many quarters. One of these prayers runs: "My lord, bring me through the year. Guard me. If you keep me this year in peace and bring me through the year, I will give you more." Certain individuals are on especially good terms with the devil. They pray to him often, and he visits them from time to time and does favors for them; they are his "friends." When such a person dies, his son often continues the relationship.

Another kind of spirit producing ill effects is the *zār*. *Zār* spirits are of many kinds: they may be male or female, Christian or Muslim, educated or unschooled, mischievous or somber. *Zār* are depicted as resembling the handsome, light-complexioned Abyssinians. They are not necessarily evil: sometimes a person is inspired by the sound of *zār* singing far off in the woods to add a new song to the local lore. But they are the great carriers of physical and mental illness. Many of the contagious diseases in Abyssinia, like typhus and smallpox, are referred to as *"zār* sicknesses." Above all, the *zār* is the bringer of seizures. When a *zār* lands on somebody's back the victim may go into a trance, succumb to melancholia, or break out in hysteria. Women are most often subjected to fits caused by *zār*—usually by male *zār,* who perform some kind of magical coitus with them and try to compete with their husbands. When a freak is born to a woman, it is often attributed to the malicious effect of a *zār* jealous of her husband.

Though some kinds of *zār* only desist from molesting their victims through constant propitiations, others can be won over to serve as powerful protecting spirits. Thus an initial discomfort can be turned into a permanent advantage, offering the erstwhile victim magical protection and, as one student has suggested, affording women a temporary escape from their depressed social status through the companionship and opportunities for self-expression found in associations of *zār* "patients."[6]

Human beings with supernatural powers are of two kinds: those who manipulate the spirits and practice magic, and those who are themselves possessed. The possessed are called *ṭayb* or *budā*. *Ṭayb* (or *ṭabib*) in its original sense means "manual worker," but it has acquired the connotation of "one with the evil eye," the primary meaning of *budā*. By looking at someone the *budā* or *ṭayb* "drinks his blood" through the magic power of his evil eye. The victim will first feel a severe headache and fatigue, then show hysterical frenzy, and finally intestinal cramps. His fingers will be clenched around his thumbs, a sign that the *budā* has grasped the thumbs and does not want anyone to see him taking his "food" from the victim. If the victim is not cured he will eventually waste away and die.

The *budā* is helpless to check his malevolent power, and if he enters the home of a friend who is not a *budā* he will shout ahead to get the children out of the way for fear he might unwittingly infect them. People who eat pork are thought invulnerable against the evil eye, the pork in their systems serving as a kind of antibody against the infection. Potters and metalsmiths have been kept in a low caste position in Abyssinia partly because of the belief that such artisans inherit this evil power along with their craft from their parents. It is important in selecting a spouse for one's child to make sure that there is no *budā* blood in the family, and to be called a *budā* or *ṭayb* is one of the more serious insults.

The Amhara peasant has many beliefs about the malevolent beings in his world. Some are purely descriptive, like the notion that *budā* turn into hyenas after dark or ride hyenas like horses, or the belief that when red spots appear on the side of a clay pot when it is heated over a fire it means that the *ṭayb* who made the pot are fighting each other. Others guide him in warding off the evil ones, such as the idea that evil spirits can be kept away when a female child has been born by placing something of iron at the head of the mother's bed. But for serious trouble—when someone has been afflicted by a *zār* or infected by a *budā*—the folk wisdom does not suffice, and a specialist is sought.

The *ṭanquāy,* or "sorcerer," is consulted for exorcising demons as well as for physical ailments. In treating a *zār* patient his task is to discern, by clever interrogation, what manner of *zār* is riding the patient and then to determine what sort of gift is required to propitiate this *zār*. For a patient who has been "eaten" by the evil eye, he may succeed in summoning the guilty *budā*—identified when the patient calls out his name during a trance—and inducing him to spit on his victim; or he may resort to such techniques as transferring the demon from the victim to the body of a chicken and then killing the chicken. The *ṭanquāy* has other supernatural powers. He can summon the devil to liquidate the enemy of a client. He can interpret dreams and predict the future. For this he boils coffee, burns incense, and, sitting on a white sheepskin with freshly cut grass spread about the room, speaks out whatever comes to him.

The *dabtarā,* thanks to his knowledge of books and the lore acquired sub rosa while attending the church schools, wields many more powers than does the *ṭanquāy*. He can write amulets to keep away sickness and evil spirits. He knows formulas that can protect one from bullets and instill insatiable passion in the breast of one's beloved. He has the power to bring rain or make it stop, and to plague the householder by turning all of his possessions against him. Like the *ṭanquāy,* his expert knowledge of plants and herbs can heal the sick or poison the client's enemy. His superiority over the *ṭanquāy* is shown by the different manner in which he arranges a divination: he consults his heavy books, brews and interprets leaves, and then writes out his predictions on paper. For all this the *dabtarā's* fees are usually higher, but his status is perhaps more precarious, for he is after all a man of the church. The peasant feels none too easy in dealing with one who both serves the church and deals with devils.

Time and Space[7]

Devils, *zār,* evil eye, and sorcery are hidden in the crevices of Amhara mentality. They are spoken of, if at all, somewhat fearfully, and some Amhara pretend that such things no longer exist or are of little account in their culture. The sacred spirits, on the other hand, loom large in the public mind.

Besides dominating Abyssinian ritual activity, they constitute the major foci for the organization of time and space.

In the Abyssinian world view, time is not rationalized for secular purposes. Some peasants calculate the hour by the shadows on mountains, but the effort is not taken very seriously. Units of time are of little concern in the workaday world. When a man says he is going on a trip "tomorrow," everyone assumes that he means he *may* be leaving a few days later. Many appointments are made, but few are kept literally; so that the phrase *hābashā qaṭaro* ("Abyssinian appointment") has come to signify an appointment to which one comes quite late or not at all. There is little sense of time in the abstract. When an Amhara peasant is asked how long a certain trip takes, he does not reply "ten hours," but rather: "If you leave here at dawn you will arrive there before it turns dark"; and his estimate of the arrival time tends to vary according to whether or not he wants the questioner to make the trip.

Historical time is still more vaguely conceived than local time. The Amhara peasant has little sense or knowledge of history. He considers all that happened before Menelik's day as "ancient times," and more or less as an undifferentiated period. He knows very few of the earlier emperors, no historical dates, and often not even the exact year, let alone date, of his own birth. He has no idea when the church in his area was built and no interest in preserving such historical monuments or mementos as may exist in his country.

When, as often happens, anecdotes about historical figures are retold around the fireplace, the interest is not in the historical context or significance of the story but in the cleverness or heroism of the characters. Much attention is paid to genealogical lines insofar as they are relevant to potential litigation regarding rights to the use of land, but not with any concern for an objective account of historical connections. In fact, the same man may give differing accounts of the way in which he is related to a given ancestor, depending on the practical interest which underlies his recitation.[8]

With regard to his religious calendar, however, the Amhara peasant is acutely conscious of the passage of time. This concern is symbolized by a ceremony held in the churches after Mass at the beginning of each new year. A *dabtarā* stands before the people and calculates the dates for the important holidays and fasts during the coming year. Sometimes this exercise is preceded by relating the story of Demetrios, the man who after long struggles succeeded in discovering the formula by which the Orthodox calendar can be computed—so that, for example, the short fast before Lent will begin on a Monday.

The symbols of this calendar are the names of the saints. Each group of four years is named after the Four Gospels, with that of St. John (*Yohānnes*) representing leap year. The customary greeting at New Year's is of the form:

"May He bring you safely from the year of Mark to the year of Luke!" Nearly every day of the month, moreover, is dedicated to some holy figure, the main ones being:

Day of Month	Name	Meaning
1st	*Ledatā*	Birth of Mary
5th	*Abbo*	St. Gabra Manfas Qeddus
7th	*Selassie*	Trinity
12th	*Miḵā'ēl*	St. Michael
16th	*Kidāna Maherat*	Covenant of Mercy (for Mary)
19th	*Gabre'ēl*	St. Gabriel
21st	*Māryām*	St. Mary
23rd	*Giyorgis*	St. George
24th	*Taḵla Hāymānot*	St. Takla Hāymānot
27th	*Madhānē Alam*	Savior of the World
29th	*Bāla Wald*	Festival of the Son

This schedule is well implanted in the peasant's mind, so much so that the names of these holy days come to take the place of calendar dates. Thus, instead of saying "He fell sick on the fifth" or "He is due to come on the twelfth," the Amhara normally says "He fell sick on Abbo" or "He is due to come on Mikā'ēl."

Time for the Amhara is thus not a morally indifferent and qualitatively undifferentiated continuum. It is a series of occasions with more or less sacred significance. These occasions are arranged in the form of cycles. In contrast to the Catholic calendar with its different saint for each day of the year, every month in Abyssinia repeats the same set of saints' days. Each year, of course, repeats the same cycle of annual holidays. The years themselves do not run on continuously, but follow the cycle—Matthew, Mark, Luke, and John—again and again. For the more learned, finally, there is a twenty-eight-year cycle which must elapse before the same year begins on the same day of the week again.

The Amhara's experience of time is thus essentially cyclical. The religious calendar, the most important dimension of time for him, consists of a series of epicycles, in which the monthly rounds play themselves out within the larger circles of annual and quadrennial rounds. Historical events are at best secondary: the seasons come and go, generations come and go, but there is not much new under the sun. The better-known prophecies foretell the return of some state of things that obtained in the past. Kassa chose the throne name of Tēwodros II because of the prophecy that a king with that name would arise to repeat the mythically fortunate reign of Tēwodros I of the fifteenth century. In this century has arisen the prophecy of another Tēwodros to come. Still another prophecy—of a short-lived invasion of Ethiopia by a Muslim from the East—suggests a repetition of the Grañ episode. Finally, there is the previously mentioned conception of the end of the world as a time of renewal, when those who died first will return to life and history will begin again.

Space, like time, is not regarded as an amoral and homogeneous continuum to be submitted to systematic measurement. Land is not something to be bought or sold at will, but belongs by right to a family, a church, or a ruling line. Land titles are defined loosely, by convention and approximation, and the Amhara peasantry have objected to attempts by the government to make exact measurements of their land. The reluctance to rationalize space is conspicuous even in the capital of Ethiopia, where to this day there are no street numbers, so that places can only be identified roughly as near a certain police station or past a certain hospital. Directions are indicated with difficulty. The points of the compass are almost never used, though there are words for the four directions. Instead, the vague terms for "up" and "down" serve to answer almost every question about location.

Though the peasants are often unclear about the precise boundaries of various place names in the countryside, they do know just where the several churches are located over a wide area. It is customary for them to locate a given place by reference to the nearest church. Thus they will say: "He lives below Abbo" or "We must travel above Mikā'ēl." As a result, locations in space are identified by the same set of co-ordinates as are events in time, namely, the names of the saints. Moreover, just as certain months each year are occasions for special celebrations in behalf of each sacred figure, so in the countryside certain churches are considered especially holy shrines. Thus, there is special veneration for *Ṭerr Māryām* ("St. Mary's Day in the month of Ṭerr") and Gishēn Māryām ("St. Mary's Church in the district of Gishēn").

The dominant configuration in the Amhara's experience of space is that of concentric circles. Whether or not we try to relate this to the cyclical organization of time, the fact remains that the pattern of a charged center surrounded by circles of decreasing significance recurs in the main areas of Amhara life.

It appears, first, in his architecture. The traditional peasant home is round, with a conical roof supported by a pole that rises in the center of the circle. This is the domestic inner sanctum, a room for eating and talking and getting warm by the fire. It is often separated by a circular partitition from sections that serve for storage, cooking, and animals. The compound in which the home stands is surrounded in some regions by a stone or brush fence, a boundary that separates the residential kin group from the whole outside world.

This pattern is more fully developed in the churches, which are round like the huts but larger and contain two concentric circular partitions inside. The holy ark stands in the center of the church, an area restricted to priests and deacons and consecrated to the performance of the Mass. The second circle is reserved for those few who are privileged to partake of Communion—young children and rare adults who have been married according to the church laws. The third circle is where ordinary people stand during the Mass and where the clergy sing and dance on special holidays. The church itself stands in a compound ringed by an outer wall, representing still another grade of ritual impurity. Those who have eaten before the Mass or have had sexual relations the night before are not supposed to enter the church at all, and must stand outside the outer wall during services.

This spatial pattern is likewise found in the arrangement of people out of doors. The outstanding instance of this is the traditional organization of the military camp of a *negus* or *rās*. In the center of the camp is the large, round tent of the chief, together with tents for the holy ark, high-ranking visitors, and supplies. Around this central area the commanding officers are stationed. They in turn are encircled by the tents of the cavalry. Beyond this ring, finally, is an outer circle composed of the huts of the common soldiery.

Spontaneous arrangements along this line appear during festivals. The person or persons who sing or dance are placed in the center and the spectators form a circle around them. During religious celebrations this circle consists of priests and *dabtarā*. At some distance the laymen watch from an outer circle. Here, as in the home, church, and military camp, concentric circles serve to segregate people according to their place in some hierarchical order.

Society and Human Nature

The Amhara's conceptualization of the human order lends itself as a whole to being articulated in terms of patterns of concentricity and hierarchy. The sociological component of the Amhara peasant world view consists, on the one hand, of a series of notions centered on the individual self and his progressively wider groupings; and, on the other hand, of a series of distinctions which rank persons in accord with criteria of superior and inferior qualities.

The Amhara peasant tends to have a pronounced awareness of his personal ego. The boundaries of his person and property appear firmly marked in his mind and are more important to him than the boundaries of any of his social egos. He likes to live on his own land, at a good distance from neighbors. If he lives in a homestead with other relatives, he prefers to dwell in his own separate building. The Amhara's proverbial comment on the subject is that "Home and the grave are by oneself." He is sensitive about his personal belongings, quick to defend his rights, reluctant to accept suggestions, and inflammable over insults. His conception of the admirable man, as we shall see in more detail below, includes the quality of leaving others alone.

This strong sense of self is confirmed and symbolized by two conspicuous Amhara customs: carrying staves and going on trips. A staff, like a pipe, affirms the ego in two ways. As a piece of personal property right at hand, it stimulates a sense of pride of ownership; as something external yet confronting the person, it makes the ego more conscious of its bounded reality. Such sensations are daily experiences for the Amhara peasant, who is rarely separated from the staff in one form or other. When he leaves his homestead he normally carries the hard *dulā,* a potential weapon of defense that likewise affirms his ego by bolstering self-confidence in a dangerous world. He braces the *dulā* against his back as he treks along, or holds it against the front of his shoulder like a rifle. Older men walk using it as a cane. A special kind of staff made of softer wood (*zang*) is carried by pious and elderly men. Participants in devotional services lean on still another type of staff (*maquāmiyā*) which is distributed in the church for that purpose.

Traveling is another custom which affirms the ego, at least when one travels spontaneously and not in organized company. As the individual moves past various stimuli, his self-consciousness is heightened by the contrast between a persisting ego and a constantly changing environment. As a traveler par excellence—and a lone traveler, unless social rank requires the presence of retainers—the Amhara peasant frequently removes himself from familiar home settings and confronts an outside world. He loves to go on the road and will travel at the slightest provocation. For him a distance of two or three hours by foot is like the American's trip to the corner drugstore. Whether to visit relatives or pay respects after death, to go to market or to court, to get holy water at a distant church, or to look after land in a far away district, the Amhara peasant is on the move dozens of times each year, often for trips involving two or three days of travel.

Because of the great emphasis on the self in Amhara experience and culture, one may for the moment say that the personal ego is the central object in the Amhara peasant's view of society. Exactly what might be meant by this statement and in what respects it needs qualification are questions that will be taken up in the concluding chapter. If it is so, certainly the next most prominent social object in his world is the circle of close ones, or *zamad.* *Zamad* refers in the first instance to consanguineal kin, and is distinguished from the category of those who are strangers, or *bā'ed.* This is perhaps the most important of all the sociological distinctions made by the Amhara: the former, *zamad,* are seen as entitled to the warmest hospitality, while toward *bā'ed* indifference and suspicion are appropriate responses.

This does not mean that the kin group is a corporate entity whose interests and identity transcend that of the individual. On the contrary, the notion of *zamad* is highly subjective, and all constellations of *zamad* reflect the interests and affections of ego. For the quality of kinship can be attributed to persons who are not consanguineal relatives, and this is done without resorting to fictions of affiliation. The term *wandam,* for example, meaning "brother," is simply applied to any male person of about the same age to whom one feels closely attached. The term *zamad* itself is applied to anyone to whom one feels a close personal tie—even to a mere fellow-countryman whom one happens to meet in a distant region. It is thus not taking too great a liberty to translate the term *zamad* as "close ones."

The primarily subjective nature of the circle of *zamad* derives not only from the fact that it includes friends as readily as actual blood relatives. Within the bounds of consanguinity, the composition of the kin group with which a person identifies fluctuates according to his current needs, particularly with respect to land use rights. As Allan Hoben has demonstrated, corporate descent groups are important among the Amhara in that rights to land use are allocated on the basis of hereditary claims possessed by such groups; but the fact that in this ambilineal descent system each individual may claim multiple active affiliations, and enjoys a relatively wide range of choice, means that the particular corporate descent group with which an individual affiliates in order to claim his rights varies according to what land is subject to disputation. He may claim land via his father, his mother, or his children (through their mothers' rights), and in each case may trace descent back to a variety of apical ancestors.[9]

The next most inclusive sociological concept beyond the ego-oriented circle of *zamad* is that of *agar,* or "homeland."* The co-residents of one's *agar,* like those who comprise one's circle of *zamad,* are regarded as forming an important "in-group," outside of which all other persons are a priori rejected. Yet the Amharic concept of homeland, like that of kin, does not refer to a fixed social entity; its referent varies according to the context in which the individual chooses to use it. Thus, as we have seen, the concept of *agar* may be used to refer to one's parish, district, province, or even nation.

A more specialized dichotomy of some prominence in the outlook of the Amhara peasant hinges on variation in the altitude of homelands. Inhabitants of lowlands (*qolañña*) and dwellers of higher regions (*dēgañña*) tend to be conceived as polar cultural types. Different sets of habits and traits are attributed to them. Thus, according to one set of stereotypes, the *qolañña* is viewed as a heavy drinker and hot tempered, while the *dēgañña* is viewed as a heavy eater and inclined more to litigation than to violence. Again, the

---

* The less prominent category of *wagan* is intermediate between these two. *Wagan* has a primarily political connotation; it consists of one's consanguineal and affinal kin, friends and close retainers, all who may be mobilized in the event of political or military competition.

referents are relative: a man living at 7,500 feet may be considered *qolaññā* by one living at 10,000 and *dēgaññā* by one living at 6,000 feet.

The broadest membership circle that the Amhara peasant normally thinks in terms of is that of the ethnic group consisting of all Amhara.[10] The ethnic self-conception of the Amhara is one which stresses certain physical and cultural characteristics, thanks to which he regards himself as superior to all non-Abyssinian groups in Ethiopia as well as to all non-Ethiopian nationals. With regard to race, the Amhara consider themselves distinctly more handsome than both the white man and the Negro man, to both of whom they apply derisive epithets. Their cultural identity is defined chiefly with respect to religion and language.

To all Amhara except a small minority who are Muslim, the name of their ethnic group is synonymous with "Christian." The term signifies Ethiopian Orthodox Christian; for the Amhara peasant, "Catholic" and "Protestant" are equivalent to "Muslim" and "pagan" as terms designating so many kinds of heathens. And being an Ethiopian Christian is to the Amhara a mark of superiority in at least two respects: it means belonging to a chosen people, heirs to the Jews and sole bearers of authentic Christianity; and it means being an adept in praying and fasting, which to the Amhara are peculiarly Abyssinian arts. This orientation has motivated a certain amount of exclusionism vis-à-vis non-Christian Ethiopians. The latter are disdained because they are not Christian, while at the same time the particularistic cast of Abyssinian Christianity has made the Amhara somewhat reluctant to proselytize and admit non-Abyssinians to the fold. A similar exclusiveness colors the Amhara's sentiments about his language. Knowledge of Amharic is considered another index of superiority, and the Amhara look down on Ethiopians who do not speak Amharic or who speak it with an accent.

The Amhara claim superiority over other Ethiopian peoples in connection with certain other aspects of culture besides religion and language, although most Amhara peasants have very little knowledge about the other ethnic groups in the country.[11] Occupational hunters and pastoral nomads are ridiculed, for example, because of their ignorance of the arts of farming and of eating *ĭnjarā*. Vis-à-vis Europeans, on the other hand, the Amhara's self-image tends to stress qualities of bravery and toughness. Insofar as he has had contact with foreigners, the Amhara has become self-conscious about his rugged way of life—his hot foods, endurance on trips, courage in revenge, and virile longevity—and looks down on the softness of the European.

Being an Amhara is thus belonging to a superior category of human beings. This is not simple ethnocentrism; it reflects rather a basically aristocratic orientation that is repeated within the Amhara fold. It is not only members of other ethnic and religious groups who are considered inferior,

11.—*The market: buying honey*

12.—*The market: inspecting pottery*

13.—*The market: selling salt bars*

Fig. 14.—*A group of shepherds*

Fig. 15.—*Threshing time*

but also various categories of Amhara discriminated on the basis of sex, age, and social position.

Although Amhara women enjoy considerable property and inheritance rights, their generally depressed status reflects the low opinion commonly held of them. The peasant woman's lot is as hard as that of a slave. In the wealthier families, where domestic drudgery is relieved by servants, she must still be a passive, reserved nonentity. Women are beaten as a matter of course for mistakes in their work or apparent flirtations with other men. As the proverb says: "Women and donkeys need the stick." "Woman's work" is referred to derisively by men; "woman's language" is the epithet for vulgar and trivial talk.

A common justification for keeping women at home nearly all the time is that if they are allowed to go outside they will stir up all manner of trouble, for by nature they are gossipers and deceivers. Another proverb tells us: "Mules and women will betray you." In a number of legends, including those connected with the saintly figures of Eçhē Yohānnes and Takla Hāymānot, women have been turned to stone because of their vile tongues and treacherous ways. Menstruation is viewed as the punishment incurred by womankind as a result of that first great treachery in Eden.

Children are considered inferior because they are governed by ignorance and passion. Toward infants the Amhara is lenient. Because "infants and cattle are the same," tiny children are not expected to perform reasonably. After two or three years, during which time the child has been indulged copiously by the father as well as the mother, his status begins to drop. He comes to be looked on as a servant. By about six years he has passed the first "age of reason," but he is wise enough only to stay away from fire, the edges of cliffs, and prickly plants. For most of his actions he must be given orders.

As the child grows older he is supposed to be dominated in turn by each of the four elements. The adolescent is likened to air: flighty, never settled. The young man is like fire: hot in picking quarrels as he is hot chasing after women, and altogether not worth very much. Only as a man approaches forty does he begin to gain respectability. He becomes cool, like water. This is a time when he minds his own business, does his work properly, and is not so prone to go about insulting others. This is the advent of the real age of reason, when a person arrives at an understanding of what is right and wrong in life. Most esteemed of all is the elder, the man of sixty or seventy. Like earth, he is settled and stable. He is sober, wise, indifferent to insults, pious, and ready to mediate rather than take part in quarrels. Children soon learn that older folk, not themselves, are the hope of the earth. This lesson was conveyed by the little boy who, when asked what he wanted to become when he grew up, replied: "I want to become an elder."

Still another invidious distinction of considerable importance in the Amhara outlook is that between the "big man" (*ṭïllïq saw*) and the commoner (*terā saw*). "Bigness" may be measured in terms of political power, economic wealth, ecclesiastical status, or any combination thereof. Though the peasant frequently has little affection for the big man, he customarily treats him with the greatest show of deference. No matter how unfamiliar a big man may be or from what part of the country he comes, the Amhara peasant sees him as entitled to unquestioning courtesy and obeisance. Analogous distinctions discriminate between the wealthy (*hābtām*) and the poor (*dehā*), and between the genteel (*çhawā*) and the rude (*bālagē*).

Yet if the Amhara takes a dim view of women, youth, and poor folk, as well as non-Amhara and non-Christians, he suffers from no illusions about homo sapiens at his best—unless they are dark illusions. The generic word for "man" in Amharic, *saw,* is the subject of a number of negative associations and idiomatic uses.[12] At its worst, the word is found in an idiom that signifies the evil eye (*ya-saw ayn*), literally: the "eye of man" (or, more idiomatically, "the eye of others"). At its best, when used to signify a fully formed human being, the word *saw* characteristically appears in the plaintive saying, *Saw yallam* ("there is no human being"); in other words, an individual who fully embodies the concept of humanity does not exist. In general, one may say that the Amhara's view of human nature is dominated by his perception of man's inherent aggressiveness and untrustworthiness.

The Amhara believes that unformed human nature is poor raw material, and that without strict punishment throughout childhood a person will grow up to be rude and offensive toward others. As an adult, moreover, he must constantly be kept in check. The rationale commonly given for the extensive schedule of fasting is that man's nature is wicked, and only by weakening himself in this manner will he be turned away from some act of aggression against others.

The Amharic concept of *ṭegābaññā* illustrates this view. *Ṭegābaññā* literally carries the meaning of one who has been sated with food and drink, but is normally taken to mean someone who begins to insult and pick fights with others. In their use of this and related words the Amhara express the belief that aggression is the usual consequence of being sated. Insubordinate behavior on the part of a servant or political appointee is usually explained as a result of his having been too well fed. "When a peasant gets sated he hits with his stick. . . " is the first line of a number of couplets I collected among rural Amhara. The specific effect of drinking alcoholic beverages is believed to release, not Eros, but the aggressive instincts. An Amharic proverb about *ṭalla* states this directly: "One [glass] whets the appetite; two quenches it; three heats one up; four makes one quarrel; five brings fighting; six causes killing." Contrary to the view that world peace depends chiefly on filling people everywhere with plenty of food and drink, the Amhara outlook would see in such a condition the prelude to mass civil war.

The Good Life

When asked what is their chief goal in life, Amhara peasants frequently respond with the expression *sarto mablāt* ("having worked, to eat"). This response says many things. It reflects their constant preoccupation with the need to eat. It suggests that having enough to feed oneself, one's family, and one's guests is the farthest horizon toward which the peasants normally aspire. It also implies that in order to eat one should work by the sweat of his brow; it praises independence and self-reliance.

In raising their children Amhara peasants consciously strive to prepare them for making a living on their own. It is shameful to be dependent on others. It is worse yet to steal. Parents instill in their children a dread of becoming a thief. To be called *lēbā,* or "thief," is—except when in fun—a terrible insult. Stealing is felt to be somewhat worse than murder. In a survey of forty rural Amhara youths asked to name the six worst actions in the eyes of the local populace, eighty-five per cent mentioned stealing, and often under two or three different names; while only sixty per cent mentioned killing, and this answer was sometimes qualified as "killing without justification" or "killing by means of poison." One peasant commented on this question by observing, "You never kill a man unless he has done something wrong; but stealing, that is the sin."

The concept of *sarto mablāt* further implies that work is good. It expresses admiration for the industrious farmer. A majority of our TAT respondents preferred that one among twenty-five cards which showed a peasant hard at work in the fields. Agricultural work is idealized in Abyssinia because it promotes the virtues of independence and honesty. If fate concurs, it may even lead to wealth. And in any case it trains and shows one to be *guabaz,* a hero in man's work, for it is no small feat to toil from dawn till moonlight in the busy seasons or half a day on an empty stomach on fasting days.

Nevertheless, those observers are not wholly wrong who speak, like Griaule, of "the little penchant for work among the people."[13] Status considerations keep the Amhara from making a fetish of work as such. He looks down on the work of artisans because of their association with the evil eye. He avoids when possible unskilled manual labor, for traditionally that has been relegated to slaves or servants from "inferior" tribes. Work for wages is likewise deemed undignified. If one must work for someone else, it should be in the context of a more personal relationship—as a retainer, for example. Women are especially sensitive about this and much prefer to serve a man as his temporary wife than as a salaried housekeeper. Finally, although the peasant aspires "to eat, having worked," he is not wholly impervious to the appeal of the more leisurely style of life of his social superiors. He would prefer, if he could but acquire the necessary servants and corvée labor, to "cause to plow" (*ās-ārasa*) rather than to plow (*ārasa*) himself.

If, in sketching the Amhara peasant's conception of the "good life," one moves from the sphere of goals to that of norms and values, one may say that while work as such is not conceived as an absolute value, the work of plowing one's land is regarded as a primary moral responsibility. The peasant's obligations toward his land extend beyond working it, moreover. At the local level he is supposed to keep it within his family, and should be ready to defend his rights to land use against all comers. At the national level he should help to keep the land "free"; that is, out of the hands of all foreigners.

Obligations toward the deity are mostly of a ritual nature. Observing the fasts and avoiding forbidden foods are perhaps most important of all. It is also important to wear the symbol of the Ethiopian Christian, the *mātab,* a simple neckcord often holding a wrought silver cross. The church should be visited and heavy work avoided on the appropriate holy days. Prayers should not be neglected. When one passes by a church he should bow three times; when he enters a church compound he should "greet" the ark by kissing some stone or pole of the church building.

The Amhara's ideal of Christian piety does, however, include certain good works which should be carried out in order to gain God's favor—giving alms to the indigent, visiting the sick or the prisoner, and aiding the wayfarer (who is referred to as a "guest of God"). But such injunctions play a slight part in the Amhara's rhetoric of social morality when compared to his extensive code of "shames," or *nawr.* Stealing and breaking the fasts are among the very worst *nawr.* Other *nawr* include murder without good reason or by a shameful means like poison; adultery; insulting or not showing proper respect toward others; failing to observe the conventions concerning engagement and marriage; failing to revenge offenses; and gossiping about others and thereby stirring up trouble. Though the sense of being shamed before God provides some measure of internal self-control in these matters, the Amhara peasant avoids immoral acts primarily for fear of being the victim of what others will say (*yelugntā*), so that he will not be "seized by shame" (*hāfrat*) or suffer humiliation (*wardat*). His prime moral concern is not to be caught in the act of committing some *nawr.*

Positive moral obligations to persons outside the circle of close ones are thus kept to a minimum. Following the conventions of respect toward superiors and peers is all that is enjoined. The good life for the Amhara peasant is lived within a minimal, Hobbesian order. The ideal neighbor is defined as one who does not touch others (*saw aynakām*). He does not touch another's land, wife, money, or personal feelings.

Among *zamad,* however, a much warmer ideal of human relations obtains.

Loyalty is proclaimed all around. Conviviality is the norm among peers, though the authoritarian character of the Amhara family inhibits camaraderie between those of greatly differing ages. Unlimited succor in time of sickness and death and profuse commensality in happier hours are important values to the Amhara peasant and ones about which he is self-conscious and articulate.

Reverence for one's fathers is perhaps the key legitimating principle in the structure of Amhara morality. This is the outgrowth and foundation of a social system which makes children devoted servants of their fathers and keeps men under their fathers' control until they are fully adult. The fierce loyalty to the symbols and practices of the church is experienced as being true to "the faith of our fathers," and it is an analogous devotion to "the land of our fathers" that moves the Amhara to a steadfast defense of his hereditary farmland and the borders of his country.

The chief areas of conflict within the Amhara peasant's conception of the good life are those of sex and aggression. These conflicts appear to reflect the mixture of Christian and pagan cultures in Abyssinian history. From Christianity come beliefs that marriage is sacred, divorce is not legitimate, and adultery is taboo. The Amhara peasant, while respecting the embodiment of these norms in the lives of priests, feels justified in having sexual relations outside marriage and in getting a divorce whenever the need arises. Perhaps it can be argued that this represents a conflict between norms and practice, but the legitimate tone of the non-Christian behavior suggests that it might well be considered an alternative norm, a carry-over from the ancient culture which legitimized polygamy.

Attitudes concerning the use of violence represent a clear instance of conflict of norms. The precepts "Do not kill" and "Love thy neighbor," though not regarded as constituting the crux of Christian ethics, are known and acknowledged in Abyssinia. The rare priest or elder who embodies the classic ideal of Christian love is appreciated as a man of the highest virtue. The fearless killer, on the other hand, embodies another ideal of no less importance— that of being *guabaz*, brave and manly. The peasant who assaults his neighbor because the latter has usurped his land, committed adultery with his wife, injured his *zamad*, or insulted him grievously is following an ethic of cardinal importance in Amhara culture.[14]

The Central Confrontation

The foregoing has indicated some of the main concepts through which the Amhara peasant perceives the common objects of human experience, and what meaning they have for him. Since it is an exploratory account, it lacks the unity that would come from the consistent application of a rigorous observational procedure or of a coherent, analytic conceptual scheme. Yet even at the present stage of inquiry it is possible to move toward a more unified statement on the subject, by following some of the suggestions advanced by Robert Redfield for the comparison of world views.[15]

"What does a people confront as it looks out on the world?" Redfield asks. After proposing a triangle of general objects confronted by all peoples—man, nature, and God—he goes on to suggest two specific questions: (1) Are these objects viewed as parts of a common matrix, each infusing the other, or are they viewed as separate and distinct entities? (2) Are they viewed as equally significant, or is special attention paid to one at the expense of the others?

As a point of departure for discussing the world view of the Amhara peasant as a whole, we may consider Redfield's characterization of the "primitive world view." In his account of a generalized primitive world view, Redfield posits that man, nature, and God are perceived as parts of an indissoluble unity, lacking really distinct identities. In the primitive outlook nature is personalized; the supernatural infuses the natural; and man's actions and traits resemble those of the deities. If this is so, then one may say that the Amhara peasant has passed beyond this primitive conception in the direction of differentiating man, nature, and God; but he has not proceeded very far. His God is conceived as a transcendental, self-sufficient Being, abstracted from particular earthly manifestations, and dwelling only at the crown of heaven. He sees nature as having a character and imposing demands of its own, not as a bearer of divine and human properties. He sees man as lacking the powers and virtues of divine beings and at the same time different in kind and higher in status than anything which exists in nature. Yet while these three objects are endowed with distinct identities and autonomous natures, they are conceived as closely and continuously interdependent. Much of what takes place in nature, such as a flood or a bad harvest, is attributed to divine agency, and the character of certain natural objects, like groves of trees and pools of water, is colored by associations with the supernatural. In human affairs, supernatural beings of various sorts are constantly active, and in the case of the *tābot*, the holy ark, a divine object has been thoroughly personalized. Man's life, moreover, is seen as intimately bound up with the vicissitudes of nature, and a personal relationship subsists between man and his friends and enemies in the animal world. In short, the Amhara looks on man, nature, and God as *separate but closely interconnected entities*.

While each of these three entities is an object of great significance to the Amhara peasant, moreover, it may be said that man is regarded as the most significant of the three; and in particular, the problem of *human aggression* may be identified as the dominant theme in the Amhara peasant's outlook on life.

Nature, to the Amhara peasant, presents no outstanding challenge, no perplexing problem, no compelling attraction. Nature is to be adjusted to carefully and quietly. God and other supernatural beings become crucial objects in time of crisis, but otherwise occupy an inconspicuous place in the Amhara's world. His prayers and oaths, his calendar, and his simple precautions against evil spirits are matters of habit. He has no driving concern with the super-natural in his daily life.

In the human realm, collective symbols and endeavors are not a major focus of attention. The demands of family, church, and state are, like the seasons, familiar and unproblematic; like nature, these institutions call for simple adjustment. On the personal side, sexuality plays a modest part in the Am-hara's outlook. Sex as such is not talked about much. It is enjoyed, beneath the surface of social life, with little fuss or problems other than the usual practical ones.

By contrast, the phenomenon of man's aggression is seen, discussed, pon-dered, and worried about to a considerable extent. The Amhara sees himself and his fellows as prone to aggression as soon as hunger no longer checks them or festivity has raised their spirits. He is wary of the stranger, forever fearful that the unfamiliar *saw* may attack with the evil eye. He sees the out-sider as bent on aggrandizement, constantly plotting to seize his patch of earth. How to keep man's potential for aggression under control is a recurrent question in Amhara experience. The Amhara considers a pitiless regime of fasting to be the only way he can keep his hostile impulses subdued, and be-lieves that children must not be spared the rod lest they be rude and aggres-sive. He withholds esteem from young men on the grounds that they are prone to throw insults and pick fights. On the other hand, he sets up occasions, like the whipping battles on Buhē and the rough play and insulting at Christmas, when the acting out of aggressive impulses is controlled through being carried on in a legitimate context. He idealizes the men of peace, the priest and the elder, for their work in putting moral pressure on people to observe the fasts and to reconcile quarrels.

At the same time, the Amhara peasant is greatly concerned about ways and means of improving his capacity for aggression, both through the technique of litigation and through violent means. He trains his sons to be brave and to fight well, and chants with enthusiasm the inflaming martial verses of *shīllalā*. He idealizes the fighter as much if not more than the man of peace. Litigants, hunters, and warriors keep vital the Amhara ideal of masculinity, which every peasant must cultivate in order to protect his land and his honor.

The Amhara peasant is simultaneously preoccupied with the stimulation and the control of aggressive behavior. The previously mentioned conflict of norms regarding violence is perhaps the chief area of moral conflict in his thinking about the good life. Though nature, God, and other aspects of man's life occupy much of his attention from time to time, it appears that the phenomenon of human aggression dominates the confrontation between the Amhara peasant and the objects of his experience.

MODERNIZATION AND THE PEASANT

At the beginning of this chapter we alluded to stereotyped views of the peasantry held by modern-educated Ethiopians who have no meaningful communication with them. It may be fruitful at this point to consider the relationship between the peasant's world and Ethiopia's quest for modernity in the form of a series of critical responses to these stereotypes.

Three views of the peasantry are of particular relevance. One sees the peasant as exploited, hence potentially progressive; one sees the peasant as uneducated, hence reactionary; and a third sees the peasant as traditionalist, hence irrelevant to Ethiopia's modernizing culture. In responding to these opinions we shall discuss, first, the peasant's conservatism; second, areas of the peasant's receptivity to change; and, finally, aspects of peasant culture which may have a positive value for Ethiopia in transition.

Peasant Conservatism

Those who eulogize the simple integrity of peasant life and regret the peasant's suppressed condition in a social order pejoratively termed "feudal" at times maintain that with a radical change of leadership in the government the peasantry would respond with renewed economic initiative and progressive orientation. Given leaders they can trust, it is argued, the Amhara peasants would support radical efforts to restructure their lives and would participate meaningfully in democratic political procedures designed to promote social change.

This view overlooks the fact, which has impressed travelers of many centuries in Ethiopia, that the Abyssinian peasant clings to his traditional ways with unruffled tenacity. The flavor of his conservatism may be illustrated by the following conversation with an unusually open-minded peasant in Manz. The man was complaining about the dangers presented by a little stream between his home and the local church during the rainy season. "If you can't put up some kind of bridge," I suggested, "why do you not stretch a heavy rope across it so people can hold on to something and not be swept away?" "That is a good idea," he replied, "but we just do not do that sort of thing around here."

Such behavior has been explained by many observers, Ethiopians and foreigners alike, as due to simple laziness. No peasant can afford to be simply lazy, however. The roots of this inertia go deeper. They touch a number of fundamental features in Amhara peasant culture which orient the peasantry against the introduction of novelty.

One of these is the concept of fate (*eddïl*) which the Amhara invoke to account for the ups and downs of their lives. *Eddïl* appears to signify the working of God's will insofar as it affects human purposes, and is to be regarded as more important than human effort in attaining one's goals. "If a man works hard, he may remain poor. If he does not work hard, he may become wealthy. The outcome is due to fate." The peasant is discouraged from determined efforts to make changes in his environment because of the feeling that no matter what he does, God's disposition is what really counts.

In addition to feeling that innovation is ineffectual, the Amhara peasant tends to feel that it is immoral. Reverence for fathers and forefathers is, we observed, a key element of the Amhara ethos. This patriarchal sentiment informs the Amhara's defense not only of his land and his religion, but of the procedures of daily living as well. It is not good to deviate from the familiar ways of doing things because they, too, have been handed down by "our fathers"; this is a phrase which interlards Amharic conversation.

A number of other, more specific, norms have had the effect of discouraging inventiveness among the Amhara. Experimentation with matter was inhibited by the disdain for puttering about with one's hands—doing anything, that is, similar to the activities of the socially dejected artisans and slaves. Hence the peasant retains the same rudimentary tools for wresting a subsistence from nature that he has used for millennia, and searches about the woods for a properly shaped piece of wood rather than improve his art of carpentry.[16] Experimentation with ideas was inhibited by the anti-intellectual cast of Amhara culture, which discredits the pursuit of ideas for their own sake. Ideas pertain either to the unchangeable mysteries, as expressed in the religious literature, or to the unchanging verities of human experience, as expressed in folk proverbs. Ideas are not entertained as "adventure," to use Whitehead's term—as a source of novel possibilities in life, a guide rather than a justification of custom.

Two factors are especially significant in accounting for the Amhara peasant's reluctance to use ideas drawn from experience and insight for the purpose of reshaping custom. One is the fact that the primary medium for the elaboration and dissemination of such ideas—the written word—was affected by a number of restrictions in Amhara culture.[17]* As a consequence, although writing has been known in Abyssinia for two millennia, it had almost never

---

* The act of writing was considered to be inherently shameful: like any manual activity other than farming and fighting, writing was regarded as degrading work, the business of scribes whose status was thereby not much higher than that of potters and metalsmiths. Only a small percentage of the clergy learned to write, and those who did were rarely adept at it. The products of writing, moreover, were deemed either too sacred or too nefarious to warrant giving laymen easy access to their medium. Script belonged above all else to the realm of scripture. The awe felt for holy writs was a deterrent against using that medium for other than devotional purposes. The chief private use of writing was for the magic formulas of the *dabtarā*, another connection with the supernatural that discouraged its lay practice. The *dabtarā*'s art served injurious as well as beneficent purposes, and the fear that those who learned to write might stumble onto potent phrases was reason for restricting that skill to a small group of the initiated.

been employed as a medium for promulgating new ideas or discussing contemporary problems. Another feature of Amhara culture that helps to account for the mental inertia of the peasantry is its emphasis on the value of deference and obedience to authority. The Amhara typically rely on legitimate authority figures to define appropriate responses to new situations, and regard the delegation of powers as a diminution of the status of such authorities. The peasant has thus refrained from initiating changes in the public domain because the prerogative of taking initiative is generally reserved to ecclesiastical and political authorities.

Receptivity to Change

Consideration of the peasant's readiness to follow the lead of legitimate authorities already points to an inadequacy of the second stereotype we have mentioned: that which sees the peasant as hopelessly ignorant and backward, hence intractable from the viewpoint of a program of modernization. For while the Amhara peasant is likely to resist the efforts of some unknown official from Addis Ababa to introduce change in his local environment, he does tend to follow the directives and imitate the example of the local authorities whom he knows and who shape the course of decisions and sanctions at the local level. Thus it is, for example, that the eucalyptus tree—imported by Emperor Menelik, taken to the provinces by nobles, and eventually planted by individual peasants—has come to dot the Amhara countryside. How quickly such change can take place is shown by the recent acceptance of photography in many provincial regions. In 1950, peasants in many Amhara areas strenuously objected to having their pictures taken, in part at least for fear of the camera as bearer of the evil eye. By 1960, visitors to some of these same areas were being deluged with requests for photographs. In the interim these peasants had been exposed to numerous photographs of the Emperor and high government officials and had observed their local authorities seizing every chance they could to be photographed.

Yet it is clear that the Amhara peasant will not imitate everything that is accepted by his traditional authorities. When a new custom strikes him as too outlandish his resistance can become adamant, as was abundantly demonstrated when the court of Susneyos carried out its ill-fated conversion to Catholicism. In analyzing the peasant's receptivity to change it is important to distinguish as independent variables: (1) the degree of acceptability of the *agents* of change, and (2) the extent to which the proposed change is congruent with traditional beliefs and values.

The whole question of the nature of peasant opposition and receptivity to modernizing programs may be discussed most realistically by focusing on a concrete area of attempted change. The material I have assembled is most detailed for the case of public health, an area to which the government has paid increased attention in recent years. A new phase of public health endeavor in this decade was marked by the imposition of a nationwide health tax in 1960.

Health has become a prime objective in Ethiopia's modernization program because of a growing realization that the wide prevalence of malaria, tuberculosis, typhus, intestinal parasites, syphilis, trachoma, leprosy, and other diseases continues to sap the vitality of the nation's productive forces and to visit misery on countless peasant families. The public health forces in Ethiopia (Ministry of Public Health, WHO mission, and AID Public Health Division) have long understood that Ethiopia's health needs cannot be met by piecemeal therapy. They have undertaken a program of preventive measures by preparing public health teams in the medical college at Gondar. The college trains health officers, community nurses, and sanitarians within a common framework, so that when they go into the field they will understand each other's tasks from the start. The first public health center employing such a team was opened in the late fifties; Ethiopia's Second Five-Year Plan envisions one such center for every fifty thousand people by 1967.

The objective of these public health workers is to transmit a number of instructions—concerning personal hygiene, environmental sanitation, early care for illness, and isolation of contagious diseases—which are at variance with customary beliefs and practices. Experience with comparable programs elsewhere suggests that the success of such health teams is by no means assured.[18] What are the forces working for and against the acceptance of these new instructions by the Amhara peasantry? Both negative and positive factors may be identified with respect to each of the three general categories previously referred to: the general outlook regarding change; attitudes toward the agents of change; and degree of compatibility between the new cultural items and the old.

The Amhara peasant's general resistance to change may be presumed operative here as elsewhere, particularly since health practices are often associated with religious beliefs and sentiments. Defense of indigenous therapies has in fact become a significant channel for the expression of traditionalist sentiment, a channel that has even been utilized on occasion in the Addis Ababa newspapers.[19] And a general posture of resistance to changes in the field of health is supported by the interests of traditional practitioners, *dabtarā* and *ṭanquāy,* who are in danger of losing clientele if modern-trained health workers come to win their allegiance.

Counter to this conservative drag, on the other hand, is the peasant's powerful desire for one basic change in his life circumstances, namely, the reduction of morbidity and mortality. Despite his idyllic conception of paradise and his frequent contention that life on earth is something of little value, the Amhara wants to avoid death. Even from the religious point of view he is motivated to live as long as possible: the monk wants to live longer in order to get closer to God by prayer, and the worldly man wants to live long enough to atone for his sins so that he may enter paradise. Health thus rates as one of the most important values. The expressions for greeting and farewell stress health. Most of the prayers and vows offered have to do with achieving health. Long, painful pilgrimages are made for cures, and much money is spent for the remedies of native practitioners and for amulets to ward off illness. This powerful desire for health and life operates as a lever to overcome the resistance to change.

Toward the bearers of new ideas designed to satisfy this desire for reduced morbidity and mortality, however, the peasant's stance is suspicious and unsympathetic at the outset. He regards Ethiopians who have been educated by Westerners as contaminated by alien norms and beliefs. They appear to him as Ethiopians, but also as strangers—as "black *faranj*"—with their European clothes and their unorthodox eating and smoking habits. He tends to distrust their motives, to suspect them of being out to take advantage of him in some way. And he resents their overt or implicit disparagement of his way of life, particularly his practices in so sensitive an area as sanitation.

Against such obstacles one cultural factor that serves to present the health worker as an acceptable agent of change is the Amhara peasant's deference to the man of learning. The public health worker is in a position to inherit some of the awe felt for the learned *dabtarā,* especially since the health teams operate out of centers which provide therapy as well as instruction, which gives them the benefit of association with the quasi-magical powers attributed to one who performs successful treatment. In addition, he can be aided by the Amhara peasant's personal devotion to someone who has helped him and won his confidence. Whether this devotion can be stimulated depends, in the last analysis, on the character and resourcefulness of the public health workers themselves. Those who are able to communicate in a dignified manner with the peasants, who avoid dealing with them as an inferior and backward people, who refrain from flaunting the most important local norms, and who are on good terms with local authorities and respected men, have a substantial chance of being accepted after an initial period of suspicion and alienation. Thus it was that a Gojjami peasant, asked why some of the local people were hearkening to the advice of the public health team at Dabra Marqos, explained: "We have come to realize that what you tell us to do is for our own advantage, not yours." Elsewhere in Gojjam, a similar response was the eventual issue of a more pronounced initial rejection of public health workers. In the village of Dajan doors were closed against a venereal disease team which was taking blood samples of the entire population for Kahn test analysis. Popular suspicion was voiced in a number of ways; the health workers were accused of selling blood, of being missionaries, and of otherwise trying to cheat the locals. The health officer in charge of the team then brought some of the objectors to the mobile laboratory, patiently explained what was going on, and how it would benefit the people. Before long word got around that these outsiders were not so evil after all, and the doors of Dajan opened.

Given the possibility that the Amhara peasant may come to acknowledge the public health worker as a legitimate agent of change, what about the discrepancy between the ideas advanced by the public health workers and the ideas of his traditional culture? The conception of the causation of illness is radically different in the two cultures. Since the peasant views the etiology of disease as a function of the will of supernatural beings, on what grounds could he adhere to prophylactic measures based on naturalistic conceptions?

Valid though our characterization of the peasant's concept of causation may be, it is nevertheless a very simplified one. It is unlikely that any world view is totally devoid of some sort of naturalistic explanations, just as, conversely, well-educated moderns often cling to residues of "superstition." Though the Amhara's general framework for understanding causation is not naturalistic, he does possess a number of specific notions which can be interpreted as naturalistic or protonaturalistic. Here are some examples:

(1) The belief that an excessively dirty house brings sickness (even though in practice animals are permitted to urinate and defecate indoors and strings of soot to hang from the rafters).

(2) A vague notion that the daily washing of hands, mouth, and feet is related to health.

(3) The concept of *metch,* an ailment involving fever and pains, believed to come from exposure to dirty places as well as excessive exposure to the sun (though the devil is often thought to be the conveyer of the ailment).

(4) The concept of *gershā,* a notion that a convalescent is liable to relapse unless he refrains from eating unaccustomed foods, resumes work slowly, stays out of the sun, and washes his body and clothes.

(5) A latent concept of contagion, found in: (a) the belief that smelling the urine of another will give one a cold, (b) the belief that the breath of a typhus patient will communicate his disease, and (c) the custom of referring to all diseases which can be given by one person to another as "*zār* sickness."

Even when the explanations set forth by the health workers deviate too much from what the peasant can possibly conceive as plausible, there may still be grounds to justify his accepting some strange advice through an appeal to more familiar beliefs and interests less directly related to the matter at hand. Thus, while peasants have been reluctant to accept the sanitarian's argument that diseases will be prevented by sanitizing the water supply through building wells, they have often been persuaded to build wells by the prospect of securing a more convenient source of water.

Measuring the relative strength of forces supporting and opposing change among the peasantry in public health and other fields of planned development is a task that requires intensive empirical studies.[20] But it should be sufficiently clear from the foregoing that the view of the Amhara peasantry as incorrigibly recalcitrant and reactionary is a rather shallow one. Amhara peasant culture contains potentialities for change that are as real as its most rigid beliefs and its substantial antipathy to change. The challenge to social statesmanship and social science alike is to understand the peasant's world in a more analytically precise way so that the diverse potentialities for change can be identified, but in the context of the total structure of peasant life.

The Legacy of Peasant Culture

Our discussion so far has treated the peasant as a wholly passive entity in contemporary Ethiopia. Whether the emphasis has been on the peasant's resistance to innovation or on his receptivity to change, he has been considered from one point of view: that of the Modernist anxious to transform Ethiopian society according to secular ideals. Common to both the modern-educated Ethiopians, who consider the peasant primarily an object for manipulation and coercion, and to those who think more in terms of providing friendly leadership and perhaps securing future political support, is the assumption that they really have nothing to learn from peasant culture, that peasant culture has nothing of substance to contribute to an Ethiopia in transition.

Whether this assumption is just or not can only be decided by Ethiopians themselves. Ironically, it is easier for an outsider to question it and to search for aspects of peasant culture that might contribute to a more meaningful national experience during the coming decades of transition. The type of possible contribution to be explored here concerns the mode of defining and responding to the situation of rapid change which Ethiopia has entered.

The social environment of contemporary Ethiopia is very tense and affords few outlets for the constructive release of tensions. The discrepancy between the growing desire for aspects of modern culture and the persistence of many old customs and problems has generated much impatience, anxiety, and ennui among the modern-educated. Their sense of inadequacy vis-à-vis Western "metropolitan" standards is no less painful for their having escaped a long heritage of colonial domination, and combined with a sense of failure to move rapidly toward aspired goals has created in many of the modern-educated marked self-destructive tendencies. Insofar as this destructiveness has not turned inward it has been projected outward against other elements inside Ethiopia and without.

One of these targets is the uneducated mass of the people, who, as we have seen, are often regarded as so backward that the only way one can bring progress to them is through coercion and authoritarian manipulation. Another target, naturally enough, has been the higher officials of the government. Of particular interest here is the fact that these officials have frequently been condemned in total terms for their alleged "selfishness" and "hypocrisy." Indeed, one of the outstanding characteristics of the modern-educated is a highly moralistic disposition which leads to a constant evaluation, and unmasking, of everyone within the broad orbit of Ethiopian political life in morally uncompromising terms.

The sources of this disposition are complex and not fully to be explained here. One factor would seem to be the ascendance of a concern for rationality and its related insistence on integrity, in opposition to the traditional patterns of deviousness and equivocation symbolized by wax and gold. Another would seem to be a growing Rousseauan concern for the "natural rights" of the people, and the related view of the powers supporting the *ancien régime* as selfishly and hypocritically depriving the people of these rights. What the consequences of this disposition may be is a question of greater urgency. For it leads to the insistence on purity of heart as the essential political virtue, a demand which necessarily results in demoralization of public life and political fanaticism.[21]

While this sort of disposition is natural to the situation of the modern-educated, hence not simply to be wished away, it is clearly out of touch with the traditional Amhara mentality. Insofar as the modern-educated may seek alternatives to a purist, sentimental, and somewhat hysterical approach to politics, they may find themselves nourished by contact, through personal communication or through the medium of literature, with the "cooler" approach of the Amhara peasant.

A feature of Amhara peasant culture discussed earlier in this chapter is the centrality of its orientation to man and to the phenomenon of human aggression in particular. To know the Amhara peasant at all closely is to appreciate how cautious he is about the intentions of others. He does not assume that he can count on others, though they may make promises. Before engaging in any secular transaction, such as lending money to a neighbor, entering into litigation, or taking on a servant, he insists on securing a guarantor (*wäss*) who agrees to make good for damages caused by the man he is backing. He does not assume that others may be benevolently disposed toward him; he suspects that behind every protestation of admiration and fealty lurks some quest for personal advantage. He does not assume that superior social status entails superior moral worth. Wryly commenting on his ambivalence toward superiors toward whom he shows such deference, he describes his posture as one of "bowing in front, and passing gas in the rear." In short, he is on guard at all times, coping with the presumed selfishness and hypocrisy of others and pursuing his own interests in a very sober and manipulative way.

At the same time the Amhara peasant's low estimate of man's potential does not bring him to a position of rejecting man. On the contrary, man is accepted, with all his frailties, for what he is. The Amhara's patterns of life are shaped, neither to overwhelm man with guilt for his shortcomings, nor to pressure him into personal or social reform, nor to deprive his worldly existence of all enjoyment and significance; but rather to accommodate human realities and transcendent values to one another in such a way that neither is seriously compromised. He honors the value of non-violence, but indirectly, by relegating its observance to a morally differentiated role, the priest. He honors the value of marital fidelity, embodied again by the priest; but he lives comfortably, following the inclinations of the old Adam, in a status defined as technically excommunicate. He accepts the reality of hostility in human relations and adjusts to this reality by encouraging it where socially useful, curbing its socially disruptive aspects through fasting, and by channeling its expression where possible through litigation before judges, argumentation before elders, and games on festive occasions.

The Amhara peasant's outlook is both realistic and humanitarian. He does not expect political leaders to be morally pure, for he understands that all men are imperfect; *saw yallam*. He is not upset by the "selfishness" and "insincerity" of *Realpolitik*—awareness of which has sometimes been a demoralizing factor among the masses in Western countries—because *Realpolitik* is the stuff of his daily life. At the same time he seeks practical arrangements whereby human interests can be furthered and human conflicts can be contained. Insofar as this characteristic orientation of Amhara peasant culture comes to permeate the outlook of Ethiopia's modernizers—and it has never been wholly absent—it may help to reduce the intensity of those unrealistic demands and inhumanitarian impulses which are endemic in a society in transition to modernity.

4

Tꞕe Emerging Aꝺolescent

While it is clear, as we have argued thus far, that a modernizing society stands to benefit from retaining or redefining many aspects of its traditional culture, it is also clear that in certain areas discontinuity is indispensable if significant change is to be brought about. Just what these areas are is something which presumably varies from nation to nation, though cross-cultural regularities may perhaps be uncovered in the course of further research. In the case of Ethiopia's incipient modernization, at least two subsystems of the traditional social system of the ruling Amhara have already undergone some sort of structural change: that of "secondary socialization," the complex of processes whereby skills and values necessary for adult life are imparted to adolescents; and that of the stratification system—the complex of arrangements whereby status is allocated to members of a society in accord with the various values upheld by the society.

An important precondition for the changes which have taken place in both of these areas was the establishment of a permanent capital: Addis Ababa, founded by Menelik in 1887[1] and now home for nearly half a million Ethiopians. Menelik's institution of the first government school in Addis Ababa in 1908 marked the beginning of a slow but steady process of introducing some of Ethiopia's youth to the novel skills and norms of modern Western culture. The concentration of power in Addis Ababa through the reign of Haile Selassie has diminished the status of the traditional Amhara elites and brought to the fore men whose prestige and influence rest to some extent on new criteria. In this chapter and the one which follows, these two areas of structural change will be examined with respect to their continuity and discontinuity with the Abyssinian past.

In Amhara culture, adolescence scarcely exists as a concept, let alone as a problem. While there are Amharic words which signify "young person," there is no word in Amharic that specifically denotes a *transitional* stage between childhood and adulthood. The goals of a stage of transition to adult status, which to us have become problematic—continuity of the social order and crystallization of personal identity—are customarily attained among the Amhara as a matter of course.

In Ethiopia's modernizing sector, however, society and the individual have been affected by numerous changes all at once. Adult standards have become confused; available roles have multiplied beyond comprehension; new agents and techniques of secondary socialization have supplemented the old. Overnight, adolescence has become both a category and a challenge.

COMING OF AGE IN ABYSSINIA

In according the individual recognition as an adult, society tends to bring some of its most powerful and explicit integrative forces to bear upon him. In many societies the transition to adulthood is accomplished in part by means of some formal ceremony in which the society corners the young person and puts its stamp upon him. Whether by way of earlobe piercing or ritual whipping, confirmation or graduation, the adolescent generally undergoes some rite which marks his coming of age and obliges him to fulfil himself as an acceptable member of adult society. In some societies, the rites are so devised that they literally represent the "death" of the child and his symbolic resurrection in a new, adult status.[2]

Such transition rites are conspicuously absent from Amhara culture. Quite the contrary: as a young Amhara approaches puberty he is unobtrusively withdrawn from participation in his culture's most solemn ritual, celebration of the Eucharist. Girls of about twelve and boys about fourteen, if they ask for Communion, are simply refused by the priests and told to go away. Thenceforth, until they marry in the church or, if they marry civilly, until their dying hour, they are not permitted to partake of the Holy Sacrament. The only exception to this rule is in the case of some deacons, who earn the right to continued participation in the Mass at the expense of remaining celibate until marriage (a price not always paid in practice).

Another way in which societies tend to mediate the transition to adulthood is through the institution of adolescent peer groups which in various ways help the young person prepare for adult status. Such groups have taken a wide variety of forms. There have been, for example, the several types of age sets in African age-graded societies; mystic orders for youths attached to

Egyptian mosques; youth dormitories and community houses in certain tribes in India; the academic and athletic youth organizations of ancient Athens and Sparta; not to mention the numerous teen-age associations of modern Western society.[3]

Here again, the adolescent Amhara is not involved in any such social forms. The advent of puberty is associated with the growing up and out of childhood groups, the gangs of shepherds who spend their days together in work and play. The girl of eleven or twelve is expected to spend all her time at home, under careful supervision. The boy of thirteen or fourteen has abandoned the shepherd's life for farming, in the company of older relatives, and soon becomes increasingly preoccupied with his private economic and erotic interests. His family elders are likely to warn him not to make friends with other youths outside the family.[4] For a number of adolescent boys to get together outside of festive occasions is, to the traditional Amhara mind, a sign that something wrong is afoot.

The absence of adolescent rites and age groups reflects the individualistic character of Amhara social organization, a subject to which we shall turn in chapter vii. Nevertheless, Amhara society catches young people in its grasp and guides them to adulthood just as firmly and surely as does a society which has many collective arrangements for its adolescents. It does this by means of a well-ordered program for growing up. The road from childhood to adulthood is one series of informal, unproblematic stages through which the growing person adjusts to progressively increased responsibilities and progressively detailed norms. After infancy, there is normally no break in continuity in the whole process.

Toward Adult Work Roles

Following a long and indulged infancy, the Amhara child is early taught the rudiments of work responsibility. At the age of three or four, children are given simple chores, such as shooing chickens from grain drying in the sun or collecting bits of firewood. Somewhat older children are expected to protect the crops against birds, farm animals, and baboons. The Amhara becomes apprenticed in the main vocation of his childhood—tending the herds—almost as soon as he can run about, and six-year-old shepherds play a crucial part in the Amhara economy.

Boys retain the responsibility for tending the herds at least until the age of twelve, but by then they have already been initiated into a number of adult work activities. At about eight or nine years the Amhara boy begins to do his share of the harvesting, sickling the wheat, barley, *téff*, or beans and loading the crops in piles he will help transport to the threshing place. He becomes adept at directing the cattle round and round the threshing floor and at winnowing the grain from the chaff. At times he helps with the weeding.

Somewhat later, when he reaches ten or eleven, the Amhara boy begins to accustom himself to the plow, perhaps trying his hand at it from time to time while his father rests for lunch. Intermittently his ability increases, and by the age of fourteen or so—earlier if the family is short of help—he is given a regular share of the plowing. This may be limited to one or two hours a day at first, but before many seasons elapse he is ready to undertake a full day's work, along with his older relatives.

In his mid-teens the Amhara boy is normally given a small part of his father's land to use for himself. The boy has full charge of plowing and harvesting this land and selling the crops at market. The crops or money he earns thereby is referred to as *gulammā* ("private possession") and is set aside for helping him to get started on his own later on. Eventually the *gulammā* will be used to purchase new clothes, an ox, and presents for his bride. Year by year the father may add a bit more land for the boy's private management, though all together it does not often amount to a very large quantity; he may produce, say, 150 to 200 liters of grain for his *gulammā* in a year (in the Amhara system of measures, about 2 *dāwlā*). When he has saved enough grain to fill a *riq,* a large wicker storage bin plastered inside with cow dung, he is considered ready to get married and strike out on his own.

By the time a boy begins to accumulate his *gulammā* he has learned nearly everything he needs to know for performing the work which will be expected of him as an adult. In his late teens the education is completed, through the mastery of such special techniques as fashioning the yoke and wooden attachments for the plow, and constructing the walls and roof for a house.

The work life of the Amhara peasant is thus a simple continuation of activities with which he has long been familiar. The same is true, *mutatis mutandis,* for those who, following their fathers' footsteps, become priests or sorcerers, governors or warriors, artisans or traders. In these cases, moreover, the foregoing pattern applies to a great extent, since the latter roles are often combined with an agricultural economic base and way of life. (Special aspects of some of these variant patterns will be discussed below.)

This pattern of gradually increased work responsibility is conspicuous in the case of girls. While shepherding and other childhood tasks are shared by both sexes, the Amhara girl begins to do distinctively female work at about six or seven. First she learns to clear seeds from cotton, and to spin, by hand. Later on she is introduced to the more taxing female chores, like fetching water and grinding grain. The progressive increase of the girl's work load is visibly illustrated by the graduated sizes of clay jugs used for carrying water. When she begins to fetch water, the young girl carries a tiny jug, called a *gambo*. As she becomes older and stronger she is given a larger size, a small *enserā*. Finally, the mature female carries the large *enserā,* a jug that holds as much as twenty liters.

At around ten years the Amhara girl leaves the shepherd's work once and for all and spends all her time about the house. She becomes increasingly useful with kitchen work—chopping onions, grinding pepper, baking *ïnjarā*. Bit by bit she learns all the arts of the housewife, including how to make good *doro waṭ*, a hot chicken stew, the dish that really proves the mettle of an Amhara bride. By the age of twelve or thirteen she knows enough to manage a home by herself and is ripe for marriage, though her training is often capped by a period after marriage during which she works alongside her mother-in-law in the home of her husband's parents. Thus the Amhara social system sees to it that the adolescent girl, as well as the adolescent boy, is familiar with adult work responsibilities and prepared to shoulder them without much ado.

Toward Marital Roles

The transition to adult status in Amhara culture is related above all to the assumption of marital roles. The three events which more than anything else establish one as an adult are marriage, moving into one's own house, and begetting a child.

Preparation for the roles of spouse and parent is more or less continuous throughout childhood, so that nearly all Amhara enter marriage as a matter of course and at an early age. Strong identifications are formed through virtually constant association with the parent of the same sex during adolescence, and to a large extent throughout childhood. When they are not out tending the herds, girls are working around the house in the company of their mothers, and boys are off in the fields or going on trips with their fathers. This identification is strengthened by experimental play within children's groups as well. It has been observed that tiny boys and girls play "marriage" and "house" with considerable sophistication, even to the point of pretending to send a messenger to the bride's parents to announce that she had been proven a virgin.[5]

With regard to premarital preparation for adult sexual functions, however, a double standard does exist. Although public norms require boys to be virgin at marriage, and one hears it said that "in the old days" this norm was strictly enforced, premarital sexual experimentation for boys is regarded as a natural occurrence.* In practice, and according to the norms of the male adolescents themselves, boys are expected to have sexual experience before marriage so long as it is carried out quietly and with discretion. If a boy is still virgin by the end of his teens he may be referred to by one of his

---

* Indeed, one of the normal functions of maidservants in the well-to-do families has been to provide sexual initiation for adolescent boys.

peers with the insulting term *sïlb* ("castrated one"). Indeed, the word that comes closest to signifying male adolescent in Amharic, *goramsä,* has the primary connotation of one who goes around with women.

The conditions attending premarital sexual experience for youths explain in part the nature of adolescent male peer relations. A *goramsä* needs at least one fairly close friend, not only as a confidant for his "secrets," but also to aid him in his affairs. When one *goramsä* goes to the home of a married woman—the strict controls against premarital affairs for girls limit his choice to married women or divorcees—the other stands guard to see that the husband or anyone else does not intrude. When he finds himself in rivalry with a competitor for the same woman, the friend assists him if the fighting gets difficult. On the other hand, the existence of a limited number of accessible females in any area implies that no alliance of friends can become very large; the competition is too great. The conflicts of interest among *goramsä* often provoke feuding and sometimes serious *dulä* fights.

The unwed girl, by contrast, must remain a virgin at all costs. It is important to the groom, not only because of the religious and social sentiments involved, but also because the Amhara male cherishes the sense of "conquering" his woman. A girl who is found not to be a virgin on her wedding night will be beaten by her husband and possibly returned to her parents. Her parents will be scandalized, and, if she is sent back, will probably give her a beating.

In order to protect the girl's virginity, she is kept under close watch by her parents after the age of ten or eleven. They do not allow her to go outside the home area by herself or to associate with boys who are not her relatives. She attends festive celebrations in the company of her parents. In some families she is kept from doing excessively heavy work in order to prevent the accidental rupture of her hymen.

The onset of menstruation is kept secret, since menstruation is seen as a shameful event for the unmarried woman. But as the girl approaches the age of puberty her mother will be advised by other female relatives that it is time to be on the lookout for a husband. Twelve or thirteen is the customary marrying age for girls, as compared with the late teens or early twenties for boys; and it has not been uncommon for girls to marry still younger, especially in former times.

This strict surveillance of the daughter does not wholly prevent a mild sort of flirting which occurs at the marketplace or on public holidays. On the latter occasions, especially Masqäl and Ṭïmqat, the girl may make some effort to appear attractive. She may wear her best clothes, dress up her hair, and, if she can afford it, put on a bit of perfume. These occasions provide a chance for the unmarried boy to spot an interesting mate, in which case he may ask around to learn the identity of her father and then present the matter hopefully to his own father.

Despite this possibility of concession to the boy's amorous desires, the interests of the father are decisive in the selection of a marriage mate, and traditionally the boy has not even known what his bride looks like until the wedding itself. The boy who dares to choose a wife on his own commits an offense for which the father has the moral right to curse and disinherit him. Marriage is regarded as a bond between families, not individuals, and the families of prospective brides are carefully inspected before the father agrees to a contract of betrothal. In making his choice, the father looks for a family whose economic level is at least as high as, if not slightly higher, than his own. He makes certain that the family does not have members who are leprous or who practice the manual crafts associated with the evil eye. He sends a messenger to visit the family on some pretext, for the purpose of determining the character of the girl and her parents. If there is any consanguine relation between the two families, he makes sure that the prospective bride and groom are separated by more than seven generations; that is, they must not have a common great-great-grandparent. A further consideration might be whether there has been any strife or rivalry between the two families, in which case the father may want to try to resolve it by means of a "political" marriage.

Once the father has decided upon a suitable mate for his son, with the advice of the mother and perhaps other relatives, he sends one or more intermediaries, usually elders, to speak on his behalf with the girl's father. The interview is conducted with considerable circumlocution, the petitioners veiling their true purpose until late in the conversation and the girl's father displaying reluctance to grant their request. Often no agreement is reached at this meeting, and the petitioning party must wait to ask a second time. If the girl's father is unwilling to give her hand, he will beg off with some polite excuse, such as that the girl is too young or that he has already promised her to someone else. If he is willing, a date for a formal betrothal is set, at which time the boy and his father together with a group of elders and other relatives repair to the home of the girl's father. After the boy gives presents to the girl's parents, the two fathers discuss their respective contributions of land, cattle, and other goods to the prospective household. When these economic arrangements are settled, a contract for marriage is sworn before witnesses and a date for the wedding is agreed upon, leaving ample time for the two families to vie in preparing sumptuous feasts for the occasion. If the girl is quite young, as long as two or three years may elapse between engagement and marriage.

The wedding festivities commence at the home of the girl's father. After a certain amount of ritualized delay, the groom and his party are admitted. The groom is not supposed to have seen his bride previously, and is at first shown only a number of similarly dressed maids, among whom sits his fiancée. The maids are then concealed by a curtain or in another room while one of the best men, called *mizē,* determines through various ruses which of the girls is the bride. She is revealed to the groom by being carried out on the back of the *mizē*.

The civil service itself is quite simple, consisting of an oath in the name of the emperor or of some deity that "she is my wife" and "he is my hus-band," the latter often uttered in so faint a voice that it must be interpreted by one of the bride's relatives. After the oaths and a certain amount of feast-ing, the couple and the groom's party depart for the home of the groom's parents, where another celebration is under way.

After the festivities the bride and groom retire to a hut which has been set aside for them for the first week or so of their marriage. The experience of the wedding night cannot be very pleasant for the bride. For the first time in her life she is far from the familiar setting of her parental home. She has had little or no sexual instruction, other than the knowledge that sexual matters are "rude" and that she is supposed to resist her husband's advances as fiercely as possible. The groom, on the other hand, has been taught to regard the nuptial night as a battle in which the bride must be forcibly overcome. If somewhat anxious himself, he at least has the moral, and some-times the physical, support of his two or three *mizē*. If he is unable to accomplish the defloration, he may call in the first *mizē*—usually a married relative or friend with some experience—who will perform the task. When at last the bride has been conquered, the *mizē* take the bloodstained cloth as proof of the girl's virginity. Their triumphant chant—*ber ambār sabara-lewo,* "he has broken the silver bracelet for you" (for the bride's parents)—is the signal for further rejoicing and revelry among the wedding guests. On the morrow groom and friends discuss the conquest with masculine glee, and the bride remains embarrassed and cowed.

The trauma of the wedding night does not appear to do irreparable dam-age to the girl, however, for Amhara women have the reputation for enjoy-ing sexuality as fully as the men. Indeed, some Amhara maintain that the girl will respect neither her groom nor herself if she does not put up a fight until subdued. With the consummation of her marriage, moreover, the Amhara girl has become a woman, a *sēt*. This represents a considerable ele-vation of her status and permits her to acquire certain distinctively adult possessions, usually presented to her by the groom. Traditionally these have included a dress, a double-layered toga (*kutā*), a headband, a mirror, a leg bracelet, a ring, an umbrella, and, in wealthier families, a colored silk robe.

For the groom, too, marriage means a gratifying boost toward adult status, symbolized by his receiving from the bride's parents distinctively adult male possessions—a *kutā*, perhaps a *barnos,* and a rifle if they can afford it.

Such is the basic pattern of betrothal and marriage among the Amhara, though many of the details vary from province to province.[6] There are, in addition, certain traditional alternatives to this standard procedure. One of these involves the solemnization of the marriage oath by taking Communion, a rite necessary for a marriage to be counted as legal by the Church, and followed by the ordained clergy and the most pious families. Another form requires no oath at all; the husband is simply expected to provide a salary and clothes for his wife. This procedure is followed chiefly by soldiers and traders, and by those who are marrying for the second time.

Still another type of marriage is that known as *qoṭ assǐr* ("ten beds") in which the boy goes to live with the girl's family while both are quite young. In this case the boy has his work apprenticeship under the girl's father. After several years, when the girl reaches puberty, a second wedding ceremony will take place—this time at the home of the groom's parents—and the union will be consummated. This type of arrangement tends to be made when the boy's family is too poor to provide enough to get him started on his own, or if the girl's father has no son to help him with the work.

There is, finally, a form of marriage by abduction. If the girl's father does not grant the request of the emissaries of the boy's father, and if the boy's father is still interested, the boy may go with two or three friends to capture her when she is on the way to market or fetching water. When this happens, the couple will approach the girl's parents after they have been married for some time and seek a reconciliation. Occasionally poor families have deliberate recourse to this form of marriage, arranging in advance a bride capture so as to avoid having to prepare the expensive wedding feasts.[7]

Although marriage marks the termination of childhood for the Amhara, it does not by itself signify the full attainment of adulthood. The newly wed couple lives at first in the home of the boy's father, and to truly "arrive" they must establish their own separate household. If the boy's family is wealthy, he may have his own house ready by the time of the wedding. More often, the couple spends a certain amount of time—a few months, or in some cases as much as two or three years—living in the home of the groom's father until their own house is built. To tarry unduly in the father's house, however, is considered a mark of laziness and a great shame.

Furthermore, because of the somewhat arbitrary manner in which the spouses are chosen for each other, there is often a serious problem of postmarital adjustment, a problem not rendered any less difficult by the proximity of the girl's mother-in-law. The divorce pattern is well known among the Amhara. Both partners enter the marriage with the full understanding that if they do not get along they will be able to separate without much difficulty, each partner taking half the goods that were accumulated during the marriage as well as the land and other private property each brought into the marriage. Only after several years of married life, which have resulted in children, and probably a separation followed by rapprochement or else divorce and remarriage, is the Amhara defined by his culture as a complete adult, a *mulu sēt* or *mulu saw*.

From Generation to Generation

Through the agency of his family of orientation, then, the Amhara adolescent automatically is prepared for adult work responsibilities and launched into married life. Continuity of the social system, however, also depends on the maintenance of a moral order that transcends the narrow commitments of kinship units. What of those sentiments that should dispose the young Amhara to conform with the more general norms of adult society?

The Abyssinian moral order rests primarily upon two pillars: the profession of Christianity and the institution of respect. These dispositions are firmly implanted during childhood and receive steady reinforcement during the transition to adulthood.

Maintenance of the fasting and dietary laws appears to be the central symbol of Christian identity in Amhara culture. Here again one may discern a pattern of progressively increased inculcation of norms throughout maturation. The taboos against pork and other unclean foods are taught at an early age and supported by references to unclean heathens ever after. More important, the Amhara learns step by step how to chasten his stomach in the traditional way. As soon as he is old enough to observe what goes on in his home, he is aware that meat products are not served to anyone on fasting days. Around the age of seven he begins his first regular fast, which means avoiding all food before noon, by observing the sixteen-day fast of *Felsatā*. The Wednesday and Friday fasts are supposed to be observed following this, though in practice it may be a few more years before the child keeps these weekly fasts regularly. Observance of the most trying fast of all, the eight-week fast of Lent, begins at about the age of fifteen.

At the same time, the adolescent comes increasingly under the jurisdiction of a member of the ordained clergy known as his *nafs abbāt* ("soul-father" or confessor). This is particularly so after marriage, when the young man may either continue to be attached to the soul-father of his own father or else may choose another one for himself. (The wife always takes the soul-father of her husband.) The soul-father serves as an agent of moral control by prescribing penance for his confessants when he learns of such infractions of the Christian rules as breaking the fasts. By adjusting to the adult fasting schedule and submitting to the moral authority of the soul-father the young person's membership in the Amhara religious community is being solidly established. With the advent of full adulthood, around the age of thirty, the Amhara is ready to observe the most severe fast of all, the forty-eight-hour period of total abstinence before Easter.

Forms of obedience and respect comprise the principal fiber of the Amhara social fabric, as we shall see more clearly in chapter vii. They are perhaps the most fundamental lessons of Amhara socialization. As soon as the child is capable of understanding he is made aware that all individuals older than he is, and all those in higher social positions, must be shown the most fastidious deference. Not to do so is a sign of being *bālagē* ("rude"), a trait which is corrected by harsh physical punishment. The readiness to respect superiors appears as early as in children's play groups, where the oldest boy spontaneously dictates the activities of the group and receives unquestioning obedience from the others.

For girls after ten and boys after twelve the training for obedience and respect is stepped up as they come under a more constant regimen of control by their parents and other elders. They are ordered to do a considerable amount of work for the household and are expected to be at the beck and call of any individual of higher status who tells them to do something. Thus they become conditioned to show automatic subservience to any figure of authority in later life, be it the family patriarch, community elder, priest, or political official.

His family of orientation is thus the primary agent for transmitting to the Amhara adolescent the more general societal norms as well as for readying him for his adult roles. In order to secure continuity of the Abyssinian social system from generation to generation, specific mechanisms outside the family, such as puberty rites or adolescent age groups, have not been required to mediate the transition to adulthood.

Personal Identity and Variant Patterns[8]

The most important single determinant of the personality of an Amhara appears to be his identification with the parent or parent-figure of the same sex. "Like father, like son" is both ideology and reality in Abyssinia. The attainment of ego identity is therefore normally a matter of imitation rather than discovery or invention. It represents an unfolding of dispositions that have been long internalized and steadily nursed by the consistent regards of an approving milieu.

Assuming the appropriate psychosexual identity is, it appears, hardly ever problematic. Although members of the same sex typically kiss upon greeting, hold hands when talking, embrace each other when walking, and sleep in each other's arms, there seems to be neither practice nor knowledge of unsublimated homosexuality among the traditional Amhara. Boys often address one another in the feminine intimate form, and girls sometimes use the masculine form among themselves or call each other "brother," without having their own sexual identities in the least confused thereby. Amhara males, in particular, have a proud cult of virility, though it is not compulsive in the sense that they must boast of sexual conquests; to talk of sexual exploits in front of others in such a manner would be a great shame, and such matters are simply taken in one's stride. (The other side of masculinity, physical courage, is the subject of a great deal of boasting. The term for masculinity, *wandnat,* is synonymous with *guabaznat,* or "bravery.")

The advent of puberty therefore makes the young Amhara simply more self-conscious about the characteristics proper to his or her sex. Girls begin to groom themselves and think of finer clothes. Boys proudly take on a "man's share" of the work; and, what is more, become somewhat unruly, tempestuous, quick to pick fights, and vaunt their new powers. The *goramsä* often carries a special kind of *dulä* that is symbolic of his youthful masculinity. Unusually short, stout, and hard, it is convenient for concealing beneath his clothes when he goes out at night on sexual adventures, and dangerous enough to convince himself that he is quite brave. As soon as conditions permit, adolescents of both sexes enter their first marriage with alacrity.

With respect to psychosocial identity, the situation is slightly more complex, in that Abyssinian society does provide a variety of social roles for its males. For the most part, boys faithfully follow the examples of their fathers. This is true in the case of noblemen, priests, traders, and artisans, as well as for the great peasant majority concerning whom the following remarks are presented.

The pattern of peasant life is broad enough to fit the dispositions of most of those who are called on to continue it. The typical Amhara adolescent boy therefore seeks no more in life than to be given a pretty wife whose father has a lot of land, to work so well that his father will be generous in giving him land and cattle when he marries, to produce abundant grain so he can eat plenty, and to become renowned in the land as an outstanding litigant.

Under certain conditions, however, this pattern may not fit. The reason may be chiefly economic: too many siblings and too little land in the family may force him to seek some other livelihood. Or it may have to do primarily with resentment with his lot under an especially rigid and unkind father. Still another motive may lie in the boy's yearning for a more suitable identity.

Whatever the reasons for his marginality may have been, the adolescent boy in traditional Abyssinia could respond to such a situation by pursuing a different identity. Religion and warfare were the two spheres most likely to attract him. Although trade and manual arts were possibilities for those whose industry exceeded their status-consciousness, they were considered the business of other ethnic groups and normally rejected by a self-respecting Amhara. When the Amhara youth left home for a new life, he was usually heading either for the school of some church teacher or the quarters of some chieftain.

Today, as in former times, the role of priest is known from childhood as a possible model for the peasant boy. He and his companions often imitate the clergy and their ceremonies in their play. The wish to become a priest is kindled by a number of interests—desire for the material benefits accorded the clergy; curiosity about the mysteries of the church; envy of the great prestige of the clergy; hope for a better chance of going to heaven after death. During adolescence the outlook of the boy who seeks to become a priest deviates from that of the *goramsā* described above. Instead of the shrill, blood-heating *shïllala* war chants he prefers the gentle hymns of the church; instead of the frenzied dancing and singing of the young braves he prefers the schooled dance of the clergy; instead of pursuing women, he is inclined to turn his head the other way when a girl appears.

The military alternative does not seem to be an ideal of Amhara children. They rarely see soldiers; and when they did in former times, it was usually in the unhappy circumstance of seeing the family's reserves plundered. It is not until the time of puberty and after that the great upsurge of aggressive instinct has turned the thoughts of many an Amhara youth to fighting. Chafing under parental domination or bristling with resentment because of being an illegitimate offspring or a stepchild, he may be anxious to turn his hostility against some enemy. He may imagine the free life of a soldier more attractive than the drudgery of the peasant's lot. In the days of feudal armies, he may have heard news about some warlord on the rise and thus have hopes, by attaching himself as a follower, of winning booty and the laurels of a hero, perhaps eventually the powers of a chieftain.

Whether the peasant boy chooses church school or the warpath, his move has frequently been an all-or-none move. The peasant boy can do nothing without the consent of his father, and normally his father will not permit him to do anything except carry on the farmwork and prepare himself to care for his parents in their old age and to inherit the family land. If there should be some sign that the son does not want to continue in his father's footsteps, the latter will do everything he can short of disinheritance—and ofttimes that—to persuade him otherwise.

And so, some restless day, eyes fixed on some alluring goal, the Amhara youth might run away and not be seen again. If he should return, it would be many years later, as a learned priest or *dabtarā* or as a successful warrior or official, and some sort of reconciliation might be effected with his family. In either case, from a sociological viewpoint, the rebellious youth is merely preparing himself to take over one of the more specialized functions on which the wider social order depends. His break with his parents does not signify a revolt against society, but, if anything, a closer attachment to society through more intimate alliance with its highest values, religion and warfare.

Thus there has always been some room for the attainment of a new social identity in Abyssinia. Although the rigidity of paternal authority often meant that it must be attained through rebellion, the adolescent could eat his cake of defiance and still have his cake of loyalty; and the social system was well served thereby.

ADOLESCENCE IN CHANGING ETHIOPIA

The foregoing description of adolescence still obtains for the vast majority of Amhara youth today. Side by side with this traditional pattern of "growing up on the farm," however, a quite different pattern of childhood and adolescence has been developing in Addis Ababa and in some of the provincial capitals. This new pattern follows the course of experience provided by participation in the government school system. It has radically interrupted the traditional rhythm of growing up and has posed more integrative problems than it has yet been able to solve.

The Welfare School

Public education in Ethiopia prior to the Italian invasion represented a small but significant trickle of activity alongside the mainstream of traditional institutions. Perhaps some six to seven hundred boys and girls received the beginnings of a modern education in the government schools of Addis Ababa by 1935.[9] Many others received some elementary education in government provincial schools and in schools operated by foreign religious missions, though the latter never played as significant a role in Ethiopia as they did in colonial Africa.

During the occupation, Ethiopians were prevented from acquiring anything higher than elementary education, but the Italians did construct a number of school buildings for their own nationals which facilitated the growth of the Ethiopian school system after 1941. By 1944 there were some 25,000 pupils enrolled in government schools, a figure which rose to 60,000 by 1950 and reached 234,000 in 1963.[10]

The base of the Ethiopian educational program has been an eight-year elementary curriculum, the first four years being taught in Amharic and the second four in English, although Ethiopian teachers often continue to teach in Amharic in the latter years.* This standard curriculum is supposed to be followed by all schools in the country—church, mission, and private schools, as well as those staffed by the government. In practice, a scarcity of teachers and materials in the provincial schools means that the curriculum is followed less closely there than in Addis Ababa. (The exceptional case of Asmara, capital of Eritrea which federated with Ethiopia in 1952 after sixty-two years under Italian administration, will not be considered here.) This elementary program culminates with a general examination that covers the five main fields of Amharic, English, mathematics, science, and social studies. Successful completion of this exam has been required for virtually every type of training beyond the elementary level.

At the secondary level, by contrast, the Ethiopian student faces a bewildering array of educational programs. As listed in the flow chart of the Ministry of Education, they include theological secondary, academic secondary, elementary teacher training, handicraft teacher training, commercial school, technical school, agricultural secondary school, nurses training, community nurses training, sanitarians, naval cadet training, air cadet training, civil aviation, and inservice technical training. Admission of students to these schools is the responsibility of the individual directors, who take into account the students' own preferences when feasible.

A similar procedure obtains at the college level, for which successful completion of the secondary school-leaving examination has in most cases been mandatory. During the 1950's a number of schools were opened at the postsecondary level: the Arts and Science Faculties of the University College of Addis Ababa, the Agricultural College, the Engineering College, the Public Health College, the Building College, and the National Defense Colleges. Some of these have now been combined into a single institution, the Haile Selassie I University.

For students who have gone as far as the upper grades of elementary school, the desire to get into one of the secondary level schools—no matter which one—has usually become the uppermost concern in their lives. They have become obsessively aware of the "value" (*ṭiqem*) of further schooling, namely, as the surest way to a job that pays well. Perhaps they have become fired with idealism to help advance their country and hope to gain some special competence that will enable them to do so. Until 1962, moreover, the rewards of being a secondary school student included material fringe benefits that gave many a powerful motive for prolonging their education. Above all,

---

* In 1963–64 the system was changed to one with six years of elementary education followed by two years of junior secondary education.

they have come too far along the road of modernity to return to what they regard as the hard and thankless lot of the traditional adolescent, and so are forced to find some place in the modernizing sector of society. Since Ethiopia's modernizing sector has so far provided only the secondary school system as a means of integrating its youth, the eighth-grade examination certificate constitutes a ticket to the future which must be obtained at all costs.

At the same time that this examination was acquiring its momentous significance in the lives of Ethiopia's youth, the proportion of students who passed it was becoming progressively smaller. By 1959, efforts by Ministry of Education officials to raise academic standards and to adjust the number of eligible students to the number of openings in secondary schools resulted in the failing of some sixty per cent of those who took the examination, a situation which provoked nearly riotous protests by students in Addis Ababa.[11]

Such conditions have laden the eighth-grade examination with more awesomeness and terror than a puberty rite. Worries about the exam preoccupy most seventh and eighth graders, and their anxiety is compounded by the attitudes of their school directors, for whom the proportion of passing students has tended to become the primary index of success. The weeks before the exam are filled with frantic cramming on the part of teachers as well as students. It is no wonder that such pressures have on occasion led students to purchase actual or alleged copies of the exam in advance from ministry employees or their go-betweens, an offense which has been sternly dealt with by the ministry.

Those students who do not pass the eighth-grade exam or who, because of family pressures, low ability, or other reasons, leave school before completing the eighth grade, move to the margin of Ethiopian society. If attendance at a secondary school or beyond may be taken as the defining characteristic of a "modern adolescent" in Ethiopia, since that signifies their participation in the one institutionalized pattern of secondary socialization in the modern sector, these young people are neither traditional adolescents nor fully modern, but fall in an interstitial category. Having caught a glimpse of some brave new world in their early schooling, they find themselves cast adrift, in the prime of their adolescence, in a no-man's region between traditional society and the promised land. In some cases they manage to make a rapid adjustment; more often, only their youthful energy saves them from total despair.

These marginal adolescents normally drift to Addis Ababa, if they are not already there, and lead the most precarious sorts of lives. They live as loiterers on the streets and byways of the capital. They go from school to school, begging for a place; or from office to office, looking for some sort of work, which they are unlikely to find if they do not have a relative in an influential position. It is so hard to find employment without at least an eighth-grade certifi-

. 16.—*The procession on Tĭmqat Day*

. 17.—*Tĭmqat procession: detail*

FIG. 18.—*Ten-year-old boy plowing*

FIG. 19.—*Mother and daughter carrying water pots*

cate that boys sometimes borrow the certificates of more successful friends and enter jobs under those assumed names. Often they live for many months with no livelihood at all. Eventually, some find work as houseboys, shine shoes, or peddle merchandise on the streets; others, on an impulse, sign up for life in one of the military services. Still others are reduced to begging, or stealing, or concocting stories with which to extract help from sympathetic foreigners.

The lives of such boys, whose number is large and steadily growing, are among the chief casualties of Ethiopia's transition to date. As they increase, their misery will become more vocal, and they may constitute an element of political unrest. Whether or not they become a political problem, they are already a social problem.

The modern adolescents, by contrast, comprise a small and determinate number.* In 1958–59, the year in which my research on them began, there were all together about 3,900 students in the academic secondary schools, 3,350 in other special schools at the secondary level, and 760 students at the post-secondary level. One source of information on these students was a questionnaire which was completed by 700 students: 500 at the secondary level, including 40 female students, in a total of 15 schools, and 200 male students in five colleges.[12] Some of the findings from this survey will be woven into the following text where appropriate.

Compared to the rest of their countrymen, and certainly those of the same age, the modern adolescents have lived in luxury. Most students at the secondary level, and all those at the college level, have been boarding students. At no cost to themselves or their parents, they have received full board and room, a token allotment of clothes, and their books. Day students have received instead a monthly allowance of Eth$20,† approximately the same amount that unskilled laborers earn for full-time work. Tuition is also free for all full-time Ethiopian students at all levels.

These "welfare school" conditions were designed to make further education attractive and possible for Ethiopian students, nearly all of whose families either can not or are unwilling to support their children for many years in school. In this, the parents are following long established Amhara custom, for in the traditional society boys who went off to church schools often did so, as we have seen, without the support of their parents, and in any case were expected to gain their livelihood by begging. Nowadays, if their children are admitted to one of the government secondary schools, even tradition-minded

---

* And one that grows steadily. In 1958 there were twenty-eight government secondary schools in the empire. By 1964 the number had increased to forty-seven.

† One Ethiopian dollar is equal to (U.S.) forty cents.

parents who may have objected to their children's spending so many years in elementary school are not a little proud to have them in so prestigious an institution, and are delighted to have them so well financed by the Ministry of Education.

Needless to say, the students who make the grade into one of the secondary schools are jubilant. The relative hardship of their elementary years gives way to an easy and stimulating life. For those who grew up in provincial schools, the move to Addis Ababa has been an especially exciting prospect—so much so that when secondary schools were newly established in some of the provincial capitals in the late 1950's, a number of students who were supposed to attend them preferred to stop their education instead.[13]

The pattern of adolescence embodied in the government schools differs from that in traditional Amhara society in two fundamental respects. In the traditional pattern, adolescence is a time when the Amhara are subjected to the strictest controls by their parents. At the same time, they are expected to prepare for independence by assuming increasing amounts of responsibility. In the modern pattern, the welfare school has the effect of removing the student as far as possible from parental controls. At the same time, it puts him in a more passive and irresponsible role than ever. He is given virtually everything he needs and obliged to do nothing in return. He is asked only to prepare himself to serve his country well later on. This obligation is in fact firmly implanted in the minds of many students, who acquire the sense of a personal debt to the government which they want to repay in later years. Ethiopian society is not yet organized, however, in a way that will bring such motives to realistic expression. During and after his school experience, little opportunity is provided for the student to mature out of an essentially passive, receptive, dependent posture. Critical of this state of affairs, one Ethiopian college student was moved to declare in an oratorical contest: "Ethiopian students are like college students the world over, with two differences—they get everything free, and their selfishness is pushed to frightening exaggeration."

Be that as it may, modern adolescence in Ethiopia does provide the essential minimal conditions for fulfilling its function. It is a moratorium for the young, in which relative freedom from traditional controls and a relatively carefree existence facilitate the acquisition of habits, beliefs, and values which their fathers never knew.*

---

* The above description applies only until 1961–62, after which secondary students no longer received room and board or stipends and Addis Ababa College students were no longer housed in dormitories. Some implications of this change are considered in the concluding section of this chapter.

New Agents of Socialization

In Amhara society, as we have seen, the agents of primary socialization—parents and older relatives—likewise prepare the young person for adulthood, by teaching him work skills, arranging his marriage, and conditioning him to the mores of adult society. In changing Ethiopia, these traditional managers of adolescence are unable to impart the skills and values needed for a modern life. Their role as agents of secondary socialization is taken for the most part by teachers and peers in the government schools.

Schools at the post-elementary levels in Ethiopia have been staffed mainly by teachers brought under contract from foreign countries—chiefly Canada, England, India, Sweden, and the United States. Together with a growing number of Ethiopians who have studied abroad, and some graduates of Ethiopian colleges, these teachers have been the principal medium through which Ethiopian adolescents have been exposed to Western culture, not only by teaching subjects like science and English literature, and skills like drafting and stenography, but also by imparting attitudes and values important for Ethiopia's modernization.

High among these new values is that of rewarding an individual solely on the basis of performance. Although the long arm of "connections" has occasionally reached into the school system, to save, for example, the relative of some dignitary from dismissal despite substandard performance, the day-to-day operation of school life follows general standards which are applied without regard to family connections, class position, or tribal and religious affiliations.* The degree to which the students have accepted the sovereignty of universal norms is reflected in their response to the question: "In general, what will help you most to get ahead, ability or 'pull' (that is, personal contacts or influence, through family or friends)?" Nine-tenths of the students at both secondary and college levels expressed the belief that ability would help them more to get ahead.

Another modern value promoted by the school staffs is that of Ethiopian nationalism. In the elementary schools outside of Addis Ababa, pupils tend to associate chiefly with members of their own tribe and religion. In the post-elementary schools, they inevitably have considerable intercourse with members of other groups. On the basis of our sample, the ethnic composition of the post-elementary schools may be estimated as in Table 2. This ethnic pluralism would seem at first to intensify particularistic sentiments among

---

* This reflects deliberate government policy. Before the occupation, sons of noblemen were segregated at Tafari Makonnen School and received preferential treatment. After the liberation, the Emperor not only discontinued this policy but took pains to eliminate favoritism in the schools to a large degree.

TABLE 2

ETHNIC AND RELIGIOUS AFFILIATIONS OF ETHIOPIAN
SECONDARY AND COLLEGE STUDENTS

Ethnic Group	Percentage	Religious Group	Percentage
Amhara............	55	"Orthodox".........	67
Tigre..............	22	"Protestant"........	6
Galla..............	15	"Catholic".........	5
Gurage............	4	"Christian".........	15
Others*...........	4		
		Total Christian....	93
		Muslim...........	4
		Others†..........	3

* Adari, Somali, Danakil, Wollamo, Kambata, Mensa, etc.
† Baha'i; agnostic; "no religion"; etc.

COMMENTS:

1. The ethnic figures must be regarded with some caution, since as many as 17 per cent of the 700 respondents failed to answer the question. It is difficult to know whether this is due primarily to the reluctance of non-Amhara students so to identify themselves, even anonymously; to the general sensitivity about mentioning anything directly related to the "tribal question"; or simply to misunderstanding of the question. I suspect that the first-named factor may not be the most important. At any rate, if one compares the secondary school replies, in which 20 per cent failed to indicate their ethnic identification, with the college replies, in which only 10 per cent failed to do so, the greater percentage of response among the latter is accompanied by a slight *increase* (53.3 to 56.7 per cent) in the Amhara category.

The figures on religious affiliation are more reliable, since only 3 per cent of the entire sample failed to answer that question.

2. Fifteen per cent of the students who indicated their ethnic affiliations are the offspring of mixed marriages, nearly two-thirds of which were between Amhara and Galla. These students were entered in the above classification according to the ethnic group of the father.

3. The students were also asked to indicate whether their own religion differed from that of their parents. *Ten per cent indicated such a change.* Of these, 28 per cent became agnostic or indicated "no religion"; 25 per cent converted to Protestantism; 17 per cent to Catholicism; 18 per cent went from "Orthodox" to "Christian" (which probably means to Protestantism in most cases); and 7 per cent changed to Baha'i.

4. A comparison with the ethnic and religious composition of the country as a whole naturally suggests itself. Unfortunately, national figures have not yet been calculated to any comparable degree of reliability. If one refers to the crude estimates in common currency, certain disproportions are readily apparent.

Thus, the Amhara proportion of the national population has been estimated at 25 to 30 per cent. It is clear that they are disproportionately represented in the school system; but not so greatly as has been at times alleged. In view of the statistics and considerations presented above, it would seem that 50 per cent is the upper limit of enrolment by "pure Amhara" in the post-elementary schools.

The disproportions with regard to religious affiliation speak for themselves. The most recent published estimates are: Ethiopian Orthodox, 35 per cent; Muslim, 35 per cent; pagan, 25 per cent; other, 5 per cent. (Lipsky, *Ethiopia* [New Haven: Human Relations Area Files Press, 1962], p. 101.)

the students. Rivalries and hostilities tend to get channeled along these lines, particularly along the Amhara-Tigre axis, and petty fights have erupted from time to time among groups of students so divided. The Amhara students, moreover, tend to interpret their numerical majority in school as self-evident justification of their political superiority in the country, an interpretation sullenly rejected by non-Amhara students who tend to be more aware of the Amhara's much smaller percentage of the national population. However, the students are regarded by their teachers, not as members of tribes, but as Ethiopians. The school authorities thus act as a countervailing force in behalf of national symbols, and their effect is considerable.[14] While entering students naturally tend to identify in the first instance with their tribes, sixty per cent of the secondary school seniors and seventy-five per cent of the college students questioned about political identifications indicated that they considered themselves Ethiopians before they considered themselves members of tribes.

The teachers also provide practical information of various sorts to assist the acculturation of their charges. They teach the etiquette of modernity, including the importance of punctuality and the keeping of promises. The objects and events in their own lives quietly demonstrate to the students much about modern Western culture, while their use of English in and out of class accustoms the students to the use of their country's official European language. Thus, besides promoting respect for impersonal standards and the sense of Ethiopian nationalism, the teachers fulfill a third extracurricular function of some importance: that of making the schools a vehicle for social mobility, a place to acquire that minimum of European habits which is essential for attaining high status in a modernizing society.

The total accomplishment of the teachers, however, falls short of giving the modern adolescents a coherent orientation to life. The cultural lessons they transmit are neither consistent among the various schools nor closely related to the situation of changing Ethiopia. The organization of education, as of everything else in Ethiopia, reflects the abiding anxiety of the government about permitting any one foreign nation to gain a monopoly in any sphere of activity. Each secondary school and college has heretofore been virtually autonomous, pursuing those policies and teaching those lessons which best fit its point of view, a point of view now guided by British culture, now by American, now by Swedish, now by French, now by Jesuit. As Margery Perham long since observed, this created a situation in which Ethiopian students have gotten "fragments from the experience and ideals of each [nation] without getting the fullest and best influence from any one national tradition."[15]

Another shortcoming of the educational program has been the relative paucity of materials relating to Ethiopian realities. As one Ethiopian educator has written: "School children are at times more familiar with the history of

Rome and the life of Abraham Lincoln than with the geography of their immediate community or the history of their own native country."[16] While a certain amount of concentration on remote matters may be essential for introducing modern adolescents to the substance and background of modern culture, it is doubtful whether they are being prepared to relate meaningfully to the society of their adulthood if that society is not made a subject for careful consideration during their schooldays.

Still another limitation on the effectiveness of the teachers stems from a quite different problem, the Ethiopian's ambivalence toward foreigners. This will be overcome with the gradual Ethiopianization of the teaching force, but that cannot be achieved for at least another generation. One area in which this problem manifests itself is linguistic nationalism. English, the official language of all post-elementary instruction, is still regarded as an outsider's tongue in Ethiopia, unlike other African countries where the European language in question serves the native peoples as a *lingua franca;* and many Ethiopians hope that the day will come when it will be replaced by Amharic as the medium of instruction.[17] Due to their ignorance of Amharic or other Ethiopian languages, foreign teachers are rarely able to gain the sort of closeness to their students that promotes the more profoundly beneficial sort of relationship. Because of this and a tradition of suspiciousness regarding foreigners, all but the radically Westernized students maintain a lingering mistrust of the teacher *qua* foreigner.

The gaps in the socialization of the modern adolescent left by the nature of his teachers and their teaching are filled to some extent by his peers. In this respect, too, modern adolescence contrasts with the traditional pattern: not only has the role of mentor and model been taken over by foreign teachers in place of the parents, but also the modern adolescent has become dependent on his peers to a degree unthinkable in traditional Amhara society.

It has been natural that the modern adolescent turn to those his own age for moral support. However much they may support the idea of his going to school as a means to a higher salary, his parents have little understanding of the new directions inherent in modern education. His foreign teachers are, at worst, preoccupied with their own narrow interests or else, at best, out of tune with the Ethiopian ethos and mentality. Older modernized Ethiopians, who should be the most sympathetic, are usually too preoccupied with their own adjustment problems to pay much attention. His schoolmates thus become his only reliable allies in the battle of growing up.

Association with age-mates is informal for the most part. There have been almost no formal youth associations or clubs in Ethiopia. The teen-age gang, with its sharp boundaries and tight controls, has scarcely come into being. Relations with peers thus takes the form of small groups of friends. More than half the secondary students questioned, and well over a third of the college students, stated that the number of their friends was only one, two, three, or four.

Almost all the students indicated that they prefer close, intimate, and enduring friendships to casual, impersonal, and frequently changing relationships. There is thus something of the traditional *goramsä*'s companion about these relations, in that these boys define their friends as confidants, as individuals with whom they can disclose "secrets" and discuss personal problems. But the modern relationship is much broader, for it also includes such activities as studying together; going on walks; playing athletic games; going to the movies; visiting the brothels; talking about education, life, and the future; seeing the sights around town.

The great sociological significance of these small clusters of companions, or *bälïnjarä* as they are called, is that they play a crucial part in mediating the transition from a childhood that is essentially traditional, despite exposure to certain modern subjects in school, to an adulthood that will be lived essentially in the modern sector. At the same time that they help the newcomer adjust to each local school community, they are helping him adjust to the broader subculture of modernizing Ethiopia—explaining the strange things and ideas he encounters; correcting his behavior, for example, by showing the proper use of silverware at the table; and refining his language, when necessary, from that of the rustic to that of the urbanite. Their creative function is no less important. Through countless conversations, some idle and some intense, they work to interpret and integrate stimuli coming from many sources—from movies; magazines; the example of Europeans living in Ethiopia; the behavior of government officials, as well as from their teachers—and thus form a sort of buffer between the lone adolescent and the various authoritative influences in his life.

Despite the radical changes in the position of the Amhara adolescents described above—their complete dependence on the government school system, their tutelage under foreign instructors, and their great reliance on age-mates —the traditional pattern of adolescent submission to parental authority still runs strong. Even though most students live as boarders or in rented quarters, they maintain contact with their parents on occasional visits or at vacation time. However far removed, they remain deeply attached to their families and sensitive to the wishes of their parents. How to acquire money to send to their families is often a dominant concern in their lives. Though in most cases the parents can not provide meaningful orientation regarding adjustment to changing conditions in Ethiopia, they do give advice about how their children should behave and try to keep them faithful to traditional norms. The fact that parents still wield considerable moral influence over the modern adolescents, more so even than their peers, is shown by the figures in Table 3.

This persistence of parental influence keeps the Ethiopian adolescent anchored in his traditional culture and accounts in part for a noticeable conservatism among Ethiopian students generally. With respect to such matters as morality, etiquette, family solidarity, and religion, students are strongly inclined to follow their parents' precepts.

While this deep-grained attachment to their parents gives the modern adolescents a sense of stability and security, it is also responsible for consider-

TABLE 3

RELATIVE INFLUENCE OF PARENTS AND
FRIENDS ON STUDENTS

EXTENT TO WHICH STUDENTS SAY THEY FOLLOW ADVICE	SECONDARY SCHOOL		COLLEGE MALES (per cent)
	Males (per cent)	Females (per cent)	
Of parents:			
Always..........	46	35	17
Usually..........	43	60	65
Not often........	11	5	18
Of friends:			
Always..........	19	8	8
Usually..........	47	61	53
Not often........	34	31	39
Number........	(396)	(40)	(197)

able strain in their lives. For there are few families—less than three per cent of our sample—in which the students do not remark some significant area of disagreement between their parents and themselves. The modest steps toward modernity that Ethiopia has taken have already kindled a smoldering conflict between generations, perhaps for the first time in Ethiopian history. It is against that background of conflict that we now examine the condition in changing Ethiopia of the three main sociological functions of adolescence: preparation for adult work roles, preparation for marriage roles, and integration into the adult intellectual and moral order.

Preparation for Work

The most conspicuous function of the secondary schools and colleges in Ethiopia is to train young people for careers unknown in their traditional society: to create engineers and mechanics, doctors and nurses, economists and educators. With regard to the familiar occupations of the old order, the schools' task is to engender a new breed of practitioner—farmers versed in modern methods of agriculture, soldiers disciplined and geared to modern techniques, clergy cognizant of ecumenical Christianity, clerks who can type and take shorthand, and government officials with some modern education.

What is most revolutionary is that the schools introduce not only new subject matters for careers, but the very notion of vocation itself—of life work as

TABLE 4

SOURCES OF FUTURE SATISFACTION CONSIDERED MOST IMPORTANT BY STUDENTS*

SOURCE FROM WHICH STUDENTS EXPECT MOST SATISFACTION IN LIFE	SECONDARY SCHOOL				COLLEGE MALES (per cent)	
	Males (per cent)		Females (per cent)			
	1st choice	2d choice	1st choice	2d choice	1st choice	2d choice
Career or occupation................	34	12	30	9	44	17
Improvement of local community......	30	27	16	36	22	28
Religious beliefs and activities.........	13	20	16	21	5	7
Participation in national and international affairs.........................	10	24	13	20	8	26
Family relationships.................	8	10	20	9	17	14
Leisure-time, recreational activities.....	5	7	5	5	3	8
Number.....................	(394)		(40)		(195)	

* Based on question 27 in the Gillespie-Allport questionnaire.

something which one *chooses,* trains for in a specific manner, and derives satisfaction from pursuing.* This orientation departs radically from the traditional expectation of inheriting the work of one's father as a matter of course. Whereas, as we have noted, the Amhara son traditionally carried on his father's work, except in rare cases where there were special reasons for not doing so, only *seven per cent* of the boys in my sample indicated that

* When asked what they expected to give most satisfaction in their lives, the students most frequently named "career or occupation" (out of six alternatives). When asked what they considered most desirable in choosing an occupation, they named "work that is really interesting" most frequently (out of six alternatives). See Tables 4 and 5.

they expected to enter the same occupation as their fathers. This figure is much smaller than that obtained from a cross-cultural study of youth by James Gillespie and Gordon Allport, who found that "approximately a third of the male students in all our samples [a total of 1,168, drawn from the United States, New Zealand, South Africa, Egypt, Mexico, France, Italy, Germany, Japan, and Israel] expect to enter the same occupations as their fathers, or ones closely related."[18] In part, the Ethiopian figure simply reflects the preparation for types of work which did not exist for previous generations.

TABLE 5

OCCUPATIONAL CONDITIONS MOST DESIRED BY STUDENTS

Conditions Which Students Consider Most Desirable in Choosing Future Occupations	Secondary School				College Males (per cent)	
	Males (per cent)		Females (per cent)			
	1st choice	2d choice	1st choice	2d choice	1st choice	2d choice
Interesting work....................	56	24	63	17	63	18
Job security........................	19	26	23	11	14	31
Chance to acquire much money........	12	11	3	11	10	16
Prestige...........................	7	9	8	17	7	5
Pleasant work companions............	4	26	3	30	3	27
Good boss..........................	2	4	0	14	3	3
Number........................	(325)		(40)		(113)	

But since it also represents numerous cases where the boy's occupational interest is a traditional one—where, in other words, one finds sons of soldiers and government officials planning to become farmers, sons of farmers planning to be teachers, and sons of priests and teachers planning to be soldiers and administrators—this figure may be interpreted as indicative of a very general rejection of parental influence with respect to occupational choice.

Parents of the modern adolescents are unhappy about this diminution of their traditional authority, especially so when their children opt for some of the more "outlandish" modern occupations. Their disapproval sometimes takes the form of urging their children to quit school and get married. Often it is expressed in the form of direct criticism of the occupation in question. Nearly two-fifths of the secondary school males questioned about this indicated that their parents did not approve of the occupation they wished to enter. As might be expected, the incidence of disapproval was highest among the students of the Gondar secondary school (fifty-eight per cent), whose parents are presumably more traditionalist than those of the Addis Ababa boys, and the students of the technical school (fifty-six per cent), whose occupational interests, involving manual labor and technical skills, are felt to resemble those artisan pursuits traditionally disesteemed by the Amhara.

Time is on the side of the students. As Ethiopia develops and education spreads, the advantages of prolonged training and modern occupations will become increasingly apparent to the parents. For some time to come, however, their resentment of the dependence of youth on foreigners and Western-educated Ethiopians for occupational guidance will continue to generate social tensions and impede the socialization process.

The harmonious pattern of preparation for adult work roles found in traditional Amhara society has been further disrupted under the new school system at at least two points: the point at which occupational commitments are made, and the point of entry into the work force.

The modern adolescent is supposed to choose which of several kinds of schools, representing a variety of vocational commitments, he wishes to enter upon successful completion of the eighth-grade exam. Quite often his choice is dictated by wholly irrelevant factors. For example, it may be made on the basis of which of the available schools promises the best standard of living.[19] Or it may be made for him by the school system, for one finds cases where the student's preferences are disregarded and he is placed in whatever school and vocational program happens to be able to accommodate him.

Even when the student's choice is relatively free from such extraneous determinants, however, it is usually difficult for him to make a meaningful decision. Eight grades of a rudimentary curriculum is hardly an adequate basis for choosing from a variety of unfamiliar vocations. So it is "fate" that guides most youngsters into one or another of the secondary school programs. The problem of choice recurs, for a much smaller number, when commitments are again required for entrance into the colleges. At this point meaningful decisions are often made, but perhaps more often they are spun from a skein of bewilderment. One secondary school graduate summed up the situation by saying, "Foreigners frequently ask young educated Ethiopians, 'What do you want to become?' How do we know? This whole business of *choosing* is entirely new to us, and we know very little about the alternatives that we have now. It is all very confusing."

So far the modernizing sector has provided little, beyond vocational pamphlets in the school libraries and an occasional school debate on the respective values of different occupations, to help orient the students on these matters.

Programs of vocational guidance and counseling have not yet been instituted.*
Students who manage to form clear and definite ambitions also suffer for
want of help, if for some reason they have been shunted away from the appropriate training program, or have been deprived of opportunities to prepare
adequately for the vocations to which they aspire. Two research findings bear
on this. In one study it was found that "few secondary school administrators
when questioned are aware of the ambitions and desires of their students,"
and that less than twenty per cent of the group of secondary school students
surveyed felt they had received training "suitable to their ambitions."[20] In my
own survey it appeared that fewer than twenty per cent of the secondary
school students expect to enter the occupation they actually want to.

In addition to this discontinuity between childhood experience and the
hitherto unknown necessity of making some sort of vocational choice, modern
adolescence also involves a sharp break between the experience of post-elementary school and the process of getting on a payroll. Here the Ethiopian youth
faces the problems of students everywhere as they leave school for the "real
world." In at least two respects, however, his dilemma is more acute than that
of his counterpart in Western societies. Because virtually all jobs are controlled
by the government, and because the government is still organized along traditional lines, the Ethiopian graduate must suddenly forget the universalistic
criteria of school and acclimate himself to the traditional pattern of ingratiating oneself with those in positions of power—a pattern referred to as *daj ṭenāt*
—if he is to gain and retain a decent job. For many graduates there is no
machinery that might assist them in locating a job: no job advertisements,
employment bureaus, not even effective personnel departments in most quarters.

The school system itself, however, does manage in certain cases to find
jobs for its graduates. For the foreign-educated returnees a special placement
board was set up within the Ministry of Education. The locally educated are
placed, if at all, by their individual schools, depending on the policy of the
school, the resourcefulness of its director, the demands of the market, and current political emphases.

The outlook for graduates of the various specialized vocational programs
has been in recent years as follows. A consistently high demand for teachers
has assured jobs for graduates of the various teachers training programs.
Graduates of the commercial school have been in great demand because of the
increasing bureaucratization of government and the slight expansion of commerce. The public health college had great difficulty in the placement of its

---

* Since this was written the University's Department of Education has begun to produce a
series of career pamphlets for secondary school students.

graduates in the late fifties, but the government's implementation of a program of public health centers has opened up increasing opportunities for their employment. Graduates of the school of social work have been placed in positions with little difficulty.

On the other hand, in those areas in which the government has shown little or no interest the school authorities have been hard put to find employment for their graduates. This was shown most dramatically in the case of the now defunct community development training project at Majete, whose graduates were allowed to drift into oblivion due to the absence of an effective community development program in the country. Those who have completed courses of study in agriculture have not been extensively employed by the government because of chronic disorganization and neglect in the Ministry of Agriculture, while lack of capital and know-how has tended to keep them from private agricultural enterprise. Graduates of the technical and engineering schools have been having some difficulty in entering the work force due to the slow pace of Ethiopia's industrial development. Graduates of general academic programs, finally, and those who drop out before completing some course of study, tend to be left to their own devices.

While the modernizing sector, then, has introduced the revolutionary notion of vocation and has institutionalized means of training young Ethiopians for modern work roles, it has not yet provided adequate mechanisms either for guiding them into and through the training programs or for employing them properly once they are trained.

Preparation for Marriage

Conditions of growing up in the modernizing sector have disrupted the harmonious pattern of Amhara adolescence also with respect to entrance into adult family roles. Conflicts arise both from postponement of the normal age for marriage and from radically new ideas about the nature of marriage.

The modern adolescent typically expects to marry at an age that is at least eight to ten years older than his traditional counterpart. While Amhara girls have traditionally married in their early teens, girls in the senior class of secondary school now say they expect to marry in their early twenties. Amhara boys have traditionally married around the age of twenty, but those in post-elementary schools now expect to marry in their late twenties or early thirties.

This shift is due to a desire to attain as much education as possible, and above all, for the boys, to the precarious economic position of modern adolescents. While living on his father's farm an Amhara boy could marry early with the assurance of having enough land to work to support his family at least at subsistence level. The modern boy who finishes secondary school or college, however, has no assets beyond his diploma in most cases. He must wait a number of years to achieve the beginnings of financial stability.

The students' conception of marriage, moreover, reflects a still more profound change. They are no longer content to regard the selection of a mate as a matter to be arranged by parents in accord with their own interests and standards. They reject the old-fashioned Amhara marriage in which romantic love plays no part and divorce is common. Most of them insist on the right to choose their own spouses, and they tend to approach that choice with criteria

TABLE 6

QUALITIES MOST DESIRED BY STUDENTS IN A FUTURE WIFE OR HUSBAND*

QUALITY	PER CENT CHECKING QUALITY AS EITHER FIRST OR SECOND CHOICE		
	Secondary Schools		College Males
	Males	Females	
Educated......................	48	75	41
Shares my opinions and beliefs..	44	48	43
Religious......................	34	25	19
Good companion................	25	30	45
Beautiful......................	15	0	22
Kind and generous..............	15	13	9
Wealthy.......................	4	2	5
Will impress my friends socially...	3	2	2
Number...................	(385)	(39)	(191)

* Related to Gillespie-Allport question No. 17.

which differ from those of their parents. Instead of following such traditional criteria as good upbringing, family background, and wealth, a number of modern adolescents aspire to find spouses who, above all else, are educated, who share their opinions and beliefs, and who will be good companions. (See Table 6.) Even such strong aversions as those against tribal and religious exogamy have receded somewhat before the new ideal of marriage founded on romantic love.* The figures in Table 7 are indicative of the diffusion of this ideal as well as of the growth of a sentiment of Ethiopian nationality.

* Although Amhara men have customarily had sexual relations with non-Amhara women and produce countless offspring from them, the latter have not been considered appropriate choices for marriage, except in very high strata where the marriage served a purpose primarily political.

These changes in the definition of marriage have produced tremendous tensions and heartache in the relations between generations. Deprived of authority in the occupational sphere, parents of modern adolescents cling with all the more pride to their traditional rights and obligations in the sphere of getting their children properly married. They often nag their children to leave school and get married while young. They stand determined to select their children's mates. If they do admit some consideration for their children's desires on the matter, they insist that any prospective spouse measure up to traditional criteria. As a result, disagreements between students and their parents revolve around the subject of marriage more frequently than anything else.

TABLE 7

DISPOSITION OF STUDENTS TOWARD TRIBAL AND
RELIGIOUS EXOGAMY

		SECONDARY SCHOOL		COLLEGE MALES (per cent)
		Males (per cent)	Females (per cent)	
Willingness to marry a person of a different religion.	Yes	29	33	60
	No	71	67	40
Willingness to marry a person of a different tribe....	Yes	64	73	84
	No	36	27	16
Number...		(392)	(40)	(194)

Modern adolescents, however, have by no means wholly rejected traditional attitudes and sentiments concerning marriage and courtship. Although a number of students say they want to marry for the modern reason of finding personal happiness through a satisfying love relation, many more indicate that they are chiefly inspired by the traditional motives of wanting to beget children. Most of them wish to continue the custom of having large families, the most frequently mentioned numbers of children desired being "four" and "more than six."*

The modern boys still widely share the traditional expectation that their

---

* The mean number of children desired by the college students in my sample is 4.23. This figure exceeds those of all the national college groups reported by Gillespie and Allport except Egypt and South African Bantu.

brides be virgin. Related norms greatly restrict their quest for romantic love. Since Ethiopian society still expects its maidens to be shy and retiring, and to avoid social relations with boys outside their families, the boys find few opportunities for getting to know members of the opposite sex. Even in those few situations where sociability between the sexes is publicly permitted, ingrained tendencies to segregate the sexes persist. The most liberal context for such sociability, the University College campus, has witnessed relatively little interaction between male and female students. In spite of their occasional resolutions to act more boldly, the college boys have in the past tended to shy away from the co-eds except during such rare formal events as a college dance or off-campus parties.

This is not to say that modern adolescent males have no opportunity for premarital sexuality. On the contrary, their opportunities in this regard are perhaps better than ever. The proliferation of brothels in Ethiopia's urban centers makes sexual initiation easy, almost a routine event.* Students also frequent these houses for social entertainment, dancing to swing and Latin rhythms, and sipping beer or soft drinks. Thus the continued sanctions against social intercourse in more respectable forms work to sharpen the Amhara dichotomy between decency and sexuality, and leave modern boys with a double standard that separates the marriageable girls from the enjoyable ones.

The idea that marriage should be founded on romantic love has brought greater anxiety as well as hope into the lives of Ethiopian adolescents. This anxiety is due in part to the above-mentioned inhibitions against that easy commerce of the sexes which so facilitates the discovery of a suitable love object. It also reflects a certain ambivalence toward the new ideal, based on a lingering attachment to the authority of the old system. This was manifest, for example, in the response to a college debate on the topic, "Resolved: that the custom of letting the parents choose a spouse for the children should be maintained," that took place in 1959. Although on anonymous questionnaires *90 per cent* of the college students said they will probably decide whom to marry themselves, and only 3 per cent said the decision would be made by parents or other relatives, in voting on the matter after the debate the students (in contrast to the judges who awarded the negative debaters) publicly declared themselves 42 per cent affirmative, 41 per cent negative, with 17 per cent abstaining.

Anxiety regarding the new conception of marriage, finally, is also connected with a new-fashioned fear of divorce. The mind of the modern adolescent vacillates between the ideal of an abiding marital relationship based on

---

* Due perhaps to the greater importance of their peers, sexual accomplishments have now become a frequent topic of conversation and a matter for boasting among modern adolescent boys.

love and the image of the traditional Amhara marriage, likely as not to end in divorce. This sort of concern was expressed in a revealing way in the following statement by a twenty-year-old college student:

> The main thing I want in my wife is good character. Beauty is not so important. Of course she will be an excellent cook. But mostly I am concerned that she be the *right* one for me; I do not want to get divorced. But you can't really know if she is the right one until after ten years of married life. If after having about five or six children it turns out troublesome, I will have to leave her. A person cannot go on living that way.

In some instances, ironically, this quest for the perfect marriage leads to a rejection of the very institution of marriage itself. Seven per cent of the students questioned indicated that they do not want to get married eventually—either because they "could never afford it," they "would be happier living single," or they just *do not want to enter a relation that will end in divorce.* Thus at a time when the stability and warmth of family life are needed more than ever, the very possibility of family is doubted.

Some Ethiopian students blame the deteriorated family and an alleged increase in divorce in their country on the impact of Western civilization. True, the introduction of the Western concept of marriage and of the rudiments of a modern occupational system have dislocated the traditional arrangements for marriage; and other related problems, to be discussed in the next chapter, plague the Western-educated elite. But Western civilization has also developed resources to begin to cope with analogous problems in its own societies, and perhaps it is not too soon to acquaint Ethiopia's youth with some of these: for example, the recent developments in man's understanding of the dynamics of marriage as well as more sophisticated conceptions of the ideal and importance of family life in modern society.

CULTURAL ORIENTATION

A generational conflict manifests itself further with respect to questions of belief, taste, and value. Because of differences on such issues, students and their parents have grown far apart. The more traditionalist of the older generation refer to the modern youth as *ya-sĭmmĭntaññā shi lĭjjotch* ("children of the eighth millennium"); that is, of that corrupt time the Amhara believe will precede the destruction of the world. The latter, in turn, refer to the old-fashioned as ignorant, uncivilized, sometimes even "savage."

Yet, as we have been suggesting, this conflict is by no means total. Amhara adolescents are too deeply attached to many aspects of their traditional culture to engage in wholesale rebellion. Because of strict childhood training they remain basically respectful toward their elders. In addition, they often prefer to champion their own traditions in the spirit of a freshly excited nationalism.

So the orientation of the modern adolescents is a complex one, demanding detailed analysis. In this section we shall discuss data that give some indication of their attitudes regarding religion, science, taste, morality, and politics.

Religion.—With regard to a general commitment to religion Ethiopian students today remain in good part tradition-directed. They mention "religion" more frequently than any other matter except success in school as the question on which they are most in accord with their parents. Religious themes are mentioned more frequently than any other in response to the question, "As a parent, what specific lesson will you try hardest to teach your children?"

Table 8 describes the incidence of student adherence to some of the traditional religious practices in Ethiopia. As might be expected, there is a consistent decrease in conventional religiosity as one moves from the secondary to the college level. Perhaps more significant is the extent to which the modern adolescents do remain faithful to the old religious practices, in view of their considerable alienation from the institution of the Ethiopian Church.[21]

Despite its toleration of a few reforms instigated by Haile Selassie, such as permitting women to sit alongside men in some of the Addis Ababa churches and providing occasional sermons in the vernacular Amharic, the Ethiopian Orthodox Church has not yet begun to adjust to the demands of the modern era. It remains rooted in the experience of an isolated peasant civilization, fixed on the past rather than turned toward the present and future. Thus it has neglected the substantial religious needs of the modern adolescents, who are eager for a fresh treatment of the great matters which religion has traditionally interpreted. But when youth today look for spiritual guidance, they find archaic liturgy; and when they look for spiritual inspiration and social teachings, they are told only to fast and observe the other hallowed customs.

It is this state of things, as well as the natural secularization of life in the cities, that has turned a number of students away from religion altogether. Many more, however, have sought to retain some sort of religious life by making new kinds of adjustment themselves. One alternative has been a privatization of faith, making religion a primarily personal matter no longer dependent on the institution of the church. Another alternative has been to adopt one of the Western forms of Christianity through contact with one of the various missions in Ethiopia.* In recent years a third alternative has fired

---

* In this they have been attracted more by Protestantism than by Catholicism, and for two reasons. The biblical purism and evangelical fervor of the Protestant missions seem best suited to meet their needs for total commitment and reorientation. Catholicism, moreover, is represented to them chiefly by the Jesuit order, whose members have managed two important schools in Ethiopia and many have earned a bad name among students because of their political style.

the imagination of some other students: attempting to reform the Orthodox Church from within. This has been done within the framework of the Orthodox Students Association, which will be discussed further in chapter vii.

Science.—Of all the aspects of Western culture to which they have been exposed, Ethiopia's students have been most receptive to the teachings of nat-

TABLE 8

EXTENT TO WHICH STUDENTS OBSERVE
TRADITIONAL RELIGIOUS PRACTICES

PRACTICE	SECONDARY SCHOOL (per cent)	COLLEGE (per cent)
Follow the fasts:		
All the time	38	16
Most of the time	26	23
Sometimes	27	24
Not at all	9	37
Go to church (mosque):		
More than once a week	9	2
Once a week	59	40
Less than once a week	25	36
Not at all	7	22
Bow to church (mosque):		
Always	28	9
Some/most of the time	50	38
Not at all	22	53
Pray:		
Twice or more daily	64	40
Once a day	22	23
Once or twice a week	6	14
Once or twice a month	5	10
Not at all	3	13
Number	(485)	(195)

ural science. They tend to regard it as the most important single benefit which Ethiopia can gain from Western civilization. After religion, morals, and manners, "science" is the response students give most often to the question: "What specific lesson will you try hardest to teach your children?"

Disagreement on such questions as the nature of solar eclipses, the descent of man, and the etiology of disease is common between the modern adolescents and their own parents. Nevertheless, it would be wrong to assume that the scientific imagination has yet displaced traditional thought patterns in the minds of Ethiopian students, or that scientific beliefs have fully replaced "superstitious" beliefs about the world. Concerning this latter issue we are fortunate to have a substantial study carried out by Dr. Edith Lord during 1956–57—a study of the beliefs of some 1,250 Ethiopian students and teachers.[22]

The subjects of this study were asked to mark as true or false a list of 132 unscientific beliefs commonly held by Ethiopians. These beliefs dealt with nature and devils, health and disease, danger and death. In spite of a measurable trend toward increased disbelief in the unscientific statements as the level of schooling increased, it was found that a significant number of these statements were accepted by a majority both of the post-elementary stu-

TABLE 9

UNSCIENTIFIC BELIEFS ACCEPTED BY SECONDARY STUDENTS

Item No.	Belief	Percentage of Secondary Students Holding the Belief
53	Certain mineral waters can cure stomach trouble by causing a person to vomit worms, sometimes frogs or toads..............	88
35	There are some skillful persons who can summon the devil at will..	87
102	Too much charity leads to madness..........................	74
58	A child will grow better if the nerves are removed from under his back teeth..	68
84	If you go into a room which has been closed for a long time, you will be attacked by Satan................................	57
78	A man who has skill in stopping rains must not eat or drink while he is performing the ceremony to stop rain, or he will be unsuccessful.......	64
	Number...	(451)

dents and of the Ethiopian teachers. Thus, 56 items were believed by half or more of the 451 secondary students in the sample; 34 items by half or more of the 96 teachers; 9 items by half or more of the 61 student nurses and first-aid workers; and 6 of the items by half or more of the 29 college freshmen. Table 9 shows some of those unscientific beliefs most commonly subscribed to by secondary school students. These particular items are of interest for two additional reasons. The first five of them were among the beliefs held by *a majority of the twenty-nine college freshmen.* The first and the last, moreover, are among those items which showed an *increasing* frequency of belief with an increase in education, from the first four primary grades, through the second four grades, to the secondary level.

In my own questionnaire, administered three years after Dr. Lord's research and only to the highest grades of secondary school and college, three questions regarding unscientific beliefs were included. In a pilot study of sixty secondary school seniors and juniors, 42 per cent held the belief that "a person can be made sick by the evil eye of a *budā*," and 33 per cent believed that "too much learning results in madness." To the one question asked of my entire sample: "Do you believe that some learned *dabtarā* can cause rain to fall or stop?," 16 per cent of 500 secondary and 7 per cent of 200 college seniors and juniors said "Yes."

This persistence among the educated youth of traditional beliefs which run counter to the consensus of modern scientists has been attributed by Lord to the inadequacies of the Ethiopian school system. This is as might be expected, inasmuch as most Ethiopian teachers have had relatively little education themselves and the curriculum has necessarily been somewhat improvised and incomplete. Officials of the Ministry of Education have labored to overcome these deficiencies, and certain changes were in fact made in consequence of Lord's study which aim at combating the more dysfunctional of the prevailing superstitions.

It seems likely, however, that certain irrational dispositions are also involved here, dispositions to maintain the unscientific beliefs in spite of improvements in teaching methods and materials. One would predict this on the basis of general sociological understanding of the consequences of rapid social change. The disruption of the traditional belief systems brought about by the sudden dissemination of scientific beliefs inevitably creates insecurity, and a common reaction to such insecurity is to cling with increased tenacity to some of the old-fashioned beliefs which are closely identified with the traditional culture.[23]

One area in which this defensive "revivalism" can be observed in Ethiopia is that of medicine. Many Ethiopians who have received modern secondary education maintain that Western medicine, while useful in many cases, represents only one possible approach to the problem of sickness and health.[24] Thus, fifty-seven per cent of the secondary students questioned asserted that traditional Ethiopian medicines are effective all or most of the time, although such therapies include the eating of rancid butter to cure malaria or drinking holy water to cure serious functional disorders. Dr. Lord herself has reported an episode which throws much light on the psychology of this reaction:

> An Ethiopian colleague, a former teacher, warned me against drinking water in a certain provincial town on penalty of my catching malaria. He was challenged thus: "You are one of the better educated persons in Ethiopia; don't you know the cause of malaria?" He quickly, and eruditely, gave all the known scientific facts about malaria. Then he added, "You people from the United States (and the United Nations) think that this (the scientif-

ically established cycle) is the only way to catch malaria. We Ethiopians know better. We know that one can *also* catch malaria from drinking the water in places where the Anopheles breed."[25]

The ambivalence toward Western science represented by this statement and by the persistence of analogous attitudes among many educated Ethiopians undoubtedly brings the individuals in question a degree of security that would be lost were they to abandon the traditional, unscientific belief system *in toto.* Perhaps a more solid sort of security could be derived from a program of education which not only imparts scientific information and attitudes, but also educates people to adapt themselves to the changes which the introduction of science involves.

Taste.—In matters of taste, Ethiopia's modern adolescents range from extreme traditionalism to extreme Westernism, with most of them preferring both traditional and European or American patterns in varying proportions.

Of food the students tend to prefer the traditional varieties, most popular of which are *doro waṭ* and *ǐnjarā.* Among Western foods they are fondest of pastries and Italian *pasta.* On the other hand, they are more inclined toward Western beverages than Ethiopian ones. The most popular Western beverages are, for the secondary students, soft drinks, and for the college students, beer; among Ethiopian drinks they prefer *ṭallā* first and milk second.

With regard to their manner of eating, the students' taste is traditional in that most prefer to eat nowhere but within the home, and to eat with their hands rather than use silverware; but it is Westernized in that most prefer eating at their own individual places rather than all together with others out of a common *ǐnjarā* basket. Opinion is most divided on the matter of exchanging *gurshā,* a morsel of food which one places in another's mouth. The slight majority who reject this old custom do so because they find it "noisy," "childish," "unsanitary," or simply "out of fashion"; while those who still enjoy it do so chiefly because it "expresses affection."

On questions of dress it should be noted that traditionally the Amhara have sentimentalized their going barefoot as well as their national costume. But because of the practical advantages of wearing tailored clothes at work and using shoes, and perhaps still more because of their high prestige in the modernizing sector, virtually all of the students prefer the European fashion in these matters. On the other hand, with respect to women's wear and the, sort of dress to be worn on holidays, the great majority opt the Ethiopian *shammā.*

In their aesthetic interests the students' taste varies considerably according to the medium. With regard to poetry and music, Ethiopian forms are preferred to Western ones, while Western forms of painting and dance are more popular with them than Ethiopian. Poetry stands as the most appreciated of all traditional forms of expression, and nearly two-thirds of the secondary and half the college students state that they compose Amharic verse themselves, on occasions ranging from public celebrations to private moments of great joy or sorrow. This is as might be expected in view of the tremendous importance of poetry in traditional Amhara culture (see chapters vi and vii). Painting, on the other hand, has played a rather inconspicuous part in Abyssinia. (Its genuine achievement in the high culture, the often remarkable Ethiopian miniatures, is frequently repudiated by modernizing Ethiopians for being too "backward.") Those students who do prefer Ethiopian-style paintings explain their preference on the grounds that they find them more intelligible and closer to Ethiopian life, and stress their value as reminders of Ethiopia's past.[26] The majority who prefer European-style paintings offer primarily mechanical reasons; they find them more "efficient," "systematic," and "accurate"—more "up-to-date."

In response to a question on their favorite type of foreign music, the students gave a wide variety of answers, ranging from "Oriental" and "religious" to "Rose, Rose, I Love You" and "Mozart." By far the most frequently mentioned musical preference was "classical" (20 per cent). This was followed by approximately equal percentages of preference for American popular songs; jazz and swing; rock 'n' roll; and Sudanese music. Of foreign dances, the most popular are the waltz and the tango (17 per cent each), followed at some distance by rock 'n roll, cha cha cha, and jitterbug. In their movie preferences, finally, historical (17 per cent) and educational (12 per cent) films are the favorites, followed by war, detective, and adventure films.

One other area of consumption should be discussed in this context: the use of cigarettes. To the tradition-minded Amhara smoking symbolizes all that is objectionable in Western culture, while to some of the modern adolescents it symbolizes the excitement and "life" of modernity. The number of these latter is not really very high, at least not among those still in school; but it is noteworthy that emphatic rejection of smoking by most of the students is based primarily on the rationalistic arguments that it is injurious to health and wastes money, rather than on the traditional argument that it is sinful and counter to Christian custom. The most violent reactions of any, however, were aroused by the question: "How do you feel about women smoking?" In the secondary school sample to which this question was posed, disapproval was practically unanimous, and the comments included "makes me ashamed," "it is scaring," "I could choke her to death," and "worse than hell itself."

A few minor differences in taste appear in connection with differences in sex and school attended. The female students in our secondary school sample show a greater partiality to native foods than do the males, and, on the other hand, greater interest in Western music and dance. Peculiarities in the subcultures of different schools account for a few other minor variations. Thus, for example, preference for Scottish dance is expressed chiefly among students of a school run by a British staff; the only kind of foreign music preferred by students of the Theological School is Sudanese music, that is, the kind most similar to Ethiopian music; and the University College, most urbane of the Ethiopian schools, is the only one where a majority of respondents indicated that they enjoy smoking.

Of all the differences, the most conspicuous is that between the secondary

TABLE 10

AESTHETIC PREFERENCES OF STUDENTS

	PERCENTAGE OF STUDENTS WHO			
AREA OF CONSUMPTION	Prefer "Traditional" or "Ethiopian" Forms	Prefer "European" or "Foreign" Forms	Indicate No Preference	NUMBER
Dress for women....	85	15	0	(700)
Food..............	80	16	4	(700)
Cigarettes*........	71	10	19	(700)
Dress on holidays....	70	26	4	(700)
Poetry............	67	26	7	(700)
Music.............	62	35	3	(700)
Manner of eating†...	40	58	2	(700)
Dance.............	38	56	6	(700)
Drink.............	24	56	20	(700)
Painting..........	23	67	10	(700)

* "Like to smoke" versus "do not like to smoke."

† Combines responses on "gurshā" and eating in common or at individual places, which were practically identical.

school students and the college students. For in each of the areas discussed above in which traditional or Ethiopian patterns were set alongside European or foreign patterns, *the move from the secondary level to college level was accompanied by a decrease in preference for traditional patterns.*

If now we overlook these differences and calculate the total response, we obtain the profile shown in Table 10, which provides some idea of the range of variation in the students' taste with regard to items from Ethiopian and foreign cultures.

Morals.—The moral values reinforced during traditional Amhara adolescence are by no means rejected during modern Ethiopian adolescence, but their significance is somewhat attenuated due to the new conditions of life in the government schools. The weakening of family controls by the new school environment has slightly reduced the importance of loyalty to kin in the students' scheme of things, and has significantly reduced the moral authority of religious customs. A third sphere of norms—respect and obedience toward elders and persons of authority—is maintained by the hierarchical school system, officially headed by the Emperor himself. However, the ambiguous status of foreign teachers and their frequent inability or unwillingness to play the traditional authoritarian role tends to weaken this, for the possibility of informal, even joking, relations with foreign teachers gives Amhara students their first taste of a more relaxed relation to authority figures. (Unprepared by any other experience for such a relationship, their reaction tends to be one of exploiting the permissive teacher as much as possible while at the same time losing respect for him.)

Finally, the expectation of physical stamina and aggressiveness in the Amhara *goramsā* is carried over into the school setting but with definite modification. It prevails in the feeling that one must not tolerate insults or be cowardly. It also persists in altered form in the new pattern of athletic activities instituted by the schools. On the other hand, the greater camaraderie expected among schoolmates means that aggression must also be carefully controlled. An indication of the psychological difficulties to which the crowded yet sociable conditions of school life have given rise appears in response to the question: "What is the worst thing that could justifiably be said against you?" The most frequent sort of answer to this question relates to unchecked aggression: "Quick to anger," "quarrelsome," "ill tempered."

Of the new moral values inculcated by the school system, some of the main ones appear to be self-development via education; honesty; sportsmanship; and social responsibility.

Ethiopians often speak of the "value" (*t̆iqem*) of education, meaning thereby the path to a well-paying job and a higher standard of living. But one would be mistaken to suppose that this explanation exhausts the meaning that education has for the modern adolescents. The freeing of their imagination and the exercise of previously unknown intellectual capacities prove themselves thrilling experiences for each new class of students. And their most preferred pastime is "reading," their most popular films are educational ones. A number of students spontaneously declared, when asked about the real reason they go to school, "to learn about the world" and "to learn about humanity."

In the traditional culture of Abyssinia, learning was highly valued, to be sure. But its task was to produce a class of literati capable of transmitting the hallowed beliefs and symbols. Education for the sake of inquiry as such or for personal development was never permitted in its program. If the value of this new sort of education exists but dimly in the minds of the older students, that is largely because the school system has made grades and diplomas the end of scholastic activity.

The fact that the value of truth is to some extent institutionalized in the schools—at least in the demand for correct answers to examination questions —gives honesty a novel importance for the modern adolescents. It does in fact appear that "honesty" is the most highly valued of the six character traits presented in the questionnaire. (See Table 11.) Numerous teachers, however,

TABLE 11

QUALITIES PREFERRED BY STUDENTS AS
REPRESENTING THE BEST KINDS OF
CHARACTER

	PER CENT CHECKING QUALITY AS EITHER FIRST OR SECOND CHOICE		
QUALITY	Secondary School		College Males
	Males	Females	
Honest............	65	73	86
Polite.............	27	30	18
Smiling, sociable.....	26	43	28
Patriotic...........	22	10	19
Kind, generous......	21	10	12
Humble, modest.....	10	15	21
Number........	(390)	(38)	(190)

report that the students tend to prevaricate on every convenient occasion. This tendency is the product of a tradition in which the culture hero is not George Washington, who "could not tell a lie," but Alaqā Gabra Hānnā, master of deceit, and of a life outside the classroom in which equivocation and deception are the rule. The effort of Ethiopian students to shake the legacy of wax and gold and incorporate the more austere ideal of truth for truth's sake is fraught with pathos. Some of them have frankly conceded that the task belongs to another generation, by naming "honesty" as the thing they want their children most to have that they did not have.

Another ideal which the Ethiopian students have adopted—slowly, but with growing success—is that of sportsmanship or fair play. In Amhara culture the goal, not the manner of fighting, is what is important. The government school system, however, has taught students to play fairly in accord with fixed rules and to respect their opponents. Until a few years ago, the imperfect acceptance of these norms was shown by the frequent fights between opposing school teams following soccer and basketball games. But gradually a new tradition of athletic activity has been building up in the schools, and with it the related norms have started to gain greater acceptance.

Still another value that the school experience has promoted is that of social responsibility. Most students are very grateful to the government for having provided them with schooling and related benefits, and they feel a keen obligation to show their gratitude by serving their country. They have also become conscious of the great needs of their people for economic and social development. In Amhara society, service was expected in behalf of the family and, except for mass levies in time of warfare, usually stopped there. The modern adolescents are still mindful of their obligations to their parents and siblings, but have now included broader ideals of social service in their moral orientation. When asked what they expect to bring most satisfaction in their lives, the students named "improvement of local community" more often than any other category except "career or occupation." (See Table 4.) When asked what they would do with a million dollars, more than a third answered in terms of purely social enterprises, such as building schools and hospitals, helping the poor and orphaned; and many others indicated private enterprises with specifically social purposes, such as improving agriculture and building factories to provide employment.

It is difficult to determine how deeply the value of social responsibility has been internalized. In their public declarations, at any rate, the students wax eloquent in propounding ideals of good citizenship. They urge themselves to prepare for introducing modern ways to the uneducated; to return to the villages, integrate themselves with the old society, and lead them gently to better ways; to fight discrimination on the basis of race, religion, and social class; to solve the problem of corruption and bribery in the government; and to promote national solidarity.

Politics.—The Amhara adolescent has little occasion to develop specifically political attitudes, since his customary political world has been coterminous with subordination to legitimate local and national authorities, and defense of his country against invaders. Unless he was the son of a nobleman involved in struggles for power, there have rarely been any political issues to engage his attention.

A host of issues, domestic and international, have by contrast been thrust upon the modern adolescent. Yet in comparison with students from the other countries of Africa and the Middle East, his political orientation is relatively undeveloped. Ethiopian students at regional or international gatherings of students have in the past tended to feel somewhat out of place, for the political wit and activism displayed by students from other countries has embarrassed their cautious dispositions.

There are three reasons for this relative lack of politicization of the Ethiopian students. One is that, having maintained her ancient independence throughout the "scramble for Africa," Ethiopia entered the twentieth century as an independent nation; and five years of Italian rule were not sufficient to shake her spirit. Ethiopian students have thus not had to participate in the anti-imperialist movement, the great school for political activism in the colonial areas.

A second factor is the deeply rooted habit of total subordination to any legitimate authority. Because of this orientation there is a persisting disposition to relegate concern for all political questions to the highest authorities. Nearly two-thirds of the secondary students and a third of the college students maintain that one should always obey the order of a superior, arguing that "obedience is a virtue," "things would not go right otherwise," and "the Bible says so."

The third reason for the almost apolitical posture of Ethiopian students has been the absence of opportunities for political expression in their country. African students from British colonies have in the past been surprised to find that their colonial situation admitted far more freedom of speech and press than Ethiopia. Teachers are expected to keep anything remotely connected with Ethiopian politics out of the classroom, and the editors are expected to keep them out of the newspapers. Nor have the students been permitted to form any kind of politically relevant associations. Even casual discussion of domestic political problems among friends has been curtailed because of the all-pervading fear of government informers.

All this has not prevented Ethiopian students from being affected to a moderate degree by the libertarian and egalitarian ideals of the West. The teaching of European history in secondary school, evaluation of students' performance without respect to class or tribal affiliation, and the exercise of electing student officers in the colleges have acted to leaven the political imagination of the students. Many of them thus ventured a degree of political criticism in their anonymous questionnaires. Forty-three per cent indicated disapproval of the existing differences between "big men" and the common people. Thirty-nine per cent were critical of the degree of control exerted by the government, of which group two-thirds felt that governmental controls are too strict (e.g., not permitting free expression), and one-third felt they were not strict enough (e.g., with respect to corruption and provincial administration).

The abortive coup d'état of December, 1960, jarred the Addis Ababa college students into an unprecedented state of political activity.[27] In response to the rebel leaders' appeal for a show of public support, hundreds of students staged a demonstration on behalf of the coup. Except for occasional school strikes in the past, this was the first time that Ethiopian students had ever taken part in any sort of organized political process. The novelty of the experience was reflected in the confusion on many faces as they marched through the streets of the capital, chanting a militant refrain and carrying placards that celebrated "Liberty, Equality, Fraternity" and "Our Country's Peaceful Change." For some, the experience was quite unreal; it was as though they were behaving thus because that is how one is supposed to behave at a time of revolution. Not a few of the participants actually regretted the coup but went along because, as one put it: "The coup has taken place; my friends are for it; so what is one to do?"

Even so, there was a moment of genuine political engagement for all when the student demonstrators proceeded to the army headquarters with the vain plea to forestall civil violence and join the new regime installed by the Imperial Bodyguard. Though they were turned away by bayonets, that moment gave the students the intoxicating taste of direct political expression. Subsequently, the army's abrupt suppression of the rebels left these students in an awkward position. All who took part in the demonstration were required to write letters of apology to the Emperor as a condition of being readmitted to study. They did so, and returned to school; but they have never been the same again. Though on the surface they appear to have reverted to the apolitical, passive orientation of the pre-coup days, occasional oratorical contests and poetry readings have given expression to a sharpened criticism of the government and greater restlessness in the student body.

Because of the relative absence of information and discussion pertaining to domestic political questions heretofore, Ethiopian students have tended to have slightly more knowledge and interest regarding international politics. On the general question of war and peace they seem to be influenced by the high value given to warfare in traditional Ethiopia. As many as forty per cent of all the students consider war "sometimes a good thing." This sentiment is somewhat stronger among the secondary school students than among the college students, but even the latter show a higher percentage of choice for this response than any of the national groups in the Gillespie-Allport study—except perhaps Egypt. (See Table 12.)

In their attitudes toward the "big three" world powers, the Ethiopian students seem to be most favorably disposed toward the United States, secondly toward the Soviet Union, and thirdly toward Great Britain. (See Table 13.) The United States is liked because it "helps other countries," has a high standard of living, and is "advanced in civilization"; while it is disliked because of its color discrimination and its being "aggressive," "rude," "boastful," and "loud-mouthed." England is liked because it is "highly civilized" and has a "good form of government"; but it is disesteemed because of its waning power, on the one hand, and its "cunning" and "treachery," and being imperialist, on the other. Russia is admired because of its power, its achievements in science, and its rapid attainment of "civilization." It is disliked, on the other hand, for being "aggressive" and "fostering war," and because of its "bad form of government" and its "atheism."

TABLE 12

ATTITUDES OF STUDENTS FROM ETHIOPIA AND SEVEN OTHER COUNTRIES TOWARD WAR*

			War Is			
Country	Institution	Sex	Needless and Preventable (per cent)	A Necessary Evil (per cent)	Sometimes a Good Thing (per cent)	Number
Ethiopia.....	Secondary schools.........	M	46	11	43	(392)
	Secondary schools.........	F	46	18	36	(39)
	Colleges.................	M	45	20	35	(199)
Egypt.......	Higher Training College....	M	31	34	34	(29)
	Women Teachers' Institute.	F	39	35	26	(31)
France.......	University of Bordeaux....	M	65	26	9	(105)
		F	74	26	0	(23)
Italy.........	Catholic University of the Sacred Heart...........	M	61	26	13	(39)
		F	46	44	10	(37)
Japan........	Secondary school and colleges, Kyoto...........	M	72	16	8	(95)
		F	58	37	4	(119)
Mexico.......	National University of Mexico...................	M	51	23	26	(106)
		F	58	24	18	(103)
New Zealand.	Victoria University College.	M	72	16	12	(74)
		F	72	12	16	(51)
United States.	Miami University.........	M	69	22	9	(112)
		F	64	33	3	(91)

* The Japanese data appear in Stoetzel, *op. cit.*, p. 306.
For the data on the other countries I am greatly indebted to a personal communication from Professor James Gillespie.

In these attitudes one may note the persistence of such traditional valuations as the esteem for power, the stress on religion, and the concern about polite and dignified behavior, alongside such modernist valuations as the esteem for civilization (*selṭāné*) and science. With regard to the emerging world power of Africa, however, the students have been rapidly coming to reject the traditional Abyssinian viewpoint, which looks with disdain upon the Negroid peoples of Africa as racially and culturally inferior.

As recently as a decade ago, a group of Ethiopian college students responded with ridicule and evident disdain to an illustrated ethnographic account of some East African tribes. But in the late 1950's, due to the growing

TABLE 13

ATTITUDES OF ETHIOPIAN STUDENTS
TOWARD THE "BIG THREE" POWERS

Classification of Comments	England (per cent)	U.S.A. (per cent)	U.S.S.R. (per cent)
Positive......	32	59	47
Negative.....	37	19	26
Neutral.......	11	5	6
No answer....	20	17	21
Number..	(640)	(700)	(662)

prominence of the African independence movement and the decision of the Ethiopian government to take more interest in African affairs, the pan-African sentiment began to invade the heretofore aloof highland plateau of Ethiopia. The attendance in Ethiopian colleges of students from other African countries and the growing number of pan-African meetings in Addis Ababa have promoted this trend. Consequently a number of Ethiopian students now follow with growing interest the developments in other African countries, and not a few indicated that their identification with Africa as a whole was stronger than their identification with Ethiopia. All but 8 per cent of the 700 students questioned: "What do you think about Africa?" had some response that showed concern, whether sympathy for African independence and getting rid of the Europeans (28 per cent), or sensitivity about Africa's "undeveloped" and "uncivilized" state and its need to work hard (33 per cent), or pride and confidence in Africa's resources and future (24 per cent).

So deeply rooted a sentiment as prejudice against Negroid Africans cannot quickly be willed away. It does seem, however, that the emergence of the new African nations is proving to be an effective agency for reducing such prejudices among the students. The broader political identity afforded by pan-Africanism may in turn be promoting a more genuine national feeling among the younger educated Ethiopians, a feeling of solidarity that begins to encompass all the ethnic groups in their land.

Still another sphere in which the Ethiopian students have had some room for the development of political values has been the study of history. The students were therefore asked to name the persons in Ethiopian and in world history whom they most liked and disliked, and to explain why.

The three most liked figures in Ethiopian history were Haile Selassie, mentioned by 36 per cent of the respondents; Tēwodros (30 per cent); and Menelik (16 per cent). Named much less frequently were Yohānnes (mostly by Tigre students); military heroes of Menelik's day, and of the resistance during the Italian occupation; and church figures, especially Abuna Peṭros (the great Orthodox martyr of the occupation).

The reasons given for naming Haile Selassie include the wide variety of respects for which his reign has been praised. He is liked for uniting Ethiopia, supporting education, fighting for the country's freedom, introducing modern civilization, and generally "helping the country." The reasons given extend to expressions of very personal attachment, such as "he gives me education," "he supplies everything," and "he is my guardian."

The reasons given for liking Tēwodros or Menelik best are more circumscribed, and they are balanced by a number of other responses in which these two emperors are named as the most *disliked* persons in Ethiopian history (Tēwodros, 7 per cent; Menelik, 4 per cent). Tēwodros is liked chiefly because of his bravery and his attempt to unite the nation, while he is disliked because of his cruelty. Menelik is liked chiefly because of his defense of the country at Adowa and his efforts to modernize Ethiopia and introduce education; and he is disliked for having sold parts of the country to Europeans. Yohānnes is mentioned about the same number of times in both categories (2 per cent): positively, for his courage in battle and his Christian zeal and, negatively, for his intolerance in persecuting non-Christians.

Lĭjj Iyāsu (11 per cent) and Ahmad Grāñ (8 per cent) are the most disliked figures in Ethiopian history. They are associated with specific offenses: Iyāsu with being an "incompetent ruler," "encouraging Islam," and "chasing after women," and Grāñ with burning churches and massacring Christians. Three other persons in this category are Sultan Ibrahim (5 per cent), for selling the port of Assab; Dajāzmātch Haile Selassie Gugsa (4 per cent), for fighting on the side of the Italians in 1935; and Yodit (2 per cent), the legendary queen who is said to have sacked Aksum in the tenth century.

FIG. 20.—*Traditional (church) school: student huts*

FIG. 21.—*Traditional school: learning to read*

FIG. 22.—*Traditional school: learning zēmā from master*

FIG. 23.—*Clergy and government school students observing national holiday*

FIG. 24.—*Inside a secondary school library*

As many as 44 per cent of the students failed to name anyone they disliked in Ethiopian history. This may be attributed in part to their meager knowledge of Ethiopian history, perhaps still more to their fear of expressing themselves honestly on such a point even in an anonymous questionnaire. But doubtless another reason was that presented by the 2 per cent of the students who wrote: "[I dislike] none; all did good."

If the responses on Ethiopian history are analyzed with respect to the qualities or achievements of the men concerned, we find that military virtue —expressed as "brave," "defeated many enemies," or "fought for Ethiopia"— is mentioned far more often than any other (27 per cent). In second place are actions related to the modernization of Ethiopia, and the third most frequent category is that of unifying the nation. The most frequently mentioned negative categories were anti-Christian actions (burning churches, converting to Islam), cruelty, treason, and selling Ethiopian territory.

A different pattern of response is apparent in the comments on world historical personages. The interest in military prowess is still there, but not as prominent (19 per cent). It appears chiefly in the preference for Napoleon and, occasionally, for Alexander the Great. Themes of national unification and modernization occur very rarely. It is the general category of humanitarian qualities and achievements that dominates these responses (40 per cent), expressed variously as "freeing the slaves," "promoting equality," "working for peace," showing kindness or generosity, possessing wisdom or creative genius. Thus it is that Abraham Lincoln stands out as the most admired figure in world history for the Ethiopian students (22 per cent), and that following him, Napoleon, and Peter the Great, Mahatma Gandhi stands in fourth place.

Responses concerning the most disliked figure in world history are consistent with this tendency to transcend the sentiment of militant nationalism. The main charges against the villains of world history have to do with cruelty, slaughter, provocation of war (including, of course, the attack on Ethiopia), and despotism, while vices related to betraying one's nation are scarcely mentioned. The names which dominate these replies are Hitler (22 per cent), Mussolini (21 per cent), Nero (8 per cent), and Stalin (2 per cent). It appears, then, that the study of world history may have the effect of strengthening the humanitarian side of the students' political orientation by exposing them to a different set of ideals and models.

THE CHANGING CONTEXT OF MODERN ADOLESCENCE

The pattern of adolescence described in this section came quickly into being and has already undergone some substantial changes. It is, in effect, the pattern of the 1950's. The educational system before and just after the occupation was, structurally, an extension of the old pattern of schooling sons of noblemen and outstanding commoners in the vicinity of the royal court. But with the importation of hundreds of foreign teachers, the establishment of an extensive system of secondary schools and colleges, and the provision of economic support for thousands of post-elementary students, a real structural change came about. Although the school system remained completely subordinate to the throne, it introduced a number of processes that had a dynamic of their own.

As we have seen, these new socialization processes have subjected the modern adolescents to many sorts of conflict and strain. They have been placed in conflict with their parents, and hence within themselves, on the basic issues of work and, particularly, marriage. They have been subjected to the simultaneous appeal of traditional and modern patterns in virtually all aspects of culture. They have been forced to make choices in numerous areas, while their traditional counterparts have customarily been prevented from making any kind of choice at all.

It might seem that such a situation would breed a troubled generation, distraught and disoriented, knowing what we do about the psychological hazards of rapid culture change. And indeed, among the modern adolescents of the fifties, one might find classical cases of anomie and identity diffusion, boys who confess, "Nothing seems worthwhile to me . . . I am confused, being brought up as I was on the traditional beliefs without questioning and then suddenly being forced to ask questions," or, "The problem of choosing the work I should go into is my only real problem right now, but because of it I find it hard to make decisions about anything. If this suffering is the price of freedom, I am not sure it is worth the price."

Such cases, however, were the exception, not the rule. Most of the students were working hard to get ahead in the world or enjoying their newly acquired freedom and camaraderie. Almost all our respondents had ready answers concerning the sort of work they want to go into, and what they would do if they could have any wish granted. Comparing themselves with their elders, they presented a positive self-image. They regarded themselves as more "civilized," "well built," and "generous" than their parents' generation, albeit somewhat lazier and less polite; and in comparison with Ethiopians a decade older, saw themselves as "better educated," "more clever," "more adventurous," and better able to "enjoy life." Nearly all of them (92 per cent) said that they felt either "enthusiastic" or "hopeful" about their personal future. So one could characterize the Ethiopian post-elementary students of the fifties as relatively buoyant, clear-headed, self-confident, and enjoying their situation of culture contact and change far more than suffering it. How may this be explained?

One great source of their strength was a sense of dependence on the Emperor. As founder of the Ethiopian school system, Haile Selassie has appeared to the students as the source of their new goods; of their learning, health, and well-being. Because of a feeling that "he supplies everything" and "he is my guardian," students of all grades have been among the most sincere and enthusiastic supporters of Haile Selassie. So their adoption of Western patterns has from the outset been legitimated by the highest traditional authority, and the harshness of the culture clash has been softened by the symbolization of both tradition and modernity in the Imperial Person. Here the traditional pattern of "functional deviance" re-asserts itself. The adolescent rebels against the traditional demands of his parents, but expends that deviant energy on behalf of legitimate symbols of the national society.

Related to this was a strong sense of national purposiveness. *Agarēnennā negusēn tammrē iredālhu* ("Having studied, I will serve my country and my king")—this was the motto of most Ethiopian students in the forties and fifties. The conspicuous needs of their country provided clear goals in terms of which students felt they were preparing themselves.

Still another motive force was the need for personal justification. The many students who in a sense deserted their home villages or families in order to spend years in school carried with them an ambition eventually to show the folks back home that they were right after all. This involved the conviction that going to school was the right, at times the righteous, thing: a blind faith that simply by continuing along the road of education they would make good in the world and return home some day as a sort of hero. Here, too, is an echo of the old deviant pattern: the renegade returning home, after many years, as a successful churchman or warlord.

The economic situation, finally, was encouraging for students. It seemed for many years that advanced training, including study abroad, would be available for whoever qualified, and that the demand for educated personnel was so great that the job opportunities for students would be endless.

By 1961, however, all these sources of adolescent morale—royal legitimation, national purpose, personal justification, and economic opportunity—had been to some extent undercut. Some of the changing circumstances have already been referred to. The effect of the rebellion of December, 1960, and its aftermath was to weaken the tie between Haile Selassie and the post-elementary students. With his moral authority somewhat undermined, the students could no longer use him to symbolize a conflict-free transition to modernity. Nor could they any longer count on him to "supply everything" indefinitely: in the summer of 1962 the Emperor announced the immediate suspension of room and board benefits for the students of the University College.

The students' outlook has further been rendered less sanguine by the confusion attending the political crisis of the sixties. They no longer feel the keen sense of national purpose, to serve "country and king." Their ideals in this regard were already weakening before the rebellion by virtue of increased awareness of the political realities in the Ethiopian government. They had also begun to doubt the transcendent efficacy of the educational process itself after observing the behavior of those educated Ethiopians who went before them and inevitably became their ideals. The violation of various traditional and modern norms by the latter, and their evident demoralization, raised many questions in the minds of the students.

Finally, the students were made more anxious by a general constricting of opportunity. Increased numbers in the school system meant a steady intensification of the competition to gain and hold on to a place in secondary school and college, particularly since 1959. The rapid filling of jobs by the educated youth and steadily growing numbers of unemployed youth began to create anxieties about finding work in the future.

From the viewpoint of the modern adolescents, then, a very supportive and stimulating environment in the fifties has changed to a somewhat threatening and confused environment in the sixties. It is in this decade that Ethiopia's leaders of the future, that tiny fraction of one per cent of the population who reach secondary school, are coming to experience adolescence as a real normative crisis. At a time when, in the highly modernized society of the United States, observers like Friedenberg charge that the adolescent condition is becoming obsolete—that scope is no longer afforded the young person for exploration and discovery of an authentic self[28]—in the transitional state of Ethiopia this condition is being thrust on the youth. The decisions they make now, the identities they forge, will largely determine the extent to which reason and creativity will have a place in Ethiopia's future.

The effort of the Ethiopian government to provide a modern education for some of Ethiopia's adolescents illustrates a principle discussed in another context by Karl Mannheim, namely, the characterization of youth as a latent sociological resource which must be mobilized when any social system seeks to change itself. It is a resource analogous to the latent energy reserves which are available to biological organisms when they must make a fresh adjustment to their environment.[29] Thus far the effort to mobilize the resources of Ethiopia's youth in behalf of modernization has proceeded chiefly through a pattern of increased *differentiation:* establishing a structure of secondary socialization separate from that of the traditional structures and thereby transmitting new beliefs, skills, and values to the youth. As yet, relatively little has been done with respect to the problems of devising modes of *integration* commensurate with these new differentiated patterns. The analyses of this chapter suggest the presence of what might be called "integration gaps" on at least three levels. On the level of the individual personality, there is the problem of synthesizing the various aspects of traditional and modern culture which have been transmitted to Ethiopian adolescents through diverse sources. Inasmuch as the external supports which cushioned these conflicts in the fifties are no longer so secure, the adolescent individual has been thrown more on his own. He can only be helped to work through these conflicts by a transformed educational program, one which educates for self-education and seeks to enlighten students concerning the complex realities of economic development and culture change. On the level of relating youth to a modernizing occupational system, there is the problem of guiding young people into and through the relevant educational programs and helping them to find appropriate work roles once trained. On the level of planning for the whole society there is the additional problem of relating the number of individuals being trained in various fields at any period to the priority requirements of a national development program.

This last issue raises questions which for the most part lie outside the scope of this book. Yet there is one point concerning the orientation of Ethiopian students which is of immediate relevance: the disjunction between the aspiration of modern-educated Ethiopians to live in Addis Ababa and work in a government office, and the nation's needs for trained workers in more directly productive fields and for those who will work in the provinces. For at the same time that Ethiopia's youth are being trained in modern skills, they are being exposed to modern pleasures; and these—the enjoyment of modern amusements, the company of other educated people, and the excitement of proximity to centers of national power and international commerce—are concentrated in Addis Ababa. At the same time that they are being educated with modern beliefs, they are being primed for a new kind of social mobility; and this channel is concentrated in the governmental bureaucracy—the nesting ground of Ethiopia's new elites. Conflict between these new interests and the nation's deepest needs, endemic in all transitional societies, poses an integrative challenge of the highest order.

5

ThE OLD AND NEW ELITES

The disjunction between traditional and modernizing sectors that characterizes the socialization of adolescents informs most aspects of contemporary
Ethiopian society. A modern institution of Western inspiration has nearly
everywhere been superimposed upon traditional forms, and as yet there has
been relatively little interaction between the two.

In the economy, subsistence production according to traditional techniques
prevails throughout all Amhara areas. Production for national and international markets is funneled through separate channels: coffee lands and a
few tobacco farms in the southern provinces, specialized commerce in a
dozen or so provincial centers, and a small number of factories dependent
mainly on non-Ethiopian management and, frequently, capital. In the legal
realm varied forms of customary law remain authoritative for much provincial litigation, while civil, criminal, and maritime codes based on French
and Swiss ideals have been enacted as the law of the nation. The governmental structure is similarly bifurcated, between local authorities who govern
in the traditional manner, albeit with reduced powers, and a ministerial
system and parliament based on European models. In the case of religious
institutions there remains a wide gulf between the orientation of the Orthodox churches and that of such Western-inspired formations as the Theological
College and the Orthodox Students Association.

This sociological dualism comes to a head in the system of social stratification. Since the mechanism of stratification ranks all the members of a society according to the value placed on their qualities and performances by that society, the stratification system of a society is its most inclusive framework of social order. Here too, however, conflicting value orientations are embodied in more or less distinct status hierarchies, and it is no longer possible to find status evaluations which are shared throughout the society. It is in the composition and relations of the elites that the value conflicts in Ethiopia today are most explicit, and in their mutual adjustments that the movement toward new forms of integration is most likely to be manifest.

The traditional infrastructure of Abyssinian society was itself relatively stratified. Highest in status were the landowning peasants, the older and wealthier of whom merged imperceptibly into the lower stratum of the nobility. Next in order were the peasants of various situations who did not own land: sons waiting to inherit land from their parents, tenants paying rents in kind to some landlord, and agricultural laborers attached as retainers on the estates of wealthy peasants, nobles, or churches. Below them were the statuses of Abyssinians who led a more mobile sort of existence, such as weavers, minstrels, common soldiers, and beggars.

The trading class was broadly divided into two ranks, that of the merchant (*naggādē*) whose caravans brought goods from afar, and that of the small-scale peddler (*shaqātch*). The wealthier Abyssinian merchant was accorded very high status, comparable at times to that of the nobility. If an Arab, Armenian, or Muslim Abyssinian, however, his status would be tainted by that disesteem felt for all outside the ethnic pale. The peddlers as a class were in a low status, comparable to that of the weavers and minstrels. Below these were metalsmiths, potters, and tanners, who were sometimes low caste Abyssinian artisans, sometimes Falasha or Gurage tribesmen. Lowest in status were the slaves, captured in wars or raiding expeditions from the Negroid tribes in the west (Shanqalla) and north (Baria and Kunama), and from the Kaffa and other Cushitic groups in the south. Freed for a generation now, such people still work as household servants and retainers, or as laborers in the towns.

Such were the classes which performed the drudgery. They produced sufficient surplus to sustain a fairly extensive, if not opulent, leisure class, which ministered to the more general political and cultural needs of the society. The feudal nobility and the clergy represented the paramount values of warfare and religion and shared responsibility for the maintenance of legal order. Together with the emperor, to whom they were normally subordinate, they commanded the resources and respect of the Abyssinian people and set standards for their behavior.

During the reign of Haile Selassie, the infrastructure of Ethiopian society has become more differentiated. A large standing army, an air force, and a small navy have been recruited and trained by foreign military missions. The modernization of transport and communication has produced a sizable class of semiskilled operatives—truck drivers, airline employees, telephone operators, typesetters, etc. The expansion of government has produced a legion of clerks. In the towns tertiary occupational roles, like salesmen and barbers, have come into being, and the establishment of factories has engendered a small industrial labor force.

All such people tend to differ from the traditional lower classes in their relative enthusiasm for *seltānē* ("civilization"). Still more enthusiastic are those who have had more intimate and prolonged exposure to the fruits of *seltānē:* domestic servants in *faranj* homes; students of the secondary schools and colleges; Imperial Bodyguard troops who served in the Korean campaign and recently in the Congo; and highland Eritreans, whose experience under sixty years of Italian colonial administration has rendered them far more modernized than people of other provinces.

Similarly, the reign of Haile Selassie has witnessed the emergence of new elite groups. A "new nobility" of government officials and urban plutocrats has taken place beside the old. In addition, a nascent intelligentsia has attained a precarious high status, resting mostly on the esteem of students, some military officers, and resident Westerners. The integrative dilemma of Ethiopia today has more to do with conflicts among and within its various elites than with tribal enmities or masses in revolt.*

Hovering over these four groups, kindred with each but superior to all, has been the personality of the present emperor. Indeed, the history of Ethiopia in the last four decades has for the most part been the story of Haile Selassie's efforts to direct and control the destinies of the old and new elites. The considerable success with which he has done this is a tribute, not only to his own remarkable manipulative skills, but also to the majesty of the office which he possesses. The position of *negusa nagast* has traditionally monopolized the highest reaches of the Abyssinian system of social stratification; constituting, as it were, an elite of One.

THE TRADITIONAL ORDER

The Lofty Throne

The emperor comprises an elite in the original sense of the word, for to the Ethiopians he is Elect of God (*seyuma egziābhēr*) according to the

---

* Although, as was suggested earlier, tribal and religious differences *may* generate new integrative crises in the future.

conventional Ge'ez honorific. Sanctity of the imperial office is an antique theme, deriving apparently from pagan ideas of divine kingship which were transplanted from South Arabia in the first millennium B.C. along with other aspects of Sabaean culture.[1] But the working ideology which has upheld this conception during the period of Amhara hegemony draws on Semitic motifs of later origin, motifs which received their classic formulation in the fourteenth century national epic, *Kebra Nagast* (*The Glory of Kings*).

The effect of the *Kebra Nagast* is to make the Ethiopian emperor both physical descendant and spiritual successor to the kings of Israel. The genealogical tie is argued by the legendary union of the Queen of Sheba and King Solomon, whose offspring, Menelik I, is held to have fathered the line of royalty which allegedly ruled at Aksum and was restored in the thirteenth century. The transfer of religious mission is shown both in a prophetic dream attributed to Solomon, in which God's favor passes from Israel to Ethiopia, and in the story of Menelik's theft from Jerusalem of the most sacred symbol of the Judaic mission, the Ark of the Covenant.* Furthermore, while at the time the *Kebra Nagast* was written the Ethiopian monarch was presented as a friendly cousin of the "king of Rome"—an echo of the sixth-century alliance between Caleb of Ethiopia and Justin I of Byzantium[2]—thereafter he came to be regarded as successor to the latter as well, and hence the sole defender of the true Christian faith.

The Ethiopians have elaborated on this exalted conception of their monarchy in other literary forms.[3] In royal chronicles and hymns of praise which span seven centuries, the emperors are celebrated for superlative beauty and superhuman powers. In splendor of countenance they are likened to the sun; in awesomeness of power, to the lion; in religious character and divine force, to the kings of Israel and, at times, to God Himself.

In life as well as in literature the person of the emperor was clad with an aura of sanctity. Ethiopian subjects have had to prostrate themselves and refrain from lifting their eyes in his presence. An analogous show of deference was expected when they received royal messages from afar; the recipient had to hear the message outside his home, standing, and naked above the waist.[4] The emperors rarely permitted themselves to be seen in public, and were often secluded by curtains while eating or drinking. They were not addressed directly, but through an interlocutor. Zar'a Yā'qob, whose officers were said to have kissed the earth each time they heard the sound of his voice, carried the demand for social distance so far that pages attached to his court were not permitted to have contact with anybody from outside, and were put to death if they dared to fraternize with local inhabitants.[5]

---

* The orthodox still maintain that the original ark containing the stone tablets of the Law is located at Aksum. It is symbolized by the *tābot* found in every Ethiopian church.

Accession to the throne involved two rites, anointment by oil and bestowal of the crown. Authority to conduct these rites was vested in the
Egyptian archbishop, the *abuna*. The formal coronation took place in a ceremony for which in former times it was expected that the parties repair to the
ancient sanctuary of Aksum. The change in status brought about through
coronation was symbolized by the assumption of a new name, as, for exam-
ample, Rās Tafari Makonnen became Haile Selassie I. The royal insignia included a ring, worn on the right ear; the royal flag, the staff of which bore a
cross resting on a ball; and special drums, trumpets, and flutes.[6] Also included
was a red silk parasol known as *zhān ṭelā* (origin of the present-day Amharic
word for umbrella). When the emperor was in procession they included a
white horse with small silver bells at his head, a silver shield, and a white
headband of muslin or fine silk.[7]

Successors to the throne were not determined according to a fixed rule like
primogeniture. Membership in the Solomonian line was normally a prerequisite, and the unsuccessful reign of Yosṭos (1711-16) demonstrates the hazards
of rule when no pretense to such affiliation could be maintained. Usually,
however, there were several legitimate candidates for the position, and the
absence of fixed procedures for choosing among them has meant that the
death of an emperor was often a time of confusion and political improvisa-
tion. At times the monarch designated his successor and swore the grandees of
the realm to an oath of support, as when Menelik named Lĭjj Iyāsu; at times
a single powerful lord, like Rās Mikā'ēl Sehul at Gondar, was the effective
king-maker; at times the judgment and interests of a number of potentates,
including on occasion the queen mother, were determinant.

The role of the emperor was largely symbolic, a quality which André
Caquot has stressed.

> The king is guarantor of peace and prosperity for his entire country. Here
> the superhuman virtue attributed to the sovereign by the Ethiopian royal
> ideology manifests itself most clearly. It is not so much a question of his ad-
> ministering the country politically as it is that he guarantee order by his
> very presence and the virtue inherent in him.[8]

The idea that the mere presence of the monarch was a guarantee of civil order
is reflected in the idiom *agara negus* ("country of a king"), which means a
tranquil land. Related to this conception is the requirement that the body of
the emperor be devoid of any physical defect or deformity, so that the well-
being of the body politic may be properly symbolized.

But during most of Ethiopia's history the emperor was by no means merely an awesome figurehead, aloof from the works and turmoil of his realm. It
was customary for him to serve the society actively in a number of ways. He
had to organize the defense of the country and lead troops into battle—if

necessary, to die on the battlefield, as did Galāwdēwos, Yohānnes IV, and others. He had to maintain a minimum of political order, balancing off contending ambitions and subduing rebellious elements. Another important function was that of ultimate arbiter in judicial disputes.* As guardian of the church, moreover, he was active in endowing monasteries and churches and in resolving doctrinal disputes among the clergy.

To carry out these and related functions the emperor needed great wealth and political power. When the monarchy was intact he could command wealth from many sources: from the country-wide land tax (*gǐber*), in the form of honey, grain, or livestock, or such special fiscal assignments as saddles, plowshares, spears, ink, or tent pegs;[9] from assessed tithes on produce; in tribute from subject peoples, either in currency (gold, salt bars, etc.) or in kind; in revenues from traders; and from gifts from new appointees and hopeful office seekers. In theory, moreover, all the land of the empire belonged to its ruler; and, in fact, a good part of it was at his direct disposal, either for cultivation as royal estates or to distribute as compensation to those who served him.

The political power of the emperor was grounded in his command of troops supported by the royal bounty. In addition, he could command the troops of all the lords subject to his authority. Through frequent tours around the country he was able to reassert his hegemony from time to time in distant regions. But even from afar, a strong monarch could usually exert great control thanks to his authority to appoint or demote at a moment's notice any officer of the realm. As Alvares observed:

> No great lord of lands, if he is in them, can leave them, or set out for the Court on any account without being summoned by the [emperor]; and being summoned he will not fail to come for any reason. And when he sets out from the land of which he is the lord, he does not leave either wife or children or any property there, because he goes away in the expectation of never returning, since . . . [the emperor] gives when he pleases, and takes away when he pleases.[10]

The ideology of sacred monarchy served to legitimate theoretically boundless demands for wealth and power as well as to provide identity and morale for the body politic. It justified, too, occasional "deviant" behavior on the part of the monarch, virtually the only person with sufficient authority to innovate in this intensely conservative culture. The emperor has always been a primary agent of cultural innovation in Abyssinia, from the time of Ēzānā, who adopted Christianity in the fourth century; to Zar'a Yā'qob in the fifteenth

---

* To this day Haile Selassie devotes several hours a week to hearing court appeals in a session known as *chelot.*

century, who instituted a number of monthly holidays and prescribed new liturgical texts; to Menelik, who introduced vaccination and the eucalyptus tree in the twentieth century. For more than a century now kings and emperors have attempted to combat the traditional Abyssinian repugnance for manual labor by themselves engaging in arduous physical work on numerous occasions.[11] Haile Selassie has followed a pattern with abundant precedents in introducing the many changes which have characterized his reign.[12]

As object of Abyssinia's highest esteem, symbol of its most cherished values, possessor of supreme wealth and power, and author of new norms, the emperor of Ethiopia thus qualifies as an elite in the more technical, sociological sense of the word as well as in its original sense of "being chosen."[13] Indeed, if more extreme interpretations of the emperor's significance are to be credited, he might even be viewed as the fountainhead of high status for all other elites. Thus Bruce, in a famous passage, declares:

> The Kings of Abyssinia are above all laws. They are supreme in all causes, ecclesiastical and civil; the land and persons of all their subjects are equally their property and every inhabitant of the kingdom is born their slave; *if he bears a higher rank it is by the king's gift; for his nearest relations are accounted nothing better.* [Italics mine.][14]

Such an interpretation, however, is more ideological than analytic. Throughout Ethiopian history one can discern definite limits to royal authority, and bases of elite status other than imperial favor.

It is true, as Margery Perham ably sets forth, that a primitive state of technology and severe geographical obstacles prevented the realization of imperial power to the degree that the royal ideology would have permitted.[15] Yet this failure of the monarchy "to build up any kind of administrative framework through which to exercise the absolute powers with which, by tradition and consent, it was endowed" was not simply a matter of wanting techniques. It also reflected the importance of ultimate values other than that of anointed royalty in Abyssinian culture.

The primary sociological limit to imperial authority was the commitment of the Abyssinian people to the tradition of their church. Religious conversion was one change which, at least in the period of Amhara hegemony, could no longer be tolerated. Za Dengel (1603–4) and Susneyos (1607–32) were brought down because of their forthright conversion to Catholicism, and the overthrow of Lĭjj Iyāsu in 1917 was legitimated on the alleged grounds that he had become a practicing Muslim. The decline in power of Tēwodros II (1855–68) was due in no small measure to the fact that his cavalier policy toward the clergy resulted in his being branded an enemy of the church.

A second limit on imperial authority lay in the perennial tendency of certain regional families to become endowed with an aura of legitimacy in their own right. Indeed, the record of rebellions by nobility as well as clergy against the emperors of Ethiopia bespeaks a persisting dualism in the Abyssinian's disposition toward the monarchy itself. In principle, the emperor is reverenced. Widely held is the sentiment expressed in the *Kebra Nagast:* "It is not a good thing for any of those who are under the dominion of a king to revile him, for retribution belongeth to God."[16] But unquestioning deference is by no means necessarily coupled with unswerving loyalty. The Abyssinian pattern differs from the Japanese, in which total loyalty to the divine monarch calls for suicide in the wake of any disgrace one might have brought upon him. The norms of fealty to the emperor have not been so deeply internalized in Ethiopia, where the pardon and reinstatement of rebels has been a common occurrence. Among Abyssinians a veneer of genuine deference has often concealed an inner consciousness of disaffection, enabling the individual to act out rebellious wishes when the opportunity or need arises. Indeed, this ambivalence has been one of the traditional impulses behind the culture pattern of wax and gold.

The Old Nobility

The Abyssinians themselves acknowledge the existence of, in addition to the emperor, two groups of persons with pre-eminent status. These are called, both in Ge'ez and Amharic, the *makuānnent*, or "nobility," and the *kāhenāt*, or "clergy." While believing the presence of a king to be a precondition of civil order, they also regard the presence of these other elites as necessary for their good life. This attitude is expressed in the Amharic saying: "Fertility of the land [is] through the *makuānnent;* the splendor of the church [is] through the *kāhenāt*."[17]

The term *makuānnent* may be used to refer to all secular dignitaries between the emperor and the well-to-do landowning peasantry. In strict contemporary usage, however, the *makuānnent* should be distinguished from two other classes of personages, whom we may call the "royal nobility" and the "local nobility" or "gentry." The former consists of the immediate royal family (*negusāwi bētasab*) and more distant royal relatives (*masāfent*). Because of their kinship with the Solomonic line these have at times been referred to as "chiefs of Israel."[18] Although it was customary for each new king to exile all male relatives who were potential candidates for the Crown to a high mountain fortress, more distant relatives might hold provincial governorates, and women of the royal family sometimes played an important role in court politics and provincial administration. Members of the royal nobility have normally been distinguished by special titles: *ābēto* (now vulgarized as *āto*, "Mister"), *le'ul,* and *lïjj* for men; and *emebēt, le'elt,* and *wayzaro* (now vulgarized in the sense of "Mrs.") for women.

The local nobility, on the other hand, were eminences whose lives and reputations were bound to a more circumscribed locale. While the non-royal nobility, or *maķuānnent* in the stricter sense, performed as high dignitaries at the imperial court and governors of large provinces, the local nobility were district chiefs and judges, or even simply wealthy landowners, who enjoyed considerable deference. Though they might not be known outside of their home regions, these men were, for the mass of the population, the lords of existence. *Ka-Gondar negus / yāgar āmbārās,* "the petty district chief [is obeyed] more than the Gondar king"[19] expresses folk wisdom on the subject. The Amharic terms which designate this class of men are *bālābbāt* and *shum,* terms we shall want to consider more closely below.

Despite these distinctions among members of the upper stratum of Abyssinian society, with respect to their general orientation and style of life they differed only in degree. They created and shared what might be called a "gentry subculture," even though it was not so differentiated from the general culture as was the case in Europe and China. In the present context, it will be meaningful to treat them as a single status group.

Special manners and skills were self-consciously taught to children of the *maķuānnent,* most of which remain part of the gentry subculture today. An etiquette of instinctual inhibition is taught. Some attention is given, for example, to toilet training, which is spontaneous among peasant children. Spitting in public is proscribed. Physical aggression is discouraged in favor of the more subtle forms of satire and patient manipulation of others. A quiet, reserved manner of speaking is stressed, in contrast with the less inhibited and cruder self-expression of the peasantry. Dignity of comportment is expected at all times; a noble should not, for example, express great enthusiasm or surprise over anything. Sobriety is inculcated as a virtue; alcohol is *la-çhawā lïjj mādasetchā / la-bālagē māzabābatchā* ("for the nobleman's son a stimulant, for the commoner an intoxicant"). In short, the gentry subculture stresses the general ideal of bringing a child up to be conspicuously genteel, or *çhawā.*

Sons of the nobility have traditionally followed a privileged curriculum.[20] They were given lessons in horseback riding and weaponry at an early age. They were also taught how to swim, an uncommon skill among the Abyssinians. Reading would often be taught, for which schooling a man of the church might be brought in as a tutor, or the boy might be sent for a while to a monastery. He might also learn how to play the *baganā,* the ten-stringed lyre used to accompany certain forms of religious and plaintive secular songs. Instead of spending his teen-age years at the plow, which was regarded as beneath his dignity, the noble boy would follow his father to court and observe the ways of litigation and the manner of passing judgments; or he might be sent as a page to the court of the king or some great lord.

The instruction of girls in noble families was not so different from that of peasant girls, though they were spared some of the menial drudgery. The *çhawā* girl would be taught all the household arts, but it was understood that she would be provided with numerous slaves to do the work after marriage. Her own adult chores would be limited to the preparation of *ṭajj,* the beverage of the nobility, and special dishes for her husband; while the preparation of *ṭallā* and food for guests would be the work of domestics.

The style of life of the nobility is colored above all by a seemingly unlimited command of deference. They are addressed as "my lord" by all comers, and waited on in a hundred ways wherever they go. Every "big man" is attended by a flock of servants and retainers, who accompany him on trips and spare him the slightest exertion. This is so elemental a feature of Amhara culture that big men are commonly referred to with the associative prefix *enna-*; for example, *enna-Dajāzmātch Hailu,* meaning "Dajāzmātch Hailu and his men."

The social space of a nobleman is crowded with the issuing of commands. When he visits the home of another, he orders the servants and young people there just as imperiously as if he were in his own home. The wives of the nobility develop much the same manner, though from a more passive position. They spend a good deal of their time sitting on their beds and issuing orders. This sort of indolent, vegetative existence has produced the obese figure and morose countenance for which some Abyssinian ladies have been noted. On the other hand, from her particular vantage point the noble lady has often played an influential and enlightened part in court and regional politics.

Conspicuous consumption among the *makuānnent* thus takes the form of a surfeit of servants. The household of a nobleman of modest rank might boast, in addition to numerous maidservants who procure and prepare food and drink for the establishment, as many as ten to fifteen male servants. Plowden has left us a description of some of their functions:

> One carries your shield, and whenever you go out he saddles your mule and accompanies you, and in the house he makes himself generally useful about your person; another makes your mead, arranges it, and is also perhaps a gunner, and supplies you with game; another is doorkeeper and order-keeper generally. One or two, older and wiser, are counsellors, and their knowledge of the country, and of customs and tricks, is of the greatest service; another has charge of the corn, watching that the maidservants do not steal, and arranging the allowance of all the rest; others are grass-cutters only, according to the number of your beasts; another is a wood-cutter for firewood, very necessary in a country where they have no coal, and the wilderness is free to all.[21]

The ultimate model for these constellations of servants and retainers was, of course, the imperial court. The *makuānnent* imitated the behavior of the emperor as much as it was within their means, prerogatives, and sense of discretion to do so. Thus, like the emperor, a nobleman never traveled on foot, but on the back of a caparisoned mule; with as many retainers as possible, shouldering spears or rifles, on the run behind him. He enjoyed a number of quasi-royal privileges: the authority to have cattle slaughtered and to have *ṭajj* prepared in his home; the right to wear a *barnos,* the dark wool cloak of the nobility; the use of an imported parasol, though not of the scarlet color reserved for the emperor, and of the horsehair fly-switch. In general, the Abyssinian noble attempted to behave like a king in his own sphere of influence and to reproduce in his own court that of the emperor. As d'Abbadie noted:

> A lord of even mediocre importance names his seneschal, his provost, his guards, a foreman of domestics, a chief baker, a butler, a squire, and various captains and pages; then he sets up a hierarchy often in ridiculous disproportion to his position; his inferiors do the same, and there is no one down to the well-to-do peasant who does not institute certain offices and analogous grades in his home. The Ethiopians often laugh about it themselves.[22]

A passion for acquiring titles is the obverse of the Abyssinian's penchant for instituting offices and grades. A man's title, *ya-mā'erg sem* ("name of rank"), has been the major indicator of the deference which is due him. Honorific titles and the paraphernalia appropriate to them are perhaps the most sought after possessions in traditional Abyssinia, for they confer inalienable status. Even if fate should deprive a man of all his wealth and power, he would retain his title until death. If he should become a prisoner, he would be given deferential treatment.

The titles of the nobility were, first and foremost, military titles. The *makuānnent* were above all an elite of war lords; and in contemporary Amharic the term *makuānnent* (singular *makonnen*) is also used to refer to any commissioned military officer. Their principal ranks, in descending order, are:

rās	"head" (of an army)
dajāzmātch	"general of the (king's) gate"
fitāwrāri∗	"general of the vanguard"
qaññāzmātch	"general of the right wing"
gerāzmātch	"general of the left wing"
bālāmbārās	"commander of a fort"
bāshā†	"commander of a rifle corps"
shālaqā	"chief of a thousand"

∗ In former times the *fitāwrāri* ranked below the *gerāzmātch*.
† *Bāshā* is a Turkish loan word, introduced after the Turko-Abyssinian wars.

All these titles were conferred by the emperor. But, in addition, *maḵuān-nent* with the rank of *rās* or *dajāzmātch* had the authority to appoint lesser officers under them. The number of troops commanded by these officers varied considerably according to circumstances. Among armies, moreover, there was great variability in status; the *fitāwrāri* of an emperor naturally enjoyed much more deference than the *fitāwrāri* of a provincial *dajāzmātch*.[23]

A number of other titles represented various civil functions. These included:

āfa negus	"mouth of the king" (lord chief justice)
āzāzh *liq* (Gondar) *wambar* (Shoa)	royal judges
naggādrās	"head of merchants" (customs collector and chief official over merchants)
ṭsahāfi lām *nagāsh* *shum* *ḵāntibā*	various titles given to provincial governors
malḵañña *meslanē*	local representatives of the emperor or provincial governors

A further set of titles was that given to the functionaries of the royal court. These were given for all court posts, including such offices as Server of the Mead (*ṭajj āsāllāfi*). Some of these titles were found exclusively at the court of the emperor; others were imitated in noble households across the land, though again, the same title naturally carried far less prestige in the provinces than when held at the imperial court. The list of court titles varied from region to region and century to century, both in its composition and its hierarchical order.[24] At any given time and place, however, a rank order was carefully respected, and confusion over protocol could provoke altercation, as was recorded in the Chronicle of Iyāsu I (1682–1706).[25]

Titles (and numbers) of the principal court functionaries, in the (descending) order of importance fixed at the time of Iyāsu I, were:

behtwaddad	chief counsellor and confidant (two)
blattēn getā	chief administrator of the palace (greater and lesser [two])
rāq māsarē or *west āzāzh*	majordomo, master of ceremonies
ṭsahāfi te'ezāz	royal scribe; keeper of the seal (two)
zhāndarabā āzazh	chief of the eunuchs

bajirond	guardian of royal property, treasurer (two)
liqa maḳuās	king's double and keeper of the king's mule
*āggāfāri**	protocol officer, superintendent of banquets

The status of these dignitaries may have been particularly vulnerable, depending so closely as it did on the whims of the monarch. Nonetheless their proximity to the center of imperial power gave them unique advantages. They were in a position to receive many gifts for favors and influence, as well as to come by some part of the royal revenues and to attend the royal banquets. They were consulted, together with military commanders, provincial governors, and high ecclesiastics, on important matters of state. Lands granted to them for their services enabled them to support small retinues of their own, including, in some cases, military contingents. They were normally an important factor in promoting stability and continuity during the troubled moments that usually followed the death of an emperor.[26]

The above classification of titles is meant only to provide a quick overview of their variety; no such formal compartmentation existed in the Abyssinian perspective. All the titles converged into a single hierarchy.[27] What is more, titles were not strictly connected to offices or functions, so military titles were frequently given to court or civil functionaries. This was particularly true of the court of Menelik, where, for example, the Superintendent of Royal Tents bore the title *bālāmbārās* and the Chief Hand-washer that of *gerāzmātch*.[28] For centuries before, moreover, provincial governors were often known by military rather than civil titles, and men holding civil titles were liable to be called to take part in military campaigns by the sovereign.

The sociological reality underlying this overlapping of titles among the nobility was the essentially unspecialized nature of their role. The ideal type of the *maḳuānnent* was at once governor, soldier, and courtier. In time of war he set forth at his own expense, with his own troops, to support the cause of the emperor, or perhaps simply to defend his own regional interests. In time of peace he might sojourn, if permitted, at the court of his king or overlord, eating and drinking with his peers, giving counsel to his liege when asked, engaged in intrigue and otherwise seeking to improve his station.

When not active in warfare or the affairs of court, the nobleman would repair to his lands to supervise the agricultural production and the collection of rents from his tenants. The emperors rewarded nobles who served them with grants of land. The higher chieftains in turn rewarded their own followers accordingly. These estates were usually held *in absentia,* the peasants

---

* *Āggāfāri* is an important title in the courts of provincial lords but is not mentioned in the court list of Iyāsu I, nor in that of the *Ser'āta Mangest*.

who cultivated them being required to hand over a certain proportion of their produce every year.*

A man's "bigness," however, depended more on political authority than possession of land. It was often true in Abyssinia, as in feudal France, that the most powerful lords actually possessed relatively few estates. So long as they were not out of favor, the nobility typically were given appointments as provincial and regional governors in return for their loyalty and services.

The responsibilities of governors at all levels were diffuse. As with the emperor, combined in their persons were administrative, judicial, and ceremonial, as well as military, functions. They were obliged to collect the land tax and tithes of their subjects and transmit the proper amount to the king. They communicated imperial proclamations, announced by beating the *nagārit,* a large drum which symbolized the legitimacy of their authority. They had to judge cases of litigation that originated in their court or were appealed from lower levels. They were expected to keep disturbances caused by bandits in their area down to a reasonable minimum. They had to preside informally on the occasion of religious festivals and to provide large feasts for their followers, and occasionally for the beggars and indigents of the area.

The fact that political position was granted as a reward for military activity, like so many acres of land—or to the highest bidder, as Almeida complained[29]—suggests that the benefits of office outweighed its obligations. Indeed, public authority in Ethiopia was frankly regarded as a private possession by all concerned. The incumbent might change, but the office remained—not so much a set of obligations to fulfill in behalf of the king, or the state, let alone in behalf of the subjects—but a set of opportunities for personal aggrandizement.

The opportunities, both psychic and economic, were impressive. One was expected to avail himself of all the obsequious gestures which serve to swell the ego of an Abyssinian ruler. If so inclined, the governor could indulge his sadism ad libitum; sword, lash, and rope were, besides the *nagārit* and seal, the official insignia of a provincial ruler. He could order the peasants in his area to labor for him—to plow his lands or build his houses—as well as command them to military service. He could exact tribute from them without relief, in addition to appropriating for his family and retainers part of the

---

* Each land unit worked by a given tenant farmer, or *gabbār,* would be divided according to that proportion, in order to equalize the differences resulting from variation in such factors as the size of land units or the quality of soil. The proportion paid to the landlord varied with the location of the land; thus, one-half might be exacted for ordinary *dēgā* (high) land, while in certain *qolā* (low) areas only a tenth might be required, owing to the difficulties of heat, jungle, and wild beasts.

taxes collected in the name of the emperor. Concerning the imposts for which the peasants were liable, Plowden wrote in 1844:

> They pay a certain portion in kind to the Ras, or other great chief, and sometimes a regular tax in money; besides this, they must furnish oxen to plough the king's lands. Their immediate governor then takes his share in kind of every grain (say a fifth), and feeds besides a certain number of soldiers at the expense of each householder: he has rights to oxen, sheep, goats, butter, honey, and every other requisite for subsistence; he must be received with joy and feasting by his subjects whenever he visits them, and can demand from them contributions on fifty pretexts—he is going on a campaign, or has just returned from one; he has lost a horse, or married a wife; his property has been consumed by fire, or he has lost his all in battle; or the sacred duty of a funeral banquet cannot be fulfilled without their aid.[30]

Two centuries earlier, observing similar phenomena, Almeida had concluded that "generally speaking, they are all plunderers rather than governors."[31] The only restraints on their exploitative behavior have been an occasionally keen sense of Christian propriety and the limits to what an exasperated local populace will bear.

The existence of a predatory class who serve military functions and maintain a gentry subculture is a common enough feature of traditional agrarian societies. What is perhaps less common in the Abyssinian case is the constellation of factors relating to the recruitment of members into this elite.

High secular status in Abyssinia was dependent on a complex of possessions—land, political strength, and honorific titles—which tended to reinforce one another. The possession of much land has always been a basis for considerable deference in Abyssinia. As a source of produce, rents, and revenues deflected from the Crown, moreover, it was also a source of wealth to be used in building up one's political strength by rewarding able soldiers and loyal followers, and by making gifts to one's superiors. Political power was directly obtained through the acquisition of governorships. Such offices were a further basis for much deference and, through the incumbent's access to tribute, customs fees, court fees, and gifts from his subjects, of much income as well. Titles, finally, not only were universally esteemed but also entitled the bearers to a style of life which included a presumptive right to gifts and obedience from all inferiors as well as the consumption of much wealth and power.

For all these possessions, the Abyssinian noble was directly dependent on his king (or, in the case of a lesser noble, on his overlord). His dependence was twofold: land, political office, and titles came to him as gifts from the sovereign, and, what is more, their continued possession was contingent on the sovereign's continuing favor. Abyssinian "vassals" had no legal rights to their "benefices," and lands granted them could be withdrawn and given to others as the emperor wished. At the death of a feudal beneficiary his lands reverted to the Crown unless specifically reconveyed to the heir by royal proclamation. Political office was no less precarious. Governors were made and unmade—by the traditional process known as *shum-shir* ("appoint-demote")—in short periods of time. The powerful position of governor of the maritime province (*bāhr nagāsh*) changed hands four times during the six years that Alvares spent in Ethiopia. Even when tradition assigned a certain post to the descendants of a certain lord, the emperors were able to exert control by shifting their favor from one descendant to another from year to year. Titles, unlike land and office, were granted for life, as we observed; but they were in no case hereditary, and thus every Abyssinian's hope for a title, let alone a raise in rank, depended on the grace of the king or of his major appointees.

Given these conditions, it was not possible for the nobility to become a closed, hereditary estate, or to develop a corporate identity capable of confronting the imperial will. On the contrary, thanks to the emperor's freedom to ennoble anyone whom he chose, there was a relatively high degree of social mobility, and the ranks of the upper strata were continuously being reshuffled.

Outstanding personal properties of various sorts often enabled Ethiopians of low birth to rise to high positions. The emperors and great lords conferred honors on those who served especially well in military expeditions, whatever their origins. Menelik's promotion of two Galla prisoners to rank as his highest generals is a famous case in point. The royal favor occasionally smiled on low-born Ethiopians who excelled in such qualities as physical beauty or witty repartee.[32] Unquestionable personal loyalty was another quality in high demand; freed slaves were sometimes given offices and dignities, since their lack of ties to political families made them particularly trustworthy.

Abyssinians have thus cherished the idea that they could rise to a higher station in life than that to which they were born. Comparatively few ever tried to do so, probably, but ambitious souls were never wanting. Seeking some benefice, or the glory of a title, or a position of power that would permit them to help their kinfolk or avenge themselves for a wrong suffered at the hands of some superior, they would attach themselves to the lord whose fortunes seemed brightest at the moment and hope, by valorous service and God's favor, to arrive someday at an estimable position.[33]

Nevertheless, though ability and fortune might carry any man high in the political hierarchy, he would not thereby automatically be accepted as one of the *makuānnent*. A self-respecting man of noble family would resist marrying his daughter to a commoner or person of dubious parentage, no matter how high a rank the latter obtained. For the Abyssinian nobility did form a self-conscious status group with a certain hereditary base. Its members shared a sense of superiority, a consciousness of kind, and an attitude toward commoners such as that expressed by the governor Takla Giyorgis to the Jesuit

Barradas: "Father, these villeins are like camels, they cry and groan when they are loaded, but in the end they carry the load that is put on them."[34] They set themselves off from the commoners, not only because of their style of life and subculture, but also because they came from well-known families.

Such sentiments were shared by the commoners. They would much rather be governed by a man from a noted family than by a person promoted from their own social level. The folkways expressed a disdain for the *nouvel arrivé*, for example, by poking fun at the office of *liqa maḳuās* (the king's double in time of battle). The *liqa maḳuās* was often a man from an unknown family, chosen because of his handsome features and resemblance to the king. The office permitted him to strut about in the king's clothes and inclined him to assume haughty airs. In some places it was customary to ridicule this upstart by referring to the minstrel, or *azmāri,* as *liqa maḳuās;* for the *azmāri,* too, was entitled to wear the kind of dress appropriate to the lord in whose banquet hall he performed, but the *azmāri* was a person of low prestige in Abyssinian society.

In other words: although the emperors could appoint and depose whenever they pleased, with or without cause; and though "the land and persons of their subjects are equally their property, and every inhabitant of their kingdom is born their slave"; by itself the principle of royal favor is clearly inadequate to explain the Abyssinian pattern of social stratification. For, unlike the neighboring kingdom of Buganda, Abyssinia was not a straightforward despotism in which the dispensation of a *ḳabaḳa* was sufficient to elevate a man into the highest social stratum.[35] The claims of a quasi-hereditary noble status group have also had to be satisfied.

How did this status group arise, and how have its claims been expressed and justified? What has been the history of its relationship with the monarchy? The existence of this class is anchored in the actual tendency for lands, office, and titles to be given to members of the same families. In reality, the emperors frequently let such possessions pass from father to son, either because they were in too distant a region or because there was no good cause for taking them away, and on occasion drew up written charters assigning grants of land to a man and his future descendants.[36] Indeed, one form of land tenure, known as *rĭsta-gult,* was precisely a sort of hereditary fief, given in exchange for military service over the generations. In certain areas, moreover, it was a matter of tradition that the governorship be given to members of a certain family. Finally, although no man inherited a title, as son of a nobleman he might inherit the culture and facilities that would give him a much better chance than any commoner to obtain a title of his own.

Two other aspects of Abyssinian society supported this tendency toward the development of what amounted to local dynasties of nobility. One was the prestige attached to the "chiefs of Israel," any of the nobility who could demonstrate some affiliation with the Solomonic line; the marriage of one of these into a local dynasty contributed an added buttress to its traditionalist claims. The other was what seems to be a still more deeply rooted disposition for decentralized hegemony based on the ancient character of the society. For, as Cerulli has recently suggested, the origins of the Ethiopian state were such as to lay the foundation for a persisting order of feudalism. The movement of South Arabs to the Eritrean coast and highlands took place, not through the conquest of an indigenous population by a united invader, as in the Norman Conquest of England, but by the intermittent emigration and settlement of distinct tribes from South Arabia into various parts of the African territory. Thus, Cerulli concludes, we see in Ethiopia "a feudalism expanded from the roots: a number of principalities or peoples which, independent on African land after their emigration, have finally been regrouped in a higher political unity, yet still conserving in the feudal system thus constituted part of their autonomy and their individuality."[37] If this is so, it would constitute an added traditional element in the sense of legitimacy of local dynastic interests.

All this suggests that we must look to two sources for the prestige of the *makuännent*—that recruitment into the secular elite came from "below" as well as from "above." These two bases of noble status are indicated by the etymology of two Amharic words commonly applied to the local nobility, *shum* and *bālābbāt*. *Shum* (or *seyum*) comes from a root which means to invest with high position. The emperor, as we have seen, is *seyuma egziābhēr* ("invested by God") and he in turn is the source of authority for investing other dignitaries. The status associated with the word *shum* is therefore based on the act of investiture by a sovereign. *Bālābbāt*, on the other hand, has the literal meaning, "one who has a father"; in other words, one who has a significant father, a notable ancestry. This status refers to claims to deference which are based on birth.

Claims based on birth, moreover, were closely tied to the ownership of land and supported by local territorial allegiances. This appears most strikingly in the office of *çhïqā shum,* the lowest level official, who is appointed, to be sure, but by the local people themselves from a small number of *bālābbāt* whose eligibility for the office rests on their inheritance of rights to certain specified pieces of land. Other local offices, like *malkañña* and *meslanē,* were normally given by regional governors to *bālābbāt* indigenous to the area. The sacred sentiment of fealty to a monarch, whose charisma rested both on membership in a hallowed dynasty and the hallowed act of coronation, thus competed in Abyssinian souls with deeply felt sentiments of attachment to members of noted families who symbolized local rights and traditions. Abyssinian political structure at any given time was determined by the relative strength of the forces supported by these two principles of legitimacy.

Neither principle was ever realized in pure form. No matter how great his authority, the emperor could never afford to ignore the hereditary claims of regional *bālābbāt* in dispensing favors and making appointments. He needed a minimum of support from regional lords who commanded devoted followers, and he could not with impunity alienate any number of these at a given time. In practice, imperial favor was accorded *both* on the basis of personal loyalty and military ability, and of ascriptive claims to rank based on birth. The exercise of imperial authority was often a question simply of confirming the leadership of a locally successful *bālābbāt*.

With regard to regionally based strength, on the other hand, birth was not a sufficient factor to assure a man a high position. (It was not even necessary, strictly speaking. Any man could attempt to build up a position of power by attracting followers. He had a much better chance, however—a chance to attain authority, and not merely force—if he came from a noted family.) If, as the son of an important lord, he inherited his father's position, he had to prove himself a suitable leader or risk being deposed by the men of the area. At the very least he had to withstand competition from his brothers. Thus, as we saw in the history of Manz, two of Nagāssi's sons were deposed before the men of Manz found in Sebstē a leader worthy of his father's mantle. Military ability, political shrewdness, and lavish generosity toward one's followers were the decisive characteristics which, together with strong ambition, could enable the son of a *bālābbāt* to attract followers and make claims of his own. With adequate forces, he could even depose a regional governor and take his place, so long as he took possession of the official drum (*nagārit*) of the office.[38] For complete legitimation, however, it was usually necessary to secure confirmation of the rule of a locally successful *bālābbāt* by the emperor. This was the reason why Nagāssi is said to have journeyed to Gondar.

In terms of the distribution of political authority, then, Abyssinian history may be viewed as an oscillation between the emperor's efforts to define local nobles as his agents and their own efforts to attain continuity and autonomy. The available sources concerning the emperors of the fifteenth and early sixteenth centuries suggest that their efforts were to a large extent successful. The ensuing "barbarian invasions" so weakened the empire that a more locally centered distribution of power became inevitable. At first only the scope of the monarchy was reduced, as the emperor came to govern a smaller area. In consequence, in outlying regions such as Manz, Gishē, and Merhābetē in northern Shoa, virtual sovereignty was wielded by the local *bālābbāt*. Nevertheless, for a good century after its founding Gondar served as a real imperial capital, and its emperors retained authority over the lords in their shrunken empire. Then, as the monarchy began its inexorable decline due to internal rivalries and the movement of Galla into court and capital, localism triumphed. Ethiopia's Age of the Princes (1769–1855) was as decentralized a political system as was twelfth-century France or fourteenth-century Japan.

It was at this time that the *maḵuánnent* came into their own. More un-abashedly than ever they constituted, not a hereditary aristocracy in corporate opposition to the king, but a plurality of proud centers of rank—partly in-herited, partly achieved—enjoying virtual autonomy. To move toward a modern nation it would be necessary to brake their centrifugal force.

The Clergy

Like the nobility, the clergy may be divided into those who are significant at the national level and those who are primarily local dignitaries. The former reside close to the imperial court, while the latter are thickly distributed around monasteries, churches, and wildernesses all over the country.

The highest ecclesiastical authority in Abyssinia was the *abuna* who, from the time of Frumentius in the fourth century until the death of Abuna Qerlos in 1949, was with few exceptions an appointee of the Coptic Patriarch at Alexandria. Chosen from the Egyptian monks of the convent of St. Anthony near the Red Sea, the *abuna* was brought, at great expense to the emperors, to live out his life in an alien land. Ignorant of the language and customs of the country, he played little part in the conduct of church affairs or in affairs of court; and when he did try to do so, his efforts were usually abruptly checked by jealous clerics and suspicious kings. His functions were purely ritual, but indispensable: he alone had authority to anoint and crown the emperor, to confer orders, and to absolve vows. From numerous revenues, rents, and fees, the *abuna* enjoyed a considerable income. Like the emperor, he was regarded as sacred because of the charisma of his office, and spent most of his time secluded from the public.[39]

Second in rank was the *eçhagē,* an appointment made by the emperor. This was the traditional title of the abbot of the convent of Dabra Libānos in Shoa, which in the course of the fourteenth and fifteenth centuries gained hegemony over Abyssinian monasticism. The *eçhagē* served as administrative head of the church and had jurisdiction over all monks and monasteries. The most esteemed of the Ethiopian clergy, he tended to wield more actual power than the *abuna.* His provincial deputies, called *liqa ḵāhenāt,* controlled the secular clergy. This office was also bestowed by the emperor, and its functions included presenting candidates for ordination and deciding ques-tions of protocol in connection with religious ceremonies.

In addition to these supreme dignitaries of the church, a small number of churchmen enjoyed pre-eminent status by virtue of their activities at the imperial court. These included the *aqābē saʿāt* ("guardian of the [canonical] hours"), the chief ecclesiastic at court, and during part of the reign of Zarʾa Yāʿqob the only official with unrestricted access to the king; the *qēs hātsē* ("king's chaplain"); the *liqa dabtarā* ("chief of the *dabtarā*"); and *liqa mammerān* ("chief of the learned men"). These four served as the four supreme judges at the royal court, and the *aqābē saʿāt* ranked third—in some lists, first—in the official order of precedence of all court dignitaries.[40]

One other church dignitary, finally, was the *nebra ed,* chief of the sacred district of Aksum, who always enjoyed a high position at the royal court. When appointed by the emperor (instead of by the provincial governor who sometimes possessed that authority), the *nebra ed* enjoyed the rare privilege of being permitted to sit while speaking in the event of his involvement in litigation.

The status of the highest ecclesiastical dignitaries was based on approximately the same factors as those which determined the status of secular nobility: royal favor; family background, in the case of those whose fathers were important nobles or noted churchmen; and the possession of wealth, political power, and imposing titles.[41] The same was true of their regional counterparts, the *alaqā,* "chiefs" of large churches and monasteries, whose wealth, power, and leisurely mode of life gave them, in Plowden's opinion, "perhaps the most enviable position in Abyssinia."[42]

The status of the clergy as a whole, however, rested on three other principles which are not affected by royal favor, birth, or worldly possessions. These were: contact with the most sacred symbols of religious authority; ascetic piety; and religious learning. Broadly speaking, in Abyssinia these three principles have been embodied primarily in three distinct roles, namely, those of priest, monk, and *dabtārā.*

A normal preparation for these roles—necessarily so, in the case of the priesthood—is service as a deacon. Ability to read is, now as before, a requisite qualification for the diaconate, but that requirement has in the past often been overlooked. More important has been the requirement of ordination by the *abuna.* Ordination formerly took place in the company of hundreds of other aspirants and, when there was uncertainty about the future availability of an *abuna,* even babes in arms were admitted.[43]

The traditional garb of the deacon is a yellowish cape made of sheepskins, though on holidays the officiating deacons may be dressed in richly colored silk robes like the priests. The duties of the deacon—and they are accounted great and secret privileges—are to prepare the sacramental bread, fetch the holy water, and assist at the Mass (the performance of which normally requires two priests and three deacons).

On reaching puberty a deacon is no longer supposed to serve in the church, for fear that he will become "impure." At that time he may decide to prepare for the priesthood. For this two qualifications must be met. He must have completed his study of reading and, ideally, of *zēmā,* the chants that are intoned in the liturgy of the Mass. These matters he may learn from the older clergy during his service as a deacon, or from his father, who, in many cases, is a priest himself. Otherwise, he goes off in search of a master. He builds a tiny thatch hut near the home of his tutor, wears ragged, unsheared sheepskins, and gets his meals by begging. He lives thus for a year or two, until he has mastered the fourteen varieties of chants used in the various masses, and perhaps special chants like the *Praise of Mary* (*Weddāssē Māry-ām*) which are sung on holidays.

The other, and more important, qualification for the priesthood is marriage according to the law of the church. After a deacon has been married in the customary manner and lived with his wife for at least forty days, their marriage must be solemnized by the celebration of the Eucharist. Thereafter he may not divorce her or remarry if she dies.

With these conditions satisfied, the candidate for priesthood may travel to the *abuna* and be ordained. He acquires thereby the power to bind and to absolve, and is granted full knowledge of the mysteries of the *tābot*. The new priest attaches himself to a church, and is given his share of the monthly assignments for conducting the Mass. This is his main responsibility, though as he grows older he will also acquire confessants to whom he will give advice and assign penances.

Apart from these duties, the life of an Abyssinian priest in many ways resembles that of his lay neighbors. He plows his fields and harvests his crops. He may do business at the markets, or add to his income by weaving. Perhaps the chief difference in his manner of life is the habit of spending time in the "gate of peace," a little building near the church where the clergy assemble after services for hours of drinking *ṭallā* and idle conversation.

In reward for his services—and this is normally the chief inducement to become a priest—the priest is given a share of the revenues in kind brought in from lands owned and managed by the church. He may also be given some land owned by the church to cultivate for himself. In addition, he receives gifts in kind from his confessants periodically, is entitled to take part in the various feasts to which priests are regularly invited, and is likely to receive some bequest from time to time.*

The insignia of the priest are modest, but they suffice to inform the stranger that here is a man to be shown special respect: a white turban wrapped around the head and a cross carried in the hand, to be kissed by all comers. Older priests often carry a fly-whisk made of horsehair, and a wicker sun umbrella.

Though there are devout and kindly men among them, the Ethiopian priests have never been particularly noted for their moral qualities. Often they are ungenerous and scheming, and ready to exploit their position at the expense of the laity. They are poorly educated in their own tradition, stuttering

---

* A sheep, or at least a sheepskin—insurance that the Memorial Mass will be properly performed on the fortieth day after the donor's death.

and misreading sacred texts in a language they have never understood. They are notorious drinkers, so much so that a modern Ethiopian novelist has one of his characters, a priest, ask: "If one stops drinking, what else is left in this world?"[44]

Nevertheless, the prestige of the priests was unassailable in Amhara culture. Whatever their personal life, they represented the value of ritual sanctity, which made it possible for the Mass to be performed in the local churches. So long as they had been duly ordained and did not break their lawful marriage bond, they were part of a sacred class. Combes and Tamisier remarked upon this in the 1830's:

> Despite all their vices, these priests manage to make themselves respected; when they pass along the roads, the faithful bow deeply to them, and in no matter what gathering they appear, everyone rises and hurries to kiss their hands.[45]

Privileged contact with the sacred symbols of the church—ordination by the sacrosanct *abuna,* exclusive access to the *tābot,* and officiation at the Eucharist —gave the priests an authority that was independent both of political dispensation and of personal accomplishment.

Other groups within the clergy have been highly esteemed for quite different reasons. Those who become monks carry great weight because they embody the virtue of ascetic piety. The *dabtarā,* on the other hand, are respected for their erudition.

Monks usually come from two kinds of background: unwed deacons desiring to spend their lives as monks, and priests whose wives have died. But previous ecclesiastical connection is not necessary for the monastic calling, nor is the ability to read required. The essential qualification is the willingness to renounce the world. The word for becoming a monk (*manakwasa*) means to renounce earthly things. A prospective monk may be of the sort described by one of Walker's informants:

> An old man who has married many wives and divorced them one by one, may say, "Henceforth it suffices me! Let the world remain lost to me! I am to turn my face to God!"[46]

In earlier times the monastic life was sought by men from all walks of life, including lords, soldiers, even emperors, in consequence of some grievous affliction, or perhaps a vow made in time of trouble, or excessive *Weltschmerz.*

Heads of monasteries have the jurisdiction to confer the monastic status. One who desires this status bequeathes his worldly possessions and goes through a ceremony in the church in which his body is declared dead. The symbol of the monastic state is a little cloth skullcap (*askēma*). Once he has become a monk, an Ethiopian is a legal nonentity. This frees him from all tax obligations and any debts he may have incurred, for which advantage many have become monks for other than spiritual motives.[47]

No specific duties or obligations are required of a monk. Abyssinian monks have spent their years in a variety of ways. One extreme is anchoritism. Many have become hermits, feeding only on roots and herbs, and have sought even greater self-mortification by such practices as standing for long periods in icy water or wearing iron girdles lined with points. Others have lived somewhat closer to human society, wandering about the country as mendicants or making the pilgrimage to Jerusalem. Others have attached themselves, for shorter or longer periods, to monasteries, spending long periods in prayer and fasting and doing some humble work like collecting wood or, if formerly a priest, assisting at the Mass with the other priests. A few have proselytized in non-Christian areas. Some monks, on the other hand, have left the world only to rejoin it at a higher level. These become advisers to grandees or themselves serve as governors of districts.

Whatever the shortcomings of individual monks, the monastic calling as a whole has enjoyed the highest esteem in Ethiopia. Monks have exerted a great influence on the thinking and behavior of the people. Itinerant hermits have harangued the people to live more pious lives. The counsel of monks has been of help to rulers in time of trouble. The prophecies of monks have been influential in setting the pattern of hopes and fears about the future.

The role of the *dabtarā* is quite different. The *dabtarā*'s combination of functions is unusual—he is at once chorister, poet, dancer, herbologist, scribe, and wizard. It is also remarkable that so indispensable a functionary in the Ethiopian Church has no formal position in the church hierarchy.

With its characteristic forbearance toward human frailty, Amhara culture has established in the *dabtarā* a religious vocation in which special knowledge is required but holiness is not expected. The vocation is thus sought by those who do not care to be bound by the strict conditions of the priesthood, or by priests who have found these conditions too much to live with, so have been divorced or remarried. Recruitment into the role is informal: there are no rites of ordination, nor is there any particular point at which a man becomes or ceases to be a *dabtarā*.

Becoming a *dabtarā* mainly entails a course of study beyond that minimal level required for the priests. The full course of traditional studies includes the vast corpus of religious chants; *āquāquām* ("religious dance"); Ge'ez grammar and *qenē;* and study of some two dozen religious books. Mastery of the entire curriculum, which takes at least twenty to thirty years according to traditional methods of pedagogy, is rarely accomplished. In addition the student acquires other knowledge sub rosa from private tutors: knowledge of writing, preparation of magic formulae, and the use of herbs.

The *dabtarā*'s way of life is more variable than that of the monk, his possibilities for income more diverse than those of the priest. He may be attached to a church as a chorister and receive a share of the church's revenues, as do the priests. Or he may donate his services to the church and earn his living by secular employment. He may work as a scribe at the court of a king or nobleman. He may spend most of his time teaching, gaining support from some large church or monastery. Like many priests he may cultivate land. In any case, he is likely to derive some income from the sale of amulets and from medical therapies. Some *dabtarā* are even said to have wandered about the country as hunters, performing magical services for clients as they go.

Dabtarā are not set off from the populace by special insignia. Some wind a turban around their heads, as do many priests; but others may dress like ordinary peasants. If holding more prestigious posts they may be seen with fly-whisks or wearing a *barnos*. But they are known by the people, who fear and respect them. They are feared because of their magical powers, which are believed capable of rendering bullets harmless and turning *ĭnjarā* to dust. They are respected because of their learning, for they are the only educated status group in traditional Amhara society. If the commoner's relatively impulsive *manner* of speaking is contrasted with the quiet reserve of the nobility, his relatively simple *language* is contrasted with that of the *dabtarā*, who is noted for a studied and circumspect use of language (*qāla-dabtarā*) and for larding his Amharic with literary (i.e., Ge'ez) expressions (*ya-dabtarā amārĭññā*).

In the case of the religious elite, then, status is in all cases achieved. While there is a natural tendency for sons of priests and *dabtarā* to follow their fathers' example, they arrive at the status in question only by fulfilling the same norms that are applied to the sons of laymen. These norms, however, differ among the different groups within the clergy. Investiture by an authority emanating from the seat of religious charisma, the Alexandrine Patriarchate, and the related ritual requirement of marriage with Communion, were the basis of priestly status, almost irrespective of the personal attainments of the candidate. Personal attainments were *all* that mattered, on the other hand, in the case of monk and *dabtarā*, but they differed radically for the two statuses.

The qualifications and characters of monks and *dabtarā* are almost diametrically opposed. The monastic state is entered only by means of a sacred rite; the *dabtarā* is in no way ordained, and might even be a "defrocked" priest. The monk's life is normally given to sensual renunciation; the *dabtarā* is normally an acknowledged sensualist (as appears, for example, in the proverb *ķa-mesā ya-talaya dabtarā / yādargāl serā* ["a *dabtarā* who is kept from lunch / will work intrigues"][48] and in stories which celebrate the *dabtarā*'s use of his knowledge for private erotic ends). In the monk the virtue of ascetic piety is stressed at the expense of knowledge. The monk need not even know how to read, though if a lifelong monk he is likely to have devoted much time to traditional studies. The *dabtarā,* by contrast, lives by his lore and his learning. At his best, the Abyssinian monk conveys a real sense of spiritual purity, of profound mystical bearing, of an utterly mild manner. The *dabtarā,* at his best, is a subtle conversationalist and an operator of wondrous effects.*

Thus, while the status of members of the old nobility was a compound resultant of simultaneously operating criteria—family and region, royal favor and accumulated power—the several criteria relevant to the status of the clergy operated more or less independently. This made the religious elite a more differentiated stratum.

This statement need be qualified only by the fact that, in addition to the considerations of ritual purity, ascetic piety, and traditional learning, a fourth factor influenced the status of the clergy, namely, royal favor as expressed in appointments to the high ecclesiastical offices. This factor crosscut the others, for such favor was dispensed to members of all three status groups. The *eçhagé* was always a monk; the *aqābē sa'āt* would seem to have been a *dabtarā;* the post of *alaqā* could be given to members of all three groups.

Just how these types of local clergy were related to the clergy at the national level in the traditional order is a question that is difficult to answer. In any case, it is likely that there were conflicts among their representatives in the competition for royal favor. In the fourteenth century, the ecclesiastics of the royal entourage included only secular clergy, and their deportment was sharply criticized by Eçhagé Fileppos, who charged that "those who live in the dwelling of the Sovereign, go about proudly in subtle raiment and with ornaments of gold and silver—perishables—and are very arrogant."[49] However, once Zar'a Yā'qob had established the custom of bringing members of the convent of Dabra Libānos to the court, the monastic order was always well represented in the royal entourage as well. In the present period one sometimes hears of competition among the different groups for influence in

---

* The association of impious properties with the main representative of traditional religious learning may be seen as an expression of the Abyssinian's ambivalence toward knowledge as such. The whole tenor of Ethiopian Orthodox religion runs counter to ratiocination and inquiry. It stresses mystery and discourages curiosity with tales like that of the man who tried to probe the mystery of the Trinity and was swallowed up by the earth—a tale commonly told to students who are learning to read. For this reason Orthodox students have frequently been quite upset by the rational theodicy taught by the Jesuit fathers at the University College.

As observed in the previous chapter, moreover, it was traditionally believed that too much learning results in madness, a belief no doubt based on the fact that older church students often drink a certain medicine to quicken their mental faculties, which sometimes deranges them (as the author has witnessed). The *dabtarā,* for their part, would seem to have thrived on this belief, benefiting from the exclusive powers and privileges gained from their esoteric knowledge.

the contemporary church hierarchy, the *dabtarā* stressing their special intellectual qualification for high positions, the monks their greater piety.

The Traditional Balance

Whatever the internal fragmentation of the church—which was compounded by regionally based doctrinal controversies—it may for the moment be considered as a unified estate vis-à-vis the secular powers. This permits us to raise the question of the integration of politico-military and religious elites in traditional Abyssinian society, a question that may be discussed in terms of two relationships: that between the values represented by the two elites, and that between the interests of their respective institutions.

The social teachings of the Ethiopian Church were couched in terms of practical justice, not universal love. Thus the pacifistic strain in Christianity barely made itself felt. The priests, to be sure, were forbidden to shed blood, animal or human; but this is more in the nature of a necessity for the maintenance of ritual purity than a symbol of moral principle. They went along willingly to the battlefield in ceremonial capacity. In fact, comments d'Abbadie, most of them would reject the interdiction of their taking part in military expeditions as a denial of their rights.[50]

Far from opposing warfare, Ethiopian Christianity served rather as an inspiration and justification for wars; since much of the fighting was directed against Muslim, Judaic, or pagan peoples, the warfare took on something of a crusading tone. As for internecine war, it was commonly justified in terms of *lex talionis*, a religiously sanctioned punishment for the sins of the enemy. In this respect, then, the two elites gave impressive support to each other. The warlords were serving the church by fighting the heathen. The fate of their military expeditions, on the other hand, was assisted by the prayers of the accompanying clergy. This reciprocal dependence was symbolized by the custom of taking some *tābot* along with the army to the battlefield, and by the custom of "greeting" the church as the first thing a warrior does when he returns home.

The values of warfare and religion were further harmonized by the symbolism of the emperor, Lion of Judah. The emperor combined in his person the figures of indomitable warlord and devout—and divinely guided—Christian. This combination was an integral part of the self-image projected by many emperors, as reflected, for example, in the identification with Constantine the Great manifested by Zar'a Yā'qob and Eskender (1478–94) in their choice of throne name, and by Tēwodros II in his coronation speech.

With regard to civil policy, moreover, the nobility and clergy were in basic accord. Both groups felt a special responsibility for adjudicating disputes. Both felt that their superior status entitled them to receive substantial amounts of rent and revenues from lands granted them by the king, and to

Fig. 25.—*Provincial nobleman and wife*

26.—*"Big men" journeying with retainers*

FIG. 27.—*A deacon*

FIG. 28.—*Group of* dabtarā

FIG. 29.—*An old* ƒ

innumerable gifts and services from the rank and file of the peasantry. Differences normally arose only when the secular powers deviated from what were generally the established norms. Thus, certain extremes of exploitation were on occasion strongly condemned by the clergy—usually the monks—as were certain transgressions of Christian custom by the secular powers, including at times the emperor himself. Amda Ṭseyon (1314–44), for example, was publicly rebuked, early in his reign, for having seduced one of his father's concubines and two of his own sisters. More generally, the clergy tended to react against flagrant misbehavior on the part of the military—such as looting the homes of those giving them quarter, or violating the right of asylum.

The extent to which the religious and secular powers stood in economic conflict seems to have depended largely on the amount of land available at any given time. Both groups were interested in the acquisition of rights to land revenues. The rights of the church to land are anchored in a traditional agreement, attributed to Yekuno Amlāk (1270–85), according to which the church was to receive one-third of the land in the realm. It is clear that the holdings of the church grew progressively larger from that time to the sixteenth century. With the subsequent diminution of Abyssinian territory and related social disorganization, the church's claim to its lands was not so scrupulously respected. Thus, Barradas observed that the emperors of the seventeenth century were as anxious to regain lands from the church for distribution to their soldiers as those of previous centuries had been generous in presenting them, while Takla Hāymānot decreed in 1771 that "all lands and villages, which are now or have been given to the Abuna by the King, shall revert to the King's own use."[51] Tēwodros, too, was anxious to recapture as much land as he could from the church. Later in the nineteenth century, however, as Menelik carried out his great territorial expansion, the church systematically acquired one-fourth of all lands in the annexed areas.

In general, it may be said that the clergy and nobility worked to further each other's interests. The nobility supported the clergy by giving endowments to churches and monasteries, setting up churches in newly conquered lands, and observing religious ceremonies as state functions. The clergy, in turn, served secular authority by providing a communications network for relaying and supporting official policies, excommunicating enemies, and providing counsel and morale in connection with military expeditions. Altogether, there was an easy commerce between the two elites. They felt common cause in their responsibilities and privileges vis-à-vis the masses. Occasionally there was even an exchange of personnel, when warlords ended their careers by becoming monks, or clerics acceded to high civil positions, like the Rās of Angot, for example, who in Alvares' time was an ordained priest.

When expectations of mutual support were not satisfied, however, conflict did erupt between the secular and religious powers. In that event both groups had recourse to powerful weapons: the former, violence; the latter, excommunication. The history of Ethiopia records numerous instances of the flogging or execution of clergy by secular authorities. The action of Fāsiladas (1632–67), who reportedly "caused seven thousand priests to be thrown headlong from the top of the mountain Balbau for having revolted against him,"[52] would represent but one of the more extreme instances of such violent retribution. Short of violence, the kings at least had other means at their disposal for controlling the clergy: the power to withhold benefices, the right to imprison church officials, the final authority on doctrinal questions, and the ability to block a united front on the part of the clergy by pitting high church officials against each other.

On the other hand, infringement on the rights of churches and monasteries, gross civil injustice, or radical departure from religious tradition could on occasion evoke surprisingly effective retaliation by the clergy. D'Abbadie provides some extremely illuminating passages on this matter, from which the following have been extracted:

> More than once have I been present at debates of this nature; I have seen these men of the church, weak and without arms amidst men of war, pleading in the name of the law, indicting the menacing covetousness of the surrounding soldiery, invoking eloquently reprobation against their powerful adversaries, and leading them to disavow themselves that force which constituted their pride. . . .
>
> In the case of an open violation of an asylum, the regular clergy got aroused; the most venerable monks abandoned their solitude, assembled the parish clergy, went into the camps, and generally they obtained justice. When the real culprit was the Dajāzmātch, they brought him to repentance, or else excommunicated him, threatened his servants with anathema if they continued to serve him, put the province under interdict and, aided by the monks of the neighboring provinces, stirred up national reprobation against him.[53]

The clergy had other resources which it could employ against the emperor himself. It could influence royal policy through highly placed advisers. Through the *abuna* it could exact certain promises from a prospective emperor as a condition of coronation. Perhaps most important, the clergy could, through its hold over public opinion, turn the populace against the sovereign. As we have seen, this power proved decisive in the encounters between church and monarch in the reigns of Za Dengel and Susneyos, and contributed significantly to the downfall of Tēwodros and Lĭjj Iyāsu.

While therefore the emperor may well have been "supreme in all causes, ecclesiastical and civil," he was far from being the sole, or even the decisive, source of the influence enjoyed by the clergy. The latter constituted a largely autonomous status group which no emperor could afford to antagonize indefinitely. The attempt to build a more powerful central government and introduce cultural reforms thus required some alteration of their independent status as well as that of the old nobility.

THE FEUDAL ORDER IN TRANSITION

The Decline of the Old Nobility

It must always have been the policy of the Ethiopian emperors, except for those few who did not relish the political side of their office, to seek to maximize their control over the regional nobility. They did this, we have seen, either by granting land, power, and rank to men who were completely dependent on them, or else by controlling, through military and diplomatic means, those lords whose birthright and regional strength gave them strong claims to their positions.

During the past century, however, the idea of subordinating regional nobles to imperial control has come to be conceived more radically and has become the core of a slowly emerging ideal of a modern nation-state. Some such vision was certainly behind the tortuous career of Tēwodros II, whose policy was a reaction against the desperate disunity which the Age of the Princes brought to Abyssinia and to the growing threat from foreign powers. In Plowden's official report to the British government in 1855, he described Tēwodros' work as follows:

> The arduous task of breaking the power of the great feudal chiefs—a task achieved in Europe only during the reigns of many consecutive kings—he has commenced by chaining almost all who were dangerous, avowing his intention of liberating them when his power shall be consolidated. He has placed soldiers of the different provinces under the command of his own trusty followers, to whom he has given high titles, but no power to judge or punish: thus, in fact, creating generals in place of feudal chieftains, more proud of their birth than of their monarch, and organising a new nobility— a legion of honour dependent on himself, and chosen specially for their daring and fidelity.[54]

The task of displacing the great feudal chiefs proved to be scarcely less arduous in Ethiopia than in Europe, however. Tēwodros' high hopes were shattered against the opposing forces of regional ambitions and clerical disaffection. The national unity he won through conquest and reform did not survive to the end of his reign.

Yohānnes IV (1871–89) likewise aimed at uniting the nation, but was distracted from serious internal reform by the need to fight off the encroachments of Egyptians, Mahdists, and Europeans. His domestic policy was more concerned with the imposition of religious uniformity than with political transformation.

Menelik revived Tēwodros' policy of creating a band of generals loyal only to himself. He did this partly by raising capable men with no connections to high position: Rās Gobānā and Fitāwrāri Hābta Giyorgis, two of his most important generals, were originally Galla prisoners. The power of the feudal chieftains he manipulated by traditional techniques, sending them to posts far removed from their home bases, and arranging political marriages. But Menelik did not decisively undercut the authority of the great provincial lords, and at his death the old political structure was still more or less intact.

The experience of these emperors was not forgotten by Haile Selassie, who seems to have made it his primary and unceasing ambition to assure his position by breaking down every sort of autonomous power where it previously existed or threatened to develop. Thanks to his policies of centralization and to modern means of transport and communication he was able to become more of an effective autocrat than any of his predecessors.

The main development during the period of his regency as Rās Tafari (1917–28) was the stiffening of his military posture. To start with he had the regional forces of Harar Province, formerly his father's governorship, which he had acquired through the favor of Empress Taitu (Menelik's wife) following Menelik's paralysis. He built up his strength by making improvements in Harar that increased his revenues and the number of his soldiers, and acquired fiefs elsewhere. Following the death of Empress Zauditu's commander of the imperial troops in 1926, he took command of these troops and brought some of his own forces into Addis Ababa. By 1928 he was strong enough to demand the title of *negus* from Zauditu and, as is well known, acceded as emperor upon her death two years later.

During these years Rās Tafari was gradually promoting the idea of a transformation of the position of the old nobility. As early as 1926 a letter published in his weekly newspaper, *Berhānennā Salām,* suggested that the prevailing feudal system of provincial government be replaced by a system based on salaried administrators.[55] An actual change of that order was out of the question at that time. A contemporary American observer thus described some of the obstacles:

> Ras Hailu of Gojjam, Ras Guksah, chief of Amhara, Dejasmatch Ayalu, powerful head of Simien, Dejasmatch Gabra Salassy of Tigre, and Ras Kassa of Shoa, are supreme lords in the rough highlands of the north country. Far removed from the central authority, thirty to forty days' journey, some of them, they are out of touch—living in a different world from that of Addis Ababa. Hundreds of lesser chiefs rally to their standards, each

with his numerous following. In the South it is the same and we heard that Dejasmatch Balcha . . . ruling thousands of square miles and no one knows how many subjects with a hand of iron, pays no taxes, no tribute, no share in the upkeep of government. It is common talk that he has been summoned to Addis Ababa upon more than one occasion and has sent back the reply: "If you want me, come down here into Sidamo and get me."[56]

The most that Rās Tafari could do to realize his political ambitions then was to work patiently within the existing structure, attempting whenever possible to fill the posts of provincial governors with men of his own.

After his coronation, Haile Selassie continued to be faced by considerable opposition from provincial lords. The governors of Tigre and Gojjam were particularly troublesome, and some nobles from those regions joined their lots to the Italian cause during the occupation. Not until the restoration was Haile Selassie able to effectuate policies which would strip the old nobility of their autonomy once and for all.

Three major innovations of the years after 1941 accomplished this end. One was the establishment of a standing military force under the Emperor's direct control that rendered the existence of separate regional armies unnecessary and possessed a capability clearly superior to that of any force a rebellious lord might muster. This included the national army, trained for a number of years by a British mission; and the Imperial Bodyguard, reestablished after the liberation on a new and expanded basis. These troops monopolized the modern weapons in the country and the limited air power, later developed into a separate air force. In a short time there appeared a new class of military officers, trained with modern techniques, and living as salaried employees of the government. The traditional function of the noble as military commander was thus made obsolete.

Second, under a governmental decree of 1942 a new fiscal system was set up under the Ministry of Finance. In this system the peasants have been obliged to pay a fixed quota of taxes in money, for which they are given a written receipt (*ḳārnē*). These taxes are collected by employees of the Ministry of Finance and transmitted directly to the provincial capitals or to Addis Ababa. This has been a popular reform among the peasantry, who are no longer required to submit arbitrary amounts of goods and labor to their district rulers. For the nobility, however, it means that their legitimate income is restricted to what they produce on their own lands, the rents they receive from their tenants, and—if they hold office—to what they receive from the government as a monthly salary; though in practice it continues to be supplemented, in many cases, by bribes and illegally imposed fees. Thus, they can no longer support a significant number of followers.

Finally, by reorganizing the provincial administration through the bureaucratic machinery of the Ministry of Interior, the power and prestige of
regional appointments have been reduced. The authority of the central government has been enhanced by redrawing the provincial boundaries so as to
cut across, in many cases, what were traditional administrative regions. Governors at all levels have been made ordinary employees of the Ministry of
Interior, with assistants and secretaries provided by the Ministry, who serve
as a constant check on their activities. Earlier in his reign, Haile Selassie
deprived the great provincial governors of the right to order capital punishment and of the prerogative of conferring lesser titles.

Stripped of their military functions, large revenues, and other means of
building up their positions, members of the most important noble families
have had no alternative but to submit totally to the sovereign authority of
Haile Selassie. This has meant, in most instances, their relegation to posts of
high prestige but little consequence: diplomatic posts abroad and, more commonly, the senate. Established by the Constitution of 1931 as the upper house
of parliament, the senate was to consist of members "appointed by His
Majesty the Emperor from among the Nobility (Mekuanent) who have for
a long time served his Empire as Princes or Ministers, Judges or high military officers." The institution was re-affirmed in the revised Constitution of
1955, and has provided, as one of its continuing functions, an outlet for
dignitaries with too much prestige of their own to be trusted with administrative positions or permitted to reside in their home regions.

Many lesser nobles have remained in the provinces with appointments as
regional governors and judges. Because of the shift of political authority to
Addis Ababa, they tend to feel forsaken and dispossessed. They regard the
behavior of those who occupy high governmental posts in Addis Ababa as
selfish and corrupt, and view with no little bitterness the fact that youngsters
with college degrees earn a great deal more than they. (A subdistrict governor, for example, earns Eth$50 per month, while those with an A.B.
automatically start any government job at Eth$450.)

Nevertheless, these lesser nobles continue to comport themselves in the
aristocratic manner of the old nobility and retain their high status in the
eyes of the local populace. However modest their resources now—and many
continue to enjoy quite sizable holdings of land—they are proud of whatever titles and offices have been given them. Though their part in the national
political structure and status system is not so weighty as that of their fore-
bears, they remain the only fully accepted secular elite in the provinces. It is
they who issue the day-to-day commands to the people, and they alone for
whom the peasantry has unflinching respect. Short of a brutally totalitarian
program that is willing to ignore the sentiments of the mass of tradition-

directed peasantry, and suffer the consequences, no dynamic program of agricultural and social development can take place in Abyssinian areas that does not enlist the active cooperation of the local *bālābbāt* and *shum*.*

The Decline of the Clergy

Although the church was instrumental in bringing Rās Tafari to power—by relieving the nobles of their oath of allegiance to Lĭjj Iyāsu—it was as a whole not sympathetic to his policy once he began to rule. Foremost champions of tradition, the clergy viewed with suspicion Rās Tafari's interest in modern education and other reforms. So pronounced was their conservatism that his weekly *Berhānennā Salām* found it newsworthy to report the fact that the clergy of one important provincial church were actually reading the Addis Ababa newspaper each week.[57] He was wise to act gingerly at first, limiting ecclesiastical reform to such matters as publishing religious texts in Ge'ez and Amharic, and encouraging the work of foreign missionaries.

In the past three decades, however, changes of many sorts have had the effect of reducing the degree of independent authority which the clergy traditionally enjoyed. These changes included the achievement of independence from the Alexandrian Patriarchate; the weakening of the church under the Italian occupation; subjection of church administration to the central government; and competition from the secular government schools.

Rās Tafari initiated the policy of seeking independence from Alexandria in 1929, when he secured the investiture of five Ethiopian bishops. This gave indigenous clergy, for the first time, the right to ordain priests and deacons, although they remained subordinate to the Egyptian archbishop. In 1950 an Ethiopian bishop, the *eçhagē*, was consecrated as archbishop; and in 1958, culminating Haile Selassie's patient and skillful negotiations, complete autonomy from Alexandria was achieved.

The attainment of ecclesiastical independence has heightened the prestige of national church officials in Ethiopia. It has brought about a re-organization of the national church hierarchy, in which fifteen bishops now hold office, one for each of the fourteen provinces, and one in Jerusalem. At the same time it has reduced the effective freedom of the clergy as a separate status group. Deprived of the external source of legitimacy which the Egyptian *abuna* formerly provided, the clergy are now entirely subordinated to the power of the Emperor. This condition was formally articulated in the Constitution of 1955, which made the election and appointment of archbishops and bishops

---

* A potentially significant medium of communication between them and the central government is the Chamber of Deputies, which since 1957 has brought popularly elected notables from the provinces to Addis Ababa.

"subject to the approval of the Emperor" and gave him "the right to promulgate the decrees, edicts, and public regulations of the Church, except those concerning monastic life and other spiritual administrations."

The general position of the church had already been weakened by the events of the Italian occupation. Italian policy resulted in the destruction of many church buildings and the massacre of numerous monks, including those of the hallowed monastery of Dabra Libānos. Of the national leaders, the Egyptian *abuna* was out of the country from 1937 on; two of the bishops were put to death, including the much venerated martyr, Abuna Pēṭros;* and the remaining two compounded the demoralization by openly supporting the invaders. One of these went so far as to anathematize resistance fighters and forbade Ethiopian priests to give Christian burial to those who died as patriots. In some areas, moreover, it is said that the local clergy lost much prestige by welcoming the invader with open arms.

Haile Selassie thus had a much stronger hand in his dealings with the clergy when he returned from exile in 1941. The next year he issued a decree which sharply restricted the perquisites of the local clergy. Their landed properties were no longer tax free, but now carried the obligation to pay taxes at the normal rate into a central church treasury. The church was deprived of temporal jurisdiction over its ordained and lay members, including the authority to inflict fines, and was denied the right to corvée labor from peasants living on their lands. (In practice these latter restrictions of authority are frequently ignored in the provinces.)

The development of a nationwide system of government schools, finally, has broken the clergy's monopoly of educational facilities. Wherever government schools have invaded traditional Abyssinian regions, the clergy tend to be defensive and resentful. The specific issues have been the decreased prestige of certain traditional religious subjects, which are not taught in these schools, and the comparatively lower income of church teachers. Thus, a full-time teacher of reading attached to a monastery may receive Eth$15 a month from the central church treasury, whereas a government school teacher in the same area teaching the same subject may earn Eth$150 a month.

Despite all these blows, the clergy still retain much the same prestige as ever in the provinces. Their influence over public opinion is considerable, and has been a major factor in discouraging families in traditional Christian areas like Manz from sending their children to government schools.† Despite

---

* A statue of Abuna Pēṭros has been raised in the center of Addis Ababa. His fate has been celebrated in the verse drama by Makonnen Endālkātchaw, *Ya-dam Demṭs,* translated into English as *The Voice of Blood* by Endālkātchaw Makonnen.

† When the Ethiopian government is ready to inaugurate a major program of provincial education, it should not prove difficult to overcome this opposition. A number of provincial priests, with whom the author has discussed this matter, have signified their willingness to serve as

recent restrictions on their income, it remains considerable. It is conservatively estimated that they possess at least fifteen per cent of the arable land in Ethiopia, and their general inertia with regard to agricultural reform remains a significant conservative factor.

In the modernizing sector, the position of the clergy has been much more vulnerable. The traditional forms of erudition and piety seem to bear little relevance to the intellectual and moral needs of the modernizing elements. The church's reputation for hostility to change further alienates them from it. But it is by no means certain that the church's position will only decline with the passage of time. Ethiopia will be profoundly susceptible to the appeal of traditional revivalist sentiment as the strains attendant on modernization increase; and by its publication of two monthlies, since 1947, the church has already shown, albeit in a limited way, its capacity to employ modern media for traditionalist purposes. On the other hand, if the tiny band of Western-educated church leaders succeed in promoting some degree of modernization in the church, through institutions like the Theological School and the Orthodox Students Association, the clergy may yet play a constructive part in the social and moral life of transitional Ethiopia. It remains to be seen whether its leadership will be effective enough to move the traditionalist clergy to make those adjustments necessary for survival as a respected status group in the modernizing sector.

The New Men of Power

After curbing the independent power of the *makuānnent,* Haile Selassie was careful to prevent others from taking their place in the political structure, determined as he was to consolidate in his own hand all the powers they once wielded. As a result of his centralization of government in Addis Ababa, however, a new group of men have gained pre-eminent status at the national level. We may call this group the "new nobility": "new" because of their development of an urban style of life, and because their influence as an elite is largely directed to the modernizing infrastructure, and "nobility" because of their perpetuation of the traditional hierarchical image of a superior and privileged status group. The core of this status group consists of government officials with the ranks of minister, vice-minister, and assistant minister, who function essentially as a personal administrative staff for the monarch.

As observed above, Tēwodros clearly saw the need for creating a new class of nobles, freed from regional interests and acting solely according to the

---

elementary instructors in the government schools, and at salaries much lower than the better trained Ministry teachers. The presence of just one or two priests in these schools would eliminate the traditionalist opposition to them that is now so strong. The situation may be compared to that in Ceylon, where the opposition of Buddhist monks to government schools was eliminated by incorporating them as teachers in those schools.

royal will. A solid foundation for such a class was not possible, however, until the central government had been sufficiently stabilized and expanded. These conditions began to be met under Menelik, who established Addis Ababa in the last decade of the nineteenth century and in 1907 created a number of ministries. Housed in buildings inside the palace compound, the ministries were initially regarded as little more than an ornament to dress up the imperial court. Although men of some stature, like Afa Negus Nasibu and Fitāwrāri Hābta Giyorgis, were named to the posts, the offices themselves did not acquire much prestige. It was no great matter when, five years after the death of Menelik, the ministers were turned out of office by a group of military officers at the instigation of Rās Tafari and sent home to their provincial estates.

After becoming emperor himself, however, Haile Selassie revived and enlarged the ministerial system. Since the restoration, it has expanded into a complex bureaucratic structure. In addition to some sixteen ministries, a number of specialized government agencies have been formed, and the military and judicial hierarchies and the diplomatic corps have been considerably expanded. The rapid growth of the central government in the past two decades is reflected in its budgetary expenditures, which went from about US$10 million in 1942 to an estimated US$110 million in 1962.

The growth of this governmental machinery has provided a new basis for elite status in Ethiopia. Mobility channels now run in terms of appointments in the government bureaucracy. The periodic announcement of appointments by the Emperor has become the focus of public interest in Ethiopia since the liberation. Every new list of appointments provides the occasion for intense gossip and *de rigueur* congratulatory parties at the homes of the favored.

The new class of high governmental functionaries under Haile Selassie may be regarded as a transitional elite: partly traditional, partly modernizing. With regard to basis of recruitment, values represented, and style of life, the new nobility present, on the one hand, a direct continuation of the old nobility; and, on the other hand, many features novel in Abyssinian society.

To some extent recruitment of members of the new nobility was not a creation of new dignitaries, but rather an absorption of members of the old nobility into the new political organization. The recruitment of *makuānnent* into the senate, which after all is an organ of the central government, may be taken as an ambiguous instance of this. Some others were given important posts in the civil and military administrations. These include members of the princely families of Shoa, Tigre, Wag, Lasta, and Gojjam; the Bakere clan, royalty from the Galla province of Wallaga; and scions of the *makuānnent* who were important in Menelik's day or before, members of aristocratic clans which go by the names of Bēzā, Mojā, Sofanē, and Addisgē. Such persons are likely to have been awarded the old military titles for purely honorific purposes. They have been led to renounce extreme particularistic ambitions, thanks to marital connections, intimidation, the lure of new benefits, and a degree of nationalism, but to some extent they remain spokesmen for regional and para-dynastic interests.

Men who did not belong to the old nobility were recruited into the new nobility on the basis of two criteria, loyalty and ability, with loyalty clearly the more important of the two. Some men from very humble backgrounds have been thus raised to the highest governmental positions through their "loyalty" to the Emperor, manifested in great part by their readiness to inform on the words and deeds of others and their obsequious and flattering manner. These have normally not been given the traditional military titles but only the titles of their office. In contrast with the carry-overs from the old nobility, still known as *masāfent* and *makuānnent,* these men have been called *bāla-selṭān* ("holders of power"). They have included a number of men who were active in the fight against the Italians, either through the Hagara Fiqer ("National Patriotic Association," a group organized in 1935 to promote Ethiopian unity and combat Italian propaganda) or as patriotic fighters in the resistance. The Emperor also promoted to high position some men who collaborated with the Italians, relying on their earlier record as an insurance against latter-day disloyalty, and using their antagonism against the patriots as a check against excessive ambitions of the latter.

On the other hand, the new nobility includes those who, whether from high family background or not, are so placed because of outstanding ability. This consideration is no longer primarily a question of military ability, but of competence in dealing with technical modern subjects and with foreign diplomats. This group may be equated with the older generation of European-educated Ethiopians. The categories of adjusted aristocrats, ambitious parvenus, and intellectual bureaucrats have thus constituted a latent subdivision among the new nobility; and tensions have from time to time been expressed along those lines.

Despite the elaboration of modern governmental structures under Haile Selassie, the dominant principle of the social order has been that of royal sovereignty. The entire staff of government officials has been the direct sociological descendant of the traditional court retinue. This was conspicuous in the titles given by Menelik to a number of the original ministers: *Afa Negus* for Minister of Justice; *Azāzh* for Minister of Palace; *Bajirond* for Treasurer; and *Ṭsahāfi Te'ezāz* for Minister of Pen. These and other court titles remain in use today. The primacy of the court over all other functions appears in periodic audiences at the palace, when all high government officials and other notables are expected to pay their respects no matter what business may be pending in their offices. The chief value embodied in the status group of the new nobility as a whole has been that of loyalty to the sovereign.

So long as they remain loyal, the Emperor has tended to let members of the new nobility help themselves to the spoils of office. Some of them retain the view that public office is a private possession, a reward from the emperor rather than an obligation to the nation or people, and that it is, therefore, appropriate to use governmental position primarily to help one's relatives, inflate one's ego, and multiply one's wealth.

For the new nobility, however, wealth is no longer measured primarily in terms of land and cattle, but of money. If they own land, it is of interest chiefly as a source of income, and they tend to prefer using it for cash crops like coffee and *çhat* (a narcotic plant sold in quantities to Arabs) than for the traditional grains and pulse or for experimental crops. They prefer to speculate in real estate rather than to increase the output of their farmlands. Indeed, because of the heightened prestige of money, many officials have been grateful—or would be grateful—for the opportunity to leave government service and become entrepreneurs. They feel very close to that small number of Ethiopians outside the government who have acquired much wealth through commercial enterprise, and who may also be included in the status group of the new nobility.

Commercial entrepreneurs came into prominence on the Ethiopian scene in the 1920's, when monopolies in alcohol, matches, salt, and tobacco, as well as trade in coffee and skins, enabled a small number of Ethiopian families, Christian as well as Muslim, to accumulate wealth. Such people became prisoners of their wealth during the occupation, since they felt obliged to collaborate with the Italians in order to protect their privileges. Many more Ethiopians have profited from the modest economic activity in the country since the liberation, although most of Ethiopia's trade remains in the hands of Arabs, Greeks, and Armenians (at least nominally). Their social level approximates that of the higher government officials. They are expected to pay their respects at court along with the *makuännent* and *bäla-selṭän*. They are often related to high government officials, and attempt to make use of their relatives in office to help them secure commercial advantages. Above all, they share the same style of life.

As an urban group, the new nobility enjoy a style of life notably different from that of their predecessors who lived on mountainous estates and in army tents. Even if assigned to provincial posts, members of the new nobility tend to maintain homes in Addis Ababa. They have been quick to incorporate the more conventional urban Western forms of conspicuous consumption. Automobiles and chauffeurs, expensive European clothes, modern houses, Scotch whiskey, and Western-style banquets and dances have become the common ingredients of their subculture.

At the same time, traditional symbols of prestige are still in evidence. The households are staffed with numerous servants and retainers, who make certain, for example, that the lord does not work in the garden or carry a package into the house from his car. Expectations of this sort of attendance are carried with the new nobility wherever they go. Similarly, members of the new nobility are frequently followed about, or waited for, by young relatives and other aspiring young men, who hope to establish a sort of civil master-retainer relationship and thereby secure a position, promotion, or loan.

The new nobility also attempts to instill in its children the refined manners and reserve of the old noble subculture. Some of the wealthiest have retained the tradition of private education, in its modern counterpart of sending their children abroad for secondary school or to private schools in Addis Ababa. They would like to control their children in the old fashion, but because of growing cultural confusion have in many cases assumed a more permissive stance. Thus their children increasingly run about freely, ignore traditions, and exhibit less fastidious manners.

Owing to their small numbers and the fact that they meet one another so often—at the palace and at social events like weddings—the members of the new nobility tend to be well acquainted with each other. They seem conscious of their status as a privileged stratum but do not form a solidary group. They divide into strongly competitive cliques, a division that itself tends to dissolve into the anxious struggle of each to maintain or improve his position at the expense of the others. The chief way to accomplish this has been to report something incriminating about another person—above all, something that impugns his loyalty to the Emperor. The consciousness of the new nobility has been dominated by the fear of arousing the Emperor's displeasure. The proximity of the throne—a phone call can summon anyone to report to the palace within ten minutes, reason unspecified—makes this a more formidable sanction than in previous generations.

How has Haile Selassie been able to prevent the new nobility from acquiring that relative autonomy of status and self-esteem which the old nobility formerly enjoyed? Why is it, despite the burgeoning of a new "power elite," that the question most earnestly asked by thoughtful Ethiopians and foreign observers for the past several years concerns a probable future "power vacuum"?

Sensitive to encroachment on his "absolute" authority by anyone else, Haile Selassie has kept his officials in a state of weakness through the strategy of his appointments. In this he has been inspired by the traditional methods of Abyssinian rulers who periodically assigned offices to different men through the process of *shum-shǐr*. Haile Selassie's policy has been to rotate officials in office every one or two years, in some cases after six months. This has prevented officials from acquiring a significant following in any one position. At the same time it has made certain that none of them will undertake any program not supervised by the Emperor, since any official's budding projects tend to be undone by his successor, whether because of personal vendetta, orders from the Emperor himself, or simply difference of approach. Thus has Haile Selassie been able to make sure that no one besides himself demonstrates any sort of leadership that might be attractive to the public.

At the same time his appointments have been made in such a way as to insure a balance of power—or impotence—favorable to his absolute control. By consistently appointing enemies to adjacent positions he has built in checks upon the behavior and sentiments of his higher officials. He has relied on mutual jealousies and conflicting ambitions to cause each to report anything incriminating he can find on the other. When appointees in the same branch of government have shown undue co-operation and friendliness, he has at times provoked friction between them.

In addition to the checks and balances of the *shum-shĭr* system, the Emperor has made use of an extensive intelligence system to keep watch over those in office and out. Not only the operations of the regular security departments of the Ministry of Interior and the police, but also some of his closer advisers have had their own personal networks, financed by moneys diverted from various government departments.

Other measures have been used to check the independence of businessmen. Money has been arbitrarily taken from them by the imposition of fines, confiscation of property, and through requests for contributions for charitable causes. A few private entrepreneurs who have been too successful have been forced into government service. Licenses have been revoked, in some cases given to foreigners rather than to prosperous Ethiopians. Dividends from commercial enterprises have been withheld, or given to others whom the Emperor favored. (Rather than appear unduly wealthy, some Ethiopian investors have preferred to use Greeks, Armenians, and Arabs as the nominal heads of their enterprises.)

Due to their relative proximity to the Emperor, their patronage powers, their wealth, and in some cases their family background, the members of the new nobility command considerable deference, particularly in Addis Ababa. Their Westernized style of life (itself modeled to a great extent on the Emperor's habits) has set new standards for modernizing Ethiopia. At the same time they are the objects of much stereotyped hostility. The people in the country, and the commoners of the towns, regard them as oppressive and unsympathetic. Their logic often runs: "The big men around the court are no good; only the Emperor is for us." The intellectuals see them as reactionary, selfish, and corrupt. The massacre of some fifteen members of the new nobility as the final act of the abortive coup d'état in 1960 was an expression of this latter judgment.

The chief advantage of the new nobility—their relative enjoyment of imperial favor—has also been their great dilemma. Those who have been conscientious in seeking to carry out their proper responsibilities have been torn by the need to do what they regard as improper in order not to incur the disfavor of the sovereign. Those with narrowly opportunistic motives have been rendered no less uneasy by the need to counter the offensives of their enemies at court.

This dilemma and the related "immorality" is a natural consequence of Ethiopia's attempt to begin modernization under a traditional despotic authority. The behavior of the new nobility that is so bitterly attacked by the intellectuals will continue to reproduce itself until the process of modernization renders it obsolete—until the specialized standards which control economic and governmental activities have been firmly institutionalized, with controls that operate independent of expressions of loyalty to the sovereign.

Standards of competence have been more firmly institutionalized in the case of a special group among the new men of power—members of the military profession. The officers corps should in fact be considered as an elite group in its own right, in view of its distinct status and functions as well as the size and political importance of Ethiopia's security forces. The regular armed forces number nearly thirty thousand; there are also an estimated twenty thousand men in the police force and an unknown number in the recently reactivated territorial armies. The number of men with the rank of major or equivalent and above is thus probably close to a thousand.

Ethiopian military officers are recipients of the special esteem their countrymen have always felt toward men of war. They have also acquired prestige from the military's efforts to defend and liberate the country during the Italian period and more recently for their backstopping of Ethiopia's claims on the Somali border. They have at the same time been objects of an undercurrent of civilian hostility, based on the feeling that they are "parasites" and doing nothing positive to enrich the country. Their style of life lends itself readily to provoking the latter sort of objection. While dissatisfaction over income on the part of non-commissioned military personnel has been a major source of tension in Ethiopia during the past decade, the perquisites of higher officers compare quite favorably with those of their civilian counterparts. They have been given substantial salaries—and in addition, free housing, free cars, and servants and retainers drawn from the rank and file. Keeping in mind his particular need to insure the loyalty of the military elite, the Emperor has furthermore presented personal gifts to individual officers directly from time to time.

As a result of intimate contact with European and American personnel who have trained them in Ethiopia, experience abroad as trainees or in United Nations military missions, and the emphasis on rationalization inherent in the modern military profession, members of the military elite tend to be more eager and impatient to modernize Ethiopia than do members of the new nobility. This contrast was already apparent at the time of the Italian invasion, when Ethiopian officers were condemning the archaic practices of civilian officials who, they charged, were holding back the defense efforts. Yet the image of a progressive, solidary military elite in Ethiopia is justified no more than the image of a reactionary, solidary ministerial elite; nor should the military leaders be seen as standing in fundamental opposition to their civilian counterparts. There is much friendly intercourse between the two groups. Army officers are often related to civilian officials, by blood or by marriage. Military personnel have in a number of cases been assigned to civilian posts in the government. While the military carry on much of their social life among themselves, they also enjoy a good deal of interaction with civilians of high status at parties, dances, weddings, and funerals.

Like the new nobility, moreover, the military officers do not form a cohesive group with common interests and ambitions. The one group which did develop a high degree of solidarity, esprit, and common political goals— the Officers Corps of the Imperial Bodyguard—was dissolved in the wake of its defeat in the 1960 rebellion. The military men have been checked and balanced by much the same techniques as have the new nobility. As a whole, they are held together by little more than the institutionalized structure of the security forces. As such, they are in any event bound to play an important part in determining the character of the future government of Ethiopia as they are crucial now in upholding the present regime.

THE BIRTH OF AN INTELLIGENTSIA

The formation of a modern intellectual class in Ethiopia is still in its earliest stages. Given the small number who have completed elementary school (a number still under one per cent of the national population) all Ethiopians who have graduated from secondary school may for the time being be considered members of a secular educated elite, those with college and graduate degrees enjoying correspondingly higher status within this elite. The total number in this group reached an estimated six thousand in 1962, about one-fourth of whom held college degrees.

Equally indicative of the rudimentary condition of the Ethiopian intelligentsia is the poverty of its institutional facilities and of its means of communication, both internally and with the international intellectual community. As of 1961, institutions with primarily intellectual purposes were limited to the small college of arts and sciences, four vocational colleges, two small research centers (the Pasteur Institute and the Section d'Archéologie, both financed by France and staffed mostly by non-Ethiopians), the Haile

Selassie I theater, and the secondary level art school.* Library facilities included the National Library, with some fifty thousand volumes; the University College Library, with about forty-five; and the reading rooms of the United States Information Service, the British Center, and the Soviet Information Service. The national library also contains a historical museum, and there is a handsome and well appointed archeological museum nearby, neither of which has so far been operated with a view to encouraging public attendance.

Except for occasional lectures sponsored by the national library and the University College extension program, none of the above institutions serves as a center for intellectual communication among adult Ethiopians. It was hoped by some that with the inauguration of the Haile Selassie I University, in December, 1961, a major new center of intellectual life would be created; but the government found it difficult to push ahead with its announced concept of an integrated institution which would operate autonomously and at a high standard.

Outside these institutions, moreover, there have been few channels of communication through which Ethiopian intellectuals can develop their minds and stimulate their imaginations. There are no periodicals to serve as a medium for such communication. One possibility, the *Ethiopian Observer*, is not quite an exception. Limited resources have kept it from operating at as high a level as available talent might permit, and its basically apologetic orientation renders implausible its claims to be "A Journal of Independent Opinion." The daily newspapers which feature contributed articles—the *Ethiopian Herald*, the *Addis Zaman*, and the Amharic sections of the *Voice of Ethiopia*—have tended to exclude pieces that have anything to do with highly controversial matters. Nor are there many social occasions for the serious discussion of intellectual matters. Professional associations, clubs devoted to intellectual matters, and even informal discussion groups exist not at all or else in a very haphazard form.

Contact with the intellectual world outside Ethiopia is almost as meager. Foreign-educated Ethiopians tend to become intellectually demoralized on returning home. The loss of a taste for reading has frequently been one of the first casualties experienced by Western-educated Ethiopians on return from abroad. Only a few hardy souls attempt to maintain some sort of link with the outside world, through subscribing to such magazines as the *New Statesman, Paris Soir,* or *New Republic.* For most of them, coming home means a cessation of the most elementary intellectual functions, other

---

* In 1963 an Institute of Ethiopian Studies was established at Haile Selassie I University, including a substantial Ethiopiana library and museum.

than those necessary to perform their jobs. They do not attempt to maintain and build personal libraries, though there are a few exceptions to this. The three small bookstores in Addis Ababa offer only the most insubstantial fare.

Nor, finally, have more than a handful of private individuals taken upon themselves the charge of a scholarly or literary calling. Although Marcel Cohen heralded the birth of a printed literature in Amharic as early as 1925,[58] writing is still not very important on the Ethiopian scene.* The output of original books and pamphlets in Amharic averaged less than fifteen a year over the past two decades. The presses and bookstores distribute Amharic publications indifferently at best. Much of the literary impetus produced by the desire of many Ethiopians to write, and the obvious need for good writing that would address itself to the intellectual demands of the present generation, has been sapped by economic, political, and cultural factors.

The economic factors include the high cost of printing; the diminutive market; and the absence of publishing houses. If an author wants to be read, he must normally pay for publication himself. Those who cannot must either find a patron in the Crown—frequently a highly lucrative arrangement—or resort to mimeographic duplication, or else remain unpublished. The censorship system and anxiety about spontaneous expression of any sort which has been fostered by prevailing political conditions constitute additional obstacles to literary development.

The paucity of serious writing has been the result no less of prevailing cultural conditions. The low intellectual level of his potential audience, the absence of channels for criticism, and the dearth of precedent make it difficult for the Ethiopian writer to determine good standards of writing. The confused state of Amharic, owing to regional variations and the absence of consensus on neologisms and loan words for expressing modern concepts, poses many problems on the level of sheer vocabulary. The temptation to get into print quickly, if the financial and political barriers can be hurdled, exceeds the temptation to work long and hard on an opus of quality. The desire to pontificate frequently eclipses the quest for understanding.

Those conditions which have inhibited the growth of Amharic literature—poverty, governmental reluctance to provide sufficient freedom and support, the newness of the modernizing culture, and the motivational level of the intellectuals themselves—may be viewed more broadly as responsible for the relative barrenness of Ethiopian intellectual life as a whole. Insofar as these conditions change in the coming decades, a radical change in the quality and organization of Ethiopian intellectual life may be expected. As a sociological

---

* This is no longer due, however, to the negative attitude toward writing as such which was discussed in chapter iii. That traditional inhibition has been largely removed—primarily, it seems, by the postwar requirement that all legal accusations and court proceedings be set down in writing.

phenomenon, however, the intellectuals are already unmistakably in evidence, and if one contrasts them as a social stratum with the new nobility their outlines become readily visible.

The new nobility came into being in consequence of Haile Selassie's policy of political *centralization*. The status of its members rests on their possession of political influence, measured partly by the strength of their personal followings but primarily by how close they are to the Emperor, and on the Westernized style of life made possible by wealth acquired through political office, rents, and commerce. Its ascendance as a status group may be located approximately in the decade after 1945, the year in which failure of a revolt in Tigre Province marked the end of attempts to assert provincial claims inspired by allegiance to members of the old nobility. The decade was marked by rapid growth of the factors supportive of centralized government and the new nobility: expansion of the bureaucracy, strengthening of the national military force, and economic advance.*

The intelligentsia, by contrast, has come into being in consequence of Haile Selassie's policy of technical *modernization*. The status of its members rests on their possession of secular Western education, status differences within the group depending on the academic degree attained and the prestige of the school attended. The development of the intelligentsia as a counter-elite has its beginnings in the present decade, beginning around 1955, the year of the jubilee celebration of the twenty-fifth Anniversary of the Emperor's coronation. This was a lavishly contrived affair which, occurring at about the time that the first sizable group of postwar college students had returned from abroad, accentuated in their minds a sense of alienation from the *ancien régime*. The present decade is marked by dramatic increase in the number of Ethiopians with college degrees and secondary school certificates, and in the general prestige of education as such in the country. For, it will be remembered, in the late forties the government found it necessary to pay families to get them to send their children to school; whereas by the late fifties, there were far too many applicants for the available places.

The pattern of recruitment of members of the new nobility has been continuous with important elements of the traditional social system. It rests on the belief in the sanctity of the emperor and the legitimacy of his unlimited political authority, and the practice of emperors sometimes to raise to high position men of low background who were *ipso facto* more trustworthy. The personnel of the new nobility, moreover, have in a number of cases been drawn from members of old noble families.

By contrast, the formation of the intelligentsia represents a break with the

---

* Due largely to trade in coffee, whose export value climbed more or less steadily from Eth$17 million in 1947 to Eth$123 million in 1957.

past. The intellectuals are the product of a secular school system which is, as we have seen, a structure foreign to Abyssinian tradition. Their members are drawn from all parts of Ethiopian society, and in almost no cases consist of Western-educated members of the old group of literati, the *dabtarā*. The question of their integration into what has remained an essentially traditional social system has thus been Ethiopia's main sociological dilemma during the present decade. We shall return to this question after considering the composition and general situation of the intellectual class.

Whatever his line of work, the Ethiopian intellectual tends to be employed by the government, since employment opportunities in the private sector are still extremely limited; and where such exist, the government has often claimed priority over the intellectual's services by virtue of its having educated him. Many of the intellectuals work as public administrators, in the middle echelons of the government bureaucracy, with the titles of "assistant," "director," and "director general"; and there has been a growing tendency to appoint them in the higher levels, especially since 1961. Hundreds of them now work as teachers in the elementary and secondary schools,* and some six dozen teach at the college level. A small but growing number are employed as physicians, medical workers, engineers, and legal advisers in various government institutions. Still another group works in the small communications field—on the staffs of the various newspapers, the patriotic monthly *Menen,* and Radio Addis Ababa. The small group holding jobs outside the government works as engineers and bureaucrats in industrial firms, as employees of the Ethiopian Air Lines, or have small commercial or agricultural enterprises of their own.

With respect to interaction among the intellectuals, however, the most important distinction among them has been the place where they received their education. Here we may speak of two main groups: those who received part of their education abroad, the "foreign-educated" or "returnees"; and those who received all their education in Ethiopia, the "local-educated" or "locals."†

The Returnees

Close to two hundred Ethiopians studied abroad prior to the Italian occupation. Since French was then the official European language in Ethiopia,

---

* About forty-five hundred Ethiopians, of varying levels of educational attainment, were teaching in government schools of all types in 1960–61, according to the Ministry of Education school census for that year.

† This term is used as a neutral descriptive category, free from any negative connotations it may have acquired when first coined by the returnees. More recently, the West African term "been-to" has been incorporated into Amharic for referring to the returnee.

quite a few of these men went to school in France and Switzerland, while others studied in Egypt, England, the United States, and Italy. In general, this first group of returnees was enthusiastic and outspoken in their desire to modernize the country. They were emboldened by the feeling that Haile Selassie was their champion, though some of them, who took plans for a Young Ethiopia movement with them into exile during the occupation, felt a need for more radical reforms than the Emperor was willing to admit.

The pre-occupation intellectuals have no significant voice as such in Ethiopia today. Many of them were massacred by the Italians following the attempt on Graziani's life in 1937. Those who survived have been scattered, some being so thoroughly absorbed in the new nobility as to lose their identity as intellectuals, others tending to lead somewhat isolated and demoralized lives. Only the handful of older military officers, who were trained at the St. Cyr Academy in France, retain any semblance of common identity based on prewar study abroad.

In speaking of the returnees, then, we speak essentially of a group whose education abroad dates to the late forties and after. The typical postliberation returnee has studied from three to five years abroad in an English-speaking institution, under the sponsorship of the Ethiopian government; though there are many exceptions to this type.

As of June, 1959, the main countries in which some five hundred Ethiopians had studied since the mid-forties were: United States and Canada, 38 per cent; United Kingdom, 20 per cent; Lebanon (American University of Beirut), 17 per cent; Western Germany, 10 per cent; and India, 4 per cent. This pattern began to change somewhat at the end of the fifties as, in addition to these countries, Ethiopians in increasingly large numbers began to attend schools in Egypt, Italy, France, Israel, and Sweden. The subjects pursued by these students covered the whole academic spectrum—from dairying and forestry to languages and theology. Most of them, however, concentrated in one of four fields: social sciences, 30 per cent; engineering, 23 per cent; education, 12 per cent; and medical sciences, 12 per cent. Notably underrepresented in their studies were the fields of business and the natural sciences.

The length of time spent abroad varied considerably. Of the three hundred students who had returned by 1958 for whom complete information is available, 15 per cent studied abroad for only one year and 18 per cent for two years; 36 per cent were abroad from three to five years, 25 per cent from six to eight years, and 6 per cent for nine or more years. The education of about half of these students was paid for by the Ethiopian government itself. Others went on scholarships given by the United States government through AID (20 per cent); by other foreign governments, chiefly West Germany and

India (10 per cent); and by international organizations, chiefly WHO and ICAO (8 per cent). The others were financed privately, either by their families (8 per cent), or, in a few cases (3 per cent), by religious groups or business firms.

Given this variety of educational background, it is not surprising that the experience of study abroad has had a variable effect on the returnees. Their images of modernity are differently colored according to the country where they have received their higher education. Their archetypes for the modern component of language vary according to the language in which they have received their technical training.

Despite such variety—which may ultimately serve to enrich their cultural life more than to fragment it—several effects of the experience abroad appear common to nearly all the returnees. These include a radical broadening of perspective; the taste for a high standard of living; greater appreciation of political freedom; a heightened sense of Ethiopian identity; and an increase in nationalistic sentiment.

Because Ethiopian students are highly motivated to learn what goes on about them in foreign countries, their travel abroad has tended to broaden their outlooks rather than to confirm their prejudices. This expansion of perspective alters their attitude toward Ethiopia in two different ways. On the one hand, by enabling them to evaluate aspects of Ethiopian life they had previously taken for granted, it has made them more aggressively critical about conditions at home. On the other hand, it has given them a greater sense of pride about Ethiopia. They have noticed that, however advanced their host country, it had certain shortcomings of its own, a sort of observation which has tended to ease the sting of cultural inferiority inevitably felt during the stay in a more modernized society.

> Before going to the United States, I pictured it as the most perfect country on earth. We students in Ethiopia believed that everything good and beautiful comes from America. After studying there, I was disappointed in many ways. For example, I found the Americans to be hypocritical—they go to church, and don't care about religion; they talk about tolerance, and are still quite prejudiced. This was a great lesson for me. I can never be so romantic about a foreign country again, and can appreciate Ethiopia's strengths as well as its weaknesses better now.

Short travel tours sometimes had a similar effect:

> I spent several weeks in Yugoslavia. . . . And I must say—despite how backward we are here, we live much more happily than the Yugoslavs. The people themselves are wonderful—warm and generous; but their lives are miserable. That experience was really quite a surprise for me.

No matter what its shortcomings, the host country inevitably accustomed Ethiopians abroad to a higher standard of living than they had known at home—except for the difficulty of having to do without servants. Those students whose rural background and limited intellectual experience had led them to consider Addis Ababa as one of the most advanced cities in the world were often shocked by the comparison. No less shocking was the moral climate, which permitted one to express oneself freely and honestly. The taste for intellectual freedom was added to that of political freedom, as students whose horizons were limited by the meager intellectual fare at home came into hungry contact with authors like Marx and Freud, Dewey and Russell.

However much the Ethiopian students abroad might seek to lose themselves in the host culture, they were not permitted to do so. In the mirror of foreigners' regards, their identity as Ethiopians took clearer shape, transcending narrower tribal identifications. Questions about Ethiopia by foreigners aroused greater interest in Ethiopia's history and contemporary problems. A number of students were thus moved to dip into the literature on their country produced by travelers and scholars in the past, and some of them came to write theses and dissertations on problems related to Ethiopia's development.

All of these factors—broadening of perspective, acquaintance with a higher economic standard, less inhibited discussions, and greater self-consciousness as Ethiopians—contributed to a spirit of nationalist dedication. This spirit was confirmed or aroused in all but two groups of the returnees. One, consisting of children of some wealthy members of the new nobility, went abroad chiefly for the prestige and pleasure involved. For them the experience was an extended holiday; they were playboys more than students. The other group consists of those who were abroad for too short a time to have a complete educational experience—in some cases, for as little as three months. These students have tended to use the tour abroad chiefly as a weapon with which to lord it over their peers on return and otherwise to serve narrow personal ambitions. Those students, however, for whom study abroad entailed a more or less serious encounter with higher education and a more modernized culture normally experienced a swelling aspiration to serve their country. They returned home deeply critical of the status quo and determined to contribute substantially to the modernization of their society.

Ostensibly, the returnees have been well situated for making such a contribution. Thanks to prudent government policy since the early fifties, they have been enabled to enjoy a minimally comfortable standard of living. Given a monthly allowance from the moment they step off the plane, they have been automatically salaried at a scale based largely on the academic degree attained, with A.B.'s starting at Eth$450 a month and Ph.D.'s at Eth$700. In addition, provisions have been made for them to borrow money from the government in order to finance heavy investments like furniture or, more usually, an automobile. All this permits returnees to live at a standard which, while clear-ly inferior to what they enjoyed abroad, is well above that of all their countrymen except the higher nobility. Their income compares favorably with the prevailing monthly wages for policemen (Eth$25–$30) and district (*waradā*) governors (Eth$100), and not unfavorably with the salary earned by vice-ministers (Eth$1,000). Compared with the more sumptuous resi-dences of the new nobility, their housing is threadbare, their staff of servants small; but usually their homes contain one or two modern appliances—a radio or phonograph, perhaps a refrigerator.

The returnees have, moreover, been shown deference from many quarters: from the modernizing sector of the public which, in its growing esteem for education, has adulated them as the most educated Ethiopians and, in the early fifties, regarded them as something of national heroes; from resident Europeans and Americans, whose perception of shared understandings with the returnees has flattered them; and from the government, which at the least has shown consistent concern for their economic security and at best has given them responsibilities and status that they would not be granted in a more modernized society without considerably more experience.

Despite such apparent advantages, however, it must be said that the re-turnees as a whole have so far done little either to modernize their country or even to establish themselves as a self-respecting status group. Their failure to do so has become one of the most widely discussed questions in Ethiopia in recent years, both among the more self-critical of the returnees and among critical Ethiopian and non-Ethiopian observers. Instead of being leaders of the new era, they have been little more than misfits in the old. If the central quality of the life of the new nobility has been anxiety, that of the intellec-tuals has been frustration. In the passionate words of one of them: "There is a wound, a boiling within each and every one of the returnees." Theirs is the frustration of modernized individuals attempting to live meaningful lives in a society that has remained essentially traditional.

The ideological aspect of this dilemma is that no synthesis of traditional and modern perspectives has yet been effected which has won the adherence of a sizable number of intellectuals and which could serve to energize their transformation of the status quo. Consensus exists only with regard to a vague sense of the inadequacy of the traditional system. There is no sense of direction. Partly this reflects deprivation due to maladjustment in personal areas, but it also represents a genuine cultural problem.

Foreign-educated Ethiopians return intellectually aware of the traditional nature of their society, but emotionally unprepared to cope with the tenacity of tradition or with the paucity of modern institutions and culture. The ex-perience of culture shock seems greater when they return to Ethiopia than when they first went abroad. Then, they were taut with anticipation, eager to learn all they could and to enjoy life in a more modern society. On return, they were dismayed to find things so "backward": "I was struck at the airport by what I saw . . . the sadness in the people's faces, their undernourishment, their despair"—and plunged into a situation where their roles are ambiguous and their convictions are assaulted daily.

The perspective acquired in the course of prolonged study and residence abroad usually generates a sharp critique of Ethiopian culture on the occasion of return. In some extreme cases, Ethiopian tradition appears devoid of any value.

> Everything in our past has been based on the oppression of the masses by the feudal lords. We must overthrow it all and start from scratch.

*   *   *   *

> There is nothing in Ethiopian traditions that I find worth while. There has been no dynamic, no development, unless prodded from the outside or above. The music and poetry are repetitive; the social order is stagnant.

Most returnees, however, stop far short of wholesale condemnation of their traditions. They become aggravated by particular customs, such as *ishi naga* —Amharic for *mañana*—or certain requirements of etiquette. Nonetheless they have retained a basic attachment to their traditions which is re-awakened in the course of a somewhat painful re-adjustment.

> The main change since returning has been my education to be Ethiopian, to view things with the eyes of an Ethiopian. At first I expected things to be as we saw them in the United States; then I came to see the real concrete problems here, to be more understanding.

*   *   *   *

> The ideas I acquired abroad have not changed, only my vim and vigor. One comes to see the setbacks, the need to take two steps back in order to achieve one forward. . . . In the major areas, I identify with the old culture—in such matters as politeness, reserve, hospitality, and being concerned about one's relatives and close friends. In the minor respects, no. The elders carry some of these things to extremes. If someone dies, they go and sit for three days; we go to pay our respects for half an hour. There are a hundred and one customs that fall into this category.

A few returnees even come to acquire a nostalgic interest in the things of the old culture. They become eager to have Ethiopian history and culture studied by scholars. Some have expressed a desire to take up the study of Ge'ez and *qenē*.

All such resolutions of the cultural problem are highly personal syntheses. They remain stable only so long as the individual's life is satisfactory in other respects. They are not anchored in a *conscience collective*. They are islands of clarity in a sea of confusion that becomes evident in remarks like the following:

> While we were in high school here, we still followed the old beliefs. We went abroad and lost them all. Nothing has yet replaced them. We have no beliefs—in any sphere—religion, social, politics.

*   *   *   *

> We are all of us confused today. Perhaps it is that the change has come too fast. At any rate, we have lost our values. We don't know what is best for us to do.

*   *   *   *

> I don't believe there is anyone in the entire country who knows where we are heading or where we should be heading.

This confusion is the confusion of all Ethiopia today, but because the returnees became so deeply involved in Western culture while abroad they alone have experienced it so acutely. Were they engaged in satisfying work and enmeshed in family obligations, moreover, such malaise would be reduced. Precisely in these fundamental areas, however, the returnees are typically frustrated.

The burden of the returnees' frustration in work has not been to locate employment, but to find meaningful employment. It is true that several of the foreign-educated have had to wait for months, in some cases for over a year, after returning to Ethiopia before they were actually given employment. With the establishment of a placement board for returned students in the Ministry of Education about 1955, this difficulty has been minimized. The more fundamental problem has been that the institutional system has been insufficiently modernized to make proper use of individuals who had acquired specialized training abroad. There has been great variability of experience in this regard. Many of the technical intelligentsia have found suitable positions, especially those in the fields of medicine and engineering, and have led quite productive and satisfying work lives since shortly after their return. Many others, however, have been demoralized by the experience of having to occupy simple administrative positions which anyone with a little common sense could handle, or by being saddled with purely administrative responsibilities even when initially placed in a technical job. In such circumstances they have found themselves forgetting most of what they learned while abroad and felt themselves not being used.

Even when located in work broadly commensurate with their training received abroad, the returnees have been frustrated by numerous hardships in the work situation and by the difficulties of reform. As might be expected, work facilities are generally inferior to those which the returnees became familiar with in more industrialized societies. Nor is there any disposition to improve improvements with what facilities are available. Little attention is paid to the condition of offices, for example, which are normally located in dark, drab, depressing rooms. Furthermore, the operating procedures of Ethiopian administration are bound to frustrate those who have been conditioned to more rationalized systems of organization. Departments frequently operate with ex post facto budgets. Filing systems are hopelessly archaic. There is virtually no public consciousness of the importance of work *time.*

> Ethiopian persons are not geared to a timetable. I have to keep telling myself: "This is how we do it here." Seeing a ten-story building go up in a month, grass and all—that is not for here. . . . I get most annoyed when I cannot finish some matter as promised. Not wanting to reveal the name of my colleague or superior who is holding up the action, I have to make up excuses. Eventually I run out of excuses and this bothers me. . . . Sometimes I get angry and say: "I have given my word to someone, and must have the matter ready today; please sign it." And am told: "Oh, well, don't rush things so."

Work relationships have frequently exasperated the returnees. There has been little inclination to give technically competent employees proper jurisdiction over the personnel in their departments. Technically uneducated superiors have tended to make unrealistic demands—for example, requesting an immediate report on a complicated question that requires weeks to prepare. On the other hand, they have tended to assume that their age and experience are equivalent to the technical knowledge of the foreign-trained, so that technically warranted projects have been casually dismissed because they do not strike the fancy of the superior.

The returnees have not been so despondent about these conditions which, after all, could be changed—than they are about the apparent futility of trying to change them. Older employees are quick to resent alterations in the accustomed order.

> My efforts to reform are opposed by most of the men who run the [postal] system now. Some of them have been working there for forty years or so, and they want to keep things just the way they were when mail came in on camels, because they have always done it that way.

Such resistance to change at the workaday level is tacitly supported by those in the upper echelons of authority—the new nobility. In them the returnees have found their main antagonists and from them have received their most painful lacerations.

The *shamäggelotch,* or "elders," as they are termed by the intelligentsia, have by no means presented a solidary front in opposition to the young modernizers. On the contrary, the attitude of the new nobility toward the returnees has generally been sympathetic, and some of them have been quite helpful to individuals or groups of students during their hard pressed days as students abroad. The situation of action, however, has kept their degree of support of the returnees to a minimum. Three patterns of elder-returnee relations can be discerned: (1) The elder is concerned above all to maintain his position and, hence, to defend himself against any encroachment on his power on the part of younger people. This type has resorted to the various techniques of court politics—false rumors, libelous accusations, etc.—in order to check the influence of the returnees and have the more reformist among them transferred to less favorable positions. (2) The elder believes that if anything is to be accomplished in Ethiopia, it must be done by the educated young people, but he must be cautious in supporting the latter, for fear of getting into trouble at the palace himself if he offends any entrenched interests. Even when a returnee has been able to get the support of such a man for some reform, he may find when the time for implementation comes that his supporter has been transferred and left no commitment in writing for his successor. (3) While generally sympathetic to the returnees, this type fears the rashness and inexperience of youth and feels itself threatened by the prospect of being displaced. His apprehension is not aggressively expressed, but tends to take the form of discrediting the returnees by blaming them for every possible mistake. Whether due to the antagonism, caution, or ambivalence of the new nobility, the returnees have found relatively little effective support for their projected reforms. The ministers typically have shown them a progressive face and just as often have pursued a stagnant policy.

Vocational malaise and ideological uncertainty thus reinforce each other. The cycle of frustration is complete when we consider the marital problems of the returnee, which revolve about the difficulty of getting to know potential spouses, financial handicaps, the changing definition of marriage, and latent warfare between the sexes in the modernizing sector.

Except for a small number of returnees whose marriages have had to be arranged ones because of political considerations, the foreign-educated men, and a few of the women, are determined to choose their own spouses. Getting to know a potential spouse, however, remains a difficult matter. The traditional mores prevail with regard to social relationships between the sexes. A girl who goes out with boys is *ipso facto* presumed to have a bad character, and many of the girls in whom a returnee might be interested are not permitted to go out by their parents. There are few places where a young man and woman can go together and have privacy. Those who attempt to follow the Western custom of dating have been embarrassed.

The cost of marriage presents another obstacle. The quality of housing that a returnee aspires to for his potential family is far beyond his means in the present-day economy. Other assumed necessities—an automobile, expensive furniture, etc.—are equally burdensome investments if the returnee does not possess them. Furthermore, the traditional large wedding is still expected in most cases. In the city this involves an enormous expense—as much as Eth$2,000-$4,000—which often puts the groom in debt for several years.*

There are many returnees for whom these factors are excuses more than insuperable obstacles, or who frankly prefer the extended bachelordom made possible by the greater freedom of the modernizing sector to an uncertain match. If, as frequently is the case, they would marry only an educated wife, they may be discouraged by the shortage of educated Ethiopian women; or beset by too much pride, if coming from a humble background, to ask for the hand of an educated girl who is likely to come from an upper-class family. They may be victims of the cycle of antagonism that has developed between educated men and women in Ethiopia, the former attacking the latter for demanding too much in the way of material things and being only superficially modernized—"half-baked"—and the latter indicting the former for preferring foreign girls and unjustly neglecting Ethiopian women.

But the root of the problem is often deeper (leaving aside, for this discussion, characterological factors). It is entwined with a basic insecurity about the whole idea of marriage in the transitional atmosphere of contemporary Ethiopia. Perhaps nowhere in the minds of the returnees do traditional and modern norms stand in such delicate counterpoise as with regard to the question of the sort of wife one should marry and the proper type of relation to have with her. Should he prefer the traditional woman, modestly dressed and inconspicuous, or the Western ideal of a sexually attractive female? Should he have a wife who stays at home all the time, or one whom he takes along to social gatherings? Should he have a wife with whom to share interests and discuss problems, or one to order about and keep in her place? The returnees have normally been attracted by the Western marriage pattern while abroad, but it is so out of place in the Ethiopian context that many are troubled by the prospect on return. The foreign-educated man feels he should have an educated wife, but he also feels threatened by a woman who is independent, especially if she is holding a job. Such ambivalence adds an additional dimension of vulnerability to the returnee's position.

In sum: the conditions of life receptive to a modernizing intellectual stratum have not yet been established in Ethiopia. The personal frustrations of the returnees are an inevitable consequence of their being the bearers of modern culture in a traditional oligarchical order—especially one that has

---

* A new custom has developed in response to this problem. It has become the practice in some offices for sheets of paper to be circulated prior to a wedding in the ministry or agency where the groom is employed. Co-workers write the amount they wish to be deducted from their salaries in their behalf. Most recently, modest weddings have started to become respectable.

been affected by modernizing agents for but a relatively brief period and in a relatively diluted fashion. The beliefs and values which the returnees acquired while abroad concern national development, technical competence, and individuality, while the norms of the social structure in which they must live are based on the values of loyalty to monarch, ascribed status, and authoritarian relations.

Of many possible types of response to such a situation of strain, four are common among the Ethiopian intelligentsia. These we may designate by the terms Opportunism, Withdrawal, Reformism, and Rebellion. With reference to the three variables of commitment to modern goals and norms, acceptance of existing authorities, and the distinction between "activity" and "passivity," these patterns may be represented schematically as in Table 14.[59]

TABLE 14

MODES OF ADAPTATION OF ETHIOPIAN
RETURNEES

	Commitment to Modern Values	Acceptance of Existing Authorities	"Activity"
Opportunism........	−	+	+
Withdrawal.........	+	−	−
Reformism.........	+	+	+
Rebellion..........	+	−	+

Opportunism is the mode of adaptation in which the returnee's commitment to modern goals and norms is eclipsed by his passion for status, power, and income. He differs from the traditional aspirant for high position in Abyssinia in that two of his status qualifications are novel—residence abroad, and a university degree—and above all in that the pursuit of his personal goals entails a *renunciation* of nationalistic ideals and universalistic standards which were nurtured while abroad. For some opportunists this is no real problem: their study abroad was all along essentially a façade to be used in advancing their careers. But for the others the process of becoming an opportunist is a gradual one and attended by chronic self-recriminations, as the returnee finds himself compulsively agreeing with his superiors and flattering them on every occasion, and performing actions primarily for the sake of advancement rather than for the sake of doing a job well.

It is impossible to go on pursuing progressive principles indiscriminately. I sometimes see my friends doing things now which we used to condemn when we were students abroad together. I wonder at times if I am losing sight of my principles altogether.

Withdrawal is the solution of those who have retained their principles at the expense of being effectual in action. The routes of escape are varied. One way is transferring attention to problems outside the country—to international relations, problems of pan-Africanism, or the gossip about London, Paris, and New York.

To me the independence of all African nations is more important than the progress of Ethiopia.

Some spend their energies in convivial relations with resident Westerners (diplomatic and technical assistance personnel, foreign businessmen) or in the traditional rounds of family visiting. Quite a few returnees lose themselves in card-playing or chess whenever they can, and a number have taken to heavy drinking. Often the returnee who withdraws shows no "symptoms" other than a general constriction of his life into narrow work routines and creature functions. At the same time he may be experiencing a fairly acute sense of estrangement.

Our generation is not really living. We are not "engaged." The simple weaver—most of the people in this country—are "engaged." We are not; we live from day to day. When I leave work I go to the Ras Hotel or somewhere else. I don't want to go home, there is nothing there for me. I have nothing to work for. I have no family, nor any interest in saving money.

The third type of response, Reformism, involves the attempt both to maintain principles and to be effective in action under the existing political order. This alternative places great demands on the personality system and might well be designated as the pattern of "moral heroism."

What we lack today is proper organization. In default of organization, we are forced to rely on morality.

The reformist returnee serves his country according to universalistic standards even though these norms are scarcely institutionalized; even though, in other words, he is likely to be criticized and even punished for maintaining standards in the face of demands by superiors and relatives to do otherwise, or for solving problems in a rational manner on his own initiative. Yet if he is officially disregarded or censured, his efforts do not go unnoticed by the patriotic modernizing elements of the population who, in a covert, informal system of communication, tend to establish severe judgments on the "bad guys" and the "good guys," and to idolize the latter as potential leaders.

In the case of Rebellion, finally, the attempt is made to be active in the pursuit of modern goals but in a spirit of basic alienation from the existing authorities. Except for a very few eccentric individuals who have seemed oblivious to the dangers of speaking out their criticism of the status quo in public, this has in the nature of current circumstances necessarily involved clandestine activity. Returnees have been involved in small conspiratorial groups since the mid-fifties. The December, 1960, coup d'état has been the most ambitious rebellious project to be acted out so far. Similarly motivated activities have included the duplication and distribution of subversive literature, and the formation of small groups as groundwork for an eventual political party.

Our data do not permit reliable estimates of the frequency of these different modes of adaptation among the returnees. It is important to note, however, that individuals often change from one mode to another in the course of their experience after return and that many follow more than one pattern at the same time. It is unlikely that the total number of returnees oriented primarily as rebels has ever exceeded two per cent. Most of them move in and out of phases of Reformism, Withdrawal, and Opportunism, depending to a large extent on the accidents of their appointments. A more concrete picture of their experience may be suggested by the following case study, that of a Western-educated Ethiopian who went from a phase of Withdrawal to one of Reformism tinged with Opportunism.

The Adjustment of "Haile": Case Study of a Returnee

October, 1958. Haile has recently returned from four years of study in a Western country. He speaks very critically about the state of things in Ethiopia. He is particularly upset by the prevailing inefficiency, the lack of industriousness, and the interminable procrastination (*ïshi naga*).

January, 1959. Haile seems deeply depressed. The ministry in which he has been placed affords him no opportunity to work effectively and the job he has bears no relation to what he was trained for. He has withdrawn more into himself, but to all outward appearances plays perfectly well, with great self-assurance, the role of the Amhara bureaucrat.

July, 1959. Now Haile is working in a different ministry, in a job somewhat more closely related to his training. He appears to feel productive and useful now, and his criticism is constructive. For example, he frequently compares the situation in the United States and Ethiopia, to show how the same sort of problem can be solved more readily in the U.S. because of its greater facilities. Though Ethiopia's comparative handicaps frustrate him, he talks of plans for the development of Ethiopia with some enthusiasm. . . . Haile complains of an

FIG. 30.—*A widower who has become a monk*

. 31.—*A group of clergy*

FIG. 32.—*Haile Selassie as a boy with his father, Rās Makonnen*

FIG. 33.—*The Emperor attending a ceremony at the University College*

overload of work, noting that he must not only do his own work but also rectify the mistakes made by others which are brought to him. In his whole branch of the ministry, he finds only two really effective workers besides himself, and they, too, are returnees. . . . He feels fortunate in having encountered no major opposition to the things he is doing in his work and points happily to the fact that his assistant minister has supported him throughout.

October, 1959.   Haile now is saying that things are fine in Addis Ababa and stresses the great improvement that has been made during the past five years. He claims that he is getting along fine in his ministry, because his job is straight "busy work." Even so, he is not a pure "ritualist"; he has already negotiated a number of reforms in the operations of his office. His general outlook seems bright—partly, no doubt, because he is "arriving" (what with printed name-cards and a smoothly functioning job) but also because he has a pretty fiancée whom he plans to marry next year. . . . At another point, however, he shows great exasperation over the considerable conflict among factions within the ministry. He decries the nepotism practiced by the heads of these factions. He says that he tries to stay independent of their intrigues.

June, 1960.   Recently Haile was given additional responsibilities in his ministry, and he expects a raise in salary soon. Although this new work is still further removed from the subjects he studied while abroad than was his previous job, he no longer complains about not being hired to do what he had been trained for or about not being used. He remains unhappy about his minister, who brings in his own men from the outside rather than promote men from the ranks—"or else I would have been a director general by now." On the other hand, he mentions with evident pleasure the fact that the Emperor sent over a gift at the time of his wedding. . . . Haile's wife is a simple, traditional sort of Ethiopian girl. He seems happy with her and with their home—an old, poorly built structure that is falling apart, but which she has taken pains to enliven with a few decorations, and has equipped with a radio. He looks forward to the prospect of building a house on their own land sometime in the future. Meanwhile, a baby is on the way. . . . The circle has come full swing. Haile talks proudly about his work, his family, and his country.

The Locals

Ethiopians with only a secondary school education comprise a group which must be reckoned as part of a burgeoning intelligentsia. Relative to the mass of the population, their intellectual attainments are high indeed. Although their cultural level is usually lower than that of the returnees, they include a few extremely cultivated self-educated men, and others whose intense intellectual curiosity would put the average returnee to shame. Apart from such considerations, however, the fact that they are among the small number of bearers of modern culture in present-day Ethiopia suffices to justify considering them as part of a secular educated elite. The very small but growing number of graduates from Ethiopian colleges who do not go abroad for graduate study may for the present discussion be included in this group, though in some respects their situation is intermediate between the locals and the returnees.

The basic differences between the returnees and locals is that the latter never lost touch with Ethiopia. Their growth has been more closely in step with the growth of their nation. Not having been accustomed to the comforts of a more modern environment, they find it less trying to live with what Addis Ababa has to offer. Not having become so deeply attached to norms rooted in an alien culture, they need not rack themselves re-adjusting. They have been spared the extremes of "soaring and collapsing enthusiasm" which inform the experience of so many foreign-educated men in traditional societies.[60]

Their cultural orientation is far less anomic than it is patriotic. They have remained enmeshed in familiar personal nexuses, to kin and schoolmates, ethnic and regional confreres, which have minimized the disruptive effect of rapid culture diffusion. Because of their essentially particularistic orientation, they are far less perplexed about the problems of institutionalizing universalistic standards than they are enthusiastic about anything that represents indigenous achievement, such as the modern secular songs created and performed by talented members of the Imperial Bodyguard or the National Patriotic Association.

Their work life is often quite gratifying: it represents, in any case, the best that they have ever known at first hand. It is not so hard for them to get used to rudimentary facilities and procedures, or to lower standards of performance. They are supplely adaptive to the moods of their superiors and the nuances of domestic political intrigue, even though they may be moved periodically to denounce such intrigue.

The locals also tend to be more content in their sexual adjustment than the returnees. The local can live happily for a long time as a bachelor, maintaining polite and distant relations with the traditional girls and frequenting the brothels for dancing and more intimate relations. (Returnees normally do not have patience for the shy, traditional girls; and they are too concerned about public opinion to be seen visiting brothels. When they or the locals do visit the brothels, it is often by way of a backdoor entrance.) When they marry, the locals almost invariably choose a traditional type of wife with relatively little education and with whom they expect to have an authoritarian relationship.

In sum: the local is not so afflicted by those problems which derive from the central dilemma of the returnee—how to fulfil himself according to modern standards in an intractable, traditional environment. The local's dilemma typically lies in a different realm, that of economic and social mobility. Whereas the returnee has been given a comparatively high income and status almost as a matter of course, the local has normally started his work life with a relatively low salary and little prestige. If the returnee has felt deprived relative to the Westerners in whose society he has lived, the local has felt deprived relative to the returnee.

The local lives on a day-to-day basis at a relatively simple standard. Though he shares the returnee's passion for woolen suits and, in many cases, for a car of his own, he is not, like the returnee, preoccupied with the quest for housing that conforms to Western standards. Except for those with extraordinary talents and family connections, the locals have had difficulty locating jobs that they feel are not beneath their dignity and which pay salaries sufficient to cover their relatively modest needs. They customarily receive a starting salary in the neighborhood of Eth$150. The more ambitious and fortunate among them have, by changing jobs, manipulating superiors, and improving skills, worked their way up to salaries in the Eth$400–$500 category. Some have become provincial teachers for a while, in order to accumulate money on which to live while shopping for a position in Addis Ababa and with which to influence some higher official to grant it to them. There remains a hard core of locals who feel they are underpaid and live in constant resentment of this situation.

This resentment has produced a general sort of negativism which characterizes many of the locals, a negativism expressed in the form of backbiting and denunciation of the higher government officials and the nobility generally. They decry social injustice and the uses of nepotism. They moralize profusely against those whom fortune has shown greater favors. But not all their social criticism is born of resentment. There are also among the locals many young men who are comfortably situated but fired by patriotic fervor with a desire for social reform.

The local is as deeply concerned about asserting his status vis-à-vis the less educated as he is to advance his position in the hierarchy. Locals are extremely meticulous about the state of their clothes. They have their shoes shined several times daily, even when they are eating only one solid meal per day. They are intent on receiving the proper deference—for example, on being served properly in a hotel. This concern for status is projected in the form of an intense nationalism that considers the speedy displacement of non-Ethiopians holding important jobs in the country a more urgent need than the establishment of effective modern institutions and universalistic standards.

Some locals can be found, of course, whose problems and aspirations resemble those of the returnees, and vice versa. However, the characteristics here associated with the two types follow logically from their basic situation and have been observed sufficiently to justify this depicting of them in terms of ideal types. The distinction is further justified on the grounds that the two groups have developed a modicum of corporate identity and a degree of mutual antagonism which was particularly pronounced in the mid-fifties.

The returnees were at first inclined to regard their locally educated countrymen with snobbish pride because of the keen sense of superiority which study abroad conferred. It was natural, moreover, for the returnees to associate most closely with those who had shared the very important personal experience of living abroad, and so they tended to neglect their former schoolmates who never crossed the seas. At times, in fact, they scarcely bothered to exchange greetings with them.

The sense that they were being regarded as inferiors embittered the locals. At the same time they were jealous that they, too, had not had the opportunity to study abroad. These mutual incriminations were heightened by economic competition, the returnees claiming that those who stayed behind had the advantage of working their way up into significant and lucrative positions, the locals believing that a degree from abroad was an automatic entree to a good job.

The latent antagonism between locals and returnees came to a head in 1957, with the simultaneous publication in the *Voice of Ethiopia* of an article by a local criticizing returnee behavior[61] and the presentation of a play by the National Patriotic Association which caricatured them. The play, for example, showed a returnee entering the office of a minister, patting him on the back, puffing cigarette smoke into his eyes, sitting back with his feet up on the minister's desk and talking on and on disrespectfully. Another returnee was shown failing to recognize his own mother when she comes into his office, exclaiming: "Woman, get out of here!" A small group of returnees protested these insults with a petition to the Emperor, who is said to have brought some criticism to bear upon the authorities involved.

With the return of increasing numbers of Ethiopians from study abroad, however, the prestige of a foreign degree has diminished, and the appearance of classes of locally educated A.B.'s, who have remained in the country to work, has further blurred the cleavage between returnees and locals. Finally, the returnees' growing awareness of their own "failure" has in many cases given them added sympathy toward the locals.

> The locals have as much right to live in the land as the returnees and as much duty to help the country. They should be given responsibility commensurate with what they are able to do. Doing serious work and being a leader do not require going abroad. We may find a leader in one of these kids. . . . In private life, I may not have much to do with them: I associate with a small group of friends, as does everyone; and you can't know everybody. But I have no contempt for the locals, and some of them are my best friends.

*   *   *   *

> The locals are the real patriots around here and the ones from whom real action will come.

The locals, in turn, seem to have become less suspicious that the returnees are looking down on them. Yet, in more recent years, they have found different grounds on which to be critical of the returnees. They see the returnees as alienated from Ethiopian life, withdrawn from public action, and consumed with private concerns, instead of living up to expectations and exercising dynamic leadership in the transformation of Ethiopian society.

> The returnees know nothing about Ethiopia when they leave, and when they come back they are just like the *faranj*. We, who have not studied much, cannot see far. We know little more than to do our daily routine. But they, who have the vision, don't do anything. They borrow thousands of dollars when they return, to buy furniture, rent a home, get a car, and so on; and that is all they think about.

The dissatisfaction of many locals with the returnees has in fact increased their own self-esteem and ambition to exert leadership themselves.

In terms of the total pattern of stratification in Ethiopia, however, the factors uniting locals and returnees outweigh those separating them. Despite differences of emphasis, they share a basic estrangement from the traditional masses and elites and a deep antagonism toward the government and most of the new nobility. They are unanimous in feeling that something is dreadfully wrong in the state of Ethiopia. Frequently they cannot articulate just what they object to, or else they seize upon some flagrant social evil as the bête noire: with the locals tending to be most outspoken against the widespread prostitution, or alcoholism, or the abuses of the courts, or the inequalities of wealth; and the returnees tending to single out inefficient practices in administration, or nepotism, or corruption in high places. Above all, perhaps, they share an increasing sense of *impatience,* a sense of being smothered in an archaic and stagnant social order, which they designate so expressively with

the Amharic phrase *ya-ḳantu weddāsē zaman*—"the era of futile flattery."
For, whatever other aspects of modern culture they have identified with,
the locals and returnees are seized with the promise of its first principle: dynamism.[62] Should they join forces, among themselves and with each other,
they might create the effective intelligentsia which is indispensable for realiz-
ing this dynamism in action. They would play complementary, and equally
necessary, parts; the locals contributing their greater drive and closeness to
traditional society, the returnees their broader perspective and skepticism
toward simplistic answers and total reforms.

There are numerous obstacles to such a progressive development. Some of
them represent the persistence among the intellectuals of a number of traditional pan-Abyssinian characteristics which inhibit both the exercise of creative leadership and the capacity for solidary action. The traditional context of
these characteristics will be discussed in the chapters which follow. The most
conspicuous obstacle, however, has been the manner in which the Ethiopian
government has sought to integrate the intellectuals in the social system. This
is the subject to which we now turn.

The Role of the Government

In the hierarchy of values which sustained the traditional Abyssinian social
order, that of the transcendental religious orientation represented by the
Orthodox Church may be said to have held the paramount position. This is
the sense in which, as has so often been remarked, religion has been Abyssinia's only truly unifying factor throughout the centuries. Religious charisma
transferred from foreign sanctuaries—the mythical Ark of the Covenant
brought from Jerusalem and the archbishop periodically imported from Egypt
—provided the ultimate source of legitimacy in the society, upholding the
authority of a sacred Christian monarch, church-defending warlords, and a
numerous and functionally differentiated clergy. It so penetrated the social
system that the basic unit of Abyssinian civil life was in fact a religious one,
the parish.

In retrospect it would seem that the most profound aspect of Haile Selassie's
accomplishment has been to dislodge the transcendental religious value from
highest place and to replace it with the system-integrative value of loyalty to
the emperor.[63] His mission has been above all a secularizing one. To accomplish it he has had greatly to increase his political and economic resources; but
insofar as his regime has been accepted, and not based exclusively on sheer
power—which to some extent is certainly the case—the paramount value in
Ethiopia under Haile Selassie has become loyalty to the emperor as a symbol
of the whole society. The autonomous significance of the church has been
reduced; its extra-Ethiopian source of charisma has been cut off, and its func-

tion has been more closely than ever tied to the service and support of the Crown.

The system-integrative value was not only subordinate to transcendental religious values in the traditional order, but it was also in competition with the separate instrumental orientations of the feudal lords. This introduced the chief instability of the traditional system. Commitment to the separate goals of the feudal lords chronically competed with that of loyalty to the emperor; and after the calamities of the sixteenth and seventeenth centuries the former decisively gained the upper hand. With the ascendance of the system-integrative value under Haile Selassie, accordingly, the semi-autonomous status of feudal nobles could no longer be tolerated, and their powers and functions were sharply reduced.

In their stead, but as arms of the emperor and living symbols of allegiance to him, a new nobility was established as the focus of national power and prestige. New goals were pronounced for the system as a whole, but integrative considerations of loyalty remained decisive: no system goals were pursued which threatened to disrupt the internal security of the regime. Finally, a generation of young men was trained in skills that would provide sufficient technical competence to provide amenities and façades to edify the emperor and his courtiers as well as to increase the nation's military strength, standard of living, and international prestige. The integrative strategy in dealing with educated Ethiopians has consistently been one of exploiting their skills without permitting the values represented by them—technical competence and national development—to be fully actualized; to make them, in effect, appendages of the court just as much as the new nobility.

Haile Selassie has sought to do this by maintaining a paternalistic relationship with the intellectuals. Government pronouncements stress that whatever advantages Ethiopians have had by way of education have resulted from his personal generosity. The Emperor has sought to make visible his paternal solicitation and bounty, for example, by visits to various secondary schools and colleges, and by sending them baskets of fruit on occasion. He has personally conferred the diplomas to all graduates of the University College. Similarly, Ethiopian students who have returned from study abroad have normally been expected to have an audience with the Emperor, in which their occupational plans are discussed and they are given some fatherly advice from the throne. The following excerpts from typical audiences of this nature were reported in the *Ethiopian Herald*.

[A speech by a returnee]:

Your Imperial Majesty!

I feel honoured and privileged to speak on behalf of my fellow students expressing our deep gratitude to Your Imperial Majesty. . . .

Thanks to the untiring endeavour of Your Imperial Majesty in the field of education, we now have not only elementary and secondary schools throughout the country but also different higher educational institutions providing the youth of our country with higher education. Besides this, competent students are selected and sent abroad for specialization, as a result of which the number of Ethiopian students in foreign countries is increasing. Those of us who are now standing before Your Imperial Majesty are only a few among those who have been given such an opportunity. . . .

Your Imperial Majesty's struggle is to enable Ethiopia to benefit from the advantages of modern education in order to improve the standard of living of Your people so that Ethiopia will play adequately its part in the international community. Consequently, the public services that are rendered in the reign of Your Imperial Majesty are enormously great compared with the past. This can be seen easily by the number of ministries and other government agencies established by Your Imperial Majesty. . . .[64]

[A reply by the Emperor]:

We have been deeply touched by what you have said on behalf of the returned students. From you, We expect devotion to your country and your Emperor. . . . Endeavour to profit your country from the fruits of your education. Men are in great need today. It is not enough to be labeled as "man"—one must be worthy of the name by being of use to the community. This is the real test of education.

You must get in intimate touch with the cultural heritage of your country. Familiarise yourselves with the modes of life from which you must have been estranged naturally by your absence. You must endeavour to purge yourselves gradually of alien influence in your daily lives, and so God help you.[65]

This sort of paternal relation has served not only to promote the loyalty of his educated "children" but also to check mild cases of dissidence. Grown men with sophisticated technical training who may have voiced some critical sentiments have been called in for mild reproof: "Why have you behaved thus? Did We not always bring you fruit and other things when you were at school?"

Such a policy was no doubt viable when Ethiopians with secondary education numbered in the hundreds, but it becomes increasingly implausible as the Emperor's family of educated youth multiplies into thousands. No less relevant to its long-run futility is the fact that knowledge, unlike wealth and political position, is an inalienable possession. Their knowledge gives Western-educated Ethiopians a kind of independence of the Emperor that is lacking in most of the new nobility, and that perhaps may be compared to the private armies of the feudal lords or the power of excommunication held by the church. It was awareness of this that prompted one returnee to say: "The Emperor will have to learn that our education is not a plaything he can turn on or off as he pleases."

But this gentle, paternal control has been backstopped by more rigorous sanctions. Censorship controls assure that anything that is published is highly flattering of the government. Intelligence networks keep intellectuals from speaking their minds and developing them through open exchange with others. Associations have in general not been permitted to form, or else have been saturated with government informers. Coupled with these repressive measures has been the policy of making appointments dependent on the extent to which one curries favor with the Emperor directly, or one of the new nobles who is high in favor at a given time. The intellectuals, no less than the new nobility, have been kept in line by *shum-shĭr* and *divide et impera*. "We have been kept from acting," said one remorseful returnee, "by fear and the sweetness of office."

In the political order sustained by the rule of Haile Selassie, the paramountcy of loyalty to the imperial government as a value has precluded the ascendance of values of national development and technical competence, values it is the peculiar burden of the intelligentsia to bear and assert. In this situation a vicious cycle of mutual mistrust has developed between the government and the intellectuals. Although the articulation of standards and the expression of criticism are important functions of intellectuals, the Emperor has tended to regard all expressions of criticism which reflect on the government, which is his personal government, as expressions of filial ingratitude at best, and at worst as signs of subversion. The intellectuals, in turn, have accepted this definition of the situation and have tended to assume—after some disheartening experiences in the course of the fifties—that is was not plausible for them to express criticism in a framework of basic loyalty to the regime. Distrust fed distrust, and antagonism mounted. The abortive coup d'état of December, 1960, was but the most outspoken and violent expression of this.

This growth of antagonism to the government has seeped down among the students. The feeling has become increasingly widespread among students at home and abroad that genuine service to the nation and the performance of technical functions are incompatible with a loyal and secure existence under the present regime. Thus, one student in a Western country said in 1961: "I am afraid to return to Ethiopia. I fear that I shall either lose all my principles, as so many of my friends seem to have done, or that I shall end up without a job or in prison."

ETHIOPIA'S DILEMMA

Haile Selassie has often proclaimed his devotion to a program of modernization. His personal achievements in this direction have been substantial: the establishment of much modern bureaucratic machinery, the institution of a parliament and electoral procedures, a mild degree of industrialization, and, above all, the provision of a modern secular education for thousands of young

people. He has been the procreator of much of what demand for modernization now exists in the country, although the Italian colonial administration
must also be credited for a certain amount of this demand. By the fifties,
however, the growth of the demand of modernization had become self-sustain-
ing, if only in a relatively small part of the population. At that point Haile
Selassie was unwilling, or at least unable, to take the next step, to raise national development higher in the societal value hierarchy than loyalty to the
Crown. Thus, a traditional oligarchy has been maintained, in which the
development of a self-respecting modern intelligentsia has been effectively
restrained and its decisive ascendance as a new elite has been prevented.

The paramount sociological problem in Ethiopia in the coming decades
concerns whether or not this pattern will be broken. There is no guarantee
that it will be. It is highly thinkable that the opportunists among the intellectuals will be absorbed into the new nobility and that a new oligarchy will
entrench itself and maintain its exclusive position by increased repression.[66]
The number of young people being given secondary and college education
will continue to be limited to a diminutive percentage, and the deeply rooted
sentiments of the mass of the population for a regime of traditional oligarchy
will not be offended. Economic development will proceed at a snail's pace,
and what additional wealth is produced will flow into the pockets of a small
minority. One possible outcome of such an eventuality would be that the
modernizing infrastructure of the society would grow increasingly restless,
culminating in a revolution which installed a modernizing oligarchy.

Alternatively, modernizing forces already unleashed in the country may
gather momentum and sustain a gradual breakthrough of the new order. If
one were to credit the reports of many who have spoken with the Emperor at
first hand, this would be his desire. But far more than imperial approval of a
distant ideal is required for it to become reality. Two conditions, above all,
would be essential. One is that the systematic, if unwitting, demoralization
of the intellectuals would have to be ended. Some sphere would have to be
created in which universalistic standards have full sway, in which a modernizing intelligentsia can maintain and develop standards and transmit them to
younger elements. The most obvious way to do this would be through a university which, by guaranteed financial support, independence from political
pressures, and determined operation at a high standard, could provide the
Ethiopian government and people with the technical and executive intelligentsia needed for effective modernization, and could provide an environment in
which a corps of "custodians of the public good," loyal to the regime but
free to express criticism, might be developed. The program for such a university was carefully drawn up by the planners of the Haile Selassie I University. It remains to be seen whether the opposition which muffled that program
shortly after its inception, in the spring of 1962, was motivated primarily by

personal antagonism toward some of the foreign academic officials intrusted with its implementation, or whether it primarily reflected natural political pressures against the establishment of an autonomous and vigorous university. Whatever the reason, the failure of the university to develop in the promising manner in which it had been conceived means that for some time to come only the continued sending of large numbers of Ethiopian students abroad will supply the intelligentsia required if modernization is to continue, and that their demoralization on return can only be reduced by instituting an effective civil service system and permitting them some degree of freedom in speech, press, and association.

The other condition is that the intellectuals themselves will have to break out of their posture of defeatism and negativism. They will have to abandon the delusive image implied by the intellectual who replied, when asked why he was sitting around in his office and doing no work: "I'm waiting until the government changes." The burden for the breakthrough rests upon them: upon their capacity to push forward in the light of developmental needs and technical requirements, maintaining a sense of affinity both with the government and with the traditional masses. Until the values of the intelligentsia are effectively institutionalized, they will get nowhere unless their ranks produce fewer "escapees" and more "moral heroes." The chances for the success of this elite would seem to rest in part on its mastery of those qualities which Edward Shils has described in analyzing the prerequisites for successful leadership in the new states—"on its capacity for self-restraint and its effectiveness in legitimating itself through modernizing achievement, through a due respect for the claims of traditional beliefs and through its recruitment of a stratum of intellectuals of intermediate level who can reinterpret traditional beliefs, adapt them to modern needs and translate them into a modern idiom."[67]

Are Ethiopian intellectuals capable of this? In the succeeding chapters we shall consider factors which work against their so doing. Yet there is no doubt that many educated Ethiopians have quietly been demonstrating such qualities for years now. Already numerous intellectuals, working as medical officers, teachers, agricultural extension workers, engineers, lawyers, journalists, and bureaucrats have shown great capacity for translating traditional Abyssinian reserve into self-restrained progressivism, and through diligent application to the task at hand and a sympathetic orientation to their tradition-minded countrymen have been laying the foundations for the great transformation. Whatever the pace and pattern of Ethiopia's political development, such work constitutes the indispensable raw material of her modernization.

6

ORALITY AND THE SEARCH
FOR LEADERSHIP

In the previous chapter we observed that modern-educated Ethiopians, particularly those who were educated abroad, acquired knowledge, skills, patriotic motivation, and social position with which they might conceivably have made substantial reforms and innovations in Ethiopia's institutions. And yet, in their own eyes as in the eyes of some high government officials and foreign observers, they have done relatively little. Their behavior has been marked by a conspicuous absence of creative leadership and solidary action.

Among many of the modern-educated this alleged sin of omission has, in turn, generated an underlying current of reproach against the government and at times against themselves. We have described some features of Ethiopia's domestic political situation which have limited the freedom of modern-educated Ethiopians to carry out progressive activities. A number of them have proceeded from awareness of those limitations to placing all blame on the government for Ethiopia's slow pace of development. Others, however, have turned some if not all of that reproach inward. "It is up to us," they say, "and we have done nothing. Why have we failed? Why have we no moral backbone, no character?"

This chapter and the next are concerned with the basis of this latter reproach, as well as with the more general task of enriching our understanding of traditional Amhara culture. We shall proceed on the assumption that insofar as modern-educated Ethiopians have failed to take decisive steps in developing their country they have been held back by other constraints and

218

limitations in addition to those imposed by the government. In the present chapter we shall deal chiefly with factors which are inhibitive of creative leadership, and in the chapter which follows chiefly with factors which affect the capacity for solidary action.

One of the most honest and perceptive of my foreign-educated informants had this to say about the absence of creative leadership among the returnees:

> Our maladjustment may be more our fault than that of the government. We have been led to expect everything from the government, and have become dependent to such a point that we can scarcely think or act for ourselves.

This is a remarkable and convincing piece of self-analysis. It falls short only insofar as it implies that the posture of dependence on governmental authority is something peculiar to the modern-educated. It is true that there have been certain conditions such as the "welfare" character of the secondary schools, which are specific to the experience of the modern-educated and which have accentuated a tendency to overdependence. But this tendency is endemic in traditional Amhara-Tigre culture, and those modern Abyssinians who exhibit it are following an inclination deeply rooted in the needs they have acquired and the culture they have internalized in their childhood.

There are various ways in which one might conceptualize this problem. It is not unrelated to what other authors have referred to variously as lack of achievement motivation or lack of innovational personality. The approach of this chapter will stress certain psychoanalytic concepts and insights. In so doing, it will not attempt to delineate an Amhara "basic personality," a task well beyond the scope of the present study.[1] Rather, we shall be concerned here solely with certain kinds of motivational orientation which are widely shared among the Amhara and which frequently inform their social behavior and their cultural symbolism.

Adopting the terminology developed by Erik Erikson,[2] we may rephrase the point about Amhara overdependence by saying that *in Amhara action and fantasy the social modality of "getting" figures very prominently*. The superior is oriented chiefly to getting food, services, and deference from his inferior;[3] the inferior is oriented chiefly to getting favors from his superior. And most interaction among the Amhara is cast in the form of superior-inferior personal dyadic relations. The prominence of this modality reflects a fixation of libido on what Erikson calls a mode of approach to the environment that is "incorporative," and that originates in connection with the infant's experience with a particular part of his body, the oral zone. The central thesis of this chapter is that Amhara behavior and symbolism exhibit a very high degree of attachment of libido, not only to the organ *mode* of incorporation, but even more to the oral *zone*.

THE PHENOMENA OF AMHARA ORALITY

Shortly after an Amhara child is born some butter is placed in his mouth. This is done in the belief that it will keep his voice from becoming harsh. From that moment on, the mouth never ceases to be an organ of extraordinary importance in his life. Its cultural importance is reflected in the attention given to it in the Amharic vocabulary: Baeteman's *Dictionnaire Amarigna-Français* lists some sixty idioms built with the Amharic word for mouth, *af*, more than are listed for any other words in the language except "eye," "heart," and "earth."[4] The organ is publicly celebrated in such proverbs as: "Cleverness of mouth, to the master; cleverness of hand, to the slave."

The oral zone is of course of universal significance. Some items of oral imagery probably appear in most languages, and manifestations of oral libido appear in many forms familiar to Westerners: the French love for gourmandism, the German passion for beer-drinking and singing, the American addiction to cigarettes, chewing gum, and "life-savers." Many of the less familiar phenomena to be related below in describing Amhara orality, moreover, are found in most of the cultures of Africa and the Middle East. But such phenomena often appear inconspicuously alongside other culturally patterned impulses and sublimations stemming from other phases of psychosexual development. What may distinguish the Amhara—and doubtless some other cultures—is the extent to which the oral zone is an object of attention and a source of behavioral modes and expressive symbolism. The Amhara, it appears, have a preoccupation with orality.

This preoccupation is manifest in three different kinds of phenomena. There are, first of all, aspects of Amhara culture which express a strong positive attachment to the infantile experience of sucking, in pure and in numerous sublimated forms. These we shall designate as the phenomena of *oral erotism*. Second, there are the aspects of Amhara culture which express a strong positive attachment to the oral zone as a center for various aggressive activities—the modes which Erikson calls "incorporation by biting," "oral retention," and "oral intrusion." These we shall collectively designate as the phenomena of *oral sadism*. Finally, there are phenomena which express a conflict about the gratification of many of these oral desires; and these we shall refer to as the phenomena of *oral ambivalence*.

Oral Erotism

Feeding at the breast is a prominent and beloved experience in Amhara life. The Amhara infant is suckled whenever he wishes, at the slightest show of desire. Since he is rarely separated from his mother it is easy for him to satisfy himself at any time of day or night. Popular beliefs about breast-feeding support this permissiveness. If a baby is not suckled whenever he wishes to be, it is believed that he will become sick or will not grow strong, and the negligent mother is looked on as one of evil character.

Not only is the infant's desire to suck freely indulged, but it is indulged for a fairly long time. The normal period for breast-feeding is two to three years. Only if a new sibling happens on the scene is weaning deliberately effected. If another child is not forthcoming, and the mother is not ill, there is no inclination at any time to deny the child the breast. In many cases nursing continues until the child is four or five, when his work obligations begin to interfere.

The attitude of oral permissiveness is manifest in other ways. Thumb-sucking is accepted with good humor, and when a baby is in a bad mood he may be given his father's or mother's thumb to use as a pacifier. Though Amhara are otherwise very modest, mothers do not hesitate to offer the breast no matter where they happen to be. When referring to the process of breast-feeding, Amhara males invariably cup one hand under an imaginary breast to depict this common and natural event. When speaking to persuade a guest to accept a second glass of beer, the Amhara host has recourse to the formula: "But your mother's breasts are two!" Another indication that breast-feeding is a very familiar part of the Amhara's social environment is that in interpreting the TAT cards, a number of respondents interpreted some scene with children as a situation of breast-feeding, although this was not depicted on any of the cards.

The emotional context of breast-feeding is more significant than the physical pleasures involved. Until he leaves the breast the Amhara child inhabits an emotional paradise. He receives much attention and is fondled by both parents and by other relatives. He remains close to his mother at all times, sleeping alongside her at night and spending the day near her when not tied in a bundle on her back. He accompanies her thus to visit relatives, attend market, or go to church. Only when the mother goes to fetch water is he separated from her, for there is not room for both baby and water jug on the mother's back, and besides, water holes are the abodes of evil spirits who may try to make the child sick.

After he is weaned, the Amhara child enters a much harsher emotional atmosphere. He must adjust to a regime of commands, responsibilities, and punishments. He is nostalgic forever after for the warmth and security of his earliest years, a condition vividly associated with the experience of sucking at the breast. The prominence in Amhara culture of this association of emotional security with breast-feeding is shown by such phenomena as the mammary symbolism of the rooftop and the institution known as the "breast-father." The former consists of a clay ornament, whose color and shape clearly replicate the female nipple, which is placed atop the breast-like conical roof which covers the Amhara home.* The latter is related to customs concerning adoption.

The adoption of children among traditional Amhara takes place through a ritual in which the child sucks the honey-dipped thumb of his intended foster parent. The latter thereby becomes the child's *ṭuṭ abbāt,* or breast-father. In some cases the child actually sucks the nipples of the *ṭuṭ abbāt.* Used metaphorically, the image of sucking someone's breast is employed to indicate becoming close to, or ingratiating oneself with, a superior; breast-feeding is so explicitly connected with emotional security that people are inclined to allude to it when finding a new source of security.

The Amhara's attachment to passive, pleasurable activities centering on the oral zone appears in a wide variety of forms. Manipulation of the lips is one of these. Amhara often stand about fingering their lips or rubbing them against some object, much as people in another culture might scratch their heads or stroke their chins. Children may be humored by having their lips played with by a relative. The frequent covering and uncovering of the mouth with a part of the toga, that is so characteristic of the Amhara, may be a sublimated form of this.

The lips are used in Amhara culture for a variety of expressive purposes. The Amhara identify persons and places, not by pointing with the finger or hand, but by distending the lips in a certain direction. Kissing, while seldom used for romantic purposes, serves a number of other expressive functions. Relatives or friends of either sex kiss each other on both cheeks after a long separation, the older or superior in status kissing first. Children and servants greet their superiors by kissing their feet, which they also do to show gratitude for some favor. One kisses one's own hands before extending them to receive a gift. Kissing one's fingers is done to signify an oath or a special appreciation of something, the meaning being "I swear by it."

Religious sentiment is typically expressed through kissing. The devout Amhara kisses his fingers and touches the table to show thanksgiving after a meal. The church is greeted by kissing a part of the building, and going to church is referred to as "kissing the church." Following devotional services the priest's cross is kissed by all present, and often the Holy Book is kissed as well. When the ark is brought outside on holidays, reverence is shown by falling to the ground and kissing the earth.

While, moreover, romantic kissing is an uncommon activity among the Amhara, Amharic literature at times represents this activity with poignant intensity. Thus, in an unwritten Amharic couplet one hears:

---

* The Gurage, by contrast, place a straight stick atop their homes. So do the Amhara of Gojjam Province.

The boundaries of your lips are like the sugar cane;
No matter how much one sucks them, one is never satisfied.

And in one of the few lyric passages in the first novel ever written in Amharic, the author resorts to the imagery of kissing in describing the beauty of an army camp at sunset:

The plain on which they had encamped was vaster than the mind's eye could measure. Except for that hill on which he stood, there were no elevations or declivities; no roots to trip or confound the foot; not a stone to discomfit the eye. It looked like a calm sea that every breeze had spared. The boundaries of heaven and earth were united by lips of love; lip to lip they were joined like the parts of fitted basketry. It appeared as though it would hurt them to separate, that they had entered a vow not to part.[5]

Talking for the sake of talking is another oral outlet of which the Amhara is generally fond. "In every country," remarked Arnauld d'Abbadie, "the plowman is miserly and sly; but the Ethiopian is, in addition, particularly loquacious."[6] The simple greeting of acquaintances evokes a barrage of ritualistic conversation, a phenomenon which stunned the Englishman Harris:

Even two old crones, who are obviously tottering on the very brink of the grave, and who are afflicted with every pain and with every sorrow entailed by the fall of our first parents, never meet in the street without indulging in a string of good wishes which are reiterated so long as their breath will permit. "How are you? How do ye do? How have you passed your time? Are you well? Are you very well? Are you quite well? Are you perfectly well? Are you not well?"—are questions which serve as the prelude to a thousand other interrogatories; and at each response the Deity must be invoked as to the unadulterated happiness and perfect felicity that has been unremittingly experienced since the last meeting.[7]

A number of other conventions provide further opportunities for this pleasure in talking. Anecdotes and gossip are not merely reported, but are expounded at length with the aid of colorful expressions and gestures. Riddle games are enjoyed by adults as well as young people. Men vie with one another at length in a semiformalized kind of playful boasting. In the church schools all reading is done aloud, a habit which persists among many students of secondary schools when they study outside of class.

A related pleasure in making sounds for their own sake appears in the Amhara's delight in repeating the words or nonsense syllables of his folk songs. On a more refined level, there is his evident pleasure in lulling over and savoring the lines of a choice couplet. We have here for a whole culture an instance of what Brill has ascribed to the poets:

Poetry is a sensuous or mystic outlet through words, or, as it were, through a chewing and sucking of nice words and phrases. The poet plays with the rhythm and rhyme of words as an epicure with a palatable viand or intoxicating old wine. . . . Like the infant, his affective state can only be pacified through a rhythmical expression of pleasurable sounds.[8]

The Amharic language itself registers a certain sensibility to the nature of poetry as an oral outlet. Agreeable and pleasing language is characterized in Amharic by the same word which is used to characterize particularly pleasing food: "*tāfata*" ("it is sweet"). The introduction to the *Chronicles* of Emperor Galawdewos is but the literary embellishment of a type of statement which could be made by any Amhara:

> We commence here this beautiful narrative, of more pleasing taste to the mouth . . . than honey and sugar, which will bring pleasure to those who hear it and will give, to those who understand it, a joy like that given by song and wine.[9]

The incorporation of knowledge no less than the enjoyment of words is conceived in explicitly oral terms in Amharic. The stomach is regarded as the seat of wisdom, and in the language of schoolboys the diligent student is one who has thoroughly "drunk his lesson." The experiencing of one's school as an Alma Mater is probably quite intense; as one tenth-grade student wrote in a contribution to his school newspaper, "Oh! Mother School! There is nothing like school! As a mother feeds her children with milk and bread, so does a school feed her children, the pupils, with education."[10]

Eating and drinking for their own sake, beyond what is required for nutrition, form perhaps the most obvious medium for oral erotism, and one that is cultivated to a notable degree among the Amhara. Feasting is called for on every possible occasion—christenings, funerals, and memorial services, as well as engagements, weddings, and annual holidays. The chief purpose of the only voluntary association in traditional Amhara society, the religious fraternal association known as the *māhebar,* is to eat and drink in honor of a certain saint on his day every month. The duration of any large celebration is said to depend on how long the food and drink last; successful ones go on for three days. Linguistic usage stresses the oral function on such occasions. One "eats at," rather than attends, a christening party; one "drinks in," rather than belongs to, a *māhebar;* one expects to "eat at," rather than dance at, somebody's wedding. The very word for Easter, "*Fāsiqā,*" literally means "great feast."

The activity of eating is colored by a number of conventions which express its great emotional significance. The mood at mealtime is supposed to be deeply serious. Food is to be masticated aloud, indicating a total involvement with the task at hand. Not to let others hear one chewing, like eating by oneself, also is taken to imply greed. The usual obligation to stand when somebody enters the room is waived when one is eating. "Grain is king," says an

Amharic proverb, and even the Emperor when visiting a school expects students to remain seated if they are at the dining table when he arrives.

Some indication of the comparative significance of this concern about eating and drinking in the Amhara psyche is afforded by a recent cross-cultural investigation of dreams. Obtained from samples of young male respondents in Ethiopia, Nigeria, and the United States, the dreams were evaluated with respect to the presence or absence of themes of "manifest orality": scenes of someone desiring, looking for, or consuming food or drink. The proportion of Ethiopian respondents (mostly Orthodox Amhara from the Gondar area) who revealed manifest orality in their dreams was found to be *64 per cent.* By contrast, the proportion of those in a sample of non-Muslim Nigerians whose dreams showed manifest orality was 38 per cent, and that in the sample of Americans was only 22 per cent.[11]

The Amhara custom of giving *gurshā* plays up the erotic component of eating. *Gurshā* means "mouthful" and, as already noted, refers to a wad of food which one places in another's mouth, usually as a gesture of affection. *Gurshā* are exchanged between husband and wife and among relatives and friends. They are often given to children, especially in families of higher status, and to favored servants and retainers as well. The *gurshā* is of such meaning in Amhara experience that it is referred to in a number of Amharic idioms. First of all it means a present or a tip—literally, *pourmanger.* It also refers to the charge of a gun: the gun is a beloved object, and a *gurshā* is what one places in its mouth. In contemporary usage, it refers to flashlight batteries.

In connection with love and many other subjects, a good deal of the imagery of Amharic verse relates in one way or another to eating and drinking. The following sample of proverbs and couplets may convey some of the flavor of this phenomenon:

Ṭajj* has no specks; a poor man has no friends.

*   *   *

[Use] proverbs in conversation; [drink] *ṭajj* in a carafe.

*   *   *

Hand and fly-whisk; mouth and *ĭnjarā*† [go together].

*   *   *

No matter how much one plows, nothing tastes so good as *goman.*‡

---

* *Ṭajj*, it may be remembered, is the Ethiopian wine made of honey.

† *Ĭnjarā* is the staple pancake.

‡ *Goman* is a kind of cabbage plant that requires no plow cultivation.

To make me forget you, this medicine is right:
Food and water, sleep and the night.

* * *

Love and porridge must be taken while hot;
Once cool, those who would taste are a lot.

* * *

The *ĭnjarā* I have, my lass;
I wait for you the *wat** to pass.†

* * *

Your father and your mother have vowed to keep from meat;
But you, their very daughter, innards do you eat.‡

Eating and drinking provide expressive symbolism in social interaction as
well as in verse. They form the primary axis of social life among the Amhara.
The exchange of *gurshā* is but a specialized form of the general pattern of
expressing sociability through feeding and being fed. Camaraderie consists to
a large extent of eating from the same *ĭnjarā* basket, and the etymology of
the word for "friend," *bālĭnjarā,* is the same as that for the English "companion," someone with whom one shares bread. At any indoor gathering
barley beer is served continuously. The visit of a guest at any time of day
calls for "a little coffee," a euphemism for as much food and drink as the
host can command. In some Amhara areas a special kind of spirit, the *ṭonin,*
is assigned the specific task of punishing persons who infringe the etiquette
of dispensing and receiving food.[12]

From this it is but a short step to politics and morals. The production of
large banquets is one of the essential arts of government in Abyssinia—
panem, if not *circenses.* The stature of a big man depends partly upon the
number of persons who customarily dine at his expense. A man's Christianity, moreover, is judged by his generosity in feeding others, a virtue that is
eulogized at times by parading his *ĭnjarā* baskets around the field. A truly
Christian Amhara is known by the regularity and scale with which he prepares memorial feasts for his departed kin, drinks in some religious fraternal
association, and holds an annual feast (*zĭker*) in which food is distributed
to the poor.

Oral activity is prominent, moreover, not only as a primary source of

---

* *Wat* is the sauce in which the *ĭnjarā* is dipped.

† The gold meaning is: "I'll wait for you until the others leave."

‡ "To eat someone's innards" is an idiom meaning: "to make him fall in love." The gold
meaning is thus: "You made me love you."

pleasure among the Amhara, but also as a typical response to situations which arouse anxiety. The crisis of death is met first of all by a prolonged ritual of wailing, and this is followed by a series of memorial feasts which occur on fixed days following the person's death. Any kind of bad news evokes repeated exclamations of "Ay! Ay!" When a child or wife is punished, the response is a prolonged and monotonous yell usually out of proportion to the actual pain felt. In the anxious hour before battle, war chants and boastful cries tune up the warriors' spirits. Moments of great awe, finally, such as the appearance of the holy ark when it is brought out of the church or the arrival of some great political personage, occasion a shrill ululation.

Response to illness was the anxiety area chosen as an index of positive fixation by Whiting and Child in their cross-cultural study of *Child Training and Personality*. They assumed that a fixation on oral gratification would express itself in a preference for therapies which involve swallowing something.[13] In this area, too, Amhara culture displays a preoccupation with orality, and not just in the form of swallowing. Something akin to a general principle for oral therapy appears in the well-known Amharic proverb: "For headache, shout on it! For stomach-ache, eat on it!"

A number of the oral therapies practiced by the Amhara are naturally functional, such as drinking a purgative made from leaves of the *kosso* tree to cure tapeworm, or eating a kind of unleavened corn bread to arrest dysentery. Beyond this, most of their magical therapies are also oral. Drinking holy water (and sometimes bathing in it) is believed to cure nearly every sort of affliction, from rheumatism and leprosy to eye and ear ailments. In some regions it is believed that eating the liver of a hyena will cure syphilis. Psychotherapy, too, often relies on oral remedies: the *zār* on a patient is often placated by feeding him, via the patient, a sumptuous meal. Oral types of prophylaxis are also to be noted. Garlic is eaten in order to prevent malaria. Certain kinds of animals are eaten on special occasions in order to ward off sickness. Finally, there is the remarkable phenomenon of the *lālibalā*, a night singer, who can protect himself against hereditary leprosy only by singing out loud in the night air.

In general, one can say that the Amhara have a tendency to attribute magical efficacy to oral incorporation and, to a lesser extent, to the adroit use of language. The latter belief appears in the assumption that human problems are solved by attaining some particularly fortunate verbal formulation, and in the association of outstanding wisdom with unusual mastery of language. The former appears in beliefs and legends which associate eating a lot with the attainment of unusual bravery, longevity, and physical strength. A legend about the invader Ahmad Grāñ, for example, relates that as a baby he was able to consume fourteen bowls of *ïnjarā* at one sitting. A number of Amhara folk tales, moreover, have as their central theme the resolution of conflict or the attainment of mastery over the environment by means of eating something or presenting food to someone.[14] It is a theme conspicuous in the legend which celebrates the ascendance of the first of the Shoan Amhara emperors, Yekuno Amlāk (1270–85). According to *The Book of the Riches of Kings,* Yekuno Amlāk ate by chance the head of a rooster which had been set out for a king of the rival Zāgwē Dynasty:

> And this youth Yakuno Amlak found the head of the cock which the woman had left by the fire-place, and he took it and ate it, and it filled his belly, and it made him an exalted person and so mighty a man that he was superior to every other man of might, and it made his face to shine like the light of the sun, and his majesty filled all the other servants of the king with awe, and all the people feared him, and they marvelled at him, and they loved him exceedingly, and they placed him in their hearts, and they recognized that the grace of God was upon him, and they said, "What is the thing which hath come upon this young man?"[15]

Oral Sadism

In addition to subserving a passive, receptive mode of relating to the environment, preoccupation with the oral zone also figures in Amhara culture as the locus of a variety of aggressive modes of behavior and fantasy. Hostility is expressed by a number of oral gestures. Sticking out the tongue and spitting on the ground in front of somebody, for example, are two forms of non-verbal insult. Biting the lower lip is an indication of anger. Touching the tongue, and then forehead, chin, and cheeks, signifies "You just wait!" When fighting, men sometimes bite one another's ears. The activation of a strong biting impulse in situations of military combat is suggested by the following refrain from an Amhara martial declaration, recorded over a century ago:

> Oh brothers, you are hungry and thirsty! Oh true sons of my mother,
> Are you not birds of prey? Come on! There is the enemy's flesh.
> And I, I will be the rider to butcher for you! Forward,
> And if you lack hydromel, I will give you my blood to drink.[16]

The theme of cannibalism appears in various forms in the Amhara imagination. One of the common subjects of traditional Amhara painting is the story of the cannibal Balaya Sab. His name is in Ge'ez, and means "Eater of Men." The story about him derives from one of the old legends collected in *The Miracles of the Blessed Virgin Mary.*[17] Balaya Sab was a wicked man who fed on the flesh of humans. At his death he appeared before St. George, who measured his evil deeds against his good deeds on a large scale. On the side of evil deeds were placed the souls of all those he had eaten, so heavy a weight that the devil began to make ready to carry him off to hell. Then

Mary intervened, placing on the empty side for good deeds a goblet of water which Balaya Sab had once given to a sick beggar out of pity; and the Eater of Men was saved. In the pictorial representation of this legend, Balaya Sab is portrayed cutting off pieces of human flesh with a curved knife in the manner in which raw beef is attacked at the Amhara table.

Most Amhara know some sort of tale about a cannibal. The topic is familiar enough that they are able to invent new ones. One boy told me he made up the following story to explain the nature of cannibals to his younger brother:

> Once there was a cannibal. He lived among many people. He had no food in his house; he was poor. But even if he had not been poor, he just liked to eat the flesh of man. In his house was a big hole which he covered with a carpet. He would invite somebody into his house and tell him to sit down on the chair over the hole. When the person sat down and fell into the hole, he would climb down by a ladder and eat him. In this way he ate all the people in his village one by one—about a hundred people. When he had eaten all the people in his village he returned to live in the forest, because there was nobody left to eat.

The cannibal motif appears in more subtle form in the parlor game known as *gabatā*, in which the aim is to accumulate as many pebbles as possible by moving them around a board with six holes on each side. In *gabatā* the active acquisition of pebbles is called "eating" and the passive acquisition is "drinking." Similarly, those who play chess or checkers refer to the process of taking a man as "eating" him. It is notable, moreover, that the Amhara version of the old riddle about how to transport a certain number of incompatible objects across the river in one boat is posed in terms of three human beings and three cannibals.

Oral sadism is further manifest among the Amhara by the nature of their speech. The Amhara are not only loquacious but also tend, both in manner of delivery and in content of conversation, to be biting and intrusive. Backbiting, insulting, arguing, and litigating are among their more characteristic modes of self-expression.

Backbiting and insulting, and the fear of being the victim of such activities, are the focus of much attention in Amhara culture. Concern about the former is expressed in a number of Amharic proverbs:

> If the mouth lacks work, it will backbite a friend.

> If you praise a man once, you will be in trouble if you backbite him later.

> If a man is a backbiter, listen for my sake when he talks to you.

Straightforward insults erupt the polite surface of Amhara social relations only under unusually heated circumstances, though it is customary for social superiors to direct a certain amount of abusive banter at their inferiors as a matter of course. In the more covert forms of expression, however, insulting is a favorite practice among Amhara. Ambiguous language and obscure allusion make possible a good deal of socially admissible, and admired, insulting. It is chiefly due to his mastery of this genre that the Amhara have come to idealize Alaqā Gabra Hānnā who, in the words of a psychologically sophisticated Ethiopian informant, by "skillful use of 'wax and gold' has defiled everything that is sacred in Abyssinian tradition: this includes Mother, God, Emperor, and Patriarch, to say nothing of the ignorant clergy, peasantry, and slaves. Gabra Hānnā . . . is the summation of the oral aggressive trend in every Abyssinian, of which the *dabtarā* in the king's court and the singer in the drink-house are only mediocre representations."

Wax and gold is, furthermore, the vehicle for the mode of expression which Erikson calls "oral retention." Just as the Amhara tends to be tight-lipped and evasive when confronted by questions he does not feel like answering, so he finds pleasure in stubbornly withholding his meaning from his audience through employing figures and allusions which no one can understand. This may be understood as a passive form of oral aggression. For the untutored, however, the active aggressive component is probably more satisfying. Most Amhara males look forward to occasions when they can insult with impunity, such as in victory after the games at Christmas or in the setting of a drink-house, where their skillfully improvised verses are repeated and sung by a minstrel. The oral sadistic spirit of this latter scene has been captured with great fidelity by a contemporary Amhara novelist. Describing the moment in a drink-house when the minstrel begins bowing his one-stringed violin and gets ready to accept verses from the crowd, he writes: "*And now every one of them prepares a bullet of verse, and gets cocked to fire veiled insults.*"[18]

Two-way communication among Amhara is frequently colored by a biting and intrusive manner as well. Amharic conversation gravitates toward a highly argumentative style. Casual disagreement, or even neutral deliberation over a common problem, often engenders a kind of protracted bickering to which the Amhara have given an onomatopoetic name, "*çhïqeçhïq.*" In its more institutionalized form, this argumentativeness becomes litigation, which has long been regarded as the national sport of Abyssinia.

As the primary means of distributing land-use rights and of reducing the likelihood of resort to violence in personal disputes, litigation serves functions of unmistakable importance in Amhara society. Yet the frequency and intensity with which Amhara take part in litigation suggests that it is motivated by non-rational factors in good part. Litigants have often lost many times the original value of some item under dispute in the course of pursuing litigation over it through the courts for many years. The language and colorful gestures of the court may be observed among Amhara in their homes or at social gatherings in the course of discussions about nearly any subject. One cannot but conclude that the Amhara litigate to a large extent because for them it is an intrinsically pleasurable activity. At times, in fact, the forms of litigation are acted out as in a game. *Teṭāyaq*, for example, analogous to the Western process of cross-examination and a beloved feature of traditional court procedure, is sometimes practiced at parties though it has been outlawed in modern courts.[19] Two men will face a "judge" and try to bedevil each other with sly questions and preposterous claims. The content of the dispute is of no matter; it may be sheer nonsense.

Amhara litigants are ingenious at expressing themselves. They do so with gestures, intonation, and timing that achieve considerable dramatic effect. They are delighted to perform at the slightest provocation. The following incident, recorded during a morning at court in Manz, illustrates that dimension of Amhara litigation which consists of the inherently gratifying expression of oral aggression:

> The defendant had been accused of plowing the plaintiff's land without permission. In fact, however, the plaintiff had given the defendant previous permission to plow there—in front of a group of elders who testified accordingly. The judge therefore ruled against the plaintiff. The plaintiff said he would appeal this decision, because the permission he granted had not been registered in the governor's office and, besides, he had some other complaint to bring against the defendant.

> At this point someone in the audience rose and said: "That is all. The judge has ruled against you, and the case is finished." Whereupon the plaintiff told this speaker that he should keep quiet, that his speaking out was against the law, that he had bothered him when the case was tried before a lower level judge previously and should bother him no more. Instead of hushing up, the speaker left his position against the wall and stood next to the defendant, asserting that he would speak in behalf of the latter.

> The plaintiff then accused this man of talking out of turn. The judge acknowledged this accusation and called for witnesses. Instantly half a dozen or more men jumped to their feet, eyes bursting with excitement and pride as before a battle, and volunteered to witness against the speaker. One by one, with a great show of oratory, they said their pieces against the man who had spoken out of turn. More than once the judge had to urge these witnesses to stop talking after the evidence had been presented. By this time the substance of the original dispute seemed to have been completely forgotten.

Oral Ambivalence

Much as the oral zone is favored by the Amhara as a center for positive gratifications, both of the passive-receptive and the active-aggressive sort, such gratifications are not enjoyed wholly without conflict. In actuality, traits which reflect anxiety about the prospect of oral gratification are no less conspicuous in Amhara culture than the phenomena we have just been discussing.

Negative attitudes regarding oral gratification appear, first of all, in the scope and variety of the restrictions placed on eating. From both their Judaic and their Christian traditions the Abyssinians have taken over nearly every restriction on eating available. The chief exception to this is the Judaic injunction against eating blood, which Abyssinian custom permits. But they have retained intact the Semitic ban on unclean animals—those which lack a split hoof, upper teeth, or do not chew the cud. Their dread of pork is so strong that to some extent they feel closer to Muslims, who also avoid pork, than to Western Christians.

They have likewise retained and elaborated on the norms concerning fasting found in early Christianity. With respect to the number and harshness of the fasts it prescribes, Amhara-Tigre custom is probably the strictest in the world. In the rigor of its fasting laws the Ethiopian Church surpasses its sister religions of Eastern Orthodoxy—the Coptic, Syrian, Armenian, and Indian Orthodox Churches. On fasting days no food or drink is to be tasted before early afternoon. Thereafter, no sort of meat, fowl, milk, or eggs may be eaten, which reduces the Amhara's post meridiem diet on fasting days to grains and pulse.

Such fasting days occur on every Wednesday and Friday of the year, except those which come during the eight weeks after Easter. There are, in addition, many special fasts in the course of the year. Some of these, like the month-long fast before Pentecost and the two months prior to Christmas, are observed only by clergy and elders. Others must be observed by everyone, though children are led into them gradually. These universal fasts include the eight weeks before Easter, plus a three-day fast during the week before Lent; two days before Christmas; and sixteen days preceding the festival of the Assumption of Mary in August. Total abstinence is prescribed for a period of forty-eight hours before Easter. All together, the ordinary Amhara is supposed to fast 165 days each year; for the devout person the total approaches 250 days.

The taboo on the use of tobacco presents another area in which oral gratification is suppressed. Two myths are told to explain this taboo. One is that the tobacco plant originally grew out of the intestines of the heretic Arius. The other is that on the day of the Crucifixion all plants except tobacco withered and died. In any case, smoking is regarded as a grave sin among traditional Amhara, and one who has been suspected of using tobacco is not permitted to kiss the Cross.

One could argue that these taboos and fasting customs are simply cultural phenomena, traits inherited from earlier traditions and retained through inertia, and that no psychological processes need be invoked in describing them. But this argument fails to explain why, in view of the harmful physical and political consequences of their excessive fasting, the Amhara should have developed in the direction of increasing rather than alleviating their fasting burden. For Abyssinia's commitment to fasting was well known by her enemies, and used to her disadvantage: Ahmad Grāñ took advantage of the country's weakness during Lent to launch his attacks at that time year after year, and the Galla hordes who succeeded him did likewise. The argument also fails to explain why the taboos on pork and tobacco, and the fasting prescriptions, should have been pushed to the forefront of Amhara Christian consciousness. For observance of these mores is considered the very crux of Christianity by traditional Amhara. Amhara often refer to fasting as the most important part of their religion. If a person fails to fast, his relatives are technically absolved from the duty of providing memorial feasts for him when he dies; let his soul wander in darkness! Fasting more than anything else protects them from the devil and enhances the likelihood of their entering paradise.

Apart from their adherence to these cultural norms, moreover, the Amhara also manifest anxiety regarding oral gratification at the purely psychological level. There is, on the one hand, a constant undertone of concern among Amhara about getting enough to eat, even under favorable agricultural conditions. On the other hand, there is a good deal of concern about the consequences of eating too much. There is much worry among the Amhara about the dangers of excessive eating at the conclusion of periods of fasting. There is also the fear that if one indulges in eating and drinking he may become uncontrollably hostile, a fear expressed in the previously mentioned notion of *ṭegābaññā*. These and other forms of anxiety about oral gratification are expressed in a number of folk tales, in which eating, drinking, singing, talking, or simply opening one's mouth result in such misfortunes as sickness, loss of property, and death.[20] A similar theme appears in the epic *Glory of Kings*: the Queen of Sheba, in satisfying her thirst by drinking from a goblet which King Solomon had placed in her bedroom, thereby forfeited her right to immunity from his amorous desires and was obliged to yield to his embrace.

Ambivalence regarding oral aggressiveness, finally, may be discerned in the Amhara's anxiety about being eaten, an anxiety which should probably be interpreted as an externalization of unacceptable oral-sadistic impulses. Traditional Amhara have a morbid fear of being "eaten" by those with the evil eye, *budā* and *ṭayb,* men who are believed to destroy their victim by invisibly sucking his blood. It is largely because of this fear that children are kept away from strangers. Similar projections appear in connection with other well-known figures in Amhara culture. Another fearful object is the *çhirāq,* a giant

cannibal with eyes in the back of his head. (The specter of the *çhirāq* is sometimes evoked in order to frighten children into behaving properly.) Still another figure is the *salābi,* a person who is imagined capable of spiriting away
a man's harvested grain by means of magic incantations.

Without delving into questions on the cultural origins and social functions
of oral ambivalence among the Amhara, one can understand how it comes
into being in the individual by looking at what happens during childhood in
Amhara society. It is true that, if one abides by the hypothesis on this
subject supported by Whiting and Child's cross-cultural study, the phenomenon remains puzzling. Their theory attributes a high degree of anxiety
about oral gratification to a low level of indulgence of oral gratification in
early childhood and a high level of frustration during weaning. This particular hypothesis is not consistent with the data on the Amhara. As we noted
earlier in this chapter, oral gratification is indulged among infants to a very
high degree by Amhara mothers. There is considerable variation in Amhara
practice with regard to weaning, moreover. At times the advent of a new
baby or a mother's sickness may require abrupt weaning, in which case a
bitter substance is put on the mother's nipple to discourage the infant. In
many cases, on the other hand, weaning occurs so gently and spontaneously
that little or no frustration is involved for the infant. The relative frequency
of these two procedures is a question for which adequate data have not
been assembled, but the norm seems to be a gradual departure from the
breast, after the child has been happily adjusted to eating other food for more
than a year.

Even if the Amhara child is not frustrated by too little indulgence of sucking and too severe weaning, he is nonetheless deprived in two other respects
as he emerges from infancy. One is nutritional. Medical studies of Abyssinian
children suggest a dietary deficiency beginning in the second half of the first
year, and persisting throughout early childhood.[21] It is possible that this
relative decline in biological well-being contributes to a sense of deprivation
toward the end of the breast-feeding period.

The emotional situation of the child after weaning presents a more visible
area of frustration. Amhara childhood is marked by a fairly sharp discontinuity. This may be illustrated by the fact that many Amhara boys are
nurslings at the age of three and shepherds at five. The narcissism which has
flowered during the nursing stage is dealt a series of blows as the young
child becomes subject to the responsibilities, punishments, and suppressed
status which are the lot of Amhara children. According to contemporary psychoanalytic theory, this sort of change in emotional support has far more
significance for the development of behavioral tendencies than the mechanics
of the weaning process; and what psychoanalysts have posited as a possible

consequence of substantial loss of accustomed mother love at the time of weaning—a mild but chronic state of mourning which gives a depressive undertone to the rest of life—is certainly one of the more evident characteristics of most Amhara.[22] At the same time the Amhara child is made anxious about his actual oral gratifications. He no longer eats whenever he wants to, but only after he has waited for the adults to finish their meal. He is no longer entitled to the choicest food, mother's milk, but to poorer food and leftovers. And he is made increasingly aware of the adult anxieties about eating connected with the fasting requirements, and with the food shortages of the rainy season.

Applying the Whiting-Child hypotheses in the light of these observations one may characterize the development of an ambivalent preoccupation with the oral zone by Amhara as follows: an initially very high level of oral satisfaction enjoyed during the nursing period makes oral gratification a particularly attractive source of pleasure as well as a desired refuge for the psyche under the pressure of later deprivations; while the emotional and nutritional deprivations which the Amhara child experiences toward the end of the nursing period and thereafter undermine the sense of security acquired during his indulged infancy and make him anxious about the fount of that security, oral gratification.*

Whatever the precise ontogenetic basis of this phenomenon may prove to be, the Amhara's ambivalent preoccupation with orality is projected at the *cultural* level in the form of two contrasting human ideals. The secular masculine ideal in Amhara culture is a hero of oral gratification and prowess. He is a man who eats much and drinks much, and who excels in litigation, in declaiming the martial chants, and in composing veiled insults. The religious ideal, on the other hand, is a hero of oral renunciation. The most devout Amhara are considered those who keep all of the fasts, even the esoteric ones; or even, as monks and ascetics, live on a fasting diet the year round— in the extreme case, feed on leaves as hermits. The association of religious virtuosity with oral renunciation reaches its logical climax in legends about Gabra Manfas Qeddus ("Servant of the Holy Spirit"), the most hallowed Amhara saint. In contrast with the normal Amhara boy who nurses for close to three years, Gabra Manfas Qeddus is said to have been at his mother's breast for only three months, when a bird swept down one day and carried him away.

---

* While this formulation may leave more questions unanswered than it solves—a purely behaviorist formula inevitably neglects the dynamics of defensive operations and the significance of ambivalence—it carries us as far as our data permit and may provide a useful point of departure for further discussion and investigation of Amhara psychology.

ORALITY AND MODERNIZATION

The preoccupation with orality which appears in their traditional orientations has not disappeared among those Abyssinians who have acquired a modern education. In some respects, that experience has tended to intensify it. A state of prolonged dependence was institutionalized in the government school system. The hiring of most educated Ethiopians by the government has meant that most of them live in a position of waiting to receive their salary— or *ïnjarā,* as they themselves put it—from the central authority. Thus the image of a bountiful father-figure has become the more firmly established. While in his own person the Emperor has projected an image of vigorous leadership, he has at the same time taken pains to promote this old pattern of oral dependence, by sending gifts of food to students and of champagne to educated officials when they marry; by continuing to provide politically relevant feasts at the palace; and, like the traditional Amhara father-feeder, by frequently reminding his subjects that everything they have they owe to him. This pattern is replicated to some extent in the relations between members of the new nobility and their younger relatives and retainers.

Part of the self-reproach of some of the modern-educated Ethiopians is directed against this passive, receptive aspect of their motivational orientation. Their criticism says in effect: instead of drafting proposals to reform our departments, teaching or writing in order to educate our countrymen, or seeking to understand better the complexities of Ethiopia's current situation, we are far more likely to be found sitting about drinking coffee in our offices, sipping beer at some hotel, playing chess, savoring felicitous phrases, and going to parties where eating and drinking are invariably the main order of business.

Insofar as they are moved to take a more active approach to their situation, moreover, their effectiveness is blocked by a tendency to fall into the traditional oral aggressive patterns of behavior. Their manner of criticizing the government, or certain officials, is frequently one of wholesale insulting. When confronted by a difficult problem, whenever they do not fall back to a posture of dependence on superiors, they incline toward argumentation, *çhïqeçhïq,* backbiting, and mutual incrimination. Experts in debate, they are unaccustomed to the arts of creative discussion.

It is not my intention to suggest that the phenomena examined in this chapter are in total conflict with the Ethiopians' search for leadership. Many aspects of Amhara orality are not in the least inconsistent with the demands of a modernizing culture. Many aspects of Amhara orality would appear to be of enduring value—the excellence in debate and the appreciation of literary subtlety, the preparation of fine feasts and the enjoyment of the table. And it is not necessary for a very large number of Amhara to change their orientations in this regard for creative leadership to be effective. What is suggested is: that by tending to relate to their environment either in a passive-receptive mode of getting, in an active-sadistic mode akin to infantile petulance, or in a state of guilt and anxiety concerning elementary gratifications—that minority of Amhara and other Ethiopians who are in a position to introduce constructive change follow a type of adjustment which is inadequate to the challenge of their present situation. Adaptive as these modes may have been in the past, they are archaic in the present.

The search for leadership in Ethiopia today is partly a search for new ego ideals. It is a search for persons and images embodying a more productive and procreative type of orientation, capable of inspiring a creative minority of Ethiopians to build on, not abandon orality, and to move beyond.*

---

* That this search goes on at a time when the epigones of modernity, living in an age of high mass consumption, appear to be relaxing into a more passive, incorporative mode—the mode of television-watching and supermarket shopping—is but one of the many manifestations of what is perhaps the central irony of the human condition at this point in history.

7

iNÖiviÖuAlisM ANÖ The
quest for social progress

A deep-going process of individualization has commonly been regarded as one of the characteristic features of the early stages of modernization. Whether hailed as a basis for economic rationalism and the embodiment of libertarian ideals or decried as the solvent of communal solidarities and traditional identities, this emergent individualism tends to be viewed against the image of a base line traditional society whose members are enmeshed in various solidary associations, bound by collective obligations, and encompassed by communal restraints.[1]

While it is probable that such an image exaggerates the degree of corporateness that obtains in most traditional societies, in the case of Abyssinia it is demonstrably wide of the mark. A characteristic individualism has impressed more than one observer of Abyssinian society in the past. Perhaps not by accident, those who have been most responsive to this characteristic have been of French nationality. Arnauld d'Abbadie, writing more than a century ago, depicted the Abyssinian as an irrepressible foe of uniformity and despotism.[2] More recently the noted linguist, Marcel Cohen, in one of his rare but highly perceptive sociological essays, described the Abyssinian as *"membre d'une société individualiste."*[3] In so doing he has suggested an interesting perspective from which to examine Amhara society as a whole, a perspective which may also throw some light on the previously raised question concerning the obstacles to solidary action among modern-educated Ethiopians.

238

FIG. 34.—*Offering a* gurshā

FIG. 35.—*Singing out the master's* qenē

IG. 36.—*Amhara litigants*

Fig. 37.—*St. Gabra Manfas Qeddus*

THE CONCEPT OF INDIVIDUALISM

What does it mean to characterize Amhara society as "individualistic"? In its most general sense, the concept of individualism refers to a condition in which primacy is given to personal interests at the expense of collective concerns. In applying this concept to Amhara society, or to any other, certain refinements are clearly necessary.

In the first place one must distinguish between individualism as the moral basis of a relatively integrated society and individualism as the consequence of social disintegration. In the latter sense it represents a breakdown in the customary standards of society and may be viewed as one form of anomie.[4] Anomic individualism may be seen as an underlying propensity in all societies against which moral sentiment and social institutions must constantly combat. It is liable to appear when any social order has been sufficiently corroded by economic want, warfare, cultural or political dislocations, or natural disaster. In Ethiopian history anomic individualism has often appeared at the death or absence of a ruler; for example, following the assassination of Wassan Sagad of Shoa in 1813,[5] and during the anarchic interval between the departure of Haile Selassie from Addis Ababa and the arrival of Italian troops in May, 1936.

In describing traditional Amhara society as an individualistic one, however, the intention is to evoke an image of a relatively stable social order that has been informed by an individualistic ethos. In this effort two further precautions are called for. There is, on the one hand, the danger that use of a general concept like individualism may obstruct our perception of areas in which the concept does not apply. No single abstraction does justice to the complexities of any society, and it is self-evident that no society can survive in which group interests are not granted priority over individual interests in certain minimal respects. Our aim, in other words, should not be to establish or refute the thesis that Amhara society is individualistic, but rather to determine in what respects it may properly be so regarded and in what respects not.

On the other hand, the concept of individualism as it pertains to a kind of moral order suffers from ambiguity. It has been used to refer to a variety of phenomena which *may* appear concurrently but which in reality are independently variable. These phenomena will be distinguished here in terms of three different usages of the concept: individualism as a psychological disposition, as a mode of social organization, and as a cultural value.

In the first sense of the term, individualism refers to a socially accepted disposition to pursue one's own goals without regard to the goals of society, whether the latter be defined in terms of collectivities or simply of one's fellow men. This is the sort of individualism De Tocqueville had in mind when defining it as the "feeling which disposes each member of the community to sever himself from the mass of his fellows and to draw apart with his family and friends, so that after he has thus formed a little circle of his own, he willingly leaves society at large to itself."[6] In the more extreme instance of this disposition, feelings of attachment even to family and friends would be fairly tenuous. It is difficult to find a neutral term with which to designate this notion. The term *egoism* will be used here, with the understanding that it refers only to the primacy of the ego's personal interests and does not imply either self-conceit or a perverse selfishness.

The concept of individualism may also be used to characterize a type of social system, one which embodies the principle of laissez faire. It is a system in which social norms are directed primarily toward setting the minimal assurance of order and regulating the clash of individual interests and have little to do with promoting consensus and co-ordinating individual activities in behalf of collective goals. In this sense of the term, individualism is comparable to the concept of social freedom: the reduction of constraints on action due to external forces. The term *independence* will be used in this context to designate this sociological concept of individualism.

Taken as a cultural value, finally, individualism may be defined as a positive valuation of the individual as such, with special emphasis on the realization of his human potentialities. As Simmel has suggested, individualism in this sense may stress one of two forms: the attainment of personal distinction by virtue of excellence according to universal standards, or differentiation from others through cultivating and expressing qualities that are unique to oneself.[7] In either form this sense of the concept may be conveyed by the term *individuality*. Both these forms of individuality were described by Burckhardt in his famous discussion of the individualism of the Italian Renaissance.

While there may be a tendency for these three kinds of individualism to appear together in any historic situation, such an association is by no means necessary. A high degree of independence is compatible with a low degree of egoism; witness the case of liberal Quakers. Similarly, individuality may flourish when independence is sharply restricted, as Burckhardt himself suggested when observing that in despotic states "political impotence does not hinder the different tendencies and manifestations of private life from thriving in the fullest vigour and variety."[8] Again, individuality may be high even when egoism is low, as in cases when individuals are led to fulfil their unique selves with the primary aim of enriching the common life—the situation, for example, of certain artists and mystics.

We shall thus be well advised to pursue the analysis of individualism in Amhara society one step at a time. We shall proceed by examining in turn the prevalence of the three kinds of individualism just defined: in the first instance, as contrasted with sentiments of mutuality and solidarity; in the second, as contrasted with a condition of numerous social obligations and constraints; in the third, as contrasted with anonymity and conformity. In so doing our attention will necessarily be directed to disparate orders of phenomena. The empirical referent of these three concepts of individualism will be studied as follows:

(1) *Egoism.*—The degree of individualistic disposition among the Amhara will be examined in terms of two measures: the extent to which individuals are attached to collective symbols and interests, and the extent to which interpersonal relations take non-solidaristic forms.

(2) *Independence.*—The degree of individualistic social organization will be examined with reference to the different institutional foci of Amhara life, and measured by the extent to which role definitions are permissive rather than prescriptive; the possibility of voluntary as opposed to compulsory associations; and the possibilities for the protection of individual rights.

(3) *Individuality.*—The degree of individuality will be measured by the extent to which originality and heroic excellence are valued in the media of self-development and self-expression customary in Amhara culture.

EGOISM VERSUS SOLIDARISM

Self and Community

To what extent are the Amhara bound to one another by a sense of community, and to what extent are their actions guided by a sense of identification with collective symbols and needs? One conspicuous area of such commitment lies in the realm of religious affiliation. The Amhara manifest a strong sense of solidarity with their coreligionists over against all those who do not wear a *mātab* and who have not been baptized. They are deeply attached to the several symbols of the church—the church building itself, the compound in which it is enclosed, the holy ark, and all representatives of ecclesiastical authority—and react to violations of the dignity and purity of their religious symbols as to a personal affront. On certain ceremonial occasions they march in procession around the church shouldering rifles and spears, indicating their determination to defend by force the integrity of their religious objects. In cases where church membership has been channeled along the lines of schismatic orders, the Amhara—particularly the monks—have defended their doctrines faithfully and have at times suffered martyrdom.

With respect to their territorial and linguistic groups, the Amhara seem similarly attached to their collective symbols, if with somewhat less passion than in the religious case. As we have seen, the Amhara has a keen sense of identification with his native locale, or *āgar,* and is readily disposed to defend it against all comers. The expression *yāgarē lïjj* ("child of my country" or

Landsmann) regularly evokes considerable sentiment. There is also a strong sense of solidarity based on the use of Amharic—both among the Amhara as a whole vis-à-vis other Ethiopians who either do not know Amharic or speak it imperfectly, and among regional dialect groups. The people of Gojjam and of the Gondar area are particularly chauvinistic with regard to the quality of their Amharic.

This attachment to symbols of religion, territory, and language is important in providing a basis for identity and morale. Yet these attachments are of relatively little import in shaping a self-transcending orientation in the day-to-day activities of the Amhara; for the crucial context of these activities is the local community, and in the civic sphere the Amhara manifest very little solidarity. Indeed, it may be said that the Amhara have virtually no sense of "community" at all, for the concept can scarcely be rendered in idiomatic Amharic.

The absence of community sentiment among the Amhara is implied by their ecology. Not only did the Amhara fail to produce extensive and durable urban centers (with the limited exception of Gondar) but their country is even barren of that frequent cornerstone of peasant life, the village. The Amhara have distributed themselves thinly, scattering in groups of fours and fives up and down their mountains and plateaus. Larger aggregations are found on the estates of noblemen, but these constitute expanded private households rather than civic communities. The Amhara justify this dispersion of their population on the grounds that wide spaces are needed for the grazing of livestock and that a man needs to live on the land he farms. But herding and farming have been carried out well enough elsewhere by people living together in villages, and it is quite probable that this ecological pattern is due as much as anything else to the Amhara's preference for not having too much association with those outside his immediate kin group. In his own words, the Amhara prefers the kind of neighbor who "does not push the boundaries" (*wassan aynaḳām*), and believes, as noted earlier, that *bēt-ennā māqbar labetchāw naw* ("home and the grave are by oneself"). It is a preference manifest in such solitary living arrangements as that of divorced women who sometimes live by themselves in the country, eking out a living by spinning cotton or brewing spirits, and in the age-old predilection of Abyssinian monks for anchoritism.

The moral counterpart of this ecological pattern is a preoccupation with private interests that leaves little room for the consideration of communal needs. According to the Amhara vocabulary of motives, social action is motivated first and foremost by the pursuit of *ṭiqem,* or narrowly conceived self-interest.[9] This matter-of-fact acceptance of egoistic motivation among the Amhara appears during what is a common occurrence: the shameless subversion of occasions which are set up to consider communal problems and to symbolize communal solidarities by the forthright assertion of individual claims and grievances.

In virtually every instance of a consideration of communal projects or needs that the author observed or heard of, the dominant characteristic of the discussion was a vigorous and uncompromising assertion of individual claims. If it was a question of allotting spaces in a new marketplace, each discussant was vociferating that the portion allotted to him was insufficient. If it was a question of securing more land for various communal purposes, the various property owners involved orated against contributing a square foot unless reimbursed at some preposterous figure. If it was a scene in court or a police station, everyone with any personal grievance, real or imagined, felt it perfectly proper to interrupt at any point and give vent to his opinion. If it was a question of rebuilding a ravaged church or constructing a road, personal disputations undermined all efforts toward communal action. If it was simply a ceremonial occasion, the peaceful setting one might have expected was shattered by the airing of private disputes.

> Today a new church building was dedicated. It was built to replace one that had been destroyed more than two decades ago by the Italians. People from all over the area made the journey to attend this celebration. All night long and well into the morning the priests and *dabtarā* sang and danced, accompanied as usual by sistrums and drums. Later in the morning, after the church had been officially sanctified, everyone was assembled in the open space in the church compound to listen to some verses composed in honor of the event by one of the local *bālābbāt,* a man who had been a key figure in getting the church rebuilt. He had scarcely finished reciting his poem when a woman in the audience spoke up in anger, arguing that the new church would involve more taxes and in some way would affect her property rights adversely. While he was trying to pacify her, others interrupted and began airing grievances of their own. What was to have been the climax of an occasion for the expression of communal solidarity ended as a bedlam of argument.[10]

The one area in which communal sentiments have seemed fairly strong among the Amhara has been in connection with the pursuit of outlaws. It is customary—in some Amhara districts, at least—for the local inhabitants to band together in informal posses when threatened by the presence of one or more *shǐftā,* or "outlaws." Yet even here, in his attitudes toward the *shǐftā,* the Amhara reveals an ambivalence regarding the maintenance of civil order and security.

The term *shǐftā* had, in former times, primarily a political connotation. It referred to someone who rebelled against his feudal superior and was applied only to persons of relatively high status.[11] More recently the term has been vulgarized and broadened to include any sort of outlaw in the rural areas. In any case the *shǐftā* is a man apart, who makes his home in uninhabited mountainous country or lowlands and lives by stealing cattle and robbing travelers. Some Amhara become *shǐftā* because of a passion for this way of life; this is particularly true of soldiers who, after a long campaign, prefer the continuation of a predatory and free existence to a return to the hard work of the fields. Others do so involuntarily, in order to escape punishment after committing some violence in the course of a personal dispute.

The attitudes of civilian Amhara toward the *shǐftā* combine fear and dislike with a strong tendency toward idealization. The *shǐftā* is feared because he is a killer; if a person happens to witness him performing some act of theft or murder, he will usually keep quiet about it for fear of reprisal. He is disliked because he lives parasitically off the productive activities of others. But the *shǐftā* is widely admired, on the other hand, because he possesses a number of qualities that are dear to the Amhara. He is reputed to be an expert singer of *shǐllalā*. He is credited with unusually handsome features because, living at the expense of others as he does, he has plenty to eat and no arduous work to wear him down. Above all he is *guabaz,* the great Amhara virtue that embodies bravery, fierceness, hardihood, and general male competence. This is symbolized by the *shǐftā*'s letting his hair grow to the proportions of a *gofarē,* the wildly thick hair style of the warrior.

The Amhara's admiration for the *shifta* is reminiscent of American attitudes toward the outlaw in "western" films. In the Amhara case, however, this is not balanced by a corresponding idealization of a sheriff-figure as the representative of civil order. Although a feudal lord or governor who captures some *shǐftā* in his area may be admired, this admiration will be directed to his personal qualities of bravery or cunning far more than to his capacity as an agent of "law and order." There is no feeling among the Amhara that the *shǐftā* must be captured simply because he is an outlaw. Instead, a more pragmatic approach is taken: the *shǐftā* is acknowledged as a legitimate social type and is tolerated at a distance so long as his killing does not become wanton or excessive. This approach, and what, in the idealization of the *shǐftā,* appears to be a tendency to identify with someone who openly flaunts the norms of civil society, bespeaks a relatively weak commitment to the value of civil order.

The weakness of the Amhara's attachment to symbols of local community is paralleled by his parochialism with respect to more inclusive levels of community. This parochialism is manifest in diverse ways in the different social strata. Among the peasantry it appears, for example, as an aversion to arranging marriages and permitting land to pass to an Amhara from a different province. Among the clergy it has been expressed in terms of those regionally based doctrinal differences which have disrupted the church for many centuries. Among the nobility it has taken the form of incessant political animosities which have weakened the nobility as a status group both in relation to the emperor and in relation to foreign countries. Another respect in which Amhara parochialism has been expressed is the addiction to regional stereotypes, according to which the Tigrean has been depicted as flighty, irresponsible, and "dry"; the Gondarē as intolerably proud; the Gojjami as sly and treacherous; and the Shoan as calculating and untrustworthy. Despite its long history as a nation, Ethiopia probably never experienced more than the dimmest stirrings of a truly national sentiment among its people; and more than once in the past century have regional lords strengthened the hand of European powers in Ethiopia by seeking their help in the combat against other local rulers.

Self and Others

In addition to considering the extent to which the members of a society identify with the needs and symbols of their more inclusive collectivities, one may also define the individualistic disposition on the dimension of personal interaction. Egoism contrasts, in other words, not only with the disposition to perceive collective purposes as one's own, but also with the disposition to seek solidarity and mutuality in face-to-face relations.

This aspect of egoism/solidarism is studied by surveying the more important forms of interaction that appear in a given society. In the survey of elementary social behavior among the Amhara now to be reported, two criteria were used to establish the importance of any given form: (1) the frequency with which it was observed, and (2) the extent to which it was stylized or "institutionalized." These criteria were not embodied in any systematic observational procedures; the only control over the observer's bias here is my own deliberate effort to present a balanced and accurate picture.

We may begin by considering the more solidaristic forms. Interaction among the Amhara is characterized, first of all, by a sort of *sensuous camaraderie*. The Amhara enjoy bodily contact. Members of the same sex customarily hold one another's hands for long periods while conversing, or embrace one another in casual fellowship. Crowds of commoners cheerfully huddle close to one another on the floor through the night when they have assembled for some social function and cannot return home the same day. Relatives and companions of the same sex incline to sleep in one another's arms, at least in the chillier altitudes.

Both their style of dress and their manner of eating give the Amhara a ready way to express this comradely feeling. Their untailored cotton or wool cloth easily adapts itself to being shared. Except perhaps for individuals of high social status, the typical Amhara is ready to use his toga as a blanket-wrap for both himself and another whom he may scarcely know.

A similar spirit is observed in Amhara commensality. Meals are customarily eaten from a common *ĭnjarā* basket. The sauce is ladled onto the center of the *ĭnjarā,* and is consumed ensemble by those sitting around the basket as they dip into it with pieces of *ĭnjarā* broken off from the edges. Traditional Amhara scoff at what they regard as the excessively individualistic Western custom of sitting each person down to a separate place at the table and thus depriving the meal hour of what they feel should be its basically communal tone.

At a more formal level of interaction this disposition is expressed in the form of *hospitality.* Amhara hospitality is luxuriously attentive and thoughtful. For example, if there is foreknowledge of a guest's arrival, he is awaited at some distance from his destination and escorted with much to-do into the home. His mule is at once unsaddled and given to feed. The guest is given a place of honor in the home, and a glass of *ṭallā* is immediately brought for him. Amhara etiquette prescribes, moreover, that a glass is not properly filled unless it overflows; and it is repeatedly filled to overflowing whenever the guest has drunk some portion of the beverage. As a gratuitous gesture of good faith, the host—or his wife, or servant—tastes some of the beverage first, a sign that no "medicine" has been added. Before long the wicker table is produced, and the guest and his party are served copiously—no matter what time of day they arrive (unless, of course, it is a fasting day). When the guest has eaten to satisfaction, the host will insist that he eat some more, by repeatedly issuing injunctions like *tegābazu* ("Help yourselves!"), *moḳar* ("Try!"), or *àfar sehon* ("If I become dust!"—i.e., "If you do not eat you will be condemning me to death"). The Amhara host is also likely to insist that his guest spend the night. The guest's feet will be washed, and the host's bed will be given to him, or long grass will be cut for bedding on the floor. At the time of farewell, the host and his attendants follow the guest and his party a good distance along the road. The guest continually cries, "Return! Return!" and the host agrees but continues to serve as escort.

Such hospitality is not wantonly bestowed upon the casual wayfarer. Normally it is reserved for those who qualify as worthy guests: relatives, friends, or persons of high rank. Nonetheless, there does exist among the Amhara some feeling that even the unknown stranger should be shown hospitality, for he is *ya-egziābhēr engedā* ("a guest of God"). Travelers are generally assured that somebody somewhere will show them hospitality; there are no inns in traditional Ethiopia, for it is considered wrong to exchange food and lodging for money.

Related to this pattern of hospitality is a delicate sense of *respect* that the Amhara displays toward all comers; often, even toward his enemies. When two Amhara pass each other anywhere, they are expected to bow slightly and say: "How did you pass the night?" or "How did you spend the day?" If they have not seen each other for some time they will say: "How have you so-journed?" and kiss each other on both cheeks. Depending on the closeness of their relationship and the interval between meetings, this introductory question will be followed by a more or less lengthy series of other questions.[12] Even when one merely passes by the home of another, he is expected to cry out his greetings from afar.

In a number of other ways, the rough edges of social life are softened by Amhara codes of etiquette. Custom prescribes that measures of grain must be filled to overflowing at the market. Grammatical forms indicating respect are used between people who are not on intimate terms. Uncovering one's head is another way of indicating respect during the greeting. Still another form is to rise whenever someone enters the room, and wait until the new entrant has pronounced "*Bezgiēr!*" ("By God!") and sits down before reseating oneself.

On more superficial levels of interaction, then, Amhara behavior is apparently not egoistic. In the more fundamental areas of work and serious communication, a different picture appears.

Altogether there is little spontaneous *co-operation* in Amhara life. The Amhara prefers to work by himself, and, when he needs assistance, to order a subordinate to help him rather than to rely on friendly assistance from his neighbor. The distribution as well as the production of goods is carried out on an essentially individualistic basis. Each nuclear family takes care of its own provisions, even when the land being cultivated belongs to one of the parents and when more than one family lives within a single compound. (Even within the nuclear family, the proprietary sentiments of husband and wife regarding objects and land which each may own are rather lively.)

There are exceptions to this general rule. In some Amhara areas certain co-operative work forms have become institutionalized, for example. One of these forms, called *wanfal*, is invoked when there is a considerable amount of plowing or harvesting to be done, and a group of men in a given area take turns working on each other's land. Another form of co-operative work, called *waffar*, is employed when there is some extraordinary job to be done—putting on a new roof or digging land that is too steep for plowing—which cannot readily be reciprocated. In this case a man sends word around that on a certain day those who live in the area should come to work at his place, in reward for which generous quantities of *ṭallā* and *dābo* will be given them.

Despite the existence of special forms like *wanfal* and *waffar*, co-operation is only a peripheral feature of Amhara work activity. These forms involve but a temporary coincidence of individual interests. They are not used because co-operation as such is felt to be an important and natural part of social life—as seems to be the case, for example, among the Galla of Ethiopia.

Spontaneous co-operation is most in evidence among the Amhara at times of crisis. When death is announced, relatives and friends promptly repair to the home of the deceased and offer their help. They build the coffin and construct a *dāss* (a temporary shelter near the house to accommodate all the expected visitors). They bring food and drink to help provide for the many who will come to pay their respects, and will similarly provide help on the occasion of the big memorial feasts to follow. Like assistance is rendered during other crises, such as prolonged illnesses or fire. Such forms of co-operation set another significant limit to egoistic orientation among the Amhara.

It is in the realm of interaction involving serious interests, touching layers of the personality deeper than those required for the formalities of etiquette, that Amhara egoism is most conspicuous. Here everything seems to conspire against generous communication and concord of opinion. As we have already observed, the Amhara are quick to become argumentative in ordinary conversation. *Litigation* is one of the most prominent forms of interaction among the Amhara. One can scarcely spend a day in the Amhara countryside without encountering litigants, whether under a tree, at a marketplace, or in the courtyard of some lord. A nobleman can never travel about the country without being accosted on the way by litigants anxious to have him hear their stories.

Litigation is, of course, an endemic feature of peasant civilizations. Yet there can be no doubt that for the Amhara this form embodies a basic psychological disposition that differs from that of the people of other peasant civilizations. In traditional China, to take a case of marked contrast, such interpersonal conflict, far from being relished, was deliberately avoided. The Chinese considered going to court to be an extravagance, and the village judge was one of the most underemployed members of the community. In China, parties to a dispute preferred to assemble at the teahouse and to seek a solution through discussion and negotiation. The Amhara, on the other hand, seeks to maximize the opportunity for self-assertion through litigious disputes.* Ordinary sociability among the Amhara is saturated with references to litigation. Current court cases comprise one of the more common topics of conversation.

Beyond litigation, *conflict* is often expressed in more violent forms. Fights with the *dulā* erupt when altercation becomes too heated. Throwing stones is another accepted mode of combat, especially among youth. Protracted enmities tend to eventuate in such acts as house-burning, assault with swords or rifles, and (according to Amhara belief, at least) poisoning.

While it is true that Amhara culture provides means and a certain amount

---

* Some indication of the gross national significance of this phenomenon is afforded by the following comparison: twenty-seven high court judges are sufficient to handle the litigation for all of England and Wales; the corresponding number for Ethiopia is *one hundred and eighteen.*

of moral pressure for the reconciliation of conflict, it appears to place greater emphasis on the acting out of aggression. It does this, first of all, by defining a number of acts as offenses which justify violent retribution of some sort. Appropriation of one's land, seduction of one's wife, and injury of one's relatives are acts of this nature, and it is incumbent on the offended party to seek personal revenge or, as the Amhara put it, "to return the debt" (*bedder mammalas*). It is considered shameful to remain passive when so affronted, an attitude expressed in the following couplet:

> Balaw ba-dimotfar daggmaw ba-wānzā,
> Bābbāt r̈istennā yallam bamı̈st wāzzā.

> Shoot him with the dimotfar,* get him again with
>   a wanza,*
> Taking your father's land or your wife away,
>   that is no joking matter.

Aggressiveness is further encouraged by the Amhara ego ideal of masculinity.[13] The identity of Amhara males is very much bound up with their capacity for aggressiveness, by both violent and verbal means. A man who has killed someone is regarded with a certain amount of veneration, and the act of killing is itself praised in verses such as:

> Saw gadlu saw gadlu: saw magdal yebajāl,
> Saw yālgadala saw sihēd yāngolājāl.

> Kill a man! Kill a man! It is good to kill a man!
> One who has not killed a man moves around
>   sleepily.

Similarly, verbal aggression is encouraged by the inclusion of excellence at litigation and insulting in the domain of proper male behavior.[14] The bestowal of insults is a rather stylized, if dangerous, procedure among the Amhara. According to Amhara customary law, insulting is a legal offense. The new criminal code provides for a gradation of penalties according to the seriousness of the insult, including fines which run from Eth$15 to as much as hundreds of dollars. The most serious insults include *bāryā* ("slave"); *ṭayb* ("evil-eyed artisan"); and *qomātā* ("leper"). Insults of lesser to medium degrees of seriousness include the following:

hodām	"greedy" (literally, "bellied")
wafrām	"fat"
saḳārām	"drunkard"
quashāshā	"dirty"
amadām	"scaly-faced" (literally, "ashen")

---

* Types of rifles.

arām	"indolent" (literally, "full of feces")
ya-dehā lïjj	"son of a poor man"
ya-lēbā lïjj	"son of a thief"
yat abātk	"bastard" (literally, "where is your father?")
waslātā	"lazy no-good"

Other, less direct forms of insult are also widely employed. As was already mentioned, a major use of the wax-and-gold formula is to express insults in so veiled a manner that direct reprisal is unlikely. Another tactic is that of not showing someone the proper respect or in some way manipulating the forms of etiquette to his disadvantage. A favorite anecdote concerning Alaqā Gabra Hānnā illustrates the simultaneous use of both methods: the Alaqā once flattered a donkey driver by bowing quite low to greet him and calling, *Endēt adarātchu?* ("How did you spend the night?"). Only when the man proudly related the episode to his friends, so the story goes, was he made to realize that the greeting was expressed in the plural form (*-atchu*), implying that he and his donkey were being placed in the same category.[15] Still another mode of indirect insult is that known as *ashmur*, in which two friends insult each other vigorously at the top of their voices, the real object of their abuse being a third party who is within earshot.

If the Amhara is by disposition inclined to bestow insults, he is still readier to take offense at the slightest hint of one directed at him. One of the tasks of socialization among the Amhara is to sensitize the young person to the various types of insults and to motivate him to strike back when he is so offended. Insults are frequently part of a vicious circle which moves from petty disagreement to serious argument to litigation at court, *dulā* fights, and even premeditated murder. Breach of etiquette may lead to no less serious consequences. In one court case which the author observed, a man was accused and convicted for addressing his father-in-law, whom he normally addressed by the polite form *ersewo*, with the familiar form *anta* in a moment of anger.

Argumentation, litigation, insulting, and revenge comprise the hard core of social interaction among Amhara. While it is possible to exaggerate the significance of these forms in the total pattern of Amhara social life, there can be little doubt of a strongly dissentious disposition just below the surface, and often at the surface, of Amhara interpersonal relations. Still another axis along which this individualistic disposition tends to be manifest is that of deception and suspicion.

The Amhara is a master at *deception*. With straight face and convincing manner he will relate the most preposterous fictions. The Amhara themselves tend to be aware that this is one of their characteristic activities. When, for example, I replied to the query of an Amhara gentleman that some horn goblets (which I had purchased for one dollar) had cost five dollars each, he remarked: "Ah, I see you have learned this country's art of lying well."

The phenomenon in question is not an unmixed expression of egoism. At times the Amhara employ deception chiefly for reasons of considerateness, not wanting to tell the other person something that will offend him. Thus a person will agree to honor a request made by his neighbor even though he has no intention in the world of doing so; his neighbor probably understands this but still prefers an insincere "Yes" to an out-and-out "No."

Most of the time, however, deception is obviously being used to further one man's interests at the expense of another's. A person seeking a favor will pretend to be in much poorer straits than he actually is.* A needy traveler may pretend to be an important personage or otherwise disguise his identity in order to secure lodging for the night. An artisan, in order to obtain business, will tell his prospective customer that a certain job will be finished in two days when he has no intention of completing the work within a fortnight. To refer once again to my own experience: when I once needed to rent a mule for a week, and it was felt that the local mule owners might be reluctant to rent one for more than two or three days, I was advised by some respected Amhara men in the area that the only thing to do was to say that the mule was wanted for a few days, then on return to say that unexpected factors prevented my getting back on time. Far more imaginative plays of deception are attributed, again, to Alaqā Gabra Hānnā, who is renowned for the episode of sending word to Menelik that he was dead so that the Emperor would send money on his behalf to Gondar.

Like the indirect forms of insulting, deception has its more subtle, passive forms; deceptiveness by omitting the truth rather than committing a falsehood. One might render the basic principle that informs communication among the Amhara as: *Avoid binding commitments; maximize the degrees of freedom left after any utterance.* Questions and answers are typically couched in extremely oblique language. Unless there is some overwhelming personal advantage to be obtained from providing information, the Amhara tend to give answers—when they do not pretend not to understand the question—in terms so ambiguous as to be worthless; for example, replying to a question about the location of a certain place or person with the word *mādo* ("yonder").

The natural complement of so much deception is pronounced *suspiciousness.* Amhara are constantly on the lookout for latent meanings and hidden motives.

---

* One Amhara priest, for example, showed me that he had no clothes other than his single blanket in order to gain sympathy and induce me to give him something. But when he learned I had a camera, he went home promptly to get dressed for a photograph.

Our people always speak indirectly, in secrets. For example, a man will come, asking for the glass he loaned another man. The debtor says he will bring it in a week, that it has been broken and he will send for a new one. The man may say: "Oh, never mind. It doesn't matter to me, don't bother." The debtor will then be scared; thinking that the owner of the glass is in his stomach quite angry and ready to kill him, he will take his gun and get the man first.[16]

The suspiciousness which so colors interaction among the Amhara has been viewed by some observers primarily as an adaptive response to some very real dangers with which Ethiopia has chronically been confronted: the threat of conversion to Western forms of Christianity by European missionaries, the threat of European imperialism, and the threat of encirclement and occupation by a militant Islam. These factors have undoubtedly intensified the apprehensiveness of Ethiopia's leaders and strengthened the much publicized xenophobic attitude of the Amhara people, just as the proliferation of security networks during the postliberation period has intensified the generalized distrust on the domestic scene. But these attitudes flourish as they do because they are nurtured on the soil of a basic disinclination to trust one another that is endemic in traditional Amhara culture.

That culture is marked, *au fond*, by a sense of despair about the possibilities of concord and enduring consensus among men, and, in more practical terms, by a realization that people who spend so much of their time deceiving one another are not to be trusted very much. *Sawen māmman baḳantu naw* ("it is futile to trust in man")—so runs an Amharic epigram sometimes woven ornamentally into wool rugs; and it carries a secular-practical as well as a religious-speculative meaning. This disposition is institutionalized in the custom of *wāss*, according to which any sort of civil transaction—hiring a man as a servant, or lending money, or litigating in court—involves as one of the first steps the securing of a *wāss*, or "guarantor," who agrees to make good for any damages caused by the man he is backing.[17] It also appears in the custom of continually challenging the assertions made by someone who is relating an episode, so that the speaker is forced to interlard his narration with oaths that swear by the truth of what he is saying. The Amhara tendency to "overinterpret" and impute deception appears in their conception of the very origins of their language, for informed traditional Amhara commonly believe that Amharic originated as a secret language during the reign of the legendary Falasha Queen Yodit.

A penchant for *secrecy* is pronounced among the Amhara and constitutes still another aspect of the individualistic disposition. In culturally elaborated forms it appears in the predilection for employing secret languages, including the argots of merchants, minstrels, and *zār* victims,[18] and the secret language of shepherds,[19] as well as the secret formulae of magicians, the obscurantist constructions of wax and gold, and the use of Ge'ez itself in the presence of illiterates. Related to this is the great popularity of riddle games among Amhara. Personal relations, moreover, are consciously predicated on the harboring of secrets, or *mĭsṭir*. The Amhara assume that it is improper to reveal oneself fully, to disclose one's *mĭsṭir,* to anyone but a very close friend; and that, in fact, rarely happens.

Given the weakness of horizontal forms of cohesion among the Amhara—sociability at mealtime, stylized politeness among equals, and co-operation in time of crisis, important though they are, cannot contain the centrifugal forces just described—the dispositions which sustain a minimum of social order among the Amhara are expressed through vertical, hierarchical forms of interaction. Here both individualistic and solidaristic forms are in evidence, the latter in the forms of deference and begging, the former in the variety of authoritarian relationships.

Perhaps the most characteristic form of interaction among the Amhara is that of *domination*. The Amhara is at his happiest when he is in a position to order someone about. The sense of domination is marked not only in relations between nobles and commoners, officers and soldiers, masters and servants, but also between husbands and wives, and parents and children. Amhara children sometimes volunteer the explanation of their desire to have children when they grow up as based on the explanation that then *they* will have youngsters of their own to command.

Connected with the passion to dominate is a predilection for administering physical punishment. In all of the relationships just mentioned corporal punishment is an integral feature, particularly so on the domestic scene. With sticks or whips, masters beat servants, teachers pupils, husbands wives, and parents children. The complete acceptance of this pattern was shown by the fact that not a single Amhara TAT respondent objected to any of the corporal punishment cards. They all assumed that the punishment depicted, including that of husband against wife and mistress against servant, was deserved, proper, and would have a salutary effect. (One of the respondents even exclaimed when regarding one of the beating scenes: "What a beautiful punishment!") The only reservations expressed concerned the possibility that the punishment might be so severe as to wound fatally the person being punished, in which case the punisher would have cause for regret.

Whatever the functions of such patterns in controlling antisocial behavior and securing adherence to the norms of the situation, the sentiment that underlies them is primarily egoistic. The superior is interested primarily in having his own way and gratifying his ego through the sheer exercise of his power; and the motivation of the punisher probably often contains a strong sadistic component—a component that gets thrown into relief in such phenomena as the Amhara compulsion to stone dogs and the occasional wantonly cruel behavior of Amhara soldiers.

While hierarchical relations among the Amhara are upheld to a large degree by the subordinate's fear of physical punishment or some other deprivation, a complementary disposition of perhaps greater importance is the sentiment of *respect for figures of higher status*. Family, age, wealth, and political or ecclesiastical rank are all variables which evoke feelings and gestures of deference proportionate to the vertical distance between the two parties. Many of these gestures consist of elaborations on ordinary forms of etiquette used among peers. Thus, in greeting a superior one not only uncovers one's head but also leaves it uncovered as long as one remains in his presence. If kisses are exchanged in greeting, the superior kisses first, on the cheek, while the person of lesser status kisses the superior's foot or knee. The inferior never sits while the superior stands, and often he remains standing even when the latter is seated.

Other gestures of respect are peculiar to the inferior-superior relationship. If an inferior is seated, for example, he must rise to speak when addressed by a superior. If eating in the home of a superior, he must rise when water is brought to wash his hands. If riding a mule, he must dismount and bow when encountering a nobleman riding on the way. The ritual of respect performed when entering the house of a superior has been vividly described by an Ethiopian student in the following passage:

> When someone, let us say a man of a lower social rank, wishes to enter the house of a superior to greet him or to make some private appeal he must first of all take off his shoes and then give them to his servant if he has one with him; if not he leaves them outside in a safe place. Then he must twist his *šäma* [shammā] round his waist and holding the end in one hand enter the hall and crossing both arms at the lower chest, bow down very low to the ground before his host. Having done that he throws that end of his *šäma* which he is holding over the back of his right or left shoulder (depending on how he wears his *šäma*) and then remains standing near the wall until he is told to sit. When given permission to sit he must choose a lower place. He does not sit in any position he likes but must cross his legs, straighten himself and bow his head a bit looking most of the time at the floor.[20]

Respect is further shown toward superiors through the use of special terms of reference and address. A superior is always referred to and addressed in the third-person-plural respect form. The term *gētotch* ("lordships") is often used instead of his name or rank in reference. In addressing a superior *gētāyē* ("my lord") may be used as well as *gētotch*. Superiors with titles are always addressed by their rank rather than by name. In addition, slightly older or more prestigious males are addressed as *gāshē* ("my shield"); the corresponding term for females is *etēyē* ("my sister"). Much older people are addressed by words signifying "father" or "mother."

It is true that the forms of respect toward superiors are often repeated mechanically and sometimes serve to cover up a distinctly hostile disposition toward certain superiors. They nevertheless do represent to some extent a genuine solidaristic sentiment—perhaps the most profound and influential social sentiment in the Amhara social system. It rests in the last analysis on the fact that the Amhara family develops a pronounced sense of filial devotion as well as habits of filial obedience. Amhara society can dispense with horizontal solidarities and communal attachments because it is held together, sufficiently for traditional purposes, at least, by an infinite network of "father-son" relationships.

The egoistic element in the hierarchical pattern is further modified by a sort of joking relationship that sometimes develops between inferiors and superiors. The harsh interrogation of inferiors at times shades into a sort of wry banter; sons or servants may be called "thief" or "scoundrel" in an undertone of unmistakable affection. At times, moreover, the direction of the jesting may be reversed. Amhara servants are noted for playing practical jokes on their masters, which the latter usually appreciate when the jests are clever.[21] Here again, wax and gold is the perfect medium—for expressing aggression against a superior while at the same time appearing to maintain the respect relationship. The following couplet, attributed to Naggādrās Tassamā Eshatē, aptly illustrates this genre:

Ennānta makuānnentotch ba-mĭn waṭ balātchu?
Eññām ba-shurwātchen ennāntam bāssātchu.

What sauce, my lords, was on your plate?
We had but peas; 'twas fish you ate.[22]

Here the poet appears to be complimenting the nobles on their more elegant cuisine at a banquet; but there is a pun on the word *bāssātchu,* literally "with your fish," for it may also be taken to mean "you took more than your share."

Within the hierarchical pattern, finally, one finds expressed a certain amount of generosity which, as we have suggested, is relatively uncommon in relations among peers. This appears in connection with the *begging* and *almsgiving* which occur in many sectors of Amhara society. For church students beyond the elementary level, begging is the primary means of livelihood. Youths who have left home to study *zēmā* or *qenē* with a master wander about today, as in former times, carrying small baskets and pleading: "For the sake of Mary! For the sake of God!" in order to get their daily morsels. The activity is so organized that when a large number of students live near the same master, they divide up the neighboring countryside to avoid duplication in their begging.

The ordained clergy are themselves given to begging, for items ranging from contributions to the local church to petty personal effects. High-ranking visitors to their locale are customarily made the objects of such solicitations. Another type of begging is practiced by the minstrels who wander about the country with their one-stringed fiddles and fecund wit, coaxing contributions from any audience they can capture. In addition to these there are numerous professional beggars—the maimed, the diseased, and the poverty-stricken— who attach themselves to a well-attended church or monastery if they are unable to travel. The *lālibalā* is a notable type within this category of mendicants.[23]

In addition to honoring the periodic appeals of beggars, "big men" are supposed to provide yearly feasts (*gīber*) at which beggars of all the above descriptions are fed. In all these instances, the solicitation and bestowal of charity contributes a solidaristic element to the network of personal relations among the Amhara.

The foregoing analysis of forms of interaction among the Amhara has been undertaken in order to gain material for generalizing about a psychological disposition. Our unspoken, tautological assumption has been that the ways in which individuals typically relate to social objects (i.e., other persons and collectivities) represent the sociologically relevant aspects of their psychology. Egoism and solidarism have been used here as concepts for depicting one dimension of "social character," using this term in the specific sense of comprising those aspects of personality which are both socially shared and constitutive of those actions that are oriented to social objects. We may now attempt to summarize the preceding discussion with the following definition of Amhara social character as it relates to the concept of individualism: The Amhara is primarily disposed to structure interaction in terms of self-assertion, dissension, and distrust, and to be indifferent to the concept of civil community. At the same time this egoistic orientation is blended with a warm and kindly sense of sociability, an occasional mood of generosity, and a refined sensibility regarding differences in status and the readiness to pay deference accordingly.

INDEPENDENCE VERSUS CONSTRAINT

In the previous section we considered the nature of the individual's orientation toward others and toward collectivities in Amhara society. Our question now is the converse: what order of demands is made upon individuals by the institutions of that society? Specifically, we shall be concerned primarily with the degree to which the norms which govern institutional roles are permissive rather than prescriptive, and the degree to which individual rights are protected against the demands of collectivities.

In pursuing this analysis we shall examine in turn the three main institutional orders which were structurally differentiated in Amhara society: the kinship system, the church, and the military-political system. In conclusion we shall discuss some more general features of social organization among the Amhara which relate to the question of individual independence.

Kinship

A base line of social constraint among the Amhara is provided by the obligations inherent in their family system. The husband must work to provide food and to defend the boundaries of the family land against all comers. The wife must care for all that transpires within the home compound—preparing of food, fetching water, caring for infants, spinning cotton, tending the fire—and must avoid sexual relationships with other men. The children must tend the flocks, do other work chores, and generally obey the slightest command of any of their elders. Neglect of any of these basic obligations brings sharp reprisals: divorce of the husband, beatings of the wife and children.

Obligations toward the parents persist, moreover, long after the children have married and established families of their own. Young married men are supposed to contribute one or two days a week to working their fathers' land, and to assist them in time of litigation. They are obliged to care for their parents when the latter have become too old to provide for themselves, an obligation sometimes discharged on a rotating basis among the surviving children. There is also a solemn obligation for the children to arrange the appropriate memorial feasts (*tazkār*) following the death of a parent, especially the one that is due on the fortieth day after death.

Adolescent children are subject to the will of their parents with respect to choice of a spouse, and youths are expected to follow their fathers' wishes in connection with adult work roles. Threat of disinheritance is the powerful consideration that underpins these constraints. For their part, the parents are obliged to keep their land in the family. They may not sell it to outsiders, and must bequeath goods and land to their children, dividing them equally among the consanguine children, with perhaps a certain amount extra for the oldest son.

With regard to siblings and more distant kin, however, relations are rather casual and obligations few. Although residence tends to be virilocal among the Amhara, descent is bilateral. Except for a small number of royal and aristocratic families, therefore, there are no obligations with respect to corporate lineages. The absence of formal structure in extended kin relations is shown by the vagueness of Amhara kin terminology. The term for brother, *wandam,* also applies to all the male relatives of one's generation and even to one's close friends. Similarly, the terms for uncle and aunt (*agot* and *akeste*) are sometimes used for nephew, niece, and cousin as well; and often these terms are simply replaced by the abstract generic word for kin, *zamad.* The extent of reciprocal obligations among kin outside the nuclear family is a function primarily of the amount of spontaneous affection that exists among the individuals concerned and how close they happen to live to each other. Relatives on good terms with one another normally take turns visiting one another and eating together on holidays. They help one another in the event of sickness, death, fire, litigation, and murder. Orphaned or economically burdensome children are often farmed out to the households of more successful relatives.

These activities are based on voluntary reciprocity or good will. In its formal structure, the Amhara kinship system stresses the independence of the nuclear family. Although it occasionally happens that married brothers live in a single large compound under the moral authority of their father or an older brother, who is known as its *alaqā* and is responsible for the compound's payment of taxes, each nuclear family lives in separate quarters and produces and consumes its own supply of food by working its own separate acreage of land.

Within the nuclear family itself, the ties that bind are limited by certain fundamental safeguards of individual rights. One is the institution of private property. The land which each partner brings into a marriage or later acquires through bequests remains his own until death. If they should separate, each takes his own land, and the goods acquired by the household during their marriage are divided equally between them. There is also the provision of *gĭl,* a quantity of property that either or both of the spouses may designate, prior to getting married, as strictly private property and indivisible in case of divorce. In the event that a nuclear family enters one of the modern savings associations or *equb* (to be discussed below), husband and wife join as separate members.

The possibility of divorce is another safeguard of individual rights within the nuclear family. Only in the *querbān* type of marriage is divorce forbidden. This form is normally restricted to priests and very devout, usually older, people; and even then divorces sometimes occur, the couple preferring the displeasure of the church to a life of continued antagonism. The standard sort of marriage is the *samānya* or contract form, in which the equivalent of a simple "I do" concludes the match and a simple "I do not" legitimates divorce. The divorce may be initiated by either husband or wife. An Amharic proverb which stresses the rights of women in this regard gives the following advice:

Balāgar siṭagab yematāl ba-degger;
Tayawennā nay qitāwen yegāgger.

When a peasant gets sated he beats you with wood;
Leave and come home, let him bake his own bread!

A couple who have firmly decided upon divorce need simply call in their relatives or go before the *çhïqā shum* in order to have their property properly divided. The only recourse to judicial process is when, as often happens, disputes break out concerning the division of property. In the *damoz* form of marriage, in which there is no civil oath, divorce is yet simpler. The wife is given certain presents and a monthly salary for the duration of the marriage. When the husband has to leave for another part of the country, or if the couple quarrel, they simply separate without further ado.

Despite its heavy claim on the energies of its members, then, the Amhara kinship system is such as to make members of the nuclear family relatively independent of extended relationships, and to give the individual marriage partners important areas of independence from each other.

Religious Organization

Membership in the Monophysite Church is automatic for all Amhara except a small percentage who are Muslim. This membership is symbolized by the ceremony of baptism, performed for male infants on the fortieth day and for females on the eightieth. At that time the child receives a special Christian name in addition to his regular family name.

Certain obligations are incumbent upon every member of the church. Foremost among these is the requirement of fasting, which begins for children of both sexes at about the age of seven and introduces a considerable element of constraint into the lives of the Amhara. Second, there is the obligation to observe the Sabbaths and the main holidays by refraining from arduous physical labor on those days. In addition, each household is obliged to contribute a certain quantity of grain to the local church every year.*

Apart from the rigorous fasting requirements, and the injunction not to work on holy days—a dubious hardship—the individual is relatively free of ritual obligations. The rituals demanded by the church are so manifold, and so sacred, that responsibility for them is given to the clergy, and the laymen

---

*In some areas this is a fixed amount per household (e.g., one or two *quana*); in others it is proportionate to the wealth of the family. It is collected by a lay official of the church, the *gend alaqā*, though sometimes by the *gabaz*.

are left free to a large extent. Since every day of the month except the thirtieth is sanctified by dedication to some saint, Mass must be performed virtually every day, a norm which is actually fulfilled by churches which have a numerous clergy. The burden for individual clergymen is kept small by a system of rotation. The average parish church will have services perhaps ten to fifteen times a month, which is still too often for heavy popular attendance. Even on Sundays and the most important holidays, when the laity are expected to attend, their participation is excused by other considerations. Those who have eaten earlier in the day, who have had sexual relations the night before, or who are harboring a grudge in their "stomach" are not even supposed to come to church. If they do come, they sit outside the wall chatting with one another while the Mass is performed inside.

Customs concerning Communion and Confession likewise give the individual a wide range of freedom. Partaking of the Communion is not required of anyone; the experience simply is available to those who are ritually pure (children, and those who have married by the *querbān*), if they are so inclined. Confession is not mandatory, but according to personal inclination. Every man has the right to choose his own personal confessor or "soul-father," though if satisfied with the one of his father, he may retain him. (A woman adopts the confessor of her husband.) The soul-father's advice may be sought when a problem arises. If a man sins—breaks the fast, works on a holiday, commits theft or murder—he is supposed to confess. If he chooses to do so, the soul-father will prescribe a certain penance—fasting an extra amount, sleeping on the floor for a period, giving something to the poor or to the church. But the initiative is entirely up to the sinner and probably more often than not he keeps the offense to himself. The proportion of Amhara who keep every fast strictly, go to church a few times a month, and confess their transgressions to the soul-father is small; in the estimate of one Amhara informant, less than five per cent.

Still greater permissiveness may be observed in connection with the religious fraternal associations known as the *māhebar*. The *māhebar* consists of a group of people from the same general area, usually of the same sex, who meet once a month on the day devoted to the saint for whom the association is named. The place of meeting rotates among the homes of the members, and the soul-father of the host is always present to bless the occasion. The meetings consist of much eating, drinking, and conviviality. Membership in a *māhebar* is purely voluntary, and the individual who wishes to join one usually has a choice among several in a given area.*

For the Amhara laity, then, a few burdensome ritual and fiscal constraints

---

* There is a variant of the *māhebar* known as the *sanbatē,* whose members take turns in providing food for the clergy and poor folk on Sundays.

are balanced by a fairly permissive mode of organization. For the clergy, the constraints are heavier; the fasting requirements are increased, and the priesthood involves, as we have seen, strict marital fidelity. On the other hand, the individualistic organization of the clergy is most striking.

This individualism is conspicuous already in the church schools, which are organized not on a class basis but in a series of master-pupil relations. Students begin their courses of study whenever they arrive at the residence of the master, and proceed each at his own pace. The master spends the bulk of his time with more advanced students, who in turn are used to instruct the less advanced. The pupils are very much on their own, uncontrolled either by their families, with whom they no longer reside, nor by any formal institution. The same is true of the masters, who are not subjected to any sort of outside controls. Indeed, each teacher tends to develop his own unique method of teaching, regarding it as something of a personal monopoly.[24]

The ministrating clergy are likewise free from controls emanating from a broad ecclesiastical organization. Each parish church functions autonomously under the direction of a head (*alaqā*) chosen by the local clergy. (Heads of the most important churches have traditionally been appointed by the emperor.) The obligations of the priesthood are not very great. The chief duty of the priest is to take his turn in performing the Mass. His pastoral services are limited to occasional visits with his particular confessants, from whom he expects to receive regular rewards of food and drink. Otherwise, his life is much the same as that of his lay neighbors.

The role of the *dabtarā,* as we have seen, is still more flexible. *Dabtarā* who are associated with a parish church are expected to take their turns singing hymns and composing *qenē* in the outer ring of the church; but otherwise they exist as free entrepreneurs, and they need not be so attached unless they so desire.

The individualistic organization of the Ethiopian Church is most striking, perhaps, in the case of the monks, especially when compared with Christian monastic orders in the Western world. Ethiopian monks are bound by nothing other than the original conditions for assuming the role, namely, renouncing family ties and worldly possessions. The monk need not enter a monastery; he may continue to live in his old home or may take to the woods as a hermit. If he does go to live at a monastery, his life is not radically changed. The Ethiopian monastery is not an organized community, but a sacred place—the site of a large and important church, in the vicinity of which live numbers of individual monks. The monk comes and goes as he wishes, prays whenever he wants, and may live free of any obligations toward his fellow monastics and toward the rest of the society.*

---

* There are, however, some monasteries where a more organized and disciplined regime may be found.

Political and Military Organization (prior to 1942)

The Amhara political system was based, as has been suggested, on an interlocking hierarchy of patron-client relationships. Given the tremendous importance of domination and deference in such relationships, the demands made upon an inferior by his superior seem virtually unlimited. Nevertheless, the system as a whole was characterized by a high degree of decentralization and laissez faire, and there were safeguards for protecting the rights of individuals at all levels.

The basic dimension of constraint concerned the imposition of taxes of various sorts. The original meaning of the verb "to rule" in Amharic (*naggasa*) is "to collect tribute"; and this was the primary activity of rulers at all levels. As we have seen, provincial rulers had to deliver an annual tribute to their overlords and the latter a tribute to the monarch; local rulers, in turn, obtained income from the labors of peasants and artisans, exacting both land taxes and tithes. Peasants working land which had been granted to a noble or church as *gult* were obliged to hand over the full produce of half their land to the landlords. In addition to paying these periodically collected taxes, the peasants were liable to have their stores confiscated when required to billet soldiers or subjected to raids by passing armies.

The peasants were further required to furnish a certain amount of corvée labor each month to their rulers and landlords. This might be used for purely personal projects, like cultivating the lord's estates, or for quasi-public ones, such as constructing a new church building. There was, finally, the obligation for every adult male who was not a member of the clergy to take up arms under his local lord whenever a levy was proclaimed. Those who did not respond to such a call were subject to fines or other punishment as well as the barbs of public opinion.

The military organization of the Amhara was highly individualistic. Unlike the Galla, the Amhara did not provide for the collective training of their warriors. Each man was left to learn how to fight by himself and to provide his own equipment. A man could become a "career" soldier when he came of age simply by purchasing a shield; or he might prevail upon an established lord to arm him temporarily, with the promise of returning the equipment should he leave that lord's service. Similarly, there were no collective provisions for the supply of troops. Each man was left to fend for himself, drawing upon the supply of grain he brought along and whatever booty he could acquire on the warpath; the preparation of his food was left to the wife or servant who accompanied him to battle.

The conduct of a military operation exhibited a minimum of external constraint and discipline. Chains of command existed with respect to the general direction of troop movements, and the camping pattern was highly structured. But the marching and fighting unit seems to have been, for all practical purposes, the individual soldier and his retainers. Battles were not fought in a disciplined manner; the outcome depended on the sheer numbers of troops, their state of morale, and the chance of catching the enemy off guard. Except for the large-scale deployment of troops in accord with the customary tactic of envelopment, there was little expectation of subordinating the impulses of individual soldiers to the needs of a "team"; for the prevailing military ethic stressed rather the heroism of the individual soldier and his drive to bring back a maximum of booty and trophies.[25]

The independent status of the common soldier in mass levies was based on the fact that he was primarily a peasant and thus expected to return to his fields as soon as a particular campaign was over. Nor were members of the more permanent armies of lords greatly constrained. Loyalty to one's lord was in many cases a lasting tie, and accounts for much of the stability that existed in such arrangements. But in general it appears to have been a factor of far less moment than was the case, for example, in feudal Japan. The Amhara soldier felt he was fighting for a lord by his own free will and, therefore, had every right to leave him when conditions justified a move. One such condition was when the lord did not reward his followers liberally enough. Another related condition was when the lord had a tendency to suffer defeat in battle. Indeed, it was not uncommon for soldiers to swarm from one side to the other during a battle when defeat for their side seemed imminent. Still another basis for deserting one's chief was the ambition of a vassal to acquire greater power, in which case he might rebel—become a *shĭftā,* in the original sense of the word—and build up a military force of his own in the hope either of impressing his erstwhile master sufficiently to be reinstated with greater honors, or of taking his place by vanquishing him in combat, or simply of carrying on as a free agent.

The civilian counterpart of the soldier's right of desertion or rebellion was the right of judicial appeal which belonged to every free Amhara. This pertained primarily to the area of property rights. A man who suffered some grievous injustice in a local court had the right of appeal, in theory at least and often in practice, to higher courts at the provincial and imperial level. There was, in addition, some possibility of relief from an inordinately oppressive governor. He might be removed accidentally by the emperor, in the continuous process of *shum-shĭr;* the people under his jurisdiction might secure his deposition through appeals to the emperor or his overlord; or they might take arms behind one of his rebellious subordinates and overthrow him by force. Traditional Amhara society thus provided significant areas of social freedom for its citizens despite the feudal obligations that lay heavy upon them.

Synchronization and Privacy

The degree of independence that exists in Amhara society may be further assessed by focusing on certain abstract properties of its organization as well as on the concrete institutions just discussed. In this context two variables are particularly relevant. One, degree of synchronization, concerns the extent to which the behavior of the individuals in group activities is strictly controlled and co-ordinated. The other concerns the extent to which the individual may be free from the intrusion of others when he desires privacy.

Except in the area of protocol and etiquette at the royal court, synchronization is conspicuously lax among the Amhara. Ample scope is left for individual whim and impulse in nearly every area of concerted activity. Groups of people going on a trip, for example, make little attempt to start at the same time or to keep abreast of each other. Carefully co-ordinated teamwork is scarcely known in manual labor. Military units proceed, not in squads and platoons, but as masses of individuals.

The lack of synchronization in singing and dancing is perhaps the most striking case of all, for in these activities the participating individuals are supposed to be performing in unison. Yet the choirs of *dabtarā* sing with little regard for the standard line; each chorister sings as the spirit moves him, and the resulting cacophony is punctuated from time to time as some voice stands out by intoning a phrase with new energy a few beats before or after the majority of his fellows. A similar phenomenon occurs in dance, where what apparently is intended to be a symmetry of motion appears rather as a cohort of individual movements.* The impression left by such performances is that the Amhara accord a high degree of independence to the individual whenever he does take part in collective enterprises.

The Amhara likewise maintain a high degree of respect for individual privacy, despite the hierarchical character of their society. This is shown, first, in the expectation that each nuclear family should inhabit its separate dwelling. The individual home is regarded with great respect; no one, not even a relative, presumes to enter another's home without being properly acknowledged and escorted inside. When possible, private quarters are isolated from those where guests are entertained. The ideal Amhara household, found among the well-to-do, contains separate buildings for private quarters (*ilfiñ*) and for the hall where company is received and entertained (*addārāsh*).

---

* At times, it may be noted, when more complex ceremonies permit a plurality of musical and choreographic themes to be going on simultaneously, despite the lack of synchronization the over-all aesthetic effect is often quite impressive. Such is the case, for example, in the ceremonial procession on Ṭimqat day described in chap. iii.

Although women and children do not have so much freedom, the adult male Amhara who chooses to go off by himself for some reason is not bothered. In at least two cases, moreover, the right to solitude is institutionalized: that of the monk or hermit, who is left to his meditation and prayers, and that of the student of *qenē*, who spends hour after hour in some lonely place composing his verse for the day.

Privacy is further protected among the Amhara by the shared belief that others normally do not have a just claim to information about one's person. Even such superficial matters as one's place of origin or one's family connections are not readily disclosed on a first encounter. This differs markedly from the custom of some other groups in Ethiopia, such as the Borana Galla, among whom it is the first order of business in any conversation to identify the "vital statistics" of one another.

The machinery of wax and gold, again, exists as a useful apparatus with which to protect one's private identity and desires. In authoritarian relations, where the superior questions the subordinate with impunity, this evasive and equivocal manner of response constitutes the latter's main defense against yielding the information sought by the questioner. The superior may feel that he has a right to the information he seeks, but, if he is a good Amhara, he understands that he may never be told the whole truth.

Thus, viewed as a whole, Amhara society does not envelop the individual in a complex network of obligations and constraints. The institutional structure of the society is relatively thin. There are few collectivities to which the individual might belong, and fewer still to which he must belong. He can, if he chooses, live at the very periphery of society—as a hermit, a monk, a *shīftā*, a minstrel, a beggar, or, if a woman, as a solitary householder. For the typical Amhara, the main obligations are to fulfil work responsibilities in behalf of the nuclear family, the parents, and to provide income and services for landlords and chieftains. Here, too, there are important degrees of freedom. An oppressive family situation may be readily relieved by divorce; an oppressive landlord or ruler may possibly be brought to justice over time, or in extreme instances fled from; and for the oppressed vassal or retainer, there is always the alternative of running away to another master or of turning to one's own devices. As a Christian, the Amhara is required to fast a good deal; but attendance at church and membership in religious fraternal associations are voluntary, and for the religious scholar there is considerable freedom of movement.

It is difficult to assess the relative weight of the few but heavy constraints that do exist in Amhara social structure and of the many areas of real independence. But in view of the considerable latitude for unconstrained action that has been described in this section, it would seem valid to characterize

Amhara society as marked by a moderately high degree of independence. This is to say that Amhara society gives relatively wide rein to individual impulse in action. It is not to say that Amhara culture places a high value on the moral worth of the individual personality. That is a separate question, which we shall now proceed to explore.

INDIVIDUALITY VERSUS CONFORMITY AND ANONYMITY

The extent to which individual personality is valued in a society is reflected primarily in two aspects of its culture. One of these comprises its processes of education, in the broadest sense of the term; the other, its forms of art. The character of these aspects of culture reveal, respectively, the degree of concern for the *development* of an individualized self and the degree of concern for the *expression* of an individualized self.

Education and Socialization

Obedience and politeness are the overriding goals in bringing up children among the Amhara. After a prolonged and indulged infancy, the Amhara child from about three years on is subjected to a regime of discipline and repression. He is taught to fulfill without question any request made by any older person. He is conditioned to stand quietly whenever guests are present and to stand facing the wall while his parents or guests eat their dinner. If addressed by elders, especially those outside his immediate family, he is expected to reply in a barely audible whisper—a norm that is sometimes adhered to with such pathetic faithfulness that it has become the object of gentle satire in a short story by the young Ethiopian writer, Tadesse Liban.[26] Children who are noisy and disrespectful are referred to contemptuously by the term *bālagē,* meaning "rude."

The desires and interests of an Amhara child are not taken into account by those who raise him. He is provided with a bare minimum of clothes, and little effort is expended in procuring him playthings,[27] although in some families little dolls made of rags (*ashāngulit*) are produced. Children have a rich play-life with their peers, but this consists mostly in imitating various adult activities. Organized games occur very rarely, the chief one—*gannā*— being played as a rule but once a year, on Christmas Day.[28] The traditional songs and dances are learned from other children while tending the herds, but children are not encouraged to perform them in front of adults. The opinions of children are never expressed, let alone consulted. Indeed, in some commoners' families the children are treated little better than the farm animals, if that well. One occasionally sees a peasant woman or servant directing her child to perform some chore by throwing clods of dirt or manure at him in the same half-interested manner in which the shepherd directs cattle by throwing stones.

The effect of Amhara socialization, then, is to inhibit rather than to stimulate the development of individuality. The spirited and expressive Amhara child of two or three is conditioned to become, for the rest of his childhood and to a large extent throughout life, taciturn, fearful, and slightly morose.

The traditional system of formal education is no less indifferent to the personality of the learner. The atmosphere of the schools where reading is taught is harsh and punitive. Pedagogy at all levels of instruction is based on repetition and memorization, with strict adherence to the conventions preferred by the teacher.* The traditional ban on the teaching of writing may also be related to the desire to keep the student's mind on received formulations. Amhara formal education in no wise seeks to cultivate the individual, but aims solely to prepare cultural specialists who will be able to perform the rituals and perpetuate the teachings of the Ethiopian Church. The instruction of noble children, finally, in the arts of riding, swimming, shooting, and playing the lyre has more to do with the transmission of the manners and skills appropriate to a position of high status than with a concern for personal development.

Music and Art

Music and dance are greatly enjoyed by the Amhara, but little attention is given to the cultivation of their forms or the refinement of their performance. The music is monodic, both melodically and rhythmically, and, except for some intricately structured accelerandos in certain religious hymns, consists chiefly in the indefinite repetition of a number of very limited musical ideas. Dance forms are still more limited and repetitive. In both genres, variation and the development of personal styles are not encouraged. Innovation, particularly in religious forms, is likely to meet strong resistance; witness the vigorous rejection of Alaqā Gabra Hānnā's innovations in dance by the masters at Gondar.

Like music and dance, Amhara design provides little scope for the free play of imagination. In pottery, basketry, and even in such antique ornamentation as appears on the coins and stelae of Aksum and the churches of Lalibela, the recurring style is that of the continuous repetition of simple geometric patterns. Painting provides a richer medium, but here again individuality is carefully constricted. The subject matter of pictures is limited by tradition to scenes concerning the life of Christ and the saints, and to the *res gestae* of emperors. The manner of treatment of these themes is

---

* A partial exception to this—the teaching of *qenē*—will be discussed below.

further limited by a number of canons. For example, saints must have no shadows on their faces; "good" characters must be portrayed *en face,* "bad" ones in profile; and honored subjects must be portrayed on the right.* Virtually all aspects of the subject matter—dress, features, actions, symbolism—are prescribed by rigid conventions. That this degree of conformity reflects a cultural attitude and not a want of inventiveness on the part of Amhara artists is shown by the discoveries of Marcel Griaule, who collected hundreds of drawings in Gojjam in the form of silhouettes and graffiti, drawings based on direct observation and exhibiting an "astonishing diversity and revealing . . . a very great liberty of expression." Yet, Griaule observed, "these drawings are scorned by the people, who pay scarcely any attention to them; and by the artists themselves, who regard them as a sort of pastime of no importance, or as an activity reserved primarily for apprentices."[29]

In painting, as in the performing arts, individuality was suppressed not only by the pressure to conform to given models but also by the anonymity of the artists involved. This is more striking in the case of painting which, particularly in the form of miniatures, produced some exceptional works. But painting was carried out for the most part as a devotional activity, and its practitioners were apparently content to remain unknown.

The Written Word and the Oral Tradition

The written literature of Ethiopia provides as little scope for individuality as does its painting. Like the painters, the authors of the Ethiopian manuscripts have for the most part remained anonymous. Their subject matter has been narrowly circumscribed by the force of tradition, and their genres have been just as narrowly conventionalized.

Ethiopian literature consists primarily of religious writings, in the first instance of free translations from Greek, Syriac, and Arabic texts. Where the writings are original they tend to be either expositions of traditional beliefs and rituals of the church, eulogies of saints, or expressions of pious fantasy on religious themes. The nature of this literature is to extol sacred objects, not to express individual personality. The *Investigations of Zar'a Yā'qob,* a very personal and imaginative critique of prevailing orthodoxies dated in the seventeenth century and reminiscent of the French *philosophes,* is the exception that proves the rule; for this manuscript has proved to be a forgery, the work of a Franciscan missionary to Ethiopia in the early nineteenth century.[30]

---

* The seriousness with which such conventions seem to have been taken is shown by the episode of Brancaleone, a Venetian painter who was in Ethiopia during the reign of Ba'eda Māryām (1468–78), who is said to have provoked an uproar by painting a Madonna with the child on her left arm instead of the conventional right.

The effect of this literature has not been, as David Riesman suggests is true of the written word generally, an individualizing one. It did not serve to "help liberate the reader from his group and its emotions, and allow the contemplation of alternative responses and the trying on of new emotions."[31] It has served rather to buttress conformity, by rekindling identification with the sacred symbols of the society. Ethiopian religious literature does not invite introspection; it is a corpus to be venerated and solemnly rehearsed. When a devout Ethiopian reads his daily or weekly portion from some writing such as the *Dāwit* (Psalms of David) or the *Weddāssē Māryām* (*Praise of Mary*), he is said to be "repeating" the text— *Dāwit yedaggemāl*. Most of those who learn to read the words of these writings do not understand the Geʿez in which they are composed.

A similar function has been performed by the secular literature, which runs primarily in praise of royalty and thus has served to uphold the political status quo. The earliest Ethiopian writings are inscriptions of the Aksumite kings dating from the fourth century A.D. Here, in a style that is to persist through the ages, the royal deeds are recounted in meticulous detail and endowed with the highest morality.[32] Geʿez chronicles were composed in this manner for most of the emperors after the thirteenth century. The earliest specimens of written Amharic consist of hymns in praise of the Emperor Amde Ṭseyon (1314–44).

Two other written works put the capstone on this conservative structure. The *Kebra Nagast,* the Ethiopian national epic, has served chiefly to legitimate the royal line that came to power in the thirteenth century and to cement once and for all the union of monarchy and church. The *Fetha Nagast,* the traditional legal code based on various canon and civil laws compiled in medieval Egypt, has served not as a working code for the adjudication of court cases but as an embellishment of *de facto* decisions, imparting to the judge an increment of authority by virtue of his ritual of referring to them.

Because of the relative sterility of Abyssinian written literature, art, dance, and music, many observers have concluded that Abyssinian culture provides no outlets for truly creative expression.[33] This judgment is not just. The Abyssinian genius freely discloses itself in the stories, verse, and proverbs that make up its very rich *oral* literature. Within this oral tradition, especially in its verse, a good deal of original expression and personalized commentary may be found.

Ethiopic verse comprises a wide variety of forms which differ according to subject and occasion. Classical *qenē,* Geʿez verse in praise of some holy figure or political leader, is composed by *dabtarā* on certain religious or political holidays. More playful verses of praise are sung in Amharic by *dabtarā* or minstrels on festive occasions. In such verses the poet may insinuate insults through the ambiguities of his compliments, as was illustrated above. *Shĭllalā,* declaimed to arouse male courage before battle, is also heard at weddings and other festive occasions. Another type of exclamatory verse (*ho-berē*) is sung by the peasant at harvest time as he drives his cattle around the threshing floor. Verse of sorrow (*engurguro*) is intoned at time of bereavement or during moments of loneliness. Finally, in the conviviality of a drink-house enlivened by a minstrel, alone at work, or with a group of friends on various occasions, the Amhara finds that verse provides a medium for thoughts on almost any subject—people, places, animals, weather, love, work, and death. The following poem illustrates an important quality found in many of these verses, pessimism and irony, especially common in verses about love.

> Fish on the cliff, baboons in the sea;
> The ass after honey, while hay draws the bee;
> On a baking-pan of wax, butter to see;
> Or a monk from Zegamel monastery
> In the pagan land of Metcha to bury;
> With an unsuited person in love to be;
> Thus has it ended, my affair with thee.
> Leave it, forget it, just let it rest—
> A hapless ass at a hyena's breast.

These various sorts of verse may be either sung or spoken. The auditory effect is often enhanced by the accompaniment of musical instruments. When serious *qenē* has been recited by its author in church, it is usually repeated by a chorus of *dabtarā* singing to the slow beat of drums and sistrums. The sad strains of *engurgo* are sometimes accompanied by the mellow ten-stringed lyre, while an instrumental background for livelier subjects may be provided by the Abyssinian banjo or one-stringed violin.

Throughout these varieties of verse forms, certain conventions are followed. Most important, the lines are supposed to rhyme; that is, end with the same consonant-plus-vowel. Inferior poets achieve this rhyme at the expense of the words they use. In addition, proper rhythm must be maintained; the lines must not "break." This means that the flow of the line must be smooth and that the metrical pattern in one line—based on the number of accents, not syllables[34]—should be paralleled by the others. A poet who breaks his lines is satirized by being dubbed a "lion."

While observing these rules—and, in the case of *qenē,* the much more complicated rules pertaining to stanza forms and poetic figures—the Amhara poet *must also be original.* In the production of verse, individuality is explicitly emphasized. Poets who use verses composed by others—this is primarily true of students of *qenē*—are insulted with the term *lēbā* ("thief"). Similarly, a poet should not repeat himself. If he repeats the same word in a piece of verse, he is derided as an "ant." Once he has composed a certain verse, he is supposed to discard it and compose something new the next time.

The composition of original verse is by no means restricted to a class of professional poets. Every good Amhara is more or less adept at it. Extemporizing verse is a favorite activity at feasts, weddings, and in the aimless camaraderie of the drink-house. Sometimes a minstrel is on hand to begin the entertainment, but the usual pattern is for him to be fed verses extemporized by others present which he then embellishes with music. Even currently, with popular culture being manufactured and distributed out of Addis Ababa, urbanized Amhara place great value on the invention of new lyrics to suit the most popular tunes of the day.

Such verses customarily have not been written down. When unusually clever verses were invented, they were transmitted by word of mouth through the country and over generations. Or some individual would be noted for "owning" some couplet he composed or memorized, and people would turn to him whenever they wanted to hear it. Only in recent decades have some Ethiopians sought to preserve these verses in more durable manner by committing them to print.

Thus it is that, contrary to Riesman's correlation of the spoken word with traditionalistic functions and the written word with individualizing ones, and contrary to the common conception of the oral tradition as inherently rigid and unchanging,[35] oral literature provides the sole area in Amhara culture where conformity to existing works is shunned and the highest premium is placed on individuality.

Cultural Heroes

The last dimension of individualism to be treated here concerns the extent to which a society is inclined to single out individual personalities for special renown. We have seen that Amhara culture places little value on the moral worth of the individual as such, in that—with the limited exception of poetry—it does not encourage the development and expression of a distinctive and authentic self. And it might seem, from a superficial reading of Ethiopian history and culture, that the pre-eminent position of the emperor precluded anything like a general tendency to glorify outstanding individuals other than the sovereign. Yet our picture of Amhara culture cannot be complete without acknowledging the substantial place it has traditionally given to what may be called a "cult of the individual." For, with respect to at least three different qualities—saintliness, bravery, and cleverness—the Amhara have a marked tendency to idealize and remember outstanding individuals.

The idolization of saintly individuals has been an important part of

Amhara religious experience. The favorite written literature consists of those genres which glorify individual saints for their special powers and great deeds. The *gadel* depicts the heroic struggles of saints against temptations and persecutions; the *tāmher* relates their miraculous feats; and the *malḳa*, a verse form of some fifty five-line stanzas, consists of a rhapsodic description of the physical features and moral qualities of some saintly subject. The various *qenē* stanza types, moreover, serve largely to glorify individuals through the exotic use of religious symbolism—especially the nine-line *mawaddas*, which means "praise."

While these literary genres are accessible only to the learned few, the multitude also adores individual saints. Each of the saints has his particular following in the population, his popularity varying according to region and to the powers for which he is famed. This idolization has been directed not only to angels and legendary figures from the past, but also, to a lesser extent, to contemporaneous religious virtuosi and outstanding masters of the religious books.

Perhaps more prominent in Amhara life has been the glorification of brave men. The Abyssinian military ethic took the form of a cult of the hero. Personal bravery—not discipline, training, honor, or self-sacrificing loyalty—was the paramount virtue in Abyssinian warfare. The *guabaz* warrior was rewarded by his chief, praised by the minstrel, and esteemed by the populace. His bravery was ranked according to the fearfulness of the enemy vanquished. Thus, in Menelik's day the fanciest headdress was given to a noble who killed one of the fierce Danakil, a less fancy headdress being awarded the killer of the tough Raya Galla. Such actions constituted the one area in which personal boasting was permitted and, in fact, institutionalized in the genre known as *fukarā*.

We are indebted to Arnauld d'Abbadie for a firsthand account of the effect of this cult of the individual hero on the orientation of the Abyssinian warrior, in a passage so rare it is worth citing at length:

> The type of combat which [the Ethiopian] prefers over all others—because it gives him the most freedom to expand his personality—is that where, due to insufficiency of terrain or other circumstances, the chiefs can engage only a part of their forces. He loves to watch the skirmishers of the two armies spy out and accost one another while declaiming their martial themes. Joyously he throws off his toga to clad himself in some military ornament . . . and to mix himself in the widely spaced lines which follow one another and rise to the attack. He loves to comprehend the rationale of the manouvers of the two parties, to be able to judge the blows, to know under which hand the victims fall, to choose from among the enemy to avenge their death, to adapt his movements to the instincts which animate his companions, and to feel the earth tremble under the charges of cavalry which come as a squall

to change suddenly the whole configuration of battle. He loves to hear, amidst the crackle of rifle-fire, the huzzahs, the shouts, the challenges, the injuries, the encouragements, the allocutions, the piercing voice of the trou-badours, and the rhythms of the flutes alternating with the lugubrious wail-ing of the trumpets; to know, finally, that on the hills, behind their drum-mers who beat out the charge in place, the two rival chiefs and the two armies are following him with their eyes, and that he may at one mo-ment or another, return to his lord and, hurling before him some trophy, tell him, at the end of his war chant: "There! This is what I know how to do!"[36]

A cult of the individual obtains, in addition, with respect to the man with a genius for outsmarting others. Men who have beguiled their foes with particular cleverness, in litigation or in political intrigues, are scarcely less celebrated than religious virtuosi or heroic warriors. Anecdotes about great feats of shrewdness are the beloved stuff of Abyssinian folk history and are twice told around the fireplace.*[37] Some lords have enjoyed great reputations simply for being such successful and gifted scoundrels.

Cleverness in words counts as much, if not more, than clever deeds. Here we confront once more the phenomenon of wax and gold, but appearing in this context as a sort of finesse in personal relations. It is a question here of individuals made memorable because of their memorable lines, their talent for swiftly and surely employing the ambiguities of Amharic to satirize, at the right moment, some personality, or social type, or aspect of the human condi-tion. Military or political events are often remembered more for the witty verse composed by some personage on the occasion than for their historical significance. In the present century, Naggādrās Tassamā Eshatē has been one of the most outstanding personalities of this sort, as was Alaqā Gabra Hānnā in the nineteenth century.

INDIVIDUALISM AND MODERNITY

The Traditional Pattern

Our inquiry thus far has involved analysis of the various ways in which self-orientation is and is not manifest among the Amhara, in lieu of the more simplistic question of whether Amhara society is individualistic or not. Build-ing on this analysis, we may now attempt a more integrated interpretation of traditional Amhara society.

The predominant tendency in human relations among the Amhara is a dis-position to seek, not unity based on affection, understanding, and/or responsi-

---

* A recent study which analyzed 1,086 stories with identifiable themes, told or written by Ethiopian children in grades two through eight, revealed that "cleverness pays" was by far the most frequently recurring theme.

bility, but disunity based on the assertion of personal claims. This tendency is to some extent contained by feelings of politeness—an aesthetic of propriety— which are manifest in many ways. It is further contained by solidaristic sentiments closely tied to the feelings and experience of childhood: the euphoria of mealtime, on the one hand, and, on the other, a pervasive respect for figures of authority. But neither by virtue of identifying with social groups of any sort, nor through a sentiment of brotherhood with other men does the Amhara transcend an orientation that is directed to, and by, the narrower needs of the self.

Consistent with this type of subjective disposition, the organization of Amhara society does not rely to a significant extent on co-operative arrangements or the machinery of consensus. Nor does it involve, on the basis of either a division of labor or the sharing of diffuse obligations, the customary performance of numerous functions on behalf of territorial communities or other collectivities. Its main axis of organization, rather, is that of a highly personal relationship between superior and subordinate, with the subordinate existing essentially as an extension of the ego of the superior. This means that there is a marked discontinuity in the exertion of social constraints upon individuals. Within the segments of superior-subordinate relations—husband-wife, father-son, master-servant, teacher-pupil, confessor-confessant, lord-retainer, elder-youth—domination is virtually unlimited. Thus the main social restraints are in the form of repressive obligations—more or less "forced" labor, payment of heavy revenues, fasting—enjoined by figures of authority. Horizontally, however, there are very few obligations, and this accounts for the considerable amount of independence that appears among the Amhara. The demands of superiors, furthermore, are issued on a highly personal and spontaneous basis. They are not systematic, continuous, and detailed; the authority of superiors is not "rationalized." This accounts for the absence of discipline and synchronization, which is a further source of independence from external constraints.*

It is further consistent with the Amhara's egoistic orientation that objects which transcend the self—whether human communities or other groups or transcendent realities—are not greatly esteemed. With the exception, therefore, of those pious men whose paintings and religious studies served a truly devotional purpose, Amhara culture did not prescribe a desire for anonymity in behalf of transcendent values. On the contrary, it greatly valued the outstanding or heroic individual. In participating in this cult of the individual, the Amhara was not submerging his ego for the sake of broader realities but reasserting his ego through identification with the celebrated personality.

Yet for all this adulation of the individual, this substantial degree of social

---

* We may put all this another way by saying that while Amhara society is highly authoritarian, it is not at all totalitarian.

freedom, and this assertion of egoistic claims, we have seen that the Amhara care very little for genuine individuality. With the limited exception of the sphere of oral literature, they do not cherish originality or creativity. With the exception of the sphere of litigation, where every man is accorded the right to speak his piece before a judge, they do not honor the dignity of the human person. Individuality as contrasted with conformity is not an Amhara value.

The explanation of this seeming paradox is not far to seek. It is, to use the terms we have been employing here, that concern for genuine individuality is grounded on solidaristic sentiment. Respect for the autonomy and uniqueness of individual selves, including one's own self, is a cultural value that can only exist if supported by a socially shared disposition to respect the integrity and dignity of others. Egoism and individuality are not only independently varying aspects of individualism; they are, in the sense in which we have been construing the latter term here, largely incompatible.

The Challenge of Modernity

Characterization of traditional Amhara society in these terms leads naturally to two general questions concerning the relation between Amhara individualism and Ethiopia's quest for modernity. The first question concerns the relation between the individualistic aspects of Amhara society and the organizational requirements of national development; the second concerns the promotion of individuality.

Whatever priority is given to the various goals more or less implicit under the rubric of "modernization," all of them entail a substantial increase in the mobilization of energies in behalf of societal ends. Whether the primary emphasis is placed on increasing per capita income, raising standards of health and education, building up military and diplomatic strength, or devising governmental institutions more responsive to popular sentiments and more efficiently run, an absolute increase in the available quantum of socially deployable human resources is indispensable.

Our analysis of Amhara society indicates that its traditions are not conducive to the mobilization of energies in behalf of communal goals. In this it differs from other African societies, such as those celebrated by the spokesmen for "African socialism"[38]—not to mention those of other peoples in Ethiopia like the Galla and the Gurage—where more "communitary" traditions would seem to provide a more viable basis for economic and social development at the community level. At the national level, where the developmental tasks are those of institution-building and education, the situation is no different. Here the need is for large numbers of people with modern education working to some degree in concert in behalf of national goals. But, as we have observed, the modern-educated Ethiopians have so far refrained from exerting themselves as a strong progressive force in the national life. This is due, we suggested in the previous chapter, to a basic passivity related to the orality syndrome in Amhara culture. The considerations raised in this chapter seem no less relevant. The egoistic disposition and organizational laissez faire characteristic of traditional Amhara society affect no less their capacity for progressive action by inhibiting the uses of solidarity.

The atomism of the Ethiopian intelligentsia has been a conspicuous feature of their condition since they came into being. It is manifested in the basic distrust in their orientation toward one another as well as toward the rest of Ethiopian society. The regret of not being able to trust one's close friends is one of the more frequently heard confessions from their lips. The analysis presented in this chapter suggests that this reflects the attitudes and customs of traditional Amhara culture as much as it does the alleged saturation of the society with informers. That so few modern-educated Ethiopians have dared to break out of the vicious circle of distrust by daring to establish solidary relationships and to circumvent the prevailing fears and stagnation by establishing organizations of some sort is an illustration of the fact that, however much they may give lip service to the ideals of nationalism and populism, their hearts are primarily attached to winning new increments of prestige and income; in brief, to becoming director-generals.

Yet the total picture is by no means only one of atomism and stagnation. Some of the energies needed for Ethiopia's development can be, and have been, obtained by extending the traditional principles of domination and respect for authority into new areas of activity. Successful innovations in rural sanitation or agricultural practice, for example, have come about when local big men have been convinced of the desirability of the change and have then pressured the populace, by means of their authority and prestige, to implement the new measures. While the traditional authoritarian approach may for some time to come be the most ready method of mobilizing energies for social development, it alone cannot meet all the organizational needs of changing Ethiopia. One reason is that its effects are not continuous. To a large extent it depends on the whim and the physical presence of the relevant authority figure. It is common experience in Addis Ababa that particularly pressing problems are neglected for a long while, until the Emperor turns his attention to them; the matter then will be busily attended to for the moment, but is likely to be forgotten again when pressing matters turn the Emperor's attention elsewhere. This pattern is the model for most activity throughout the society where responsibility for specific problems is not carefully institutionalized.

Another shortcoming of the traditional political pattern is that it does not tap the potential energies now dormant in the population. Insofar as the mass of the people remain passive, involved in the developmental process only as objects of manipulation, their own creative energies will go unused. Only when their personal aspirations can be linked with co-operative endeavors or collective projects will their participation be sufficiently motivated to draw forth new sources of energy.

The traditional approach, moreover, does not take into acount the available intelligence of the population. It neither takes advantage of the understanding of immediate problems possessed by those concerned nor responds to their pressing needs and interests. The result is failure to make improvements in areas ripe for change, and antagonism or frustration of the elements of the population involved.

Given the relative ineffectuality and unresponsiveness of traditional methods of mobilization, and the new demands for concerted action unleashed by the process of urbanization and the growth of modern aspirations, it is natural that new forms of association should emerge to fill the sociological vacuum. That these new associations have been late in coming merely reflects the tenacity of traditional habits and institutions, as well as the reluctance of the government to permit the formation of groups which might have any sort of political or parapolitical ambitions. But during the past decade, and particularly since the rebellion of December, 1960, a variety of novel associational forms have come into being or have significantly diffused throughout the country. These associations may be described under three general categories: (1) formal associations of indigenous inspiration, (2) formal associations of foreign inspiration, and (3) informal associations.

Formal Associations of Indigenous Inspiration

Eddir.—Probably the oldest and most widely diffused of the modern associations in Ethiopia, the *eddir* is a form of welfare institution. Its functions are primarily to help defray the cost of funerals; to assist families in the event of the death, illness, unemployment, or imprisonment of their breadwinners; and to help in the case of loss due to fire. Members of an *eddir* are obliged to contribute to a common fund and to attend the funerals of other members. (Twenty-five cents a month is not an uncommon payment, although in rural centers the contributions are often solicited only in time of need.) The institution is said to have originated among the Gurage and to have become more widely adopted during the Italian invasion, when many people who were killed had no relatives to bury them. Since then *eddir* have been established in towns all over the country, fulfilling the vital functions which were performed by kin in the traditional countryside. They are organized on a territorial basis, in villages, towns, and city quarters; on an ethnic basis, as among the Dorze and Wollamo peoples; and even on an institutional basis, as among the employees of some government ministries. Often considerable moral pressure is exerted on townsfolk to become members—the threat of having no one come to one's funeral is particularly potent—and the transactions of the *eddĭr* are strictly governed by elected officers.[39]

Equb.—The *equb* is a form of savings association in which weekly or monthly payments of a fixed sum are exchanged for the privilege of receiving a large lump sum at some point in the life of the group. In addition to providing a means of forced saving, the *equb* offers a basis for sociability when the members come together to make their payments and are provided with food and drink. Like the *eddĭr*, the *equb* is believed to have originated among the Gurage, and acquired wider popularity following the Italian invasion when many people needed large sums of money for rebuilding homes and purchasing livestock. The mode of operation of an *equb* has been described in the *Ethiopian Observer* as follows:

> A person desiring to start an Iqub will discuss the matter with his friends; if they agree a meeting will be called to discuss the rules and regulations of the proposed new society, and in particular the amount of money to be paid by each member, the frequency of payment and the time and place of meeting. A president, or dagna [literally, "judge"], and a money collector will be elected from among the most respected and reliable members of the group.

> The President then asks every member to bring one or two guarantors who will be responsible for payment in case of default for whatever reason it may be.

> On the appointed day all the members assemble and the secretary will call the roll. Any member unable to attend is expected to send his subscription in time. The specified sum is then handed by every member (or substitute) to the President. Any latecomer will be fined according to a pre-arranged schedule, this money being kept by the President until the end of the Iqub, when it is used for the common enjoyment of the members. The collected funds are drawn by lot, the winner receiving the total subscription of all the members. The lottery is normally effected by the members writing their names on small pieces of paper which are then placed in a hat, a blind-folded non-member then drawing out the name of the winner.

> After each draw, the winner is disqualified from taking part in further lotteries, but continues to pay his fee until every member has drawn his share. If he fails in this duty his guarantors have to pay.

> When all at length have been rewarded the time has come to set up a new Iqub.[40]

Equb have been established by members of virtually all low- and middle-income groups—clerks, merchants, servants, peasants, policemen. Their rapid increase, in response to the growing importance of money in Ethiopia's economy during the past two decades, represents a significant growth of the capacity for voluntary formal organization in the modernizing sector.[41]

Māhebar (Regional Associations).—A type of formal association which has sprung up in Addis Ababa in recent years, becoming popular for the first time around 1960, is known as the *māhebar*. While its name is taken from the traditional Orthodox fraternal association, in aims and organization it is different from the religious *māhebar*. While the latter is devoted to honoring one of the saints and is convened primarily for feasting and sociability, the modern *māhebar* is organized on the basis of territorial or tribal bonds and is concerned with problems of social betterment. The first *māhebar* of this kind was established by the Gurage in the fifties.* Thereafter, the idea spread to members of other groups, and Addis Ababa residents originating in Gondar, Tigre, Harar, Manz, Tagulat, Fitche and elsewhere began to form *māhebar* of their own. The basic idea behind all these *māhebar* is to make some contribution to the welfare of the provinces through projects voluntarily financed and organized by fellow-countrymen living in the metropolis. These projects have included construction of roads, schools, and hospitals; supplying books for schools; and provision of facilities for assisting inhabitants of the provinces who come to the city. Members of the various *māhebar* convene weekly or biweekly, usually on Sunday in the vicinity of one or another of the Addis Ababa churches, to discuss their projects and make their financial contributions.

Formal Associations of Foreign Inspiration

Student Associations.—The Orthodox Students Association was founded in 1958 by a convention representing all the colleges and some of the secondary schools. Its successful establishment was due in large part to the efforts of an Indian Orthodox minister who at the time was one of the Emperor's private secretaries. There is some evidence that an earlier spontaneous effort to form such a group in the early fifties was checked by the government. Members of this association have been concerned with adapting the activities of the church to contemporary needs. They criticize the established church for its use of a dead language, excessive ritualism, and lack of teaching; and have proposed that the Orthodox Church should institute Sunday schools and

---

* The Gurage *māhebar* remains in a class of its own, with respect to size, wealth, and ambitiousness of program. The Gurage have also pointed the way to using the *māhebar* form in a way that transcends the narrow tribal or territorial passions which it has thus far tended to canalize. This has been done through the establishment of another, project-oriented *māhebar* concerned solely with building a road from Alam Gana to Wollamo Soddo, whose membership includes Galla and Wollamo as well as Gurage. This association has already collected well over a million dollars, and has completed the construction of a bridge. It is headed by a capable Gurage army general and its activities and collections are reported regularly in the Addis Ababa press.

cultivate a missionary spirit in order to reach the non-Christian peoples of Ethiopia. The association sponsors weekly religious services, featuring hymns in Amharic and talks in Amharic on religious and moral questions, and publishes a monthly journal. The Orthodox Students Association stands out as the first nationwide voluntary association in Ethiopia. It holds an annual convention which draws some three hundred students from all parts of the country.

The Ethiopian College Students Association was established in 1960 after some years of patient maneuvering by officers of the various college student governments. It attempts to represent the interests and needs of students vis-à-vis the government and to handle relations with international student organizations.

A number of student clubs have appeared from time to time within the framework of the colleges. One of the most popular and productive of these has been the Ethnological Society of the University College, founded in the early fifties by a Polish member of the college staff. Over the years it has produced several issues of an ethnological bulletin. More recently, under the framework of the new university, dramatic and choral groups have been established as well as groups like the Education Students Association and the Economics Students Association. Graduates of some of the secondary schools and colleges, moreover, have formed a small number of alumni associations.

Labor Unions.—Although Ethiopia has for some time been a paying member of the ILO, the government has until recently strongly opposed the establishment of unions in the country. Nevertheless, due to the encouragement of labor representatives from Western and other African countries, as well as to the courageous efforts of a number of Ethiopians, several unions have at last been established and have won some degree of recognition from the government.* Trade unions were first attempted among employees of the Franco-Ethiopian Railroad and in Eritrea.[42] They now include employees of a number of factories. Even household servants have formed associations that establish minimal conditions which members are obliged to demand from their employers.

Professional Associations.—The Ethiopian Teachers Association, with a large paper membership but scarcely any activity, was the only professional association in Ethiopia prior to the 1960 rebellion. If one may generalize from the frustrated attempts of Ethiopian doctors to establish a medical association, it would seem that the government was attempting to discourage groups of this sort as well as trade unions. Since 1961, however, the picture has changed. There now exists not only a medical association, which publishes its own

---

* A law establishing a legal basis for labor unions was enacted by the Ethiopian parliament in 1962.

journal, but also an engineers' association, a college teachers' association, and an Ethiopian writers' association. Earlier attempts to establish an organization of lawyers have not yet reached fruition.

National and International Service Organizations.—A final group of formal associations consists of those which include non-Ethiopian nationals as well as Ethiopians in their membership and which carry out welfare services of various sorts. The Ethiopian Red Cross, the Ethiopian Women's Welfare Association, the YMCA, and the Rotary Club of Addis Ababa have been active for more than a decade. More recently, the International Christian Fellowship was formed with an eye to discussing ways of translating Christian principles into social action, and the Social Service Society has broken new ground in the welfare field with its ambitious program of relocating and rehabilitating Addis Ababa indigents.

Informal Associations

Another significant sociological development since the 1960 rebellion has been the blossoming of what might be called "mutual confidence groups." Although the public climate remains somewhat tense and generalized suspicion still prevails, a step has been taken away from the complete atomism of the pre-rebellion era. These groups consist of numbers of friends, bound by such factors as kinship, common ethnic background, relationships formed during study abroad, and occupational ties. Perhaps the most important single bond underlying these groups derives from friendships formed during the crucial experience of attending secondary school together. While for the most part these groups carry out no organized activities or structured discussions, they do provide a context in which any of the issues of the day can be discussed with fairly complete frankness and without fear of reprisal.

There are some progressive Ethiopians who would like to see these groups become the nuclei of action groups and political parties, even on an overt basis. The prevailing view among them, however, seems to be that this is as far as they can go under the present regime.

The efflorescence of voluntary associations in Ethiopia during the past half dozen years constitutes a remarkable thickening of the fabric of Ethiopian society. It may be seen as a vast, unconscious process of arousing and co-ordinating energies to meet the novel realities of Ethiopia's current historical situation. What relationship to this collective process have the individualistic features of Amhara character and society which were discussed above?

It may be observed that in virtually none of the cases cited above were the Amhara the initiators of the associational forms in question. The territorial and "project" *māhebar* were introduced into Ethiopian life by the Gurage; so, as far as present evidence indicates, were the *eddīr* and the *equb*. The labor movement, limited as it is, has been in the hands of Eritreans on the one hand, and primarily non-Amhara workers in the south. Student associations have been formed chiefly at the instigation and under the aegis of foreign staff members; though here, as with the professional associations, modernized Amhara have sometimes played a leading role.

Once the new associations had been introduced, the Amhara like other Ethiopians were quick to adopt and expand them. Their participation in these new associations, however, has been affected, as might be expected, by the intrusion of traditional behavior patterns. Three examples of such behavior patterns come readily to mind.

(1) While the *equb* is conceived as a kind of credit union and as a focus for communal sociability, the *co-operative* sentiment tends to be lacking among members of Amhara *equb*, at least those of which the author has any knowledge. For example, in case of dire need, an *equb* member who desires the lump sum out of turn may be forced to *buy* the amount from the weekly winner, sometimes by forfeiting as much as ten or twenty per cent of the amount. By capitalizing on the crises of others, some enterprising *equb* members are able to sell their successful claims several times. Furthermore, in the early years of their existence, *equb* were frequently faced with the problem created by members who won the money early in the cycle, left town with the money, and did not return to pay their later installments. This difficulty has been met to some extent by the requirement of securing one or two guarantors for each person who enters an *equb*, but problems of this nature have led to altercations that have brought many *equb* members into court.

(2) The behavior of members of Amhara territorial *māhebar* is essentially that of a traditional social or civil gathering. The big men are seated in places of honor; the rest of the people stand quietly by. After a protracted period of exchanging greetings and milling about, the crowd listens respectfully while one or more of the big men makes a statement, and perhaps exchanges a few words with the group's secretary; and then the gathering disbands. Although the *māhebar* is organized with respect to the attainment of specific goals, the substance of the meetings is instumental to a very slight degree. The assembly rarely involves a meeting of minds to discuss an issue or a common problem, or to work out a program of action; but exists primarily as an occasion for the resonance of primordial sentiments by virtue of shared territorial attachments.

(3) In all associations, finally, certain traditional characteristics which are incongruent with the optimum conduct of groups come to the fore. This is no less true of the modern-educated than of the traditionals. Members fail to come on time to arranged meetings or neglect to come altogether.* They

---

* The *equb* has attempted to check this pattern by imposing fines on members who come late.

resist taking responsibility and showing initiative. In general, they reveal little capacity for self-discipline in a collective setting.

The need for what can be accomplished through the new associations, however, transcends the intermittent obstacles to their effective functioning posed by such individualistic behavior. As modernization proceeds and as Ethiopians gain experience in these associations, one may expect that the more disruptive aspects of such behavior will be transformed in the direction of greater compliance with the implicit norms of group functioning. Amhara in the modernizing sector have no choice now but to replace the ethos of the *shĭftā,* the litigant, and the wandering student with that of the president, secretary, and treasurer if they are to remain true to the ambitions that have been awakened within them.

There are, moreover, a number of respects in which adequate functioning in modern groups may be supported by behavioral traits inherited from the past. Three of these traits in particular deserve to be mentioned in this context. One is the fundamentally respectful orientation toward others. This serves to reduce the outbreak of dissension among group members, and in the attitude of respect and obedience toward figures of authority provides the basis, given capable and decisive leaders, for a significant amount of concerted action among group members. A second trait of some importance is the acceptance of conflict as a natural and not particularly threatening component of human relations. This means that group members are ready to admit and deal with such conflicts as do emerge in their ranks, and are experienced in the resolution of such conflicts through the agency of elderly mediators or the more formal processes of litigation. Finally, the Amhara sense of humor—wry, realistic, attuned to the ironies of existence—introduces a salutary leavening ingredient into group process. It provides an outlet for the release of tensions in group situations and adds a certain flavor to group experience that often more than compensates for the lack of a hyperinstrumental orientation.

The Question of Individuality

Although effective modernization is unthinkable without a significant increase in solidaristic sentiments and rationalized organization, in Ethiopia as elsewhere, the fate of the other aspect of individualism discussed in this chapter—individuality as a cultural value—poses a more controversial question. If the essence of modernity is the systematic effort to control rationally man's physical and social environment, then the society of *1984* may be claimed as a possible modern utopia no less than the society in which all children go to Montessori schools and all adults paint, undergo psychoanalysis, and study Great Books. The cultivation of individuality stands as but one of many possible values commonly subsumed under the notion of modernity and must compete with other values, like that of maximizing efficiency in production, which are indifferent or antagonistic to it. The modernizing elites are thus faced with the question, whether they confront it openly or not, of the extent to which their political and cultural institutions should be encouraged to emphasize the dignity, integrity, and creativity of individuals.

And yet it can be argued that individuality, while not a necessary constituent of modernity—if, from the author's viewpoint, an extremely desirable and plausible constituent—may be an indispensable means of accomplishing any of the goals aspired to by the modernizing elites. The argument is that informed and reliable leadership, on the one hand, and responsible and effective criticism, on the other, depend ultimately on the existence of at least a minority of persons who can think for themselves and can have confidence in their thinking and in the possibility of meaningful communication with others. In terms of the collective interests of the national society, one could maintain that a developed individuality is *more* important for the elite of a transitional society than of a highly modernized nation.

The weight of Amhara tradition opposes the graceful emergence of such a minority in Ethiopia. The pressures toward conformity and the inhibition of self-expression in most areas of life are, we have seen, characteristic of that tradition. The surly use of authority, the subtle sense of fatalism, the adulation of rank rather than human qualities, the distrust of innovation, the drabness of subsistence, the authority of conventional styles, the narrowness of outlook maintained by mass illiteracy and religious fundamentalism, the interpersonal aspects of the ethos of wax and gold (deception, insult, and intrigue)— these and related aspects of Amhara culture are formidable obstacles to the development of individuality among Ethiopians.[43]

Such a development is further impeded by two characteristics of Ethiopia's contemporary situation: the fear of criticism and the new "cult of personality." Given the Amhara emphasis on the deserts of status and the formalities of social intercourse, it is natural that the uses of honest criticism should have been kept to a minimum in their traditional social order. And thus it is that, from want of public habits of constructive criticism, traditions of self-examination have never emerged; rather, the ego has ever been first and foremost on the defensive to ward off all real or alleged slights to its dignity.[44] Altercation among Amhara has frequently arisen from a characteristic incapacity to accept advice and counsel, let alone criticism. This difficulty has been compounded by Ethiopia's present circumstance, for she finds herself, after centuries of living as she pleased with a mode of adjustment fairly well suited to the realities of traditional life, suddenly forced to acknowledge the inadequacy of her culture for purposes of living in the modern world. This situation has prompted the hasty erection of new self-justificatory defenses and an extreme touchiness about being considered "primitive" or "backward." This sensitivity has been exacerbated by the fact that European politicians in pursuit of their colonial interests, and foreign journalists in pursuit of sensational stories, have shown no compunctions about dwelling on and exaggerating some of the more unflattering aspects of Ethiopian culture. In such an emotional climate, the attempt to be objective about one's country and one's self, to engage in self-examination that is both sympathetic and critical, can be carried out only by efforts that are profoundly heroic.

The situation has scarcely been improved, moreover, by the form taken by the "cult of the individual" in contemporary Ethiopia. The centralization of power has been accompanied by a radical centralization of prestige. The cult of personality occasioned by the ascendance of Haile Selassie overshadows all public life in Ethiopia. It is manifest in the ubiquitous photographs; the naming of countless streets, plazas, schools, and other institutions after him; and in the unremitting praise and adulation accorded him in all public speeches and mass media. Other individuals have normally been accorded recognition only by virtue of their proximity to him, while individuals possessing attainments in their own right, and thus some claim to public attention, have deliberately been kept in the shadows. Domestic news conveyed through the press and radio has largely consisted of the minutiae of the Emperor's daily activities, including such matters as the exact time at which he performs any public function and all the words he speaks on any occasion. This cult of personality has further been advanced in the Ethiopian press by its adherence to a number of conventions respecting the person of the Emperor, such as that of placing the name of the Emperor at the beginning of any article in which he is mentioned; capitalizing all references to the Emperor, including all pronouns; and attributing all developments and progress reported in the newspapers to the initiative and foresight of the Emperor and his government.[45]

The political implications of this phenomenon need not concern us here. Whether the monopolization of prestige as well as power by the Emperor may have a primarily beneficial effect, through providing an authoritative symbol that can link the multifarious elements of the Ethiopian state; or whether, as was the case with Bismarck, the elimination of other possible pre-eminent personalities is laying the basis for a leadership vacuum for which the coming generation may pay dearly, is a question that cannot yet be answered. In this context we are concerned only with establishing the point that the ascendance of a cult of personality such as now obtains in Ethiopia eliminates not only the bestowal of public esteem for authentic individual performance, but also deprives the people of exercise in a crucial prerequisite of individuality—loyal criticism toward the government, one's friends, and one's self.

Besides the efforts of those courageous Ethiopians who, in exile abroad or living in inner exile at home, have steadfastly worked to develop their powers of integrity and their capacities of independent judgment, there is but one force that holds any promise of increasing the scope of personal autonomy and creativity in Ethiopia, and that is education. The fate of Ethiopia one and two generations hence is linked, more closely than members of large, industrialized societies can readily appreciate, with a single small institution: the Haile Selassie I University. As pinnacle of the country's educational system, it sets the standards, prepares the teachers, and devises many of the innovations to be used throughout the nation's schools. No less important, its relative independence from the national government gives it a certain leeway to pursue policies based primarily on academic considerations. The Ministry of Education, which administers all other secular schools in the country, is necessarily more subjected to the routine pressures of domestic politics. The university, on the other hand, by virtue of its many expatriate staff members and its dependence on outside financial help, is more intimately tied to international academic standards and practices. While a growing number of qualified Ethiopians have joined its staff, for some time to come the University will necessarily be greatly dependent on assistance from academic men from other countries. In any event, it is likely to remain in continuous contact with the outside world by virtue of its participation in the international community of scholars. This condition may give it a degree of autonomy and insulation that can but further the patient development of Ethiopia's most sorely needed asset: cadres of individuals who can resist the facile slogans of the day and work to provide for Ethiopia's great transformation the benefits of enlightened aims and realistic practices.

NOTES

CHAPTER 1: *Introduction*

1. E. Ullendorf, *The Semitic Languages of Ethiopia* (London: Taylor's [Foreign] Press, 1955), p. 25.

2. Elsewhere I have discussed the specific question of the influence of Amhara culture on Ethiopian national politics. Cf. "Ethiopia: Identity, Authority, and Realism," *Political Culture and Political Development,* ed. Lucien Pye and Sidney Verba (Princeton: Princeton University Press, 1965).

3. Augustus Wylde, *Modern Abyssinia* (London: Methuen and Co., 1901), p. 3.

4. Cf. Abbā Yā'qob Gabra Iyasus, *Maṭsehāfa Sawāsew Za-Ge'ez* (Asmara: Tipografia Francescana, 1920 E.C.*), pp. 288 ff.; Mars'ē Hāzan Walda Qirqos, *Yāmāriññā Sawāsew* (Addis Ababa: Artistic Press, 1948 E.C.), pp. 215–18; Alamāyhu Mogas, *Malḵ'a Ityopyā* (Asmara: Kokaba Ṭsebāh Press, 1952 E.C.), pp. 10 ff.
   For an introduction to the European literature on *qenē,* cf. M. M. Moreno, *Raccolta di Qenē* (Rome: Tipografia del Senato, 1935); also Enrico Cerulli, *Storia della letteratura etiopica* (Milan: Nuova Accademia Editrice, 1956), pp. 154–56, 226–32.

5. Alamāyhu Mogas, *op. cit.,* p. 12.

6. Cerulli, *op. cit.,* p. 154.

7. Alamāyhu Mogas, *Sawāsew Ge'ez* (Addis Ababa: Tasfā Press, 1950 E.C.), p. 117.

8. Alamāyhu Mogas, *Malḵ'a Ityopyā, op. cit.,* p. 7.

9. This subject is treated at greater length in D. Levine, "Ambiguity and Modernity" (paper presented at the Fifth World Congress of Sociology, Wash-

---

* E.C. refers to the Ethiopian calendar dating, which runs seven or eight years behind the European calendar.

ington, D.C., September 7, 1962; printed in the *Journal of the Ethiopian Students of North America,* IV, No. 1, 3–20).

10. H. Nakamura, *The Ways of Thinking of Eastern Peoples* (Japanese National Commission for UNESCO, 1960), p. 484.

11. On the concept of primordial sentiments cf. Edward Shils, "Primordial, Personal, Sacred, and Civil Ties," *British Journal of Sociology,* VIII (June, 1957), 130–45; and Clifford Geertz, "The Integrative Revolution: Primordial Sentiments and Civil Politics in the New States," *Old Societies and New States,* ed. C. Geertz (New York: Free Press of Glencoe, 1963), pp. 105–57.

12. G. Almond, "A Functional Approach to Comparative Politics," *The Politics of the Developing Areas,* ed. G. Almond, J. Coleman, and L. Pye (Princeton: Princeton University Press, 1960), esp. pp. 36–38.

13. *Op. cit.,* pp. 17–21.

14. Richard Weaver, "Individuality and Modernity," *Essays on Individuality,* ed. Felix Morley (Philadelphia: University of Pennsylvania Press, 1958), p. 77.

CHAPTER 2 : *The Legacy of Manz and Gondar*

1. Stephen Wright, "Ethiopian Literature," *Encyclopaedia Britannica.* More detailed descriptions of the literature of the period may be found in Enrico Cerulli, *Storia della letteratura etiopica* (Milan: Nuova Accademia Editrice, 1956), chaps. iii–vii; and Jean Doresse, *L'empire du Prêtre-Jean* (Paris: Librairie Plon, 1957), II, chaps. xii, xiv.

2. Cf. Otto Jäger, *Aethiopische Miniaturen* (Berlin: Gebr. Mann, 1957); and *Ethiopia: Illuminated Manuscripts* (Paris: UNESCO, 1961).

3. A revised edition of the English translation of Alvares' valuable manuscript has recently been published, and will be the text referred to in later references: *The Prester John of the Indies,* ed. C. F. Beckingham and G. W. B. Huntingford (2 vols.; Cambridge: The Hakluyt Society, 1961).

4. Job Ludolphus, *A New History of Ethiopia,* trans. J. P. Gent (2d ed.; London, 1684), p. 189.

5. Cf. Richard Pankhurst, *An Introduction to the Economic History of Ethiopia* (London: Lalibela House, 1961), p. 406.

6. Carlo Conti-Rossini, ed. and trans., "Iyāsu I, Re d'Etiopia e martire," *Rivista degli studi orientali,* XX, 107.

7. This disparaging image of Dāwit III has been perpetuated in the contemporary verse drama, *Selāsāwi Dāwit,* by the Shoan author Makonnen Endālkātchaw.

8. Sir Wallis Budge, *A History of Ethiopia* (2 vols.; London: Methuen and Co., 1928), II, 453.

9. This translation was made from the Italian translation in Cerulli, *op. cit.,* pp. 231–32.

10. Ababa Ayçhēh, *Bileçho* (Addis Ababa: Tensā'ē Za-Gubā'ē Press, 1948 E.C.).

11. The letter was made available to the author through the courtesy of an Ethiopian informant. The text paraphrases Psalm 79.

12. This and the following section draw in part on material which has been published elsewhere, together with other material on Manz not included here. Cf. D. Levine, "On the History and Culture of Manz," *Journal of Semitic Studies,* IX (Spring 1964), 204–11.

13. The boundaries of Manz proper include the Mofar River in the south, the Adabāy and Wānchet rivers in the west, the Qechenē River in the north, and in the east a long chain of mountains which pour forth the waters that drain across Manz and which divide it from the lowlands of Efrātā, Gedem, and Qawat. Accurate maps of Manz and its boundaries are not yet available.

14. Their itineraries are described in Isenberg and Krapf, *Journals* (London, 1843); and Paul Soleillet, *Voyages en Éthiopie* (Rouen, 1886).

15. A. Caquot, "L'homélie en l'honneur de l'archange Raguel," *Annales d'Éthiopie,* II (1957), 91–122.

16. *Ibid.,* p. 113.

17. *Ibid.,* p. 114.

18. Takla Tsādeq Makuriyā, *Ya-Ityopyā Tāriḳ Ka-Atsē Lebna Dengel Eska Atse Tēwodros* (Addis Ababa: Tensā'ē Za-Gubā'ē Press, 1949 E.C.), p. 20.

19. Cerulli, *op. cit.,* pp., 101–3.

20. Doresse, *op. cit.,* p. 165.

21. Chahab ad-Din Ahmad, *Futuh el-Habacha,* trans. D'Abbadie and Paulitschke (Paris, 1898), p. 342.

22. Cf. D. Levine, "On the History and Culture of Manz," *op. cit.,* p. 208.

23. This account of Nagāssi, like the accounts of his descendants which follow, has been constructed from a variety of sources, which, while differing in details, agree on the essential points presented here unless otherwise indicated. Oral traditions were obtained from Amhara informants in Manz and Addis Ababa. The chief written sources consulted include: Heruy Walda Selassie, an unpublished and untitled manuscript on the history of Ethiopia (part of which was published in his *Wā-Zēmā* [Addis Ababa, 1923 E.C.]); Takla Tsādeq Makuriyā, *op. cit.;* Tādassa Za-Waldē, *Ya-Abētohun Yā'qob Teweldennā Acher Tāriḳ* (Addis Ababa: Berhānennā Salām Press, 1948 E.C.); Guèbrè Sellassié, *Chronique du Règne de Ménélik II* (2 vols.; Paris: Librairie Orientale et Américaine, 1930–32); Antonio Cecchi, *Da Zeila alle frontiere del Caffa* (3 vols.; Rome, 1886–87); Major W. C. Harris, *The Highlands of Ethiopia* (3 vols.; 2d ed.; London, 1844); Isenberg and Krapf, *op. cit.;* and Soleillet, *op. cit.*

24. The related claim set forth by his dynasty—that Nagāssi was in the direct line of descent from Lebna Dengel—is less universally acknowledged by Ethiopians. It is still a controversial question whether or not Nagāssi was actually related to Lebna Dengel and, if so, by what route.

The official genealogy traces the descent line as follows: Lebna Dengel—Yā'qob—Segew Qāl—Warada Qāl—Lebsa Qāl—Nagāssi. This is the account set forth in Takla Tsādeq Makuriyā's history. The other Shoan authors who deal with this matter present different pictures, however. Blättengētā Heruy and Guèbrè Sellassié telescope the genealogy: Yā'qob—Segew Qāl—Nagāssi. Tādassa Za-Waldē, on the other hand, leaves the question open; he identifies Segew Qāl as one of Yā'qob's sons, and refers to Nagāssi as father of the Shoan Dynasty, but affirms nothing concerning a connection between Segew Qāl and Nagāssi.

The picture is further complicated by the fact that none of these versions was reported to European travelers in the nineteenth century prior to the ascendance of Menelik. According to information given Major Harris by Shoan informants in the 1840's, Nagāssi inherited royal blood through his mother, who was said to be a granddaughter of "a daughter of the House of Solomon." Four decades later Soleillet was told still another story, namely, that "the kings of Shoa are now of the House of David, heirs of Solomon, cousins of Christ" not through Nagāssi, but by virtue of the marriage of his great-great-grandson, Asfā Wassan, to a relative of the imperial family at Gondar. Cecchi, finally, mentions none of these legitimizing affiliations.

25. Heruy manuscript, p. 19.
26. The latter version is given by Cecchi.
27. James Bruce, *Travels to Discover the Source of the Nile* (5 vols.; London, 1790), III, 255–56.
28. Cecchi, *op. cit.*, I, 241.
29. Takla Ṭsādeq, *op. cit.*, p. 255.
30. Harris, *op. cit.*, III, 9.
31. Takla Ṭsādeq, *op. cit.*, p. 257.
32. Harris, *op. cit.*, III, 12.
33. Isenberg and Krapf, *op. cit.*, p. 301. Heruy's account of the rebellion of Matako is considerably different. We are following Harris and Krapf here since they were virtually contemporaneous with the events, and would have no particular reason not to record them faithfully.
34. Isenberg and Krapf, *op. cit.*, p. 302.
35. Harris, *op. cit.*, II, 133.
36. Arnauld d'Abbadie, *Douze ans de séjour dans la Haute-Éthiopie* (Paris, 1868), p. 173.
37. The word "Manz" (or "Manzeh"), according to local clergy, stems from a Ge'ez expression which means "land on which Christ's blood was sprinkled."
38. Ludolphus, *op. cit.*, p. 215.
39. The architecture and layout of the imperial compound are described in Monti della Corte, *I castelli di Gondar* (Rome: Società Italiana Arti Grafiche, 1938).
40. On the role of the *abuna,* cf. below, chap. v.
41. C. Poncet, "A Voyage to Ethiopia," *The Red Sea and Adjacent Countries at the Close of the Seventeenth Century* (London: Hakluyt Society, 1949), p. 61.
42. This is what has been called an orthogenetic, as distinguished from a hetero-genetic, pattern of cultural development. Cf. Robert Redfield and Milton Singer, "The Cultural Role of Cities," *Economic Development and Cultural Change,* III, No. 1, 53–73.

43. E. Combes and M. Tamisier, *Voyage en Abyssinie* (4 vols.; Paris, 1843), III, 342, call Gondar "une ville de plaisirs." Eduard Rüppell, *Reise in Abessinien* (2 vols.; Frankfurt am Main, 1838–40), II, 190, speaks of the Gondarēs' "grenzenlosen Liederlichkeit."

44. Trimingham, *Islam in Ethiopia* (London: Oxford University Press, 1952), p. 104.

45. Rüppell, *op. cit.*, II, 132.

46. Isenberg and Krapf, *op. cit.*, p. 287.

47. "Menelik's conquests," of course, were won for the most part by trusted generals, who were men from all parts of Ethiopia.

48. The figure is from a local census made by the Gondar Public Health College around 1958.

49. The Ethiopian Election Board listed 88,000 families and a registration of 35,000 voters in Manz in 1957. The figures are probably exaggerated.

50. The regional association will be discussed further in chapter vii.

51. "The Integrative Revolution: Primordial Sentiments and Civil Politics in the New States," *Old Societies and New States,* ed. C. Geertz (New York: Free Press of Glencoe, 1963), pp. 105–57.

52. "Ansprache an die Mitglieder des Vereins B'nai B'rith," *Gesammelten Werke,* XVII, 51–53.

53. *Ibid.*, and *Collected Papers,* V, 174.

CHAPTER 3: *The World of the Amhara Peasant*

1. Ernest Luther, *Ethiopia Today* (Stanford, Calif.: Stanford University Press, 1958).

2. The general methodological problem involved here is discussed in Hugo Engelmann, "The Activity Bias of Ethnography and the History of Society," *Anthropological Quarterly,* XXXIII (July, 1960), 158–63.

3. The TAT cards designed for use in Ethiopia were originally prepared by Dr. Edith Lord, US/AID, in connection with her own research there. The data on which the present study draws were obtained by administering twenty-five cards to a sample of twenty young Amhara in Manz—seventeen males and three females—ranging in age from sixteen to twenty-five years.

4. Cf. Samuel Alamayahu, "The Game of Gänna," *University College of Addis Ababa Ethnological Society Bulletin,* No. 9 (1959), pp. 9–28.

5. Cf. Akalou Wolde Michael, *"Buhe,"* UCAA *Ethnological Society Bulletin,* No. 7 (1957), pp. 57–64.

6. Simon Messing, "Group Therapy and Social Status in the Zar Cult of Ethiopia," *American Anthropologist,* LX (December, 1958), 1120–26. More extensive discussion of the *zār* may be found in Messing, "The Highland-Plateau Amhara of Ethiopia" (unpublished Ph.D. dissertation, University of Pennsylvania, 1957), and Michel Leiris, *La possession et ses aspects théâtraux chez les Éthiopiens de Gondar* (Paris: Plon, 1958).

7. This section draws on material previously published in D. Levine, "On the

Conceptions of Time and Space in the Amhara World View," *Atti del convegno internazionale di studi etiopici* (Rome: Accademia Nazionale dei Lincei, 1960), pp. 223–28.

8. Cf. Allan Hoben, "The Role of Ambilineal Descent Groups in Gojjam Amhara Social Organization" (unpublished Ph.D. dissertation, University of California, 1963), pp. 140 ff.

9. *Ibid.,* chaps. ii and v.

10. On Amhara attitudes toward nationhood cf. D. Levine, "Ethiopia: Identity, Authority, and Realism," *Political Culture and Political Development,* ed. L. Pye and S. Verba (Princeton: Princeton University Press, 1965).

11. Messing, "The Highland-Plateau Amhara," pp. 63–67, presents a detailed analysis of the ethnic hierarchy in Ethiopia "as it exists in the minds of most Amhara." Briefly summarized, this hierarchy consists, in order of descending status, of the (Christian) Tigre; Christianized Galla; Muslim and pagan Galla, and other sedentary Cushitic-speaking peoples who were self-governing prior to Menelik's conquests (Kaffa, Wollamo, etc.); peoples identified chiefly as manual laborers (Falasha, Gurage); and occupational hunters, pastoral nomads, and Negroid ex-slaves.

12. This subject is discussed in greater detail in D. Levine, "Ethiopia: Identity, Authority, and Realism," *op. cit.*

13. Marcel Griaule, "Le travail en Abyssinie," *Revue internationale du travail,* XXIII (February, 1931), p. 8.

14. This ideal is discussed at greater length in D. Levine, "The Concept of Masculinity in Ethiopian Culture" (paper presented at the Fourteenth Annual Symposium of the Committee on Human Development, The University of Chicago, May 11, 1963: to be published in the *International Journal of Social Psychiatry*).

15. *The Primitive World and Its Transformations* (Ithaca, N.Y.: Cornell University Press, 1954), chap. iv; and *The Little Community* (Chicago: University of Chicago Press, 1955), chap. vi.

16. Cf. Messing, "The Highland-Plateau Amhara," p. 540.

17. Harris observed that "the Abyssinian scribe does not hold the pen of a ready writer; and the dilatory management of his awkward implement is attended with gestures and attitudes the most ridiculous." Also, "Few of the priesthood understand the art of writing, and all regard the exercise of the pen as shameful and derogatory." *The Highlands of Ethiopia* (3 vols.; London, 1844), III, 15, 182.

18. Cf. Benjamin Paul, ed. *Health, Culture, and Community* (New York: Russell Sage Foundation, 1955).

19. See a series of articles beginning in the *Ethiopian Herald,* Addis Ababa, June 27, 1960: "Let the Victim Speak of the Magnitude of Ethiopian Medicine."

20. A long-term study of this and related problems is currently being carried out under the supervision of the US/AID Public Health Section in Ethiopia.

21. For general analyses of the nature of political life which support this assertion, cf. Edward Shils, *The Torment of Secrecy* (Glencoe, Ill.: Free Press, 1956);

and Hannah Arendt, *On Revolution* (New York: Viking Press, 1963), esp. chap. ii.

CHAPTER 4: *The Emerging Adolescent*

1. Cf. Richard Pankhurst, "Menelik and the Foundation of Addis Ababa," *Journal of African History*, II, No. 1 (1961), 103–17.

2. Cf. Mircea Eliade, *Birth and Rebirth: the Religious Meanings of Initiation in Human Culture* (New York: Harper & Bros., 1958).

3. For illustration of this phenomenon in a wide variety of societies as well as a highly advanced interpretation of it, cf. S. N. Eisenstadt, *From Generation to Generation: Age Groups and Social Structure* (London: Routledge & Kegan Paul, 1956). For additional examples cf. H. Ammar, *Growing Up in an Egyptian Village* (London: Routledge & Kegan Paul, 1954); and J. Stoetzel, *Without the Chrysanthemum and the Sword* (New York: Columbia University Press, 1955).

4. Messing, "The Highland-Plateau Amhara of Ethiopia" (unpublished Ph.D. dissertation, University of Pennsylvania, 1957).

5. *Ibid.*, p. 436.

6. In addition to Messing, the literature on betrothal and marriage among the Amhara includes Abebe Ambatchew, "Betrothal among the Säwan Amharas," *UCAA Ethnological Society Bulletin*, No. 5 (June, 1956), pp. 5–12; J. I. Eadie, *An Amharic Reader* (Cambridge: Cambridge University Press, 1924), pp. 75–79; C. H. Walker, *The Abyssinian at Home* (London: Sheldon Press, 1933).

7. Messing, *op. cit.*, pp. 459–60.

8. The conceptualization of "identity" used here follows the work of Erik Erikson, cf. "The Problem of Ego Identity," *Journal of the American Psychoanalytic Association*, IV (January, 1956), 58–121; reprinted in *Identity and Anxiety*, ed. M. Stein, J. Vidich, and D. White (Glencoe, Ill.: Free Press, 1960).

9. Margery Perham, *The Government of Ethiopia* (London: Faber and Faber, 1948), p. 247.

10. Tadesse Tereffe, "Progress, Problems and Prospects in Ethiopian Education," *Ethiopia Observer*, VIII, No. 1 (1964), 12.

11. In response to which, the government adjusted the passing grade so as to permit a larger number of students to pass the examination.

12. The exact composition of this sample was as shown in the tabulation on page 294.

13. Haile Fida, "High School and Educational Complications," *Ethiopian Herald* (Addis Ababa), August 2, 1960.

14. Thus, one American school director was celebrated by an Ethiopian student during the graduation ceremonies one year as follows:

    "When we came here, we were Tigreans, Gallas, Amharas, and so forth. Now, thanks to the director, we leave as Ethiopians, and as alumni of this school."

15. Perham, *op. cit.*, p. 256.

Name of School[a]	Enrol-ment[b]	Grades Surveyed	No. Total	No. Male	No. Female
I. Tafari Makonnen School.........	320	11th and 12th	60	60	0
II. Haile Selassie I Secondary School..	230	12th	47	47	0
III. Menelik II School..............	245	12th	15	15	0
IV. General Wingate Secondary School.	325	12th	58	58	0
V. Madhane Alem School...........	160	12th	21	21	0
VI. Empress Mennen School..........	220	12th	19	0	19
VII. The English School[c].............	....	11th and 12th	9	7	2
VIII. Madhane Alem School (Harar)....	450	12th	23	23	0
IX. Haile Selassie I School (Gondar)...	135	11th	45	45	0
X. Theological Academy............	100	12th	13	13	0
XI. Commercial School..............	335	12th	42	31	11
XII. Technical School...............	420	12th	57	57	0
XIII. Social Work Training Program[d]...	12	12th	11	3	8
XIV. Teacher Training School (Harar)..	278	12th	51	51	0
XV. Agriculture School (Ambo)........	120	12th	29	29	0
Total secondary schools..........	3,350	....	500	460	40
XVI. University College..............	420	3d and 4th	44	......	......
XVII. Engineering College.............	100	3d and 4th	31	......	......
XVIII. College of Agricultural and Mechanical Arts (Alemaya).........	172	3d and 4th	49	......	......
XIX. Haile Selassie I Military Academy (Harar)......................	138	3d[e]	38	......	......
XX. Public Health Officers Training Program (Gondar).................	60	3d and 4th	38	......	......
Total colleges.................	890	....	200	......	......

[a] These schools include all but five of the government postelementary schools which were offering full four-year programs in 1959. Schools I–IX are listed as "academic secondary schools"; X–XV as "special schools"; and XVI–XX as "institutions of higher learning." Unless otherwise indicated, they are located in Addis Ababa.

[b] The enrolment figures are for the academic year 1959–60, except for Tafari Makonnen School, where a preliminary version of the questionnaire was used during 1958–59. In schools which include elementary grades as well, the figures refer only to the secondary level enrolment. The total universe of the grades surveyed in these twenty schools was 1,150.

[c] A very small private school, attended by several Europeans as well as Ethiopians. The entire Ethiopian group of the two highest classes responded.

[d] A two-year program organized with the assistance of UNESCO. The students surveyed were the equivalent of secondary school seniors.

[e] The terminal year.

16. Mulugeta Wodajo, "Postwar Reform in Ethiopian Education," *Comparative Education Review,* II (February, 1959), 27.

17. Cf. William Shack, "Organization and Problems of Education in Ethiopia," *The Journal of Negro Education,* XXVIII (Fall, 1959), 405–20.

18. *Youth's Outlook on the Future: A Cross-national Study* (Garden City, N.Y.: Doubleday & Co., 1955), p. 9.

19. Thus, an eighth-grade student in Manz explained the popularity of the Jimma Agricultural School by saying, "The boys all want to go there because it is run by the Americans, and a school run by Americans means that everything is done right—food and clothes are properly distributed, and so on."

20. Shack, *op. cit.*, p. 417.

21. In response to a question on their attitudes toward the priests, sixty juniors and seniors of Tafari Makonnen Secondary School replied as follows (1959): 40 per cent were unequivocally proclerical; 22 per cent were ambivalent, expressing awareness of both good and bad elements in the clergy; and 18 per cent were primarily anticlerical, calling the priests "incompetent," "opposed to modernization," and "not supported by the people." (The rest were no answers or noncommittal.)

22. Edith Lord, "The Impact of Education on Non-scientific Beliefs in Ethiopia," *Journal of Social Psychology*, XLVII, Second-Half (May, 1958), 339–54.

23. Cf. Talcott Parsons, *Essays in Sociological Theory* (rev. ed.; Glencoe, Ill.: Free Press, 1954), chaps. vii and xiv.

24. Cf. chap. iii, p. 89, and note 19.

25. Lord, "The Impact of Education on Non-Scientific Beliefs," typescript version, pp. 6–7.

26. A sophisticated expression of this approach to Ethiopian painting has been published by an Ethiopian student in France. Cf. Berhanu Abbaba, "La peinture éthiopienne: point de vue d'un Éthiopien," *Cahiers d'Études Africaines*, II, No. 1 (1961), 160–65.

27. For a brief account of this historic event cf. Lipsky *et al.*, *Ethiopia* (New Haven: Human Relations Area Files Press, 1962), pp. 210–12.

28. Edgar Z. Friedenberg, *The Vanishing Adolescent* (Boston: Beacon Press, 1959).

29. *Diagnosis of Our Time* (New York: Oxford University Press, 1944), chap. iii.

CHAPTER 5: *The Old and New Elites*

1. C. Conti Rossini, "La regalità sacra in Abissinia," *Studi e materiali di storia delle religioni*, XXI (1948), 12–31.

2. A. Vasiliev, "Justin I (518–527) and Abyssinia," *Byzantinische Zeitschrift*, XXXIII (1933), 67–77; *Justin the First* (Harvard, 1950), pp. 299–302.

3. A. Caquot, "La royauté sacrale en Éthiopie," *Annales d'Éthiopie*, II (1957), 205–19.

4. F. Alvares, *The Prester John of the Indies,* ed. C. F. Beckingham and G. Huntingford (2 vols.; Cambridge: Hakluyt Society, 1961), I, 122.

5. "The Chronicle of the Emperor Zara Yaqob," *Ethiopia Observer*, V, No. 2 (1961), 153.

6. J. Varenbergh, *Studien zur äthiopischen Reichsordnung* (Strassburg, 1916), p. 3.

7. James Bruce, *Travels to Discover the Source of the Nile* (5 vols.; Edinburgh, 1790), III, 237.

8. *Op. cit.*, p. 214.
9. Gebre-Wold Ingida-Worq, "Ethiopia's Traditional System of Land Tenure and Taxation," *Ethiopian Observer*, V, No. 4 (1962), 309–11.
10. Alvares, *op. cit.*, II, 445.
11. R. Pankhurst, "Status, Division of Labour and Employment in Nineteenth-Century and Early Twentieth-Century Ethiopia," *UCAA Ethnological Society Bulletin*, II, No. 1 (1961), 30–34.
12. For an enumeration of many of these changes cf. S. Messing, "Changing Ethiopia," *Middle East Journal*, IX (Autumn, 1955), 413–32.
13. The sociological definition of elite assumed here is most fully articulated in S. F. Nadel, "The Concept of Social Elites," *International Social Science Bulletin*, VIII, No. 3 (1956), 413–24.
14. Bruce, *op. cit.*, III, 280.
15. *The Government of Ethiopia* (London: Faber and Faber, 1948), pp. 71–76.
16. Wallis Budge, trans., *The Queen of Sheba and Her Only Son Menyelek* (London: Medici Society, 1922), p. 64.
17. Afevork, *Grammatica della lingua amarica* (Rome, 1905), p. 264.
18. W. E. Conzelman, ed., *Chronique de Galawdewos* (Paris, 1895), p. 149.
19. J. Baeteman, *Dictionnaire Amarigna-Français* (Dire Dawa: Saint Lazare, 1929), p. 629.
20. Māhtama-Selassie Walda-Masqal, *Zeḵra Nagar* (Addis Ababa: Naṭsānat Press, 1942 E.C.), chap. xx.
21. W. Plowden, *Travels in Abyssinia* (London, 1868), p. 139.
22. Arnauld d'Abbadie, *Douze ans de séjour dans la Haute-Éthiopie* (Paris, 1868), pp. 374–75.
23. Lieutenant Collat, *L'Abyssinie actuelle* (Paris, 1906), p. 28.
24. Varenbergh, *op. cit.*; Gebre-Wold Ingida-Worq, *op. cit.*
25. Ignazio Guidi, ed. *Annales Iohannis I, Iyāsu I et Baḵāffā* (Paris, 1903), pp. 144–51.
26. On the ranks and perquisites of dignitaries at the court of a *dajāzmātch* in the 1840's cf. d'Abaddie, *op. cit.*, pp. 336–37.
27. The order of precedence set under Iyāsu I is reproduced in Alvares, *op. cit.*, II, 560–61; that of the Ethiopic work *Ser'āta Mengest* in Varenbergh, *op. cit.*
28. Māhtama-Selassie, *op cit.*, chap. ii.
29. E. Almeida, "The History of High Ethiopia," in *Some Records of Ethiopia, 1593–1646*, ed. C. F. Beckingham and G. Huntingford (London: Hakluyt Society, 1954), pp. 72–73.
30. Plowden, *op. cit.*, p. 138.
31. Almeida, *op. cit.*, p. 73.
32. An autobiographical account of an instance of such nobility at the court of Menelik appears in Makonnen Endālkātchaw, *Malḵām Bēta Sabotch* (Addis Ababa, 1949 E.C.).
33. Some of the dynamics of this process are described by an Ethiopian novelist in Rās Imru Haile Selassie, *Fitāwrāri Belāy* (Addis Ababa: Berhānennā

Salām Press, 1948 E.C.). This has been translated by Tadesse Tamrat in *Ethiopian Observer*, V, No. 4, 342–60.

34. Cited in R. Pankhurst, *An Introduction to the Economic History of Ethiopia* (London: Lalibela House, 1961), p. 168.
35. Cf. Lloyd Fallers, "Despotism, Status Culture, and Social Mobility in an African Kingdom," *Comparative Studies in Society and History*, II (October, 1959), 11–32.
36. Alvares, *op. cit.*, I, 17–22. Cf. R. Pankhurst, *op. cit.*, pp. 131–32.
37. E. Cerulli, "Punti di vista sulla storia dell'Etiopia," *Atti del convegno internazionale di studi etiopici* (Rome: Accademia Nazionale dei Lincei, 1960), p. 8.
38. Plowden, *op. cit.*, p. 46.
39. B. Vèlat, "Une grande dignitaire de l'Église Éthiopienne," *Les Cahiers Coptes*, No. 4 (1953), pp. 13–20.
40. Alvares, *op. cit.*, II, 560; Varenbergh, *op. cit.*, p. 10.
41. On the secular attainments of an *aqābē sa'āt* cf. Bruce's vignette: "[He is] the third dignity of the church, and . . . the first religious officer in the palace. He had a very large revenue, and still a greater influence. He was a man exceedingly rich, and of the very worst life possible; though he had taken the vows of poverty and chastity, it was said he had at that time above seventy mistresses in Gondar. His way of seducing women was as extraordinary as the number seduced . . . when he had fixed his desires upon a woman, he forced her to comply, under pain of *excommunication*." *Op. cit.*, III, 201.
42. Plowden, *op. cit.*, p. 88.
43. Alvares, *op. cit.*, II, 354.
44. Assafā Gabra Māryām, *Enda Waṭaṭch Qaratch* (Addis Ababa: Berhānennā Salām Press, 1943 E.C.), p. 84.
45. E. Combes and M. Tamisier, *Voyage en Abyssinie* (Paris, 1843), pp. 199–200.
46. C. H. Walker, *The Abyssinian at Home* (London: Sheldon Press, 1933), p. 113.
47. W. C. Harris, *The Highlands of Ethiopia* (3 vols.; 2d ed.; London, 1844), II, 304.
48. Baeteman, *op. cit.*, p. 908.
49. E. Cerulli, "Gli abbati di Dabra Libānos," *Orientalia*, XII (1943), 249.
50. D'Abbadie, *op. cit.*, p. 308.
51. R. Pankhurst, *op. cit.*, p. 198.
52. C. Poncet, "A Voyage to Ethiopia," *The Red Sea and Adjacent Countries at the Close of the Seventeenth Century* (London: Hakluyt Society, 1949), p. 123.
53. D'Abbadie, *op. cit.*, p. 145.
54. Plowden, *op. cit.*, p. 457.
55. *Oriente moderno*, VII (1927), 39.
56. J. E. Baum, *Savage Abyssinia* (New York: Grosset & Dunlap, 1927), pp. 40–41.

57. *Oriente moderno, loc. cit.*
58. "La naissance d'une littérature imprimée en Amharique," *Journal Asiatique,* CCVI (1925), 348–63.
59. This mode of conceptualization has been stimulated and influenced by the theoretical discussions found in W. I. Thomas and F. Znaniecki, *The Polish Peasant,* Vol. II, Part IV, Introduction; Talcott Parsons, *The Social System,* chap. vii; and Robert Merton, *Social Theory and Social Structure,* rev. ed., chaps. iv and v.
60. John and Ruth Useem, *The Western-Educated Man in India* (New York: Dryden Press, 1955).
61. "Ka-ĭj Āyshāl Domā," *Voice of Ethiopia* (Addis Ababa), September 16, 1957.
62. Cf. Edward Shils, *Political Development in the New States* (The Hague: Mouton & Co., 1962), p. 7.
63. The conceptual scheme assumed here is articulated in Talcott Parsons, "A Revised Analytical Approach to the Theory of Social Stratification," in *Class, Status, and Power,* ed. S. M. Lipset and R. Bendix (Glencoe, Ill.: Free Press, 1953).
64. *The Ethiopian Herald* (Addis Ababa), March 21, 1960.
65. *Ibid.,* September 12, 1959.
66. As a possibility inherent in the situation of the developing nations, this alternative has been discussed by R. F. Behrendt, "The Emergence of New Elites and New Political Integration Forms and Their Influence on Economic Development," in *Transactions of the Fifth World Congress of Sociology* (Louvain: International Sociological Association, 1962), pp. 3–32.
67. *Op. cit.,* p. 89.

CHAPTER 6: *Orality and the Search for Leadership*

1. A formulation concerning Amhara "social character," however, is presented in chap. vii.
2. E. Erikson, *Childhood and Society* (rev. ed., 1963; New York: Norton & Co., 1950), chap. ii.
3. Cf. W. Plowden's observation: "It is a saying in Abyssinia, that a chief or master is a child—signifying that it is his servants' duty to soothe him, to pet him, to advise him, to answer him, and to understand all his actions." *Travels in Abyssinia* (London, 1868), p. 61.
4. J. Baeteman, *Dictionnaire Amarigna-Français* (Dire Dawa: Saint Lazare, 1929), pp. 643–46.
5. Afawarq Gabra Yesus, *Ṭobiyā* (Addis Ababa: Cooperative Education Press, 1958), p. 30.
6. Arnauld d'Abbadie, *Douze ans de séjour dans la Haute-Éthiopie* (Paris, 1868), p. 41.
7. W. C. Harris, *The Highlands of Ethiopia* (3 vols.; 2d ed.; London, 1844), II, 40.

8. A. A. Brill, "Poetry as an Oral Outlet," *Psychoanalytic Review*, XVIII (October, 1931), 358.

9. W. E. Conzelman, trans., *Chronique de Galawdewos* (Paris, 1895), p. 121.

10. From an article in the *Tafari Makonnen Ensign* (Addis Ababa), April 12, 1951.

11. Carl O'Nell, "Manifest Orality, Hunger and Thirst in Dreams: A Cross-cultural Study of Oral Frustration" (unpublished Master's thesis, University of Chicago, 1964). A fourth group in this study consisted of a sample of Muslim Nigerians who, because of their fasting at the time of Ramadan when the dreams were obtained, presented a significantly higher proportion of respondents with dreams showing manifest orality (55 per cent) than did the non-Muslim Nigerians. O'Nell hypothesized that the Ethiopians would reveal manifest orality with greater frequency than both the non-Muslim Nigerians and the Americans, and these hypotheses were both confirmed ($p < 0.005$ and $p < 0.001$, respectively).

12. Personal communication from Allan Hoben.

13. John Whiting and Irvin Child, *Child Training and Personality: A Cross-cultural Study* (New Haven: Yale University Press, 1953), p. 194.

14. This and a subsequent reference to folk tales is based on an unpublished analysis of Ethiopian folk tales originally collected by Russel G. Davis, formerly of AID/Ethiopia. The sample contains some Galla as well as Amhara folk tales, but these are not distinguished in the analysis. The author of that study, completely independent of the present author, arrived at a conclusion concerning Abyssinian personality that exactly parallels the formulations of this chapter: "In short I would say that the Abyssinian personality centers around the oral-receptive and oral-sadistic orientations with an ambivalent regressive variant."

15. Wallis Budge, trans., *The Life of Takla Haymanot, The Miracles of Takla Haymanot,* and *The Book of the Riches of Kings* (London: W. Griggs, 1906), p. 349.

16. D'Abbadie, *op. cit.,* p. 298.

17. Wallis Budge, trans., *The Miracles of the Blessed Virgin Mary* (London: W. Griggs, 1900).

18. Assafā Gabra Māryām, *Enda Waṭaṭch Qaratch* (Addis Ababa: Berhānennā Salām Press, 1946 E.C.), p. 142.

19. *Teṭāyaq* was outlawed, the author was told, because it led to betting on the participants, and because modern legal procedure requires that everything be written down.

20. See note 14 above.

21. Woodruff and Hoerman, "Nutrition of Infants and Preschool Children in Ethiopia," *Public Health Reports,* LXXV, No. 8, 728.

22. Cf. Erikson, *op. cit.,* p. 80.

CHAPTER 7: *Individualism and the Quest for Social Progress*

1. This is a theme that runs through a century of social theory from Henry Maine and Ferdinand Tönnies to Robert Redfield and Louis Wirth. The explicit discussion of this theme in terms of the concept of individualism was perhaps most pronounced in the writings of Georg Simmel. More recently, sociologists like Karl Mannheim and David Riesman have refined the argument by viewing modern individualism as a transitional phenomenon, midway between the communalism of traditional society and the collectivism and "other-direction" of advanced industrial society.

2. Arnauld d'Abbadie, *Douze ans de séjour dans la Haute-Éthiopie* (Paris, 1868), pp. 72, 91, 114, 120.

3. Marcel Cohen, "Individu et société en Abyssinie," in *Cinquante Années de recherches* (Paris: C. Klincksieck, 1955).

4. A condition marked by the absence or loss of shared social norms. The concept was established in the literature of sociological theory by Émile Durkheim in *Suicide.*

5. W. C. Harris, *The Highlands of Ethiopia* (3 vols.; 2d ed.; London, 1844), III, 12.

6. Alexis de Tocqueville, *Democracy in America* (2 vols.; New York: Vintage Books, 1954), II, 104.

7. Georg Simmel, "Individualismus," in *Brücke und Tur,* ed. M. Susman and M. Landmann (Stuttgart: G. F. Koehler Verlag, 1957), pp. 251–59.

8. Jacob Burckhardt, *The Civilization of the Renaissance in Italy,* trans. S. G. C. Middlemore (London: Phaedon Press, 1951), p. 82.

9. *Ṭiqem* is thus comparable to the Italian notion of *interesse,* defined by Banfield as "material, short-run advantage for the individual," though the Amhara tend to emphasize increments of prestige as much as increments of income. Since Banfield's case is that of a peasant culture that has been eroded by industrialization of the larger society, and hence presents to some extent an instance of anomic individualism, his Montegrano is not strictly comparable to the Amhara. Even so, a comparison of the two cases may be instructive; cf. E. Banfield, *The Moral Basis of a Backward Society* (Glencoe, Ill.: Free Press, 1958).

10. Author's field notes.

11. J. Baeteman, *Dictionnaire Amarigna-Français* (Dire Dawa: Saint Lazare, 1929), p. 288.

12. See quotation from Harris in chap. vi, p. 223.

13. See above, chap. iii, p. 83, and note 14.

14. Cf. Simon Messing, "The Highland-Plateau Amhara of Ethiopia" (unpublished Ph.D. dissertation; University of Pennsylvania, 1957), p. 439.

15. Messing, "Ethiopian Folktales Ascribed to the Late Nineteenth Century Wit, Aläqa Gäbre-Hanna," *Journal of American Folklore,* LXX, No. 275 (January–March, 1957), 70.

16. Author's field notes; from an interview with an Amhara schoolteacher.

17. On the permeation of Amhara social relationships by the demand for guarantors, cf. Giovani Masucci, *Il garante nelle consuetudini etiopiche* (Rome, 1941).

18. Wolf Leslau, "An Ethiopian Merchant's Argot," *Language*, XXV (1959), 22–28; "An Ethiopian Argot of People Possessed by a Spirit," *Africa*, XIX (1949), 204–12; "An Ethiopian Minstrel's Argot," *Journal of the American Oriental Society*, LXXII (1952), 102–9.

19. Messing, "The Highland-Plateau Amhara," p. 445.

20. Tilahoun Paulos, "Forms of Greeting and Other Signs of Respect in Ethiopia," *UCAA Ethnological Society Bulletin*, No. 5 (1956), pp. 25–32.

21. Cf. J. I. Eadie, *An Amharic Reader* (Cambridge: Cambridge University Press, 1924), pp. 39–46.

22. Māhtama-Selassie Walda-Masqal, *Amariññā Qenē* (Addis Ababa, 1948 E.C.), p. 53.

23. For an extended discussion of begging cf. Walter Plowden, *Travels in Abyssinia* (London, 1868), pp. 404–8. On the student mendicants cf. Teshager Wube, "The Wandering Student," *UCAA Ethnological Society Bulletin*, No. 9 (1959), pp. 52–60.

24. "Il est à noter que pratiquement chaque maître a sa méthode d'enseignement qui lui est propre et qu'il considère comme un veritable monopole." Abbé Bernard Vélat, "Les Debtara Éthiopiens," *Les Cahiers Coptes*, V (1954), 26.

25. On the Amhara military ethos and behavior during campaigns cf. Harris, *op. cit.*, II, 162, 203 ff.; Plowden, *op. cit.*, 51 ff.; L. Sambon, *L'esercito abissino* (Rome, 1896).

26. Tadesse Liban, "Tïnnïshu Lïjj" ("The Little Boy"), in *Maskarām* (Addis Ababa: Artistic Press), pp. 110–18.

27. "From the adults (children) take both ideas and hand-me-down objects that have been used, worn-out and discarded, for their play activities . . . for adults rarely produce a toy for children nor give them any new, unused object." Messing, "The Highland-Plateau Amhara," p. 435.

28. Cf. chap. iii, p. 62, and note 4.

29. "En Abyssinie," *La Géographie* (November–December, 1930), p. 10. Cf. also his *Silhouettes et Graffitti Abyssins* (Paris, 1933).

30. Eugen Mittwoch, "Die Angeblichen Abessinischen Philosophen des 17 Jahrhunderts," *Abessinische Studien*, ed. E. Mittwoch (Berlin and Leipzig, 1934), pp. 1–18.

31. *The Oral Tradition, the Written Word, and the Screen Image* (Yellow Springs, Ohio: Antioch Press, 1956), p. 13.

32. Cf. Enrico Cerulli, *Storia della letteratura etiopica* (Milan: Nuova Accademia Editrice, 1956), chap. ii.

33. Thus Hans Jenny speaks of the Amhara's *erstarrte Kultur*, in *Äthiopien: Land im Aufbruch* (Stuttgart: Deutsche Verlags-Anstalt, 1957), pp. 123–26; and Ernest Luther generalizes that "the Ethiopian people have shown themselves to be remarkably uncreative," in *Ethiopia Today* (Stanford, Calif.: Stanford University Press, 1958), p. 36.

34. A. Klingenheben, "Zur Amharischen Poesie," *Rassegna di studi etiopici,* XV (1959), 5–20.
35. Clyde Kluckhohn's statement that "Where dependence on memory exists, there seems to be an inevitable tendency to emphasize the correct perpetuation of the precious oral tradition," reflects, if the Amhara case is at all typical, an exaggerated view of the rigidity of the oral tradition that is shared by many students. *Mirror for Man* (New York: McGraw-Hill, 1949), p. 30.
36. D'Abbadie, *op. cit.,* p. 313.
37. Stories with this theme numbered 27 per cent; the next highest category was only 9 per cent. The data are reported in Edith Lord, *Culture Patterns in Ethiopia* (Washington, D.C.: International Co-operation Administration, 1959), p. 28.
38. Cf. Immanuel Wallerstein, *Africa: The Politics of Independence* (New York: Random House, 1961), p. 134.
39. Cf. Richard Pankhurst and Endreas Eshete, "Self-help in Ethiopia," *Ethiopia Observer,* II, No. 11 (December, 1958), 354–64.
40. *Ibid.,* p. 356.
41. Besides Pankhurst and Eshete, cf. Asfaw Damte, *"Eḳub," UCAA Ethnological Society Bulletin,* No. 8 (1938), pp. 63–76.
42. Luther, *op. cit.,* p. 118.
43. On the inhibition of individuality as a generic problem among the new nations cf. Edward Shils, *Political Development in the New States* (The Hague: Mouton & Co., 1962), pp. 37–38.
44. The classic response of the European mentality to this trait appears in Plowden's famous remark: "Once vanquish [the Abyssinians'] idea that they are perfect, that they are the favoured people on earth, and that nothing can be taught them, and they will be quick and intelligent to learn and to imitate"; *op. cit.,* p. 396.
45. William Seed, "Censorship in Ethiopia," *Manchester Guardian,* Oct. 7, 1954.

NOTE ON TRANSLITERATION

An effort has been made to represent accurately all Ethiopian words used in the text—except for a handful of the most commonly encountered names of emperors, provinces, and ethnic groups—by means of a consistently applied system of transliteration. The system followed here is that used by the majority of English and Italian scholars.*

VOWELS

Order in Ethiopic Script	Symbol Used	Pronunciation
First	a	as in *care*
Second	u	as in pr*u*dent
Third	i	as in rav*i*ne
Fourth	ā	as in *fa*ther
Fifth	ē	as in pr*ey*
Sixth	e	as in sil*e*nt
	ĭ	as in s*i*t
Seventh	o	as in g*o*

CONSONANTS

Glottalized consonants are represented by q, ṭ, ṭs, çh, and p. Geminated consonants are indicated by doubling the consonant.

---

* For the Amharic alphabet according to this system of transliteration, see I. Guidi, *Vocabolario Amarico-Italiano* (Rome: Istituto per l'Oriente, 1953), pp. xiv–xv; or C. F. Beckingham and G. Huntingford, ed., *The Prester John of the Indies* (2 vols.; Cambridge: Hakluyt Society, 1961), I, 24–25.

GLOSSARY

Abuna	እቡነ	Archbishop of the Ethiopian Church
Afa negus	አፈ ንጉሥ	Chief judicial magistrate (literally, "mouth of the king")
Agar	አገር	Country, homeland
Alaqā	አለቃ	Chief, commander
Aqābē sa'āt	ዐቃቤ ሰዓት	Title of the chief ecclesiastic at the imperial court in former times
Aquāquām	አቋቋም	Traditional religious dance performed by *dabtarā*
Azmāri	አዝማሪ	Minstrel
Bālābbāt	ባላባት	Local notable; one who comes from a distinguished family
Bālagē	ባለጌ	Rude
Bāla-selṭān	ባለሥልጣን	One who holds delegated political authority
Bānnā	ባና	A woolen blanket worn by people in Manz
Barnos	በርኖስ	A dark wool cape worn by people of high status
Bēt	ቤት	House, room, quarter
Budā	ቡዳ	A person believed to possess the "evil eye"
Chawā	ጨዋ	Free-born; genteel

305

Chïqā shum	ጭቃ ሹም	Local headman
Chïqechïq	ጭቅጭቅ	Bickering
Dābo	ዳቦ	A whole wheat bread
Dabtarā	ደብተራ	Literatus of the Ethiopian Church, functions as chorister, poet, scribe, herbologist, etc.
Dēgā	ዴጋ	Highland
Dulā	ዱላ	Wooden staff
Echage	እጨጌ	Traditional title of administrative head of the Ethiopian Church
Eddïl	እድል	Fate
Eddïr	እድር	(Modern) voluntary welfare association
Engurguro	እንጉርጉሮ	Song genre used in times of grief
Equb	ዕቁብ	(Modern) form of credit union
Faranj	ፈረንጅ	Foreigner (esp. Western)
Gabbār	ገባር	One who pays tribute
Gannā	ገና	A hockey-like game played at Christmas
Gïber	ግብር	Tribute; a large meal
Goramsā	ጎረምሳ	A virile youth
Guabaz	ጉባዝ	Brave, hardy
Gulammā	ጉለማ	Grain which a youth produces and keeps as his own; personal possession
Gult	ጉልት	Conditional rights to the tribute and corvée labor due from the peasants on a certain piece of land
Gurshā	ጉርሻ	A wad of food placed in someone's mouth
Ïnjarā	እንጀራ	Staple food among Amhara and Tigre, a kind of pancake
Kāhenāt	ካህናት	Clergy
Kutā	ኩታ	A cotton toga of double thickness
Lālibalā	ላሊበላ	One who sings at night to ward off leprosy
Lēbā	ሌባ	Thief
Lïjj	ልጅ	Child

Māhebar	ማኅበር	Traditional religious fraternal association; now, any kind of voluntary formal association
Makuānnent	መኳንንት	Nobility
Mātab	ማተብ	A neckcord worn to symbolize membership in the Ethiopian Orthodox Church
Marĭdāzmātch	መርዳዝማች	Honorific title peculiar to Shoa province
Mizē	ሚዜ	"Best man" at a wedding
Nagārit	ነጋሪት	Drum traditionally used by authorities to signal proclamations
Negusa nagast	ንጉሠ ነገሥት	Emperor (literally, "king of kings")
Qenē	ቅኔ	Religious poetry based on use of wax-and-gold figures
Qollā	ቆላ	Lowlands
Querbān	ቁርባን	Communion
Rĭst	ርስት	Hereditary rights to the use of land
Sam-ennā warq	ሰምና ወርቅ	"Wax and gold." See text, chap. i
Saw	ሰው	Man; others
Selṭānē	ሰልጣኔ	Civilization, progress
Shammā	ሸማ	Light cotton toga worn by many Ethiopians
Shĭftā	ሽፍታ	Rebel; outlaw
Shĭllalā	ሽለላ	A genre of martial songs
Shumat	ሹመት	Appointment (to office)
Shum-shĭr	ሹም ሽር	"Appoint-demote": refers to the traditional process of allocating political offices
Tābot	ታቦት	Holy ark
Ṭajj	ጠጅ	Honey-wine
Ṭallā	ጠላ	Barley-beer
Ṭanquāy	ጠንቋይ	Sorcerer, witch-doctor
Ṭayb	ጠይብ	Metalworker believed to possess the evil eye
Ṭēff	ጤፍ	An indigenous grass cultivated in Ethiopia as a cereal grain
Ṭegābaññā	ጥጋበኛ	One who has grown arrogant from a surfeit of food and drink
Tergum	ትርጉም	Interpretation

Ṭïqem	ጥቅም	Personal advantage
Ṭïmqat	ጥምቀት	Baptism; Epiphany
Wesṭa wayrā	ውስጠ ወይራ	"Inside of olive-tree." See text, chap. i
Zār	ዛር	A spirit which brings sickness
Zamad	ዘመድ	Kinfolk; close ones
Zēmā	ዜማ	Religious music

INDEX

D'Abbadie, Arnauld, 158, 176, 223, 238, 272

Abbïyē, 22, 33–34

Abuna: influence on emperors, 177; quarters in Gondar, 41; ritual functions, 152, 168, 181; role described, 167

Abuna Petros, 142, 182

Addis Ababa: attraction of educated to, 147, 209; as focus of change, 47, 95; and mass culture, 271; peasant attitudes toward, 42

Addis Zaman, 46, 191

Afa negus, 159, 185

Afqārā, 31

African nations: struggle for nationality, 3; student attitudes toward, 141–42

Agāntchā, 31, 52

Agar, concept of, 49–50, 77

Age groups, 96–97, 116–17

Aggression: on holidays, 61–64; in Manz culture, 38–41; and moral conflict, 83, 135; oral, 228–31; in peasant world view, 79–81, 85; in social interaction, 248–51

Ahmad Grāñ. *See* Grāñ, Ahmad

Aksum, 2, 16, 24, 151, 152, 168, 267

Alaqā, status of, 168, 173

Alaqā Gabra Hānnā, 27–28, 45–46, 136, 230, 251, 267, 273

Allport, Gordon, 120, 139

Almeida, E., 161, 162

Almond, Gabriel, 16

Almsgiving, 255–56

Alvares, Francisco, 19, 153, 175

Ambiguity: and modernization, 10–11, 15–17; in wax-and-gold verse, 8–9; in Western culture, 10

Amda Tseyon, 19, 175, 269

Amharic, 2, 8, 78, 109, 116

Amharization, 3

Amhāyas, 22, 34

Ankobar, 34, 35

Anomie, 239

Architecture: of Gondar, 23–24, 26; traditional style of, 267

Asfā Wassan, 22, 34–35

Asmara, 109

Associations, voluntary: behavior in, 282–83; endogenous, 277–79; informal, 281; professional, 280–81; religious, 224, 260; service, 281; student, 279–80

Bagemder, 2, 37, 46

Baha'i, 114

Balaya Sab, 228–29